Version Control with Subversion

Marin Todorov.

Other resources from O'Reilly

Related titles   The Art of Agile Development   Making Things Happen

Applied Software Project   Python for Unix and Linux
Management   System Administration

oreilly.com   *oreilly.com* is more than a complete catalog of O'Reilly books. You'll also find links to news, events, articles, weblogs, sample chapters, and code examples.

oreillynet.com is the essential portal for developers interested in open and emerging technologies, including new platforms, programming languages, and operating systems.

Conferences   O'Reilly Media brings diverse innovators together to nurture the ideas that spark revolutionary industries. We specialize in documenting the latest tools and systems, translating the innovator's knowledge into useful skills for those in the trenches. Visit *conferences.oreilly.com* for our upcoming events.

Safari Bookshelf (*safari.oreilly.com*) is the premier online reference library for programmers and IT professionals. Conduct searches across more than 1,000 books. Subscribers can zero in on answers to time-critical questions in a matter of seconds. Read the books on your Bookshelf from cover to cover or simply flip to the page you need. Try it today for free.

SECOND EDITION

Version Control with Subversion

C. Michael Pilato, Ben Collins-Sussman, and
Brian W. Fitzpatrick

O'REILLY®

Beijing · Cambridge · Farnham · Köln · Sebastopol · Taipei · Tokyo

Version Control with Subversion, Second Edition

by C. Michael Pilato, Ben Collins-Sussman, and Brian W. Fitzpatrick

Published by O'Reilly Media, Inc., 1005 Gravenstein Highway North, Sebastopol, CA 95472.

O'Reilly books may be purchased for educational, business, or sales promotional use. Online editions are also available for most titles (*http://safari.oreilly.com*). For more information, contact our corporate/institutional sales department: 800-998-9938 or *corporate@oreilly.com*.

Editor: Mary E. Treseler	**Indexer:** Joe Wizda
Production Editor: Sarah Schneider	**Cover Designer:** Karen Montgomery
Copyeditors: Mary Brady and Audrey Doyle	**Interior Designer:** David Futato
Proofreader: Sarah Schneider	**Illustrator:** Jessamyn Read

Printing History:

September 2008: Second Edition.
June 2004: First Edition.

ISBN: 978-0-596-51033-6

[M]

1221247267

Table of Contents

Foreword

A bad Frequently Asked Questions (FAQ) sheet is one that is composed not of the questions people actually ask, but of the questions the FAQ's author *wishes* people would ask. Perhaps you've seen the type before:

> Q: How can I use Glorbosoft XYZ to maximize team productivity?

> A: Many of our customers want to know how they can maximize productivity through our patented office groupware innovations. The answer is simple. First, click on the *File* menu, scroll down to *Increase Productivity*, then...

The problem with such FAQs is that they are not, in a literal sense, FAQs at all. No one ever called the tech support line and asked, "How can we maximize productivity?" Rather, people asked highly specific questions, such as "How can we change the calendaring system to send reminders two days in advance instead of one?" and so on. But it's a lot easier to make up imaginary Frequently Asked Questions than it is to discover the real ones. Compiling a true FAQ sheet requires a sustained, organized effort: over the lifetime of the software, incoming questions must be tracked, responses monitored, and all gathered into a coherent, searchable whole that reflects the collective experience of users in the wild. It calls for the patient, observant attitude of a field naturalist. No grand hypothesizing, no visionary pronouncements here—open eyes and accurate note-taking are what's needed most.

What I love about this book is that it grew out of just such a process, and shows it on every page. It is the direct result of the authors' encounters with users. It began with Ben Collins-Sussman's observation that people were asking the same basic questions over and over on the Subversion mailing lists: what are the standard workflows to use with Subversion? Do branches and tags work the same way as in other version control systems? How can I find out who made a particular change?

Frustrated at seeing the same questions day after day, Ben worked intensely over a month in the summer of 2002 to write *The Subversion Handbook*, a 60-page manual that covered all the basics of using Subversion. The manual made no pretense of being complete, but it was distributed with Subversion and got users over that initial hump in the learning curve. When O'Reilly decided to publish a full-length Subversion book, the path of least resistance was obvious: just expand the Subversion handbook.

The three coauthors of the new book were thus presented with an unusual opportunity. Officially, their task was to write a book top-down, starting from a table of contents and an initial draft. But they also had access to a steady stream—indeed, an uncontrollable geyser—of bottom-up source material. Subversion was already in the hands of thousands of early adopters, and those users were giving tons of feedback, not only about Subversion, but also about its existing documentation.

During the entire time they wrote this book, Ben, Mike, and Brian haunted the Subversion mailing lists and chat rooms incessantly, carefully noting the problems users were having in real-life situations. Monitoring such feedback was part of their job descriptions at CollabNet anyway, and it gave them a huge advantage when they set out to document Subversion. The book they produced is grounded firmly in the bedrock of experience, not in the shifting sands of wishful thinking; it combines the best aspects of user manual and FAQ sheet. This duality might not be noticeable on a first reading. Taken in order, front to back, the book is simply a straightforward description of a piece of software. There's the overview, the obligatory guided tour, the chapter on administrative configuration, some advanced topics, and of course, a command reference and troubleshooting guide. Only when you come back to it later, seeking the solution to some specific problem, does its authenticity shine out: the telling details that can only result from encounters with the unexpected, the examples honed from genuine use cases, and most of all the sensitivity to the user's needs and the user's point of view.

Of course, no one can promise that this book will answer every question you have about Subversion. Sometimes the precision with which it anticipates your questions will seem eerily telepathic; yet occasionally, you will stumble into a hole in the community's knowledge and come away empty-handed. When this happens, the best thing you can do is email *users@subversion.tigris.org* and present your problem. The authors are still there and still watching, and the authors include not just the three listed on the cover, but many others who contributed corrections and original material. From the community's point of view, solving your problem is merely a pleasant side effect of a much larger project—namely, slowly adjusting this book, and ultimately Subversion itself, to more closely match the way people actually use it. They are eager to hear from you, not only because they can help you, but because you can help them. With Subversion, as with all active free software projects, *you are not alone.*

Let this book be your first companion.

—Karl Fogel
Chicago, March 14, 2004

Preface

"It is important not to let the perfect become the enemy of the good, even when you can agree on what perfect is. Doubly so when you can't. As unpleasant as it is to be trapped by past mistakes, you can't make any progress by being afraid of your own shadow during design."

—Greg Hudson, Subversion developer

In the world of open source software, the Concurrent Versions System (CVS) was the tool of choice for version control for many years. And rightly so. CVS was open source software itself, and its nonrestrictive modus operandi and support for networked operation allowed dozens of geographically dispersed programmers to share their work. It fit the collaborative nature of the open source world very well. CVS and its semi-chaotic development model have since become cornerstones of open source culture.

But CVS was not without its flaws, and simply fixing those flaws promised to be an enormous effort. Enter Subversion. Subversion was designed to be a successor to CVS, and its originators set out to win the hearts of CVS users in two ways—by creating an open source system with a design (and "look and feel") similar to CVS, and by attempting to avoid most of CVS's noticeable flaws. While the result isn't necessarily the next great evolution in version control design, Subversion *is* very powerful, very usable, and very flexible. And for the most part, almost all newly started open source projects now choose Subversion instead of CVS.

This book is written to document the 1.5 series of the Subversion version control system. We have made every attempt to be thorough in our coverage. However, Subversion has a thriving and energetic development community, so already a number of features and improvements are planned for future versions that may change some of the commands and specific notes in this book.

What Is Subversion?

Subversion is a free/open source version control system. That is, Subversion manages files and directories, and the changes made to them, over time. This allows you to recover older versions of your data or examine the history of how your data changed. In this regard, many people think of a version control system as a sort of "time machine."

Subversion can operate across networks, which allows it to be used by people on different computers. At some level, the ability for various people to modify and manage the same set of data from their respective locations fosters collaboration. Progress can occur more quickly without a single conduit through which all modifications must occur. And because the work is versioned, you need not fear that quality is the trade-off for losing that conduit—if some incorrect change is made to the data, just undo that change.

Some version control systems are also software configuration management (SCM) systems. These systems are specifically tailored to manage trees of source code and have many features that are specific to software development—such as natively understanding programming languages, or supplying tools for building software. Subversion, however, is not one of these systems. It is a general system that can be used to manage *any* collection of files. For you, those files might be source code—for others, anything from grocery shopping lists to digital video mixdowns and beyond.

Is Subversion the Right Tool?

If you're a user or system administrator pondering the use of Subversion, the first question you should ask yourself is: "Is this the right tool for the job?" Subversion is a fantastic hammer, but be careful not to view every problem as a nail.

If you need to archive old versions of files and directories, possibly resurrect them, or examine logs of how they've changed over time, then Subversion is exactly the right tool for you. If you need to collaborate with people on documents (usually over a network) and keep track of who made which changes, then Subversion is also appropriate. This is why Subversion is so often used in software development environments—working on a development team is an inherently social activity, and Subversion makes it easy to collaborate with other programmers. Of course, there's a cost to using Subversion as well: administrative overhead. You'll need to manage a data repository to store the information and all its history, and you'll need to be diligent about backing it up. When working with the data on a daily basis, you won't be able to copy, move, rename, or delete files the way you usually do. Instead, you'll have to do all of those things through Subversion.

Assuming you're fine with the extra workflow, you should still make sure you're not using Subversion to solve a problem that other tools solve better. For example, because Subversion replicates data to all the collaborators involved, a common misuse is to treat it as a generic distribution system. People will sometimes use Subversion to distribute huge collections of photos, digital music, or software packages. The problem is that this sort of data usually isn't changing at all. The collection itself grows over time, but the individual files within the collection aren't being changed. In this case, using Subversion is "overkill."[*] There are simpler tools that efficiently replicate data *without* the overhead of tracking changes, such as *rsync* or *unison*.

Subversion's History

In early 2000, CollabNet, Inc. (*http://www.collab.net*) began seeking developers to write a replacement for CVS. CollabNet offers a collaboration software suite called Collab-Net Enterprise Edition (CEE), of which one component is version control. Although CEE used CVS as its initial version control system, CVS's limitations were obvious from the beginning, and CollabNet knew it would eventually have to find something better. Unfortunately, CVS had become the de facto standard in the open source world largely because there *wasn't* anything better, at least not under a free license. So CollabNet determined to write a new version control system from scratch, retaining the basic ideas of CVS, but without the bugs and misfeatures.

In February 2000, they contacted Karl Fogel, the author of *Open Source Development with CVS* (Coriolis, 1999), and asked if he'd like to work on this new project. Coincidentally, at the time Karl was already discussing a design for a new version control system with his friend Jim Blandy. In 1995, the two had started Cyclic Software, a company providing CVS support contracts, and although they later sold the business, they still used CVS every day at their jobs. Their frustration with CVS had led Jim to think carefully about better ways to manage versioned data, and he'd already come up with not only the name "Subversion," but also the basic design of the Subversion data store. When CollabNet called, Karl immediately agreed to work on the project, and Jim got his employer, Red Hat Software, to essentially donate him to the project for an indefinite period of time. CollabNet hired Karl and Ben Collins-Sussman, and detailed design work began in May 2000. With the help of some well-placed prods from Brian Behlendorf and Jason Robbins of CollabNet, and from Greg Stein (at the time an independent developer active in the WebDAV/DeltaV specification process), Subversion quickly attracted a community of active developers. It turned out that many people had encountered the same frustrating experiences with CVS and welcomed the chance to finally do something about it.

The original design team settled on some simple goals. They didn't want to break new ground in version control methodology; they just wanted to fix CVS. They decided that Subversion would match CVS's features and preserve the same development model, but would not duplicate CVS's most obvious flaws. And although it did not need to be a drop-in replacement for CVS, it should be similar enough that any CVS user could make the switch with little effort.

After 14 months of coding, Subversion became "self-hosting" on August 31, 2001. That is, Subversion developers stopped using CVS to manage Subversion's own source code and started using Subversion instead.

---

[*] Or as a friend puts it, "swatting a fly with a Buick."

While CollabNet started the project, and still funds a large chunk of the work (it pays the salaries of a few full-time Subversion developers), Subversion is run like most open source projects, governed by a loose, transparent set of rules that encourage meritocracy. CollabNet's copyright license is fully compliant with the Debian Free Software Guidelines. In other words, anyone is free to download, modify, and redistribute Subversion as he pleases; no permission from CollabNet or anyone else is required.

Subversion's Architecture

Figure P-1 illustrates a "mile-high" view of Subversion's design.

On one end is a Subversion repository that holds all of your versioned data. On the other end is your Subversion client program, which manages local reflections of portions of that versioned data (called "working copies"). Between these extremes are multiple routes through various Repository Access (RA) layers. Some of these routes go across computer networks and through network servers, which then access the repository. Others bypass the network altogether and access the repository directly.

Subversion's Components

Subversion, once installed, has a number of different pieces. The following is a quick overview of what you get. Don't be alarmed if the brief descriptions leave you scratching your head—*plenty* more pages in this book are devoted to alleviating that confusion.

svn
> The command-line client program

svnversion
> A program for reporting the state (in terms of revisions of the items present) of a working copy

svnlook
> A tool for directly inspecting a Subversion repository

svnadmin
> A tool for creating, tweaking, or repairing a Subversion repository

mod_dav_svn
> A plug-in module for the Apache HTTP Server, used to make your repository available to others over a network

svnserve
> A custom standalone server program, runnable as a daemon process or invokable by SSH; another way to make your repository available to others over a network.

svndumpfilter
> A program for filtering Subversion repository dump streams

svnsync
> A program for incrementally mirroring one repository to another over a network

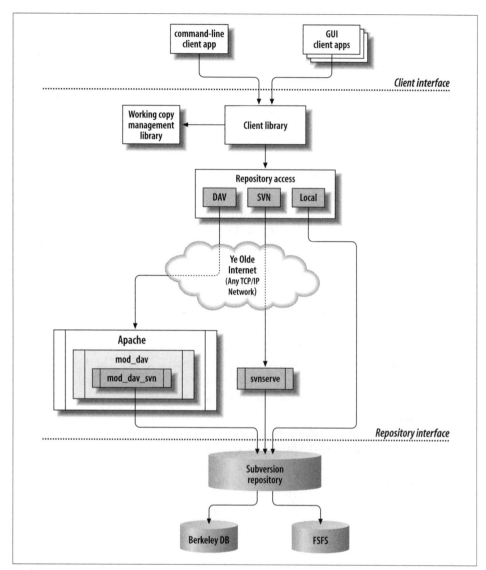

Figure P-1. Subversion's architecture

What's New in Subversion

The first edition of this book was released in 2004, shortly after Subversion had reached 1.0. Over the following four years, Subversion released five major new versions, fixing bugs and adding major new features. While we've managed to keep the online version of this book up to date, we're thrilled that the second edition from O'Reilly now covers Subversion up through release 1.5, a major milestone for the project. Here's a quick summary of major new changes since Subversion 1.0. Note that this is not a complete list; for full details, please visit Subversion's web site at *http://subversion.tigris.org*.

Subversion 1.1 (September 2004)
> Release 1.1 introduced FSFS, a flat-file repository storage option for the repository. While the Berkeley DB backend is still widely used and supported, FSFS has since become the default choice for newly created repositories due to its low barrier to entry and minimal maintenance requirements. Also in this release came the ability to put symbolic links under version control, auto-escaping of URLs, and a localized user interface.

Subversion 1.2 (May 2005)
> Release 1.2 introduced the ability to create server-side locks on files, thus serializing commit access to certain resources. Although Subversion is still a fundamentally concurrent version control system, certain types of binary files (e.g., art assets) cannot be merged together. The locking feature fulfills the need to version and protect such resources. With locking also came a complete WebDAV autoversioning implementation, allowing Subversion repositories to be mounted as network folders. Finally, Subversion 1.2 began using a new, faster binary-differencing algorithm to compress and retrieve old versions of files.

Subversion 1.3 (December 2005)
> Release 1.3 brought path-based authorization controls to the *svnserve* server, matching a feature formerly found only in the Apache server. The Apache server, however, gained some new logging features of its own, and Subversion's API bindings to other languages also made great leaps forward.

Subversion 1.4 (September 2006)
> Release 1.4 introduced a whole new tool—*svnsync*—for doing one-way repository replication over a network. Major parts of the working copy metadata were revamped to no longer use XML (resulting in client-side speed gains), while the Berkeley DB repository backend gained the ability to automatically recover itself after a server crash.

Subversion 1.5 (June 2008)
> Release 1.5 took much longer to finish than prior releases, but the headliner feature was gigantic: semiautomated tracking of branching and merging. This was a huge boon for users, and it pushed Subversion far beyond the abilities of CVS and into the ranks of commercial competitors such as Perforce and ClearCase. Subversion 1.5 also introduced a bevy of other user-focused features, such as interactive resolution of file conflicts, partial checkouts, client-side management of changelists, powerful new syntax for externals definitions, and Simple Authentication and Security Layer (SASL) authentication support for the *svnserve* server.

Audience

This book is written for computer-literate folk who want to use Subversion to manage their data. While Subversion runs on a number of different operating systems, its primary user interface is command-line-based. That command-line tool (*svn*), and some auxiliary programs, are the focus of this book.

For consistency, the examples in this book assume that the reader is using a Unix-like operating system and is relatively comfortable with Unix and command-line interfaces. That said, the *svn* program also runs on non-Unix platforms such as Microsoft Windows. With a few minor exceptions, such as the use of backward slashes (\) instead of forward slashes (/) for path separators, the input to and output from this tool when run on Windows are identical to its Unix counterpart.

Most readers are probably programmers or system administrators who need to track changes to source code. This is the most common use for Subversion, and therefore it is the scenario underlying all of the book's examples. But Subversion can be used to manage changes to any sort of information—images, music, databases, documentation, and so on. To Subversion, all data is just data.

While this book is written with the assumption that the reader has never used a version control system, we've also tried to make it easy for users of CVS (and other systems) to make a painless leap into Subversion. Special sidebars may mention other version control systems from time to time, and Appendix B summarizes many of the differences between CVS and Subversion.

Note also that the source code examples used throughout the book are only examples. Although they will compile with the proper compiler incantations, they are intended to illustrate a particular scenario and not necessarily to serve as examples of good programming style or practices.

How to Read This Book

Technical book authors always face a certain dilemma: whether to cater to *top-down* or to *bottom-up* learners. A top-down learner prefers to read or skim documentation, getting a large overview of how the system works; only then does she actually start using the software. A bottom-up learner is a "learn by doing" person—someone who just wants to dive into the software and figure it out as she goes, referring to book sections when necessary. Most books tend to be written for one type of person or the other, and this book is undoubtedly biased toward top-down learners. (And if you're actually reading this section, you're probably already a top-down learner yourself!) However, if you're a bottom-up person, don't despair. While the book may be laid out as a broad survey of Subversion topics, the content of each section tends to be heavy with specific examples that you can try-by-doing. For the impatient folks who just want to get going, you can jump right to Appendix A.

Regardless of your learning style, this book aims to be useful to people of widely different backgrounds—from those with no previous experience in version control to experienced system administrators. Depending on your own background, certain chapters may be more or less important to you. The following can be considered a "recommended reading list" for various types of readers:

Experienced system administrators
> The assumption here is that you've probably used version control before and are dying to get a Subversion server up and running ASAP. Chapters 5 and 6 will show you how to create your first repository and make it available over the network. After that's done, Chapter 2 and Appendix B are the fastest routes to learning the Subversion client.

New users
> Your administrator has probably already set up Subversion, and you need to learn how to use the client. If you've never used a version control system, then Chapter 1 is a vital introduction to the ideas behind version control. Chapter 2 is a guided tour of the Subversion client.

Advanced users
> Whether you're a user or administrator, eventually your project will grow larger. You're going to want to learn how to do more advanced things with Subversion, such as how to use Subversion's property support (Chapter 3), how to use branches and perform merges (Chapter 4), how to configure runtime options (Chapter 7), and other things. These chapters aren't critical at first, but be sure to read them once you're comfortable with the basics.

Developers
> Presumably, you're already familiar with Subversion, and you now want to either extend it or build new software on top of its many APIs. Chapter 8 is just for you.

The book ends with reference material—Chapter 9 is a reference guide for all Subversion commands, and the appendixes cover a number of useful topics. These are the chapters you're mostly likely to come back to after you've finished the book.

Conventions Used in This Book

The following typographic conventions are used in this book:

`Constant width`
> Used for literal user input, command output, and command-line options

Italic
> Used for program and Subversion tool subcommand names, file and directory names, and new terms

`Constant width italic`
> Used for replaceable items in code and text

Also, we've sprinkled especially helpful or important bits of information throughout the book (in contextually relevant locations), set off visually so they're easy to find. Look for the following icons as you read:

This icon designates a special point of interest.

This icon designates a helpful tip or recommended best practice.

This icon designates a warning. Pay close attention to these to avoid running into problems.

Organization of This Book

The chapters that follow and their contents are listed here:

Chapter 1, *Fundamental Concepts*
Explains the basics of version control and different versioning models, along with Subversion's repository, working copies, and revisions.

Chapter 2, *Basic Usage*
Walks you through a day in the life of a Subversion user. It demonstrates how to use a Subversion client to obtain, modify, and commit data.

Chapter 3, *Advanced Topics*
Covers more complex features that regular users will eventually come into contact with, such as versioned metadata, file locking, and peg revisions.

Chapter 4, *Branching and Merging*
Discusses branches, merges, and tagging, including best practices for branching and merging, common use cases, how to undo changes, and how to easily swing from one branch to the next.

Chapter 5, *Repository Administration*
Describes the basics of the Subversion repository, how to create, configure, and maintain a repository, and the tools you can use to do all of this.

Chapter 6, *Server Configuration*
Explains how to configure your Subversion server and offers different ways to access your repository: HTTP, the svn protocol, and local disk access. It also covers the details of authentication, authorization and anonymous access.

Chapter 7, *Customizing Your Subversion Experience*
> Explores the Subversion client configuration files, the handling of internationalized text, and how to make external tools cooperate with Subversion.

Chapter 8, *Embedding Subversion*
> Describes the internals of Subversion, the Subversion filesystem, and the working copy administrative areas from a programmer's point of view. It also demonstrates how to use the public APIs to write a program that uses Subversion.

Chapter 9, *Subversion Complete Reference*
> Explains in great detail every subcommand of *svn*, *svnadmin*, and *svnlook* with plenty of examples for the whole family!

Appendix A, *Subversion Quick-Start Guide*
> For the impatient, a whirlwind explanation of how to install Subversion and start using it immediately. You have been warned.

Appendix B, *Subversion for CVS Users*
> Covers the similarities and differences between Subversion and CVS, with numerous suggestions on how to break all the bad habits you picked up from years of using CVS. Included are descriptions of Subversion revision numbers, versioned directories, offline operations, *update* versus *status*, branches, tags, metadata, conflict resolution, and authentication.

Appendix C, *WebDAV and Autoversioning*
> Describes the details of WebDAV and DeltaV and how you can configure your Subversion repository to be mounted read/write as a DAV share.

Appendix D, *Copyright*
> A copy of the Creative Commons Attribution License, under which this book is licensed.

This Book Is Free

This book started out as bits of documentation written by Subversion project developers, which were then coalesced into a single work and rewritten. As such, it has always been under a free license (see Appendix D). In fact, the book was written in the public eye, originally as part of the Subversion project itself. This means two things:

- You will always find the latest version of this book in the book's own Subversion repository.
- You can make changes to this book and redistribute it however you wish—it's under a free license. Your only obligation is to maintain proper attribution to the original authors. Of course, we'd much rather you send feedback and patches to the Subversion developer community, instead of distributing your private version of this book.

The online home of this book's development and most of the volunteer-driven translation efforts regarding it is *http://svnbook.red-bean.com*. There you can find links to the latest releases and tagged versions of the book in various formats, as well as instructions for accessing the book's Subversion repository (where its DocBook XML source code lives). Feedback is welcomed—encouraged, even. Please submit all comments, complaints, and patches against the book sources to *svnbook-dev@red-bean.com*.

Using Code Examples

This book is here to help you get your job done. In general, you may use the code in this book in your programs and documentation. You do not need to contact us for permission unless you're reproducing a significant portion of the code. For example, writing a program that uses several chunks of code from this book does not require permission. Selling or distributing a CD-ROM of examples from O'Reilly books does require permission. Answering a question by citing this book and quoting example code does not require permission. Incorporating a significant amount of example code from this book into your product's documentation does require permission.

If you feel your use of code examples falls outside fair use or the permission given above, feel free to contact us at *permissions@oreilly.com*.

This work is licensed under the Creative Commons Attribution License. To view a copy of this license, visit *http://creativecommons.org/licenses/by/2.0/* or send a letter to Creative Commons, 559 Nathan Abbott Way, Stanford, California 94305, USA. See Appendix D for the full license.

An attribution usually includes the title, author, publisher, and ISBN. For example: *Version Control with Subversion*, Second Edition, by C. Michael Pilato, Ben Collins-Sussman, and Brian W. Fitzpatrick. Copyright 2002–2008 C. Michael Pilato, Ben Collins-Sussman, and Brian W. Fitzpatrick, 978-0-596-51033-6.

Safari® Books Online

Safari When you see a Safari® Books Online icon on the cover of your favorite technology book, that means the book is available online through the O'Reilly Network Safari Bookshelf.

Safari offers a solution that's better than e-books. It's a virtual library that lets you easily search thousands of top tech books, cut and paste code samples, download chapters, and find quick answers when you need the most accurate, current information. Try it for free at *http://safari.oreilly.com*.

How to Contact Us

Please address comments and questions concerning this book to the publisher:

O'Reilly Media, Inc.
1005 Gravenstein Highway North
Sebastopol, CA 95472
800-998-9938 (in the United States or Canada)
707-829-0515 (international/local)
707-829-0104 (fax)

O'Reilly's web page for this book, where we list errata, examples, or any additional information. You can access this page at:

http://www.oreilly.com/catalog/9780596510336

To comment or ask technical questions about this book, send email to:

bookquestions@oreilly.com

For more information about our books, conferences, Resource Centers, and the O'Reilly Network, see our web site at:

http://www.oreilly.com

Acknowledgments

This book would not be possible (nor very useful) if Subversion did not exist. For that, the authors would like to thank Brian Behlendorf and CollabNet for the vision to fund such a risky and ambitious new open source project; Jim Blandy for the original Subversion name and design—we love you, Jim; and Karl Fogel for being such a good friend and a great community leader, in that order.[†]

Thanks to O'Reilly and our various editors: Chuck Toporek, Linda Mui, Tatiana Apandi, Mary Brady, and Mary Treseler. Their patience and support has been tremendous.

Finally, we thank the countless people who contributed to this book with informal reviews, suggestions, and patches. While this is undoubtedly not a complete list, this book would be incomplete and incorrect without their help: Bhuvaneswaran A, David Alber, C. Scott Ananian, David Anderson, Ariel Arjona, Seth Arnold, Jani Averbach, Charles Bailey, Ryan Barrett, Francois Beausoleil, Brian R. Becker, Yves Bergeron, Karl Berry, Jennifer Bevan, Matt Blais, Jim Blandy, Phil Bordelon, Sietse Brouwer, Tom Brown, Zack Brown, Martin Buchholz, Paul Burba, Sean Callan-Hinsvark, Branko Cibej, Archie Cobbs, Jason Cohen, Ryan Cresawn, John R. Daily, Peter Davis, Olivier Davy, Robert P. J. Day, Mo DeJong, Brian Denny, Joe Drew, Markus Dreyer, Nick

---

[†] Oh, and thanks, Karl, for being too overworked to write this book yourself.

Duffek, Boris Dusek, Ben Elliston, Justin Erenkrantz, Jens M. Felderhoff, Kyle Ferrio, Shlomi Fish, Julian Foad, Chris Foote, Martin Furter, Vlad Georgescu, Peter Gervai, Dave Gilbert, Eric Gillespie, David Glasser, Marcel Gosselin, Lieven Govaerts, Steve Greenland, Matthew Gregan, Tom Gregory, Maverick Grey, Art Haas, Mark E. Hamilton, Eric Hanchrow, Liam Healy, Malte Helmert, Michael Henderson, Øyvind A. Holm, Greg Hudson, Alexis Huxley, Auke Jilderda, Toby Johnson, Jens B. Jorgensen, Tez Kamihira, David Kimdon, Mark Benedetto King, Robert Kleemann, Erik Kline, Josh Knowles, Andreas J. Koenig, Axel Kollmorgen, Nuutti Kotivuori, Kalin Kozhuharov, Matt Kraai, Regis Kuckaertz, Stefan Kueng, Steve Kunkee, Scott Lamb, Wesley J. Landaker, Benjamin Landsteiner, Vincent Lefevre, Morten Ludvigsen, Dennis Lundberg, Paul Lussier, Bruce A. Mah, Jonathon Mah, Karl Heinz Marbaise, Philip Martin, Feliciano Matias, Neil Mayhew, Patrick Mayweg, Gareth McCaughan, Craig McElroy, Simon McKenna, Christophe Meresse, Jonathan Metillon, Jean-Francois Michaud, Jon Middleton, Robert Moerland, Marcel Molina Jr., Tim Moloney, Alexander Mueller, Tabish Mustufa, Christopher Ness, Roman Neuhauser, Mats Nilsson, Greg Noel, Joe Orton, Eric Paire, Dimitri Papadopoulos-Orfanos, Jerry Peek, Chris Pepper, Amy Lyn Pilato, Kevin Pilch-Bisson, Hans Polak, Dmitriy Popkov, Michael Price, Mark Proctor, Steffen Prohaska, Daniel Rall, Srinivasa Ramanujan, Jack Repenning, Tobias Ringstrom, Jason Robbins, Garrett Rooney, Joel Rosdahl, Christian Sauer, Ryan Schmidt, Jochem Schulenklopper, Jens Seidel, Daniel Shahaf, Larry Shatzer, Danil Shopyrin, Erik Sjoelund, Joey Smith, W. Snyder, Stefan Sperling, Robert Spier, M. S. Sriram, Russell Steicke, David Steinbrunner, Sander Striker, David Summers, Johan Sundstroem, Ed Swierk, John Szakmeister, Arfrever Frehtes Taifersar Arahesis, Robert Tasarz, Michael W. Thelen, Mason Thomas, Erik van der Kolk, Joshua Varner, Eric Wadsworth, Chris Wagner, Colin Watson, Alex Waugh, Chad Whitacre, Andy Whitcroft, Josef Wolf, Luke Worth, Hyrum Wright, Blair Zajac, Florian Zumbiehl, and the entire Subversion community.

From Ben Collins-Sussman

Thanks to my wife, Frances, who for many months got to hear "But honey, I'm still working on the book," rather than the usual "But honey, I'm still doing email." I don't know where she gets all that patience! She's my perfect counterbalance.

Thanks to my extended family and friends for their sincere encouragement, despite having no actual interest in the subject. (You know, the ones who say, "Ooh, you wrote a book?", and then when you tell them it's a computer book, they sort of glaze over.)

Thanks to all my close friends, who make me a rich, rich man. Don't look at me that way—you know who you are.

Thanks to my parents for the perfect low-level formatting and for being unbelievable role models. Thanks to my kids for giving me the opportunity to pass that on.

From Brian W. Fitzpatrick

Huge thanks to my wife, Marie, for being incredibly understanding, supportive, and most of all, patient. Thank you to my brother, Eric, who first introduced me to Unix programming way back when. Thanks to my Mom and Grandmother for all their support, not to mention enduring a Christmas holiday where I came home and promptly buried my head in my laptop to work on the book.

To Mike and Ben: it was a pleasure working with you on the book. Heck, it's a pleasure working with you at work!

To everyone in the Subversion community and the Apache Software Foundation, thanks for having me. Not a day goes by where I don't learn something from at least one of you.

Lastly, thanks to my grandfather, who always told me that "freedom equals responsibility." I couldn't agree more.

From C. Michael Pilato

Special thanks to Amy, my best friend and wife of more than 10 incredible years, for her love and patient support, for putting up with the late nights, and for graciously enduring the version control processes I've imposed on her. Don't worry, sweetheart—you'll be a TortoiseSVN wizard in no time!

Gavin, you're able to read half of the words in this book yourself now; sadly, it's the other half that provide the key concepts. And sorry, Aidan—I couldn't find a way to work Disney/Pixar characters into the text. But Daddy loves you both and can't wait to teach you about programming.

Mom and Dad, thanks for your constant support and enthusiasm. Mom- and Dad-in-law, thanks for all of the same *plus* your fabulous daughter.

Hats off to Shep Kendall, through whom the world of computers was first opened to me; Ben Collins-Sussman, my tour guide through the open source world; Karl Fogel, you *are* my *.emacs*; Greg Stein, for oozing practical programming know-how; and Brian Fitzpatrick, for sharing this writing experience with me. To the many folks from whom I am constantly picking up new knowledge—keep dropping it!

Finally, to the One who perfectly demonstrates creative excellence—thank You.

## CHAPTER 1

Fundamental Concepts

This chapter is a short, casual introduction to Subversion. If you're new to version control, this chapter is definitely for you. We begin with a discussion of general version control concepts, work our way into the specific ideas behind Subversion, and show some simple examples of Subversion in use.

Even though the examples in this chapter show people sharing collections of program source code, keep in mind that Subversion can manage any sort of file collection—it's not limited to helping computer programmers.

The Repository

Subversion is a centralized system for sharing information. At its core is a repository, which is a central store of data. The repository stores information in the form of a *filesystem tree*—a typical hierarchy of files and directories. Any number of *clients* connect to the repository and then read or write to these files. By writing data, a client makes the information available to others; by reading data, the client receives information from others. Figure 1-1 illustrates this.

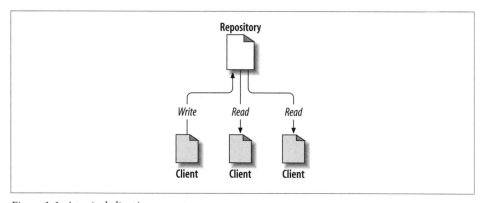

Figure 1-1. A typical client/server system

So, why is this interesting? So far, this sounds like the definition of a typical file server. And indeed, the repository *is* a kind of file server, but it's not your usual breed. What makes the Subversion repository special is that *it remembers every change* ever written to it—every change to every file, and even changes to the directory tree itself, such as the addition, deletion, and rearrangement of files and directories.

When a client reads data from the repository, it normally sees only the latest version of the filesystem tree. But the client also has the ability to view *previous* states of the filesystem. For example, a client can ask historical questions such as, "What did this directory contain last Wednesday?" and, "Who was the last person to change this file, and what changes did he make?" These are the sorts of questions that are at the heart of any *version control system*: systems that are designed to track changes to data over time.

Versioning Models

The core mission of a version control system is to enable collaborative editing and sharing of data. But different systems use different strategies to achieve this. It's important to understand these different strategies, for a couple of reasons. First, it will help you compare and contrast existing version control systems in case you encounter other systems similar to Subversion. Beyond that, it will also help you make more effective use of Subversion, since Subversion itself supports a couple of different ways of working.

The Problem of File Sharing

All version control systems have to solve the same fundamental problem: how will the system allow users to share information but prevent them from accidentally stepping on each other's feet? It's all too easy for users to accidentally overwrite each other's changes in the repository.

Consider the scenario shown in Figure 1-2. Suppose we have two coworkers, Harry and Sally. They each decide to edit the same repository file at the same time. If Harry saves his changes to the repository first, it's possible that (a few moments later) Sally could accidentally overwrite them with her own new version of the file. Although Harry's version of the file won't be lost forever (because the system remembers every change), any changes Harry made *won't* be present in Sally's newer version of the file, because she never saw Harry's changes to begin with. Harry's work is still effectively lost—or is at least missing from the latest version of the file—and probably by accident. This is definitely a situation we want to avoid!

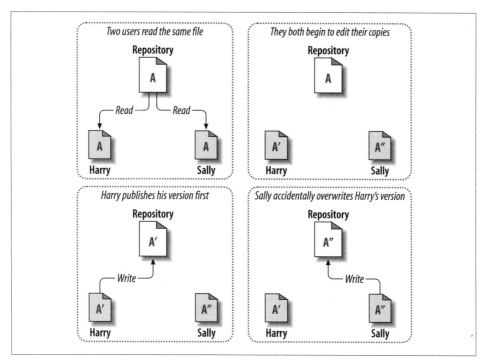

Figure 1-2. The problem to avoid

The Lock-Modify-Unlock Solution

Many version control systems use a *lock-modify-unlock* model to address the problem of many authors clobbering each other's work. In this model, the repository allows only one person to change a file at a time. This exclusivity policy is managed using locks. Harry must "lock" a file before he can begin making changes to it. If Harry has locked a file, Sally cannot also lock it, and therefore cannot make any changes to that file. All she can do is read the file and wait for Harry to finish his changes and release his lock. After Harry unlocks the file, Sally can take her turn by locking and editing the file. Figure 1-3 demonstrates this simple solution.

The problem with the lock-modify-unlock model is that it's a bit restrictive and often becomes a roadblock for users:

- *Locking may cause administrative problems.* Sometimes Harry will lock a file and then forget about it. Meanwhile, because Sally is still waiting to edit the file, her hands are tied. And then Harry goes on vacation. Now Sally has to get an administrator to release Harry's lock. The situation ends up causing a lot of unnecessary delay and wasted time.

- *Locking may cause unnecessary serialization.* What if Harry is editing the beginning of a text file, and Sally simply wants to edit the end of the same file? These changes don't overlap at all. They could easily edit the file simultaneously, and no great

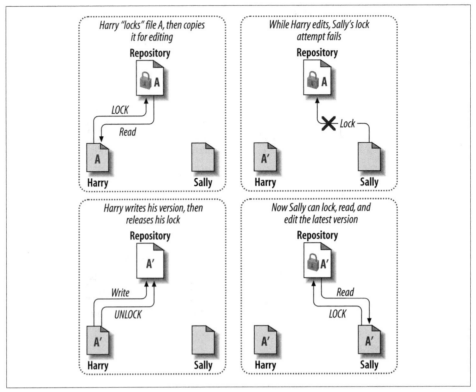

Figure 1-3. The lock-modify-unlock solution

harm would come, assuming the changes were properly merged together. There's no need for them to take turns in this situation.

- *Locking may create a false sense of security.* Suppose Harry locks and edits file A, while Sally simultaneously locks and edits file B. But what if A and B depend on one another, and the changes made to each are semantically incompatible? Suddenly A and B don't work together anymore. The locking system was powerless to prevent the problem—yet it somehow provided a false sense of security. It's easy for Harry and Sally to imagine that by locking files, each is beginning a safe, insulated task, and thus they need not bother discussing their incompatible changes early on. Locking often becomes a substitute for real communication.

The Copy-Modify-Merge Solution

Subversion, CVS, and many other version control systems use a *copy-modify-merge* model as an alternative to locking. In this model, each user's client contacts the project repository and creates a personal *working copy*—a local reflection of the repository's files and directories. Users then work simultaneously and independently, modifying

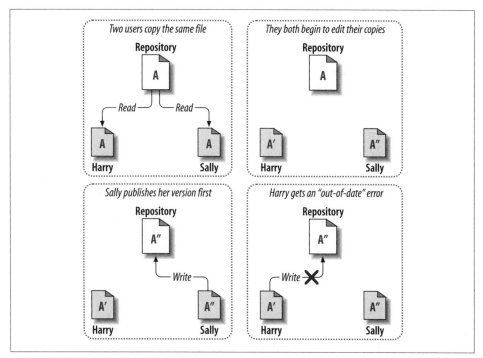

Figure 1-4. The copy-modify-merge solution

their private copies. Finally, the private copies are merged together into a new, final version. The version control system often assists with the merging, but ultimately, a human being is responsible for making it happen correctly.

Here's an example. Say that Harry and Sally each create working copies of the same project, copied from the repository. They work concurrently and make changes to the same file A within their copies. Sally saves her changes to the repository first. When Harry attempts to save his changes later, the repository informs him that his file A is *out of date*. In other words, file A in the repository has somehow changed since he last copied it. So Harry asks his client to *merge* any new changes from the repository into his working copy of file A. Chances are that Sally's changes don't overlap with his own; once he has both sets of changes integrated, he saves his working copy back to the repository. Figures 1-4 and 1-5 show this process.

But what if Sally's changes *do* overlap with Harry's changes? What then? This situation is called a *conflict*, and it's usually not much of a problem. When Harry asks his client to merge the latest repository changes into his working copy, his copy of file A is somehow flagged as being in a state of conflict: he'll be able to see both sets of conflicting changes and manually choose between them. Note that software can't automatically resolve conflicts; only humans are capable of understanding and making the necessary intelligent choices. Once Harry has manually resolved the overlapping changes—

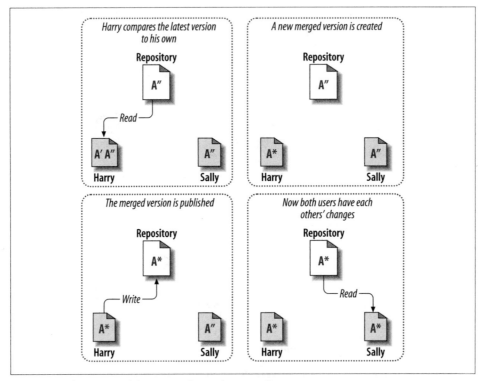

Figure 1-5. The copy-modify-merge solution (continued)

perhaps after a discussion with Sally—he can safely save the merged file back to the repository.

The copy-modify-merge model may sound a bit chaotic, but in practice, it runs extremely smoothly. Users can work in parallel, never waiting for one another. When they work on the same files, it turns out that most of their concurrent changes don't overlap at all; conflicts are infrequent. And the amount of time it takes to resolve conflicts is usually far less than the time lost by a locking system.

In the end, it all comes down to one critical factor: user communication. When users communicate poorly, both syntactic and semantic conflicts increase. No system can force users to communicate perfectly, and no system can detect semantic conflicts. So there's no point in being lulled into a false sense of security that a locking system will somehow prevent conflicts; in practice, locking seems to inhibit productivity more than anything else.

Subversion in Action

It's time to move from the abstract to the concrete. In this section, we'll show real examples of Subversion being used.

Subversion Repository URLs

Throughout this book, Subversion uses URLs to identify versioned files and directories in Subversion repositories. For the most part, these URLs use the standard syntax, allowing for server names and port numbers to be specified as part of the URL:

```
$ svn checkout http://svn.example.com:9834/repos
...
```

But there are some nuances in Subversion's handling of URLs that are notable. For example, URLs containing the `file://` access method (used for local repositories) must, in accordance with convention, have either a server name of `localhost` or no server name at all:

```
$ svn checkout file:///var/svn/repos
...
$ svn checkout file://localhost/var/svn/repos
...
```

Also, users of the `file://` scheme on Windows platforms will need to use an unofficially "standard" syntax for accessing repositories that are on the same machine, but on a different drive than the client's current working drive. Either of the two following URL path syntaxes will work, where X is the drive on which the repository resides:

```
C:\> svn checkout file:///X:/var/svn/repos
...
C:\> svn checkout "file:///X|/var/svn/repos"
...
```

In the second syntax, you need to quote the URL so that the vertical bar character is not interpreted as a pipe. Also, note that a URL uses forward slashes even though the native (non-URL) form of a path on Windows uses backslashes.

 You cannot use Subversion's file:// URLs in a regular web browser the way typical file:// URLs can. When you attempt to view a file:// URL in a regular web browser, it reads and displays the contents of the file at that location by examining the filesystem directly. However, Subversion's resources exist in a virtual filesystem (see "Repository Layer" on page 253), and your browser will not understand how to interact with that filesystem.

Finally, it should be noted that the Subversion client will automatically encode URLs as necessary, just like a web browser does. For example, if a URL contains a space or upper-ASCII character as in the following:

```
$ svn checkout "http://host/path with space/project/españa"
```

then Subversion will escape the unsafe characters and behave as though you had typed:

```
$ svn checkout http://host/path%20with%20space/project/espa%C3%B1a
```

If the URL contains spaces, be sure to place it within quotation marks so that your shell treats the whole thing as a single argument to the *svn* program.

Repository URLs

You can access Subversion repositories through many different methods—on local disk or through various network protocols, depending on how your administrator has set things up for you. A repository location, however, is always a URL. Table 1-1 describes how different URL schemes map to the available access methods.

Table 1-1. Repository access URLs

Schema	Access method
file:///	Direct repository access (on local disk)
http://	Access via WebDAV protocol to Subversion-aware Apache server
https://	Same as http://, but with SSL encryption
svn://	Access via custom protocol to an svnserve server
svn+ssh://	Same as svn://, but through an SSH tunnel

For more information on how Subversion parses URLs, see "Subversion Repository URLs" on page 7. For more information on the different types of network servers available for Subversion, see Chapter 6.

Working Copies

You've already read about working copies; now we'll demonstrate how the Subversion client creates and uses them.

A Subversion working copy is an ordinary directory tree on your local system, containing a collection of files. You can edit these files however you wish, and if they're source code files, you can compile your program from them in the usual way. Your working copy is your own private work area: Subversion will never incorporate other people's changes, nor make your own changes available to others, until you explicitly tell it to do so. You can even have multiple working copies of the same project.

After you've made some changes to the files in your working copy and verified that they work properly, Subversion provides you with commands to "publish" your changes to the other people working with you on your project (by writing to the repository). If other people publish their own changes, Subversion provides you with commands to merge those changes into your working copy (by reading from the repository).

A working copy also contains some extra files, created and maintained by Subversion, to help it carry out these commands. In particular, each directory in your working copy contains a subdirectory named *.svn*, also known as the working copy's *administrative directory*. The files in each administrative directory help Subversion recognize which files contain unpublished changes and which files are out of date with respect to others' work.

A typical Subversion repository often holds the files (or source code) for several projects; usually, each project is a subdirectory in the repository's filesystem tree. In this arrangement, a user's working copy will usually correspond to a particular subtree of the repository.

For example, suppose you have a repository that contains two software projects, `paint` and `calc`. Each project lives in its own top-level subdirectory, as shown in Figure 1-6.

To get a working copy, you must *check out* some subtree of the repository. (The term *check out* may sound like it has something to do with locking or reserving resources, but it doesn't; it simply creates a private copy of the project for you.) For example, if you check out */calc*, you will get a working copy like this:

```
$ svn checkout http://svn.example.com/repos/calc
A    calc/Makefile
A    calc/integer.c
A    calc/button.c
Checked out revision 56.

$ ls -A calc
Makefile  button.c integer.c .svn/
```

The list of letter As in the left margin indicates that Subversion is adding a number of items to your working copy. You now have a personal copy of the repository's */calc*

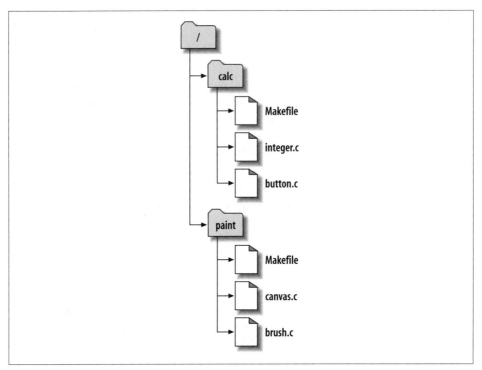

Figure 1-6. The repository's filesystem

directory, with one additional entry—*.svn*—which holds the extra information needed by Subversion, as mentioned earlier.

Suppose you make changes to *button.c*. Since the *.svn* directory remembers the file's original modification date and contents, Subversion can tell that you've changed the file. However, Subversion does not make your changes public until you explicitly tell it to. The act of publishing your changes is more commonly known as *committing* (or *checking in*) changes to the repository.

To publish your changes to others, you can use Subversion's *svn commit* command:

```
$ svn commit button.c -m "Fixed a typo in button.c."
Sending        button.c
Transmitting file data .
Committed revision 57.
```

Now your changes to *button.c* have been committed to the repository, with a note describing your change (namely, that you fixed a typo). If another user checks out a working copy of */calc*, she will see your changes in the latest version of the file.

Suppose you have a collaborator, Sally, who checked out a working copy of */calc* at the same time you did. When you commit your change to *button.c*, Sally's working copy is left unchanged; Subversion modifies working copies only at the user's request.

To bring her project up to date, Sally can ask Subversion to *update* her working copy, by using the *svn update* command. This will incorporate your changes into her working copy, as well as any others that have been committed since she checked it out:

```
$ pwd
/home/sally/calc

$ ls -A
Makefile button.c integer.c .svn/

$ svn update
U    button.c
Updated to revision 57.
```

The output from the *svn update* command indicates that Subversion updated the contents of *button.c*. Note that Sally didn't need to specify which files to update; Subversion uses the information in the *.svn* directory as well as further information in the repository to decide which files need to be brought up to date.

Revisions

An *svn commit* operation publishes changes to any number of files and directories as a single atomic transaction. In your working copy, you can change files' contents; create, delete, rename, and copy files and directories; and then commit a complete set of changes as an atomic transaction.

By atomic transaction, we mean simply this: either all of the changes happen in the repository, or none of them happens. Subversion tries to retain this atomicity in the face of program crashes, system crashes, network problems, and other users' actions.

Each time the repository accepts a commit, this creates a new state of the filesystem tree, called a *revision*. Each revision is assigned a unique natural number, one greater than the number of the previous revision. The initial revision of a freshly created repository is numbered 0 and consists of nothing but an empty root directory.

Global Revision Numbers

Unlike most version control systems, Subversion's revision numbers apply to *entire trees*, not individual files. Each revision number selects an entire tree, a particular state of the repository after some committed change. Another way to think about it is that revision N represents the state of the repository filesystem after the Nth commit. When Subversion users talk about "revision 5 of *foo.c*," they really mean "*foo.c* as it appears in revision 5." Notice that in general, revisions N and M of a file do *not* necessarily differ! Many other version control systems use per-file revision numbers, so this concept may seem unusual at first. (Former CVS users might want to see Appendix B for more details.)

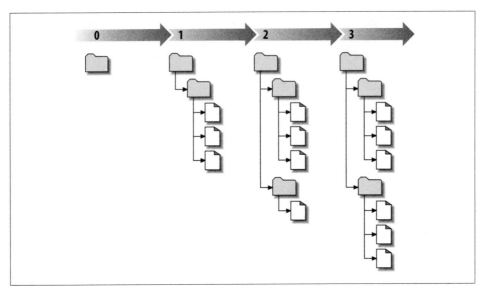

Figure 1-7. The repository

Figure 1-7 illustrates a nice way to visualize the repository. Imagine an array of revision numbers, starting at 0, stretching from left to right. Each revision number has a filesystem tree hanging below it, and each tree is a "snapshot" of the way the repository looked after a commit.

It's important to note that working copies do not always correspond to any single revision in the repository; they may contain files from several different revisions. For example, suppose you check out a working copy from a repository whose most recent revision is 4:

```
calc/Makefile:4
     integer.c:4
     button.c:4
```

At the moment, this working directory corresponds exactly to revision 4 in the repository. However, suppose you make a change to *button.c* and commit that change. Assuming no other commits have taken place, your commit will create revision 5 of the repository, and your working copy will now look like this:

```
calc/Makefile:4
     integer.c:4
     button.c:5
```

Suppose that, at this point, Sally commits a change to *integer.c*, creating revision 6. If you use *svn update* to bring your working copy up to date, it will look like this:

```
calc/Makefile:6
     integer.c:6
     button.c:6
```

Sally's change to *integer.c* will appear in your working copy, and your change will still be present in *button.c*. In this example, the text of *Makefile* is identical in revisions 4, 5, and 6, but Subversion will mark your working copy of *Makefile* with revision 6 to indicate that it is still current. So, after you do a clean update at the top of your working copy, it will generally correspond to exactly one revision in the repository.

How Working Copies Track the Repository

For each file in a working directory, Subversion records two essential pieces of information in the *.svn/* administrative area:

- Which revision your working file is based on (this is called the file's *working revision*)
- A timestamp recording when the local copy was last updated by the repository

Given this information, by talking to the repository, Subversion can tell which of the following four states a working file is in:

Unchanged, and current
> The file is unchanged in the working directory, and no changes to that file have been committed to the repository since its working revision. An *svn commit* of the file will do nothing, and an *svn update* of the file will do nothing.

Locally changed, and current
> The file has been changed in the working directory, and no changes to that file have been committed to the repository since you last updated. There are local changes that have not been committed to the repository; thus an *svn commit* of the file will succeed in publishing your changes, and an *svn update* of the file will do nothing.

Unchanged, and out of date
> The file has not been changed in the working directory, but it has been changed in the repository. The file should eventually be updated in order to make it current with the latest public revision. An *svn commit* of the file will do nothing, and an *svn update* of the file will fold the latest changes into your working copy.

Locally changed, and out of date
> The file has been changed both in the working directory and in the repository. An *svn commit* of the file will fail with an "out of date" error. The file should be updated first; an *svn update* command will attempt to merge the public changes with the local changes. If Subversion can't complete the merge in a plausible way automatically, it leaves it to the user to resolve the conflict.

This may sound like a lot to keep track of, but the *svn status* command will show you the state of any item in your working copy. For more information on that command, refer to "See an overview of your changes" on page 26.

Mixed Revision Working Copies

As a general principle, Subversion tries to be as flexible as possible. One special kind of flexibility is the ability to have a working copy containing files and directories with a mix of different working revision numbers. Unfortunately, this flexibility tends to confuse a number of new users. If the earlier example showing mixed revisions perplexed you, here's a primer on why the feature exists and how to make use of it.

Updates and commits are separate

One of the fundamental rules of Subversion is that a "push" action does not cause a "pull," nor vice versa. Just because you're ready to submit new changes to the repository doesn't mean you're ready to receive changes from other people. And if you have new changes still in progress, *svn update* should gracefully merge repository changes into your own, rather than forcing you to publish them.

The main side effect of this rule is that it means a working copy has to do extra bookkeeping to track mixed revisions as well as be tolerant of the mixture. It's made more complicated by the fact that directories themselves are versioned.

For example, suppose you have a working copy entirely at revision 10. You edit the file *foo.html* and then perform an *svn commit*, which creates revision 15 in the repository. After the commit succeeds, many new users would expect the working copy to be entirely at revision 15, but that's not the case! Any number of changes might have happened in the repository between revisions 10 and 15. The client knows nothing of those changes in the repository, since you haven't yet run *svn update*, and *svn commit* doesn't pull down new changes. If, on the other hand, *svn commit* were to automatically download the newest changes, it would be possible to set the entire working copy to revision 15—but then we'd be breaking the fundamental rule of "push" and "pull" remaining separate actions. Therefore, the only safe thing the Subversion client can do is mark the one file—*foo.html*—as being at revision 15. The rest of the working copy remains at revision 10. Only by running *svn update* can the latest changes be downloaded and the whole working copy be marked as revision 15.

Mixed revisions are normal

The fact is, *every time* you run *svn commit* your working copy ends up with some mixture of revisions. The things you just committed are marked as having larger working revisions than everything else. After several commits (with no updates in between), your working copy will contain a whole mixture of revisions. Even if you're the only person using the repository, you will still see this phenomenon. To examine your mixture of working revisions, use the *svn status* command with the --verbose option (see "See an overview of your changes" on page 26 for more information).

Often, new users are completely unaware that their working copy contains mixed revisions. This can be confusing, because many client commands are sensitive to the working revision of the item they're examining. For example, the *svn log* command is used to display the history of changes to a file or directory (see "Generating a List of Historical Changes" on page 38). When the user invokes this command on a working copy object, he expects to see the entire history of the object. But if the object's working revision is quite old (often because *svn update* hasn't been run in a long time), the history of the *older* version of the object is shown.

Mixed revisions are useful

If your project is sufficiently complex, you'll discover that it's sometimes nice to forcibly *backdate* (or update to a revision older than the one you already have) portions of your working copy to an earlier revision; you'll learn how to do that in Chapter 2. Perhaps you'd like to test an earlier version of a submodule contained in a subdirectory, or perhaps you'd like to figure out when a bug first came into existence in a specific file. This is the "time machine" aspect of a version control system—the feature that allows you to move any portion of your working copy forward and backward in history.

Mixed revisions have limitations

However you make use of mixed revisions in your working copy, there are limitations to this flexibility.

First, you cannot commit the deletion of a file or directory that isn't fully up to date. If a newer version of the item exists in the repository, your attempt to delete will be rejected to prevent you from accidentally destroying changes you've not yet seen.

Second, you cannot commit a metadata change to a directory unless it's fully up to date. You'll learn about attaching "properties" to items in Chapter 3. A directory's working revision defines a specific set of entries and properties, and thus committing a property change to an out-of-date directory may destroy properties you've not yet seen.

Summary

We covered a number of fundamental Subversion concepts in this chapter:

- We introduced the notions of the central repository, the client working copy, and the array of repository revision trees.
- We saw some simple examples of how two collaborators can use Subversion to publish and receive changes from one another, using the "copy-modify-merge" model.
- We talked a bit about the way that Subversion tracks and manages information in a working copy.

At this point, you should have a good idea of how Subversion works in the most general sense. Armed with this knowledge, you should now be ready to move into the next chapter, which is a detailed tour of Subversion's commands and features.

## CHAPTER 2

Basic Usage

Now we will go into the details of using Subversion. By the time you reach the end of this chapter, you will be able to perform all the tasks you need to use Subversion in a normal day's work. You'll start with getting your files into Subversion, followed by an initial checkout of your code. We'll then walk you through making changes and examining those changes. You'll also see how to bring changes made by others into your working copy, examine them, and work through any conflicts that might arise.

Note that this chapter is not meant to be an exhaustive list of all of Subversion's commands—rather, it's a conversational introduction to the most common Subversion tasks that you'll encounter. This chapter assumes that you've read and understood Chapter 1 and are familiar with the general model of Subversion. For a complete reference of all commands, see Chapter 9.

Help!

Before reading on, here is the most important command you'll ever need when using Subversion: *svn help*. The Subversion command-line client is self-documenting—at any time, a quick svn help *subcommand* will describe the syntax, options, and behavior of the subcommand:

```
$ svn help import
import: Commit an unversioned file or tree into the repository.
usage: import [PATH] URL

   Recursively commit a copy of PATH to URL.
   If PATH is omitted '.' is assumed.
   Parent directories are created as necessary in the repository.
   If PATH is a directory, the contents of the directory are added
   directly under URL.
   Unversionable items such as device files and pipes are ignored
   if --force is specified.
```

```
Valid options:
  -q [--quiet]            : print nothing, or only summary information
  -N [--non-recursive]    : obsolete; try --depth=files or --depth=immediates
  --depth ARG             : limit operation by depth ARG ('empty', 'files',
                            'immediates', or 'infinity')
  ...
```

Options and Switches and Flags, Oh My!

The Subversion command-line client has numerous command modifiers (which we call options), but there are two distinct kinds of options: short options are a single hyphen followed by a single letter, and long options consist of two hyphens followed by a number of letters (e.g., -s and --this-is-a-long-option, respectively). Every option has a long format, but only certain options have an additional short format (these are typically options that are frequently used). To maintain clarity, we *usually* use the long form in code examples, but when describing options, if there's a short form, we'll provide the long form (to improve clarity) and the short form (to make it easier to remember). You should use whichever one you're more comfortable with, but don't try to use both.

Getting Data into Your Repository

You can get new files into your Subversion repository in two ways: *svn import* and *svn add*. We'll discuss *svn import* now, and we'll discuss *svn add* later in this chapter when we review a typical day with Subversion.

svn import

The *svn import* command is a quick way to copy an unversioned tree of files into a repository, creating intermediate directories as necessary. *svn import* doesn't require a working copy, and your files are immediately committed to the repository. You typically use this when you have an existing tree of files that you want to begin tracking in your Subversion repository. For example:

```
$ svnadmin create /var/svn/newrepos
$ svn import mytree file:///var/svn/newrepos/some/project \
         -m "Initial import"
Adding         mytree/foo.c
Adding         mytree/bar.c
Adding         mytree/subdir
Adding         mytree/subdir/quux.h

Committed revision 1.
```

The example just shown copies the contents of directory *mytree* under the directory *some/project* in the repository:

```
$ svn list file:///var/svn/newrepos/some/project
bar.c
foo.c
subdir/
```

Note that after the import is finished, the original tree is *not* converted into a working copy. To start working, you still need to *svn checkout* a fresh working copy of the tree.

Recommended Repository Layout

While Subversion's flexibility allows you to lay out your repository in any way that you choose, we recommend that you create a *trunk* directory to hold the "main line" of development, a *branches* directory to contain branch copies, and a *tags* directory to contain tag copies. For example:

```
$ svn list file:///var/svn/repos
/trunk
/branches
/tags
```

You'll learn more about tags and branches in Chapter 4. For details and how to set up multiple projects, see "Repository Layout" on page 134 and "Planning Your Repository Organization" on page 147 to read more about project roots.

Initial Checkout

Most of the time, you will start using a Subversion repository by doing a *checkout* of your project. Checking out a repository creates a "working copy" of it on your local machine. This copy contains the HEAD (latest revision) of the Subversion repository that you specify on the command line:

```
$ svn checkout http://svn.collab.net/repos/svn/trunk
A    trunk/Makefile.in
A    trunk/ac-helpers
A    trunk/ac-helpers/install.sh
A    trunk/ac-helpers/install-sh
A    trunk/build.conf
...
Checked out revision 8810.
```

What's in a Name?

Subversion tries hard not to limit the type of data you can place under version control. The contents of files and property values are stored and transmitted as binary data, and "File Content Type" on page 57 tells you how to give Subversion a hint that "textual" operations don't make sense for a particular file. There are a few places, however, where Subversion places restrictions on information it stores.

Subversion internally handles certain bits of data—for example, property names, pathnames, and log messages—as UTF-8-encoded Unicode. This is not to say that all your interactions with Subversion must involve UTF-8, though. As a general rule, Subversion clients will gracefully and transparently handle conversions between UTF-8 and the encoding system in use on your computer, if such a conversion can meaningfully be done (which is the case for most common encodings in use today).

In WebDAV exchanges and older versions of some of Subversion's administrative files, paths are used as XML attribute values and as property names in XML tag names. This means that pathnames can contain only legal XML (1.0) characters, and properties are further limited to ASCII characters. Subversion also prohibits TAB, CR, and LF characters in pathnames to prevent paths from being broken up in diffs or in the output of commands such as *svn log* or *svn status*.

Although it may seem like a lot to remember, in practice these limitations are rarely a problem. As long as your locale settings are compatible with UTF-8 and you don't use control characters in pathnames, you should have no trouble communicating with Subversion. The command-line client adds an extra bit of help—to create "legally correct" versions for internal use, it will automatically escape illegal path characters as needed in URLs that you type.

Although the preceding example checks out the trunk directory, you can just as easily check out any deep subdirectory of a repository by specifying the subdirectory in the checkout URL:

```
$ svn checkout \
      http://svn.collab.net/repos/svn/trunk/subversion/tests/cmdline/
A    cmdline/revert_tests.py
A    cmdline/diff_tests.py
A    cmdline/autoprop_tests.py
A    cmdline/xmltests
A    cmdline/xmltests/svn-test.sh
...
Checked out revision 8810.
```

Since Subversion uses a copy-modify-merge model instead of lock-modify-unlock (see "Versioning Models" on page 2), you can immediately make changes to the files and directories in your working copy. Your working copy is just like any other collection of files and directories on your system. You can edit and change it, move it around, even delete the entire working copy and forget about it.

Although your working copy is "just like any other collection of files and directories on your system," and you can edit files at will, you must tell Subversion about *everything else* that you do. For example, if you want to copy or move an item in a working copy, you should use *svn copy* or *svn move* instead of the copy and move commands provided by your operating system. We'll talk more about these later in this chapter.

Unless you're ready to commit the addition of a new file or directory or changes to existing ones, there's no need to further notify the Subversion server that you've done anything.

What's with the .svn Directory?

Every directory in a working copy contains an administrative area—a subdirectory named *.svn*. Usually, directory listing commands won't show this subdirectory, but it is nevertheless an important directory. Whatever you do, don't delete or change anything in the administrative area! Subversion depends on it to manage your working copy.

If you accidentally remove the *.svn* subdirectory, the easiest way to fix the problem is to remove the entire containing directory (a normal system deletion, not *svn delete*), and then run *svn update* from a parent directory. The Subversion client will download the directory you've deleted, with a new *.svn* area included.

Although you can certainly check out a working copy with the URL of the repository as the only argument, you can also specify a directory after your repository URL. This places your working copy in the new directory that you name. For example:

```
$ svn checkout http://svn.collab.net/repos/svn/trunk subv
A    subv/Makefile.in
A    subv/ac-helpers
A    subv/ac-helpers/install.sh
A    subv/ac-helpers/install-sh
A    subv/build.conf
…
Checked out revision 8810.
```

That will place your working copy in a directory named subv instead of a directory named trunk, as we did previously. The directory subv will be created if it doesn't already exist.

Disabling Password Caching

When you perform a Subversion operation that requires you to authenticate, by default Subversion caches your authentication credentials on disk. This is done for convenience so that you don't have to continually reenter your password for future operations. If you're concerned about caching your Subversion passwords,[*] you can disable caching either permanently or on a case-by-case basis.

To disable password caching for a particular one-time command, pass the --no-auth-cache option on the command line. To permanently disable caching, you can add the

---

[*] Of course, you're not terribly worried—first because you know that you can't *really* delete anything from Subversion, and second because your Subversion password isn't the same as any of the other 3 million passwords you have, right? Right?

line `store-passwords` = `no` to your local machine's Subversion configuration file. See "Client Credentials Caching" on page 97 for details.

Authenticating As a Different User

Since Subversion caches auth credentials by default (both username and password), it conveniently remembers who you were acting as the last time you modified your working copy. But sometimes that's not helpful—particularly if you're working in a shared working copy such as a system configuration directory or a web server document root. In this case, just pass the `--username` option on the command line, and Subversion will attempt to authenticate as that user, prompting you for a password if necessary.

Basic Work Cycle

Subversion has numerous features, options, bells, and whistles, but on a day-to-day basis, odds are that you will use only a few of them. In this section, we'll run through the most common things that you might find yourself doing with Subversion in the course of a day's work.

The typical work cycle looks like this:

1. Update your working copy.
   - *svn update*
2. Make changes.
   - *svn add*
   - *svn delete*
   - *svn copy*
   - *svn move*
3. Examine your changes.
   - *svn status*
   - *svn diff*
4. Possibly undo some changes.
   - *svn revert*
5. Resolve conflicts (merge others' changes).
   - *svn update*
   - *svn resolve*
6. Commit your changes.
   - *svn commit*

Update Your Working Copy

When working on a project with a team, you'll want to update your working copy to receive any changes other developers on the project have made since your last update. Use *svn update* to bring your working copy into sync with the latest revision in the repository:

```
$ svn update
U  foo.c
U  bar.c
Updated to revision 2.
```

In this case, it appears that someone checked in modifications to both *foo.c* and *bar.c* since the last time you updated, and Subversion has updated your working copy to include those changes.

When the server sends changes to your working copy via *svn update*, a letter code is displayed next to each item to tell you which actions Subversion performed to bring your working copy up to date. To learn what these letters mean, run `svn help update`.

Make Changes to Your Working Copy

Now you can get to work and make changes in your working copy. It's usually most convenient to decide on a discrete change (or set of changes) to make, such as writing a new feature, fixing a bug, and so on. The Subversion commands that you will use here are *svn add*, *svn delete*, *svn copy*, *svn move*, and *svn mkdir*. However, if you are merely editing files that are already in Subversion, you may not need to use any of these commands until you commit.

Versioning Symbolic Links

On non-Windows platforms, Subversion is able to version files of the special type *symbolic link* (or "symlink"). A symlink is a file that acts as a sort of transparent reference to some other object in the filesystem, allowing programs to read and write to those objects indirectly by way of performing operations on the symlink itself.

When a symlink is committed into a Subversion repository, Subversion remembers that the file is in fact a symlink, and it also remembers the object to which the symlink "points." When that symlink is checked out to another working copy on a non-Windows system, Subversion reconstructs a real filesystem-level symbolic link from the versioned symlink. But that doesn't in any way limit the usability of working copies on systems such as Windows that do not support symlinks. On such systems, Subversion simply creates a regular text file whose contents are the path to which the original symlink pointed. While that file can't be used as a symlink on a Windows system, it also won't prevent Windows users from performing their other Subversion-related activities.

You can make two kinds of changes to your working copy: *file changes* and *tree changes*. You don't need to tell Subversion that you intend to change a file; just make your changes using your text editor, word processor, graphics program, or whatever tool you would normally use. Subversion automatically detects which files have been changed, and in addition, it handles binary files just as easily as it handles text files—and just as efficiently, too. For tree changes, you can ask Subversion to "mark" files and directories for scheduled removal, addition, copying, or moving. These changes may take place immediately in your working copy, but no additions or removals will happen in the repository until you commit them.

Here is an overview of the five Subversion subcommands that you'll use most often to make tree changes:

svn add foo

> Schedule file, directory, or symbolic link *foo* to be added to the repository. When you next commit, *foo* will become a child of its parent directory. Note that if *foo* is a directory, everything underneath *foo* will be scheduled for addition. If you want only to add *foo* itself, pass the `--depth empty` option.

svn delete foo

> Schedule file, directory, or symbolic link *foo* to be deleted from the repository. If *foo* is a file or link, it is immediately deleted from your working copy. If *foo* is a directory, it is not deleted, but Subversion schedules it for deletion. When you commit your changes, *foo* will be entirely removed from your working copy and the repository.[†]

svn copy foo bar

> Create a new item *bar* as a duplicate of *foo* and automatically schedule *bar* for addition. When *bar* is added to the repository on the next commit, its copy history is recorded (as having originally come from *foo*). *svn copy* does not create intermediate directories unless you pass the `--parents` option.

svn move foo bar

> This command is exactly the same as running `svn copy foo bar; svn delete foo`. That is, *bar* is scheduled for addition as a copy of *foo*, and *foo* is scheduled for removal. *svn move* does not create intermediate directories unless you pass the `--parents` option.

svn mkdir blort

> This command is exactly the same as running `mkdir blort; svn add blort`. That is, a new directory named *blort* is created and scheduled for addition.

[†] Of course, nothing is ever totally deleted from the repository—just from the HEAD of the repository. You can get back anything you delete by checking out (or updating your working copy to) a revision earlier than the one in which you deleted it. Also see "Resurrecting Deleted Items" on page 116.

Changing the Repository Without a Working Copy

There *are* some use cases that immediately commit tree changes to the repository. This happens only when a subcommand is operating directly on a URL, rather than on a working-copy path. In particular, specific uses of *svn mkdir*, *svn copy*, *svn move*, and *svn delete* can work with URLs (and don't forget that *svn import* always makes changes to a URL).

URL operations behave in this manner because commands that operate on a working copy can use the working copy as a sort of "staging area" to set up your changes before committing them to the repository. Commands that operate on URLs don't have this luxury, so when you operate directly on a URL, any of the aforementioned actions represents an immediate commit.

Examine Your Changes

Once you've finished making changes, you need to commit them to the repository, but before you do so, it's usually a good idea to take a look at exactly what you've changed. By examining your changes before you commit, you can make a more accurate log message. You may also discover that you've inadvertently changed a file, and this gives you a chance to revert those changes before committing. Additionally, this is a good opportunity to review and scrutinize changes before publishing them. You can see an overview of the changes you've made by using *svn status*, and you can dig into the details of those changes by using *svn diff*.

Look Ma! No Network!

You can use the commands *svn status*, *svn diff*, and *svn revert* without any network access even if your repository *is* across the network. This makes it easy to manage your changes-in-progress when you are somewhere without a network connection, such as traveling on an airplane, riding a commuter train, or hacking on the beach.‡

Subversion does this by keeping private caches of pristine versions of each versioned file inside the *.svn* administrative areas. This allows Subversion to report—and revert—local modifications to those files *without network access*. This cache (called the "text-base") also allows Subversion to send the user's local modifications during a commit to the server as a compressed *delta* (or "difference") against the pristine version. Having this cache is a tremendous benefit—even if you have a fast Internet connection, it's much faster to send only a file's changes rather than the whole file to the server.

‡ And you don't have a WLAN card. Thought you got us, huh?

Subversion has been optimized to help you with the task of examining your changes, and it is able to do many things without communicating with the repository. In particular, your working copy contains a hidden cached "pristine" copy of each version-controlled file within the .svn area. Because of this, Subversion can quickly show you how your working files have changed and can even allow you to undo your changes without contacting the repository.

See an overview of your changes

To get an overview of your changes, you'll use the *svn status* command. You'll probably use *svn status* more than any other Subversion command.

CVS Users: Hold That Update!

You're probably used to using *cvs update* to see what changes you've made to your working copy. *svn status* will give you all the information you need regarding what has changed in your working copy—without accessing the repository or potentially incorporating new changes published by other users.

In Subversion, *svn update* does just that: it updates your working copy with any changes committed to the repository since the last time you updated your working copy. You may have to break the habit of using the *update* command to see what local modifications you've made.

If you run *svn status* at the top of your working copy with no arguments, it will detect all file and tree changes you've made. Here are a few examples of the most common status codes that *svn status* can return. (Note that the text following # is not actually printed by *svn status*.)

```
?       scratch.c            # file is not under version control
A       stuff/loot/bloo.h    # file is scheduled for addition
C       stuff/loot/lump.c    # file has textual conflicts from an update
D       stuff/fish.c         # file is scheduled for deletion
M       bar.c                # the content in bar.c has local modifications
```

In this output format, *svn status* prints six columns of characters, followed by several whitespace characters, followed by a file or directory name. The first column tells the status of a file or directory and/or its contents. The codes we listed are:

A item

> The file, directory, or symbolic link *item* has been scheduled for addition into the repository.

C item

> The file *item* is in a state of conflict. That is, changes received from the server during an update overlap with local changes that you have in your working copy (and weren't resolved during the update). You must resolve this conflict before committing your changes to the repository.

`D` *item*

The file, directory, or symbolic link *item* has been scheduled for deletion from the repository.

`M` *item*

The contents of the file *item* have been modified.

If you pass a specific path to *svn status*, you get information about that item alone:

```
$ svn status stuff/fish.c
D      stuff/fish.c
```

svn status also has a `--verbose` (`-v`) option, which will show you the status of *every* item in your working copy, even if it has not been changed:

```
$ svn status -v
M            44     23    sally   README
             44     30    sally   INSTALL
M            44     20    harry   bar.c
             44     18    ira     stuff
             44     35    harry   stuff/trout.c
D            44     19    ira     stuff/fish.c
             44     21    sally   stuff/things
A             0      ?     ?      stuff/things/bloo.h
             44     36    harry   stuff/things/gloo.c
```

This is the "long form" output of *svn status*. The letters in the first column mean the same as before, but the second column shows the working revision of the item. The third and fourth columns show the revision in which the item last changed and who changed it.

None of the prior invocations to *svn status* contact the repository—instead, they compare the metadata in the *.svn* directory with the working copy. Finally, there is the `--show-updates` (`-u`) option, which contacts the repository and adds information about things that are out of date:

```
$ svn status -u -v
M       *    44     23    sally   README
M            44     20    harry   bar.c
        *    44     35    harry   stuff/trout.c
D            44     19    ira     stuff/fish.c
A             0      ?     ?      stuff/things/bloo.h
Status against revision:    46
```

Notice the two asterisks: if you were to run `svn update` at this point, you would receive changes to *README* and *trout.c*. This tells you some very useful information—you'll need to update and get the server changes on *README* before you commit, or the repository will reject your commit for being out of date (more on this subject later).

svn status can display much more information about the files and directories in your working copy than we've shown here—for an exhaustive description of *svn status* and its output, see "svn status" in Chapter 9.

Examine the details of your local modifications

Another way to examine your changes is with the *svn diff* command. You can find out *exactly* how you've modified things by running `svn diff` with no arguments, which prints out file changes in *unified diff format*:

```
$ svn diff
Index: bar.c
===================================================================
--- bar.c     (revision 3)
+++ bar.c     (working copy)
@@ -1,7 +1,12 @@
+#include <sys/types.h>
+#include <sys/stat.h>
+#include <unistd.h>
+
+#include <stdio.h>

 int main(void) {
-  printf("Sixty-four slices of American Cheese...\n");
+  printf("Sixty-five slices of American Cheese...\n");
 return 0;
 }

Index: README
===================================================================
--- README    (revision 3)
+++ README    (working copy)
@@ -193,3 +193,4 @@
+Note to self:  pick up laundry.

Index: stuff/fish.c
===================================================================
--- stuff/fish.c    (revision 1)
+++ stuff/fish.c    (working copy)
-Welcome to the file known as 'fish'.
-Information on fish will be here soon.

Index: stuff/things/bloo.h
===================================================================
--- stuff/things/bloo.h    (revision 8)
+++ stuff/things/bloo.h    (working copy)
+Here is a new file to describe
+things about bloo.
```

The *svn diff* command produces this output by comparing your working files against the cached "pristine" copies within the *.svn* area. Files scheduled for addition are displayed as all added text, and files scheduled for deletion are displayed as all deleted text.

Output is displayed in unified diff format. That is, removed lines are prefaced with -, and added lines are prefaced with +. *svn diff* also prints filename and offset information useful to the *patch* program, so you can generate "patches" by redirecting the diff output to a file:

```
$ svn diff > patchfile
```

You could, for example, email the patch file to another developer for review or testing prior to a commit.

Subversion uses its internal diff engine, which produces unified diff format by default. If you want diff output in a different format, specify an external diff program using `--diff-cmd` and pass it any flags you'd like using the `--extensions` (`-x`) option. For example, to see local differences in file *foo.c* in context output format while ignoring case differences, you might run `svn diff --diff-cmd /usr/bin/diff --extensions '-i' foo.c`.

Undoing Working Changes

Suppose, while viewing the output of *svn diff*, you determine that all the changes you made to a particular file are mistakes. Maybe you shouldn't have changed the file at all, or perhaps it would be easier to make different changes starting from scratch.

This is a perfect opportunity to use *svn revert*:

```
$ svn revert README
Reverted 'README'
```

Subversion reverts the file to its premodified state by overwriting it with the cached "pristine" copy from the *.svn* area. But also note that *svn revert* can undo *any* scheduled operations—for example, you might decide that you don't want to add a new file after all:

```
$ svn status foo
?       foo

$ svn add foo
A       foo

$ svn revert foo
Reverted 'foo'

$ svn status foo
?       foo
```

> `svn revert` *item* has exactly the same effect as deleting *item* from your working copy and then running `svn update -r BASE` *item*. However, if you're reverting a file, *svn revert* has one very noticeable difference—it doesn't have to communicate with the repository to restore your file.

Or perhaps you mistakenly removed a file from version control:

```
$ svn status README

$ svn delete README
D       README
```

```
$ svn revert README
Reverted 'README'

$ svn status README
```

Resolve Conflicts (Merging Others' Changes)

We've already seen how `svn status -u` can predict conflicts. Suppose you run `svn update` and some interesting things occur:

```
$ svn update
U  INSTALL
G  README
Conflict discovered in 'bar.c'.
Select: (p) postpone, (df) diff-full, (e) edit,
        (h) help for more options:
```

The U and G codes are no cause for concern; those files cleanly absorbed changes from the repository. The files marked with U contained no local changes but were Updated with changes from the repository. The G stands for merGed, which means that the file had local changes to begin with, but the changes coming from the repository didn't overlap with the local changes.

But the next two lines are part of a feature (new in Subversion 1.5) called *interactive conflict resolution*. This means that the changes from the server overlapped with your own, and you have the opportunity to resolve this conflict. The most commonly used options are displayed, but you can see all of the options by typing *h*:

```
  ...
  (p)  postpone    - mark the conflict to be resolved later
  (df) diff-full   - show all changes made to merged file
  (e)  edit        - change merged file in an editor
  (r)  resolved    - accept merged version of file
  (mf) mine-full   - accept my version of entire file (ignore their changes)
  (tf) theirs-full - accept their version of entire file (lose my changes)
  (l)  launch      - launch external tool to resolve conflict
  (h)  help        - show this list
```

Let's briefly review each of these options before we go into detail on what each option means:

(p)ostpone

Leave the file in a conflicted state for you to resolve after your update is complete.

(d)iff

Display the differences between the base revision and the conflicted file itself in unified diff format.

(e)dit

Open the file in conflict with your favorite editor, as set in the environment variable `EDITOR`.

(r)esolved

After editing a file, tell *svn* that you've resolved the conflicts in the file and that it should accept the current contents—basically, that you've "resolved" the conflict.

(m)ine-(f)ull

Discard the newly received changes from the server and use only your local changes for the file under review.

(t)heirs-(f)ull

Discard your local changes to the file under review and use only the newly received changes from the server.

(l)aunch

Launch an external program to perform the conflict resolution. This requires a bit of preparation beforehand.

(h)elp

Show the list of all possible commands you can use in interactive conflict resolution.

We'll cover these commands in more detail now, grouping them together by related functionality.

Viewing conflict differences interactively

Before deciding how to attack a conflict interactively, odds are that you'd like to see exactly what is in conflict, and the *diff* command (d) is what you'll use for this:

```
...
Select: (p) postpone, (df) diff-full, (e) edit,
        (h)elp for more options : d
--- .svn/text-base/sandwich.txt.svn-base     Tue Dec 11 21:33:57 2007
+++ .svn/tmp/tempfile.32.tmp     Tue Dec 11 21:34:33 2007
@@ -1 +1,5 @@
-Just buy a sandwich.
+<<<<<<< .mine
+Go pick up a cheesesteak.
+=======
+Bring me a taco!
+>>>>>>> .r32
...
```

The first line of the diff content shows the previous contents of the working copy (the BASE revision); the next content line is your change; and the last content line is the change that was just received from the server (*usually* the HEAD revision). With this information in hand, you're ready to move on to the next action.

Resolving conflict differences interactively

There are four different ways to resolve conflicts interactively—two of which allow you to selectively merge and edit changes, and two of which allow you to simply pick a version of the file and move along.

If you wish to choose some combination of your local changes, you can use the "edit" command (e) to manually edit the file with conflict markers in a text editor (determined by the EDITOR environment variable). Editing the file by hand in your favorite text editor is a somewhat low-tech way of remedying conflicts (see "Merging conflicts by hand" on page 34 for a walkthrough), so some people like to use fancy graphical merge tools instead.

To use a merge tool, you need to either set the SVN_MERGE environment variable or define the merge-tool-cmd option in your Subversion configuration file (see "Configuration Options" on page 236 for more details). Subversion will pass four arguments to the merge tool: the BASE revision of the file, the revision of the file received from the server as part of the update, the copy of the file containing your local edits, and the merged copy of the file (which contains conflict markers). If your merge tool is expecting arguments in a different order or format, you'll need to write a wrapper script for Subversion to invoke. After you've edited the file, if you're satisfied with the changes you've made, you can tell Subversion that the edited file is no longer in conflict by using the "resolve" command (r).

If you decide that you don't need to merge any changes but just want to accept one version of the file or the other, you can either choose your changes (a.k.a. "mine") by using the "mine-full" command (mf) or choose theirs by using the "theirs-full" command (tf).

Postponing conflict resolution

This may sound like an appropriate section for avoiding marital disagreements, but it's actually still about Subversion, so read on. If you're doing an update and encounter a conflict that you're not prepared to review or resolve, you can type p to postpone resolving a conflict on a file-by-file basis when you run svn update. If you're running an update and don't want to resolve any conflicts, you can pass the --non-interactive option to *svn update*, and any file in conflict will be marked with a C automatically.

The C stands for conflict. This means that the changes from the server overlapped with your own, and now you have to manually choose between them after the update has completed. When you postpone a conflict resolution, *svn* typically does three things to assist you in noticing and resolving that conflict:

- Subversion prints a C during the update and remembers that the file is in a state of conflict.
- If Subversion considers the file to be mergeable, it places *conflict markers*—special strings of text that delimit the "sides" of the conflict—into the file to visibly demonstrate the overlapping areas. (Subversion uses the svn:mime-type property to decide whether a file is capable of contextual, line-based merging. See "File Content Type" on page 57 to learn more.)

- For every conflicted file, Subversion places three extra unversioned files in your working copy:

filename.mine

> This is your file as it existed in your working copy before you updated your working copy—that is, without conflict markers. This file has only your latest changes in it. (If Subversion considers the file to be unmergeable, the *.mine* file isn't created, since it would be identical to the working file.)

filename.rOLDREV

> This is the file that was the BASE revision before you updated your working copy. That is, it's the file that you checked out before you made your latest edits.

filename.rNEWREV

> This is the file that your Subversion client just received from the server when you updated your working copy. This file corresponds to the HEAD revision of the repository.

> Here, *OLDREV* is the revision number of the file in your *.svn* directory, and *NEWREV* is the revision number of the repository HEAD.

For example, Sally makes changes to the file *sandwich.txt*, but does not yet commit those changes. Meanwhile, Harry commits changes to that same file. Sally updates her working copy before committing and she gets a conflict, which she postpones:

```
$ svn update
Conflict discovered in 'sandwich.txt'.
Select: (p) postpone, (df) diff-full, (e) edit,
        (h)elp for more options : p
C   sandwich.txt
Updated to revision 2.
$ ls -1
sandwich.txt
sandwich.txt.mine
sandwich.txt.r1
sandwich.txt.r2
```

At this point, Subversion will *not* allow Sally to commit the file *sandwich.txt* until the three temporary files are removed:

```
$ svn commit -m "Add a few more things"
svn: Commit failed (details follow):
svn: Aborting commit: '/home/sally/svn-work/sandwich.txt' remains in conflict
```

If you've postponed a conflict, you need to resolve the conflict before Subversion will allow you to commit your changes. You'll do this with the *svn resolve* command and one of several arguments to the --accept option.

If you want to choose the version of the file that you last checked out before making your edits, choose the *base* argument.

If you want to choose the version that contains only your edits, choose the *mine-full* argument.

If you want to choose the version that your most recent update pulled from the server (and thus discard your edits entirely), choose the *theirs-full* argument.

However, if you want to pick and choose from your changes and the changes that your update fetched from the server, merge the conflicted text "by hand" (by examining and editing the conflict markers within the file), and then choose the *working* argument.

svn resolve removes the three temporary files and accepts the version of the file that you specified with the `--accept` option, and Subversion no longer considers the file to be in a state of conflict:

```
$ svn resolve --accept working sandwich.txt
Resolved conflicted state of 'sandwich.txt'
```

Merging conflicts by hand

Merging conflicts by hand can be quite intimidating the first time you attempt it, but with a little practice, it can become as easy as falling off a bike.

Here's an example. Due to a miscommunication, you and Sally, your collaborator, both edit the file *sandwich.txt* at the same time. Sally commits her changes, and when you go to update your working copy, you get a conflict. You're going to have to edit *sandwich.txt* to resolve the conflict. First, take a look at the file:

```
$ cat sandwich.txt
Top piece of bread
Mayonnaise
Lettuce
Tomato
Provolone
<<<<<<< .mine
Salami
Mortadella
Prosciutto
=======
Sauerkraut
Grilled Chicken
>>>>>>> .r2
Creole Mustard
Bottom piece of bread
```

The strings of less-than signs, equals signs, and greater-than signs are conflict markers and are not part of the actual data in conflict. You generally want to ensure that those markers are removed from the file before your next commit. The text between the first two sets of markers is composed of the changes you made in the conflicting area:

```
<<<<<<< .mine
Salami
Mortadella
```

```
Prosciutto
=======
```

The text between the second and third sets of conflict markers is the text from Sally's commit:

```
=======
Sauerkraut
Grilled Chicken
>>>>>>> .r2
```

Usually you won't want to just delete the conflict markers and Sally's changes—she's going to be awfully surprised when the sandwich arrives and it's not what she wanted. This is where you pick up the phone or walk across the office and explain to Sally that you can't get sauerkraut from an Italian deli.§ Once you've agreed on the changes you will commit, edit your file and remove the conflict markers:

```
Top piece of bread
Mayonnaise
Lettuce
Tomato
Provolone
Salami
Mortadella
Prosciutto
Creole Mustard
Bottom piece of bread
```

Now use *svn resolve*, and you're ready to commit your changes:

```
$ svn resolve --accept working sandwich.txt
Resolved conflicted state of 'sandwich.txt'
$ svn commit -m "Go ahead and use my sandwich, discarding Sally's edits."
```

Note that *svn resolve*, unlike most of the other commands we deal with in this chapter, requires that you explicitly list any filenames that you wish to resolve. In any case, you want to be careful and use *svn resolve* only when you're certain that you've fixed the conflict in your file—once the temporary files are removed, Subversion will let you commit the file even if it still contains conflict markers.

If you ever get confused while editing the conflicted file, you can always consult the three files that Subversion creates for you in your working copy—including your file as it was before you updated. You can even use a third-party interactive merging tool to examine those three files.

Discarding your changes in favor of a newly fetched revision

If you get a conflict and decide that you want to throw out your changes, you can run `svn resolve --accept theirs-full` *CONFLICTED-PATH* and Subversion will discard your edits and remove the temporary files:

---

§ And if you ask them for it, they may very well ride you out of town on a rail.

```
$ svn update
Conflict discovered in 'sandwich.txt'.
Select: (p) postpone, (df) diff-full, (e) edit,
        (h) help for more options: p
C     sandwich.txt
Updated to revision 2.
$ ls sandwich.*
sandwich.txt  sandwich.txt.mine  sandwich.txt.r2  sandwich.txt.r1
$ svn resolve --accept theirs-full sandwich.txt
Resolved conflicted state of 'sandwich.txt'
```

Punting: using svn revert

If you decide that you want to throw out your changes and start your edits again (whether this occurs after a conflict or at any time), just revert your changes:

```
$ svn revert sandwich.txt
Reverted 'sandwich.txt'
$ ls sandwich.*
sandwich.txt
```

Note that when you revert a conflicted file, you don't have to use *svn resolve*.

Commit Your Changes

Finally! Your edits are finished, you've merged all changes from the server, and you're ready to commit your changes to the repository.

The *svn commit* command sends all of your changes to the repository. When you commit a change, you need to supply a *log message* describing your change. Your log message will be attached to the new revision you create. If your log message is brief, you may wish to supply it on the command line using the --message (or -m) option:

```
$ svn commit -m "Corrected number of cheese slices."
Sending        sandwich.txt
Transmitting file data .
Committed revision 3.
```

However, if you've been composing your log message as you work, you may want to tell Subversion to get the message from a file by passing the filename with the --file (-F) option:

```
$ svn commit -F logmsg
Sending        sandwich.txt
Transmitting file data .
Committed revision 4.
```

If you fail to specify either the --message or --file option, Subversion will automatically launch your favorite editor (see the information on editor-cmd in "Config" on page 239) for composing a log message.

If you're in your editor writing a commit message and decide that you want to cancel your commit, you can just quit your editor without saving changes. If you've already saved your commit message, simply delete the text, save again, and then abort:

```
$ svn commit
Waiting for Emacs...Done

Log message unchanged or not specified
(a)bort, (c)ontinue, (e)dit
a
$
```

The repository doesn't know or care whether your changes make any sense as a whole; it checks only to make sure nobody else has changed any of the same files that you did when you weren't looking. If somebody *has* done that, the entire commit will fail with a message informing you that one or more of your files are out of date:

```
$ svn commit -m "Add another rule"
Sending        rules.txt
svn: Commit failed (details follow):
svn: File '/sandwich.txt' is out of date
...
```

(The exact wording of this error message depends on the network protocol and server you're using, but the idea is the same in all cases.)

At this point, you need to run **svn update**, deal with any merges or conflicts that result, and attempt your commit again.

That covers the basic work cycle for using Subversion. Subversion offers many other features that you can use to manage your repository and working copy, but most of your day-to-day use of Subversion will involve only the commands that we've discussed so far in this chapter. We will, however, cover a few more commands that you'll use fairly often.

Examining History

Your Subversion repository is like a time machine. It keeps a record of every change ever committed and allows you to explore this history by examining previous versions of files and directories as well as the metadata that accompanies them. With a single Subversion command, you can check out the repository (or restore an existing working copy) exactly as it was at any date or revision number in the past. However, sometimes you just want to *peer into* the past instead of *going into* it.

Several commands can provide you with historical data from the repository:

svn log

Shows you broad information: log messages with date and author information attached to revisions and which paths changed in each revision

svn diff
> Shows line-level details of a particular change

svn cat
> Retrieves a file as it existed in a particular revision number and displays it on your screen

svn list
> Displays the files in a directory for any given revision

Generating a List of Historical Changes

To find information about the history of a file or directory, use the *svn log* command. *svn log* will provide you with a record of who made changes to a file or directory, at what revision it changed, the time and date of that revision, and—if it was provided—the log message that accompanied the commit:

```
$ svn log
------------------------------------------------------------------------
r3 | sally | 2008-05-15 23:09:28 -0500 (Thu, 15 May 2008) | 1 line

Added include lines and corrected # of cheese slices.
------------------------------------------------------------------------
r2 | harry | 2008-05-14 18:43:15 -0500 (Wed, 14 May 2008) | 1 line

Added main() methods.
------------------------------------------------------------------------
r1 | sally | 2008-05-10 19:50:31 -0500 (Sat, 10 May 2008) | 1 line

Initial import
------------------------------------------------------------------------
```

Note that the log messages are printed in *reverse chronological order* by default. If you wish to see a different range of revisions in a particular order or just a single revision, pass the --**revision** (-r) option:

```
$ svn log -r 5:19    # shows logs 5 through 19 in chronological order

$ svn log -r 19:5    # shows logs 5 through 19 in reverse order

$ svn log -r 8       # shows log for revision 8
```

You can also examine the log history of a single file or directory. For example:

```
$ svn log foo.c
...
$ svn log http://foo.com/svn/trunk/code/foo.c
...
```

These will display log messages *only* for those revisions in which the working file (or URL) changed.

Why Does svn log Not Show Me What I Just Committed?

If you make a commit and immediately type `svn log` with no arguments, you may notice that your most recent commit doesn't show up in the list of log messages. This is due to a combination of the behavior of *svn commit* and the default behavior of *svn log*. First, when you commit changes to the repository, *svn* bumps only the revision of files (and directories) that it commits, so usually the parent directory remains at the older revision (See "Updates and commits are separate" on page 14 for an explanation). *svn log* then defaults to fetching the history of the directory at its current revision, and thus you don't see the newly committed changes. The solution here is to either update your working copy or explicitly provide a revision number to *svn log* by using the `--revision` (`-r`) option.

If you want even more information about a file or directory, *svn log* also takes a `--verbose` (`-v`) option. Because Subversion allows you to move and copy files and directories, it is important to be able to track path changes in the filesystem. So, in verbose mode, *svn log* will include a list of changed paths in a revision in its output:

```
$ svn log -r 8 -v
------------------------------------------------------------------------
r8 | sally | 2008-05-21 13:19:25 -0500 (Wed, 21 May 2008) | 1 line
Changed paths:
   M /trunk/code/foo.c
   M /trunk/code/bar.h
   A /trunk/code/doc/README

Frozzled the sub-space winch.

------------------------------------------------------------------------
```

svn log also takes a `--quiet` (`-q`) option, which suppresses the body of the log message. When combined with `--verbose`, it gives just the names of the changed files.

Why Does svn log Give Me an Empty Response?

After working with Subversion for a bit, most users will come across something like this:

```
$ svn log -r 2
------------------------------------------------------------------------
$
```

At first glance, this seems like an error. But recall that while revisions are repository-wide, *svn log* operates on a path in the repository. If you supply no path, Subversion uses the current working directory as the default target. As a result, if you're operating in a subdirectory of your working copy and attempt to see the log of a revision in which neither that directory nor any of its children were changed, Subversion will show you an empty log. If you want to see what changed in that revision, try pointing *svn log* directly at the topmost URL of your repository, as in `svn log -r 2 http://svn.collab.net/repos/svn`.

Examining the Details of Historical Changes

We've already seen *svn diff* before—it displays file differences in unified diff format. We used it to show the local modifications made to our working copy before committing to the repository.

In fact, it turns out that there are *three* distinct uses of *svn diff*:

- Examining local changes
- Comparing your working copy to the repository
- Comparing repository revisions

Examining local changes

As we've seen, invoking `svn diff` with no options will compare your working files to the cached "pristine" copies in the .*svn* area:

```
$ svn diff
Index: rules.txt
===================================================================
--- rules.txt    (revision 3)
+++ rules.txt    (working copy)
@@ -1,4 +1,5 @@
 Be kind to others
 Freedom = Responsibility
 Everything in moderation
-Chew with your mouth open
+Chew with your mouth closed
+Listen when others are speaking
$
```

Comparing working copy to repository

If a single `--revision` (`-r`) number is passed, your working copy is compared to the specified revision in the repository:

```
$ svn diff -r 3 rules.txt
Index: rules.txt
===================================================================
--- rules.txt    (revision 3)
+++ rules.txt    (working copy)
@@ -1,4 +1,5 @@
 Be kind to others
 Freedom = Responsibility
 Everything in moderation
-Chew with your mouth open
+Chew with your mouth closed
+Listen when others are speaking
$
```

Comparing repository revisions

If two revision numbers, separated by a colon, are passed via `--revision` (`-r`), the two revisions are directly compared:

```
$ svn diff -r 2:3 rules.txt
Index: rules.txt
===================================================================
--- rules.txt   (revision 2)
+++ rules.txt   (revision 3)
@@ -1,4 +1,4 @@
 Be kind to others
-Freedom = Chocolate Ice Cream
+Freedom = Responsibility
 Everything in moderation
 Chew with your mouth open
$
```

A more convenient way of comparing one revision to the previous revision is to use the `--change` (`-c`) option:

```
$ svn diff -c 3 rules.txt
Index: rules.txt
===================================================================
--- rules.txt   (revision 2)
+++ rules.txt   (revision 3)
@@ -1,4 +1,4 @@
 Be kind to others
-Freedom = Chocolate Ice Cream
+Freedom = Responsibility
 Everything in moderation
 Chew with your mouth open
$
```

Lastly, you can compare repository revisions even when you don't have a working copy on your local machine, just by including the appropriate URL on the command line:

```
$ svn diff -c 5 http://svn.example.com/repos/example/trunk/text/rules.txt
...
$
```

Browsing the Repository

Using *svn cat* and *svn list*, you can view various revisions of files and directories without changing the working revision of your working copy. In fact, you don't even need a working copy to use either one.

svn cat

If you want to examine an earlier version of a file and not necessarily the differences between two files, you can use *svn cat*:

```
$ svn cat -r 2 rules.txt
Be kind to others
```

ocolate Ice Cream
n moderation
ur mouth open

direct the output directly into a file:

```
2 rules.txt > rules.txt.v2
```

svn list

The *svn list* command shows you which files are in a repository directory without actually downloading the files to your local machine:

```
$ svn list http://svn.collab.net/repos/svn
README
branches/
clients/
tags/
trunk/
```

If you want a more detailed listing, pass the **--verbose** (**-v**) flag to get output like this:

```
$ svn list -v http://svn.collab.net/repos/svn
   20620 harry          1084 Jul 13  2006 README
   23339 harry               Feb 04 01:40 branches/
   21282 sally               Aug 27 09:41 developer-resources/
   23198 harry               Jan 23 17:17 tags/
   23351 sally               Feb 05 13:26 trunk/
```

The columns tell you the revision at which the file or directory was last modified, the user who modified it, the size if it is a file, the date it was last modified, and the item's name.

 The svn list command with no arguments defaults to the *repository URL* of the current working directory, *not* the local working copy directory. After all, if you want a listing of your local directory, you could use just plain *ls* (or any reasonable non-Unix equivalent).

Fetching Older Repository Snapshots

In addition to all of the previous commands, you can use *svn update* and *svn checkout* with the **--revision** option to take an entire working copy "back in time":[‖]

```
$ svn checkout -r 1729 # Checks out a new working copy at r1729
...
$ svn update -r 1729 # Updates an existing working copy to r1729
...
```

‖ See? We told you that Subversion was a time machine.

Many Subversion newcomers attempt to use the preceding *svn update* example to "undo" committed changes, but this won't work as you can't commit changes that you obtain from backdating a working copy if the changed files have newer revisions. See "Resurrecting Deleted Items" on page 116 for a description of how to "undo" a commit.

Lastly, if you're building a release and wish to bundle up your files from Subversion but don't want those pesky *.svn* directories in the way, you can use *svn export* to create a local copy of all or part of your repository sans *.svn* directories. As with *svn update* and *svn checkout*, you can also pass the `--revision` option to *svn export*:

```
$ svn export http://svn.example.com/svn/repos1 # Exports latest revision
...
$ svn export http://svn.example.com/svn/repos1 -r 1729
# Exports revision r1729
...
```

Sometimes You Just Need to Clean Up

Now that we've covered the day-to-day tasks that you'll frequently use Subversion for, we'll review a few administrative tasks relating to your working copy.

Disposing of a Working Copy

Subversion doesn't track either the state or the existence of working copies on the server, so there's no server overhead to keeping working copies around. Likewise, there's no need to let the server know that you're going to delete a working copy.

If you're likely to use a working copy again, there's nothing wrong with just leaving it on disk until you're ready to use it again, at which point all it takes is an *svn update* to bring it up to date and ready for use.

However, if you're definitely not going to use a working copy again, you can safely delete the entire thing, but you'd be well served to take a look through the working copy for unversioned files. To find these files, run `svn status` and review any files that are prefixed with a ? to make certain that they're not of importance. After you're done reviewing, you can safely delete your working copy.

Recovering from an Interruption

When Subversion modifies your working copy (or any information within *.svn*), it tries to do so as safely as possible. Before changing the working copy, Subversion writes its intentions to a logfile. Next, it executes the commands in the logfile to apply the requested change, holding a lock on the relevant part of the working copy while it works—to prevent other Subversion clients from accessing the working copy mid-change. Finally, Subversion removes the logfile. Architecturally, this is similar to a journaled filesystem. If a Subversion operation is interrupted (e.g., if the process is killed or if the machine crashes), the logfiles remain on disk. By reexecuting the logfiles, Subversion can complete the previously started operation, and your working copy can get itself back into a consistent state.

And this is exactly what *svn cleanup* does: it searches your working copy and runs any leftover logs, removing working copy locks in the process. If Subversion ever tells you that some part of your working copy is "locked," this is the command that you should run. Also, *svn status* will display an L next to locked items:

```
$ svn status
  L     somedir
M       somedir/foo.c

$ svn cleanup
$ svn status
M       somedir/foo.c
```

Don't confuse these working copy locks with the ordinary locks that Subversion users create when using the lock-modify-unlock model of concurrent version control; see the sidebar "The Three Meanings of "Lock"" on page 75 for clarification.

Summary

Now we've covered most of the Subversion client commands. Notable exceptions are those dealing with branching and merging (see Chapter 4) and properties (see "Properties" on page 48). However, you may want to take a moment to skim through Chapter 9 to get an idea of all the different commands that Subversion has—and how you can use them to make your work easier.

## CHAPTER 3

Advanced Topics

If you've been reading this book chapter by chapter, from start to finish, you should by now have acquired enough knowledge to use the Subversion client to perform the most common version control operations. You understand how to check out a working copy from a Subversion repository. You are comfortable with submitting and receiving changes using the *svn commit* and *svn update* operations. You've probably even developed a reflex that causes you to run the *svn status* command almost unconsciously. For all intents and purposes, you are ready to use Subversion in a typical environment.

But the Subversion feature set doesn't stop at "common version control operations." It has other bits of functionality besides just communicating file and directory changes to and from a central repository.

This chapter highlights some of Subversion's features that, while important, aren't part of the typical user's daily routine. It assumes that you are familiar with Subversion's basic file and directory versioning capabilities. If you aren't, you'll want to first read Chapters 1 and 2. Once you've mastered those basics and consumed this chapter, you'll be a Subversion power user!

Revision Specifiers

As we described in "Revisions" on page 11, revision numbers in Subversion are pretty straightforward—integers that keep getting larger as you commit more changes to your versioned data. Still, it doesn't take long before you can no longer remember exactly what happened in each and every revision. Fortunately, the typical Subversion workflow doesn't often demand that you supply arbitrary revisions to the Subversion operations you perform. For operations that *do* require a revision specifier, you generally supply a revision number that you saw in a commit email, in the output of some other Subversion operation, or in some other context that would give meaning to that particular number.

But occasionally, you need to pinpoint a moment in time for which you don't already have a revision number memorized or handy. So besides the integer revision numbers, *svn* allows as input some additional forms of revision specifiers: *revision keywords* and revision dates.

The various forms of Subversion revision specifiers can be mixed and matched when used to specify revision ranges. For example, you can use -r *REV1*:*REV2* where *REV1* is a revision keyword and *REV2* is a revision number, or where *REV1* is a date and *REV2* is a revision keyword, and so on. The individual revision specifiers are independently evaluated, so you can put whatever you want on the opposite sides of that colon.

Revision Keywords

The Subversion client understands a number of revision keywords. These keywords can be used instead of integer arguments to the --revision (-r) option and are resolved into specific revision numbers by Subversion:

HEAD
> The latest (or "youngest") revision in the repository.

BASE
> The revision number of an item in a working copy. If the item has been locally modified, this refers to the way the item appears without those local modifications.

COMMITTED
> The most recent revision prior to, or equal to, BASE, in which an item changed.

PREV
> The revision immediately *before* the last revision in which an item changed. Technically, this boils down to COMMITTED–1.

As can be derived from their descriptions, the PREV, BASE, and COMMITTED revision keywords are used only when referring to a working copy path—they don't apply to repository URLs. HEAD, on the other hand, can be used in conjunction with both of these path types.

Here are some examples of revision keywords in action:

```
$ svn diff -r PREV:COMMITTED foo.c
# shows the last change committed to foo.c

$ svn log -r HEAD
# shows log message for the latest repository commit

$ svn diff -r HEAD
# compares your working copy (with all of its local changes) to the
# latest version of that tree in the repository
```

```
$ svn diff -r BASE:HEAD foo.c
# compares the unmodified version of foo.c with the latest version of
# foo.c in the repository

$ svn log -r BASE:HEAD
# shows all commit logs for the current versioned directory since you
# last updated

$ svn update -r PREV foo.c
# rewinds the last change on foo.c, decreasing foo.c's working revision

$ svn diff -r BASE:14 foo.c
# compares the unmodified version of foo.c with the way foo.c looked
# in revision 14
```

Revision Dates

Revision numbers reveal nothing about the world outside the version control system, but sometimes you need to correlate a moment in real time with a moment in version history. To facilitate this, the **--revision (-r)** option can also accept as input date specifiers wrapped in curly braces ({ and }). Subversion accepts the standard ISO-8601 date and time formats, plus a few others. Here are some examples. (Remember to use quotes around any date that contains spaces.)

```
$ svn checkout -r {2006-02-17}
$ svn checkout -r {15:30}
$ svn checkout -r {15:30:00.200000}
$ svn checkout -r {"2006-02-17 15:30"}
$ svn checkout -r {"2006-02-17 15:30 +0230"}
$ svn checkout -r {2006-02-17T15:30}
$ svn checkout -r {2006-02-17T15:30Z}
$ svn checkout -r {2006-02-17T15:30-04:00}
$ svn checkout -r {20060217T1530}
$ svn checkout -r {20060217T1530Z}
$ svn checkout -r {20060217T1530-0500}
...
```

When you specify a date, Subversion resolves that date to the most recent revision of the repository as of that date, and then continues to operate against that resolved revision number:

```
$ svn log -r {2006-11-28}
------------------------------------------------------------------------
r12 | ira | 2006-11-27 12:31:51 -0600 (Mon, 27 Nov 2006) | 6 lines
...
```

You can also use a range of dates. Subversion will find all revisions between both dates, inclusive:

```
$ svn log -r {2006-11-20}:{2006-11-29}
...
```

Since the timestamp of a revision is stored as an unversioned, modifiable property of the revision (see "Properties" on page 48), revision time-stamps can be changed to represent complete falsifications of true chronology, and can even be removed altogether. Subversion's ability to correctly convert revision dates into real revision numbers depends on revision datestamps maintaining a sequential ordering—the younger the revision, the younger its timestamp. If this ordering isn't maintained, you will likely find that trying to use dates to specify revision ranges in your repository doesn't always return the data you might have expected.

Is Subversion a Day Early?

If you specify a single date as a revision without specifying a time of day (for example, 2006-11-27), you may think that Subversion should give you the last revision that took place on the 27th of November. Instead, you'll get back a revision from the 26th, or even earlier. Remember that Subversion will find the *most recent revision of the repository* as of the date you give. If you give a date without a timestamp, such as 2006-11-27, Subversion assumes a time of 00:00:00, so looking for the most recent revision won't return anything on the 27th.

If you want to include the 27th in your search, you can either specify the 27th with the time ({"2006-11-27 23:59"}), or just specify the next day ({2006-11-28}).

Properties

We've already covered in detail how Subversion stores and retrieves various versions of files and directories in its repository. Whole chapters have been devoted to this most fundamental piece of functionality provided by the tool. And if the versioning support stopped there, Subversion would still be complete from a version control perspective.

But it doesn't stop there.

In addition to versioning your directories and files, Subversion provides interfaces for adding, modifying, and removing versioned metadata on each of your versioned directories and files. We refer to this metadata as *properties*, and they can be thought of as two-column tables that map property names to arbitrary values attached to each item in your working copy. Generally speaking, the names and values of the properties can be whatever you want them to be, with the constraint that the names must contain only ASCII characters. And the best part about these properties is that they, too, are versioned, just like the textual contents of your files. You can modify, commit, and revert property changes as easily as you can file content changes. And the sending and receiving of property changes occurs as part of your typical commit and update operations—you don't have to change your basic processes to accommodate them.

Subversion has reserved the set of properties whose names begin with svn: as its own. While there are only a handful of such properties in use today, you should avoid creating custom properties for your own needs with names that begin with this prefix. Otherwise, you run the risk that a future release of Subversion will grow support for a feature or behavior driven by a property of the same name but with perhaps an entirely different interpretation.

Properties show up elsewhere in Subversion, too. Just as files and directories may have arbitrary property names and values attached to them, each revision as a whole may have arbitrary properties attached to it. The same constraints apply—human-readable names and anything-you-want binary values. The main difference is that revision properties are not versioned. In other words, if you change the value of, or delete, a revision property, there's no way, within the scope of Subversion's functionality, to recover the previous value.

Subversion has no particular policy regarding the use of properties. It asks only that you not use property names that begin with the prefix svn:. That's the namespace that it sets aside for its own use. And Subversion does, in fact, use properties—both the versioned and unversioned variety. Certain versioned properties have special meaning or effects when found on files and directories, or they house a particular bit of information about the revisions on which they are found. Certain revision properties are automatically attached to revisions by Subversion's commit process, and they carry information about the revision. Most of these properties are mentioned elsewhere in this or other chapters as part of the more general topics to which they are related. For an exhaustive list of Subversion's predefined properties, see "Subversion Properties" on page 358.

In this section, we'll examine the utility—both to users of Subversion and to Subversion itself—of property support. You'll learn about the property-related *svn* subcommands and how property modifications affect your normal Subversion workflow.

Why Properties?

Just as Subversion uses properties to store extra information about the files, directories, and revisions that it contains, you might find properties to be of similar use. You might find it useful to have a place close to your versioned data to hang custom metadata about that data.

Say you wish to design a web site that houses many digital photos and displays them with captions and a datestamp. Now, your set of photos is constantly changing, so you'd like to have as much of this site automated as possible. These photos can be quite large, so as is common with sites of this nature, you want to provide smaller thumbnail images to your site visitors.

You can get this functionality using traditional files. That is, you can have your *image123.jpg* and an *image123-thumbnail.jpg* side by side in a directory. Or if you want to keep the filenames the same, you might have your thumbnails in a different directory, such as *thumbnails/image123.jpg*. You can also store your captions and datestamps in a similar fashion, again separated from the original image file. But the problem here is that your collection of files multiplies with each new photo added to the site.

Now consider the same web site deployed in a way that makes use of Subversion's file properties. Imagine having a single image file, *image123.jpg*, with properties set on that file that are named `caption`, `datestamp`, and even `thumbnail`. Your working copy directory looks much more manageable—in fact, it looks to the casual browser like there are nothing but image files in it. But your automation scripts know better. They know that they can use *svn* (or better yet, they can use the Subversion language bindings—see "Using the APIs" on page 261) to dig out the extra information that your site needs to display without having to read an index file or play path manipulation games.

 Although Subversion places few restrictions on the names and values you use for properties, it has not been designed to optimally carry large property values or large sets of properties on a given file or directory. Subversion commonly holds all the property names and values associated with a single item in memory at the same time, which can cause detrimental performance or failed operations when extremely large property sets are used.

Custom revision properties are also frequently used. One common such use is a property whose value contains an issue tracker ID with which the revision is associated, perhaps because the change made in that revision fixes a bug filed in the tracker issue with that ID. Other uses include hanging more friendly names on the revision—it might be hard to remember that revision 1935 was a fully tested revision. But if there's, say, a `test-results` property on that revision with the value `all passing`, that's meaningful information to have.

Searchability (or, Why *Not* Properties)

For all their utility, Subversion properties—or, more accurately, the interfaces available for them—have a major shortcoming: although it is a simple matter to *set* a custom property, *finding* that property later is a whole different ball of wax.

Trying to locate a custom revision property generally involves performing a linear walk across all the revisions of the repository, asking of each revision, "Do you have the property I'm looking for?" Trying to find a custom versioned property is painful, too, and often involves a recursive *svn propget* across an entire working copy. In your situation, that might not be as bad as a linear walk across all revisions. But it certainly leaves much to be desired in terms of both performance and likelihood of success, especially if the scope of your search would require a working copy from the root of your repository.

For this reason, you might choose—especially in the revision property use case—to simply add your metadata to the revision's log message using some policy-driven (and perhaps programmatically enforced) formatting that is designed to be quickly parsed from the output of *svn log*. It is quite common to see the following in Subversion log messages:

```
Issue(s): IZ2376, IZ1919
Reviewed by:  sally

This fixes a nasty segfault in the wort frabbing process
...
```

But here again lies some misfortune. Subversion doesn't yet provide a log message templating mechanism, which would go a long way toward helping users be consistent with the formatting of their log-embedded revision metadata.

Manipulating Properties

The *svn* program affords a few ways to add or modify file and directory properties. For properties with short, human-readable values, perhaps the simplest way to add a new property is to specify the property name and value on the command line of the *svn propset* subcommand:

```
$ svn propset copyright '(c) 2006 Red-Bean Software' calc/button.c
property 'copyright' set on 'calc/button.c'
$
```

But we've been touting the flexibility that Subversion offers for your property values. And if you are planning to have a multiline textual, or even binary, property value, you probably do not want to supply that value on the command line. So the *svn propset* subcommand takes a `--file` (`-F`) option for specifying the name of a file that contains the new property value:

```
$ svn propset license -F /path/to/LICENSE calc/button.c
property 'license' set on 'calc/button.c'
$
```

There are some restrictions on the names you can use for properties. A property name must start with a letter, a colon (:), or an underscore (_); after that, you can also use digits, hyphens (-), and periods (.).[*]

In addition to the *propset* command, the *svn* program supplies the *propedit* command. This command uses the configured editor program (see "Config" on page 239) to add or modify properties. When you run the command, *svn* invokes your editor program on a temporary file that contains the current value of the property (or that is empty, if you are adding a new property). Then, you just modify that value in your editor program until it represents the new value you wish to store for the property, save the temporary

---

[*] If you're familiar with XML, this is pretty much the ASCII subset of the syntax for XML "Name".

file, and then exit the editor program. If Subversion detects that you've actually changed the existing value of the property, it will accept that as the new property value. If you exit your editor without making any changes, no property modification will occur:

```
$ svn propedit copyright calc/button.c  ### exit the editor without changes
No changes to property 'copyright' on 'calc/button.c'
$
```

We should note that, as with other *svn* subcommands, those related to properties can act on multiple paths at once. This enables you to modify properties on whole sets of files with a single command. For example, we could have done the following:

```
$ svn propset copyright '(c) 2006 Red-Bean Software' calc/*
property 'copyright' set on 'calc/Makefile'
property 'copyright' set on 'calc/button.c'
property 'copyright' set on 'calc/integer.c'
...
$
```

All of this property adding and editing isn't really very useful if you can't easily get the stored property value. So the *svn* program supplies two subcommands for displaying the names and values of properties stored on files and directories. The *svn proplist* command will list the names of properties that exist on a path. Once you know the names of the properties on the node, you can request their values individually using *svn propget*. This command will, given a property name and a path (or set of paths), print the value of the property to the standard output stream:

```
$ svn proplist calc/button.c
Properties on 'calc/button.c':
  copyright
  license
$ svn propget copyright calc/button.c
(c) 2006 Red-Bean Software
```

There's even a variation of the *proplist* command that will list both the name and the value for all of the properties. Simply supply the **--verbose** (**-v**) option:

```
$ svn proplist -v calc/button.c
Properties on 'calc/button.c':
  copyright : (c) 2006 Red-Bean Software
  license : =================================================================
Copyright (c) 2006 Red-Bean Software.  All rights reserved.

Redistribution and use in source and binary forms, with or without
modification, are permitted provided that the following conditions
are met:

1. Redistributions of source code must retain the above copyright
notice, this list of conditions, and the recipe for Fitz's famous
red-beans-and-rice.
...
```

The last property-related subcommand is *propdel*. Since Subversion allows you to store properties with empty values, you can't remove a property altogether using *svn propedit* or *svn propset*. For example, this command will *not* yield the desired effect:

```
$ svn propset license '' calc/button.c
property 'license' set on 'calc/button.c'
$ svn proplist -v calc/button.c
Properties on 'calc/button.c':
  copyright : (c) 2006 Red-Bean Software
  license :
$
```

You need to use the *propdel* subcommand to delete properties altogether. The syntax is similar to the other property commands:

```
$ svn propdel license calc/button.c
property 'license' deleted from 'calc/button.c'.
$ svn proplist -v calc/button.c
Properties on 'calc/button.c':
  copyright : (c) 2006 Red-Bean Software
$
```

Remember those unversioned revision properties? You can modify those, too, using the same *svn* subcommands that we just described. Simply add the `--revprop` command-line parameter and specify the revision whose property you wish to modify. Since revisions are global, you don't need to specify a target path to these property-related commands so long as you are positioned in a working copy of the repository whose revision property you wish to modify. Otherwise, you can simply provide the URL of any path in the repository of interest (including the repository's root URL). For example, you might want to replace the commit log message of an existing revision.[†] If your current working directory is part of a working copy of your repository, you can simply run the *svn propset* command with no target path:

```
$ svn propset svn:log '* button.c: Fix a compiler warning.' -r11 --revprop
property 'svn:log' set on repository revision '11'
$
```

But even if you haven't checked out a working copy from that repository, you can still effect the property change by providing the repository's root URL:

```
$ svn propset svn:log '* button.c: Fix a compiler warning.' -r11 --revprop \
          http://svn.example.com/repos/project
property 'svn:log' set on repository revision '11'
$
```

Note that the ability to modify these unversioned properties must be explicitly added by the repository administrator (see "Commit Log Message Correction" on page 163). That's because the properties aren't versioned, so you run the risk of losing information if you aren't careful with your edits. The repository administrator can set up

---

† Fixing spelling errors, grammatical gotchas, and "just-plain-wrongness" in commit log messages is perhaps the most common use case for the `--revprop` option.

methods to protect against this loss, and by default, modification of unversioned properties is disabled.

 Users should, where possible, use *svn propedit* instead of *svn propset*. While the end result of the commands is identical, the former will allow them to see the current value of the property that they are about to change, which helps them verify that they are, in fact, making the change they think they are making. This is especially true when modifying unversioned revision properties. Also, it is significantly easier to modify multiline property values in a text editor than at the command line.

Properties and the Subversion Workflow

Now that you are familiar with all of the property-related *svn* subcommands, let's see how property modifications affect the usual Subversion workflow. As we mentioned earlier, file and directory properties are versioned, just like your file contents. As a result, Subversion provides the same opportunities for merging—cleanly or with conflicts—someone else's modifications into your own.

As with file contents, your property changes are local modifications, made permanent only when you commit them to the repository with *svn commit*. Your property changes can be easily unmade, too—the *svn revert* command will restore your files and directories to their unedited states—contents, properties, and all. Also, you can receive interesting information about the state of your file and directory properties by using the *svn status* and *svn diff* commands:

```
$ svn status calc/button.c
 M      calc/button.c
$ svn diff calc/button.c
Property changes on: calc/button.c
_____
Name: copyright
   + (c) 2006 Red-Bean Software

$
```

Notice how the *status* subcommand displays M in the second column instead of the first. That is because we have modified the properties on *calc/button.c*, but not its textual contents. Had we changed both, we would have seen M in the first column, too. (We cover *svn status* in "See an overview of your changes" on page 26.)

You might also have noticed the nonstandard way that Subversion currently displays property differences. You can still use *svn diff* and redirect its output to create a usable patch file. The *patch* program will ignore property patches—as a rule, it ignores any noise it can't understand. This does, unfortunately, mean that to fully apply a patch generated by *svn diff*, any property modifications will need to be applied by hand.

Property Conflicts

As with file contents, local property modifications can conflict with changes committed by someone else. If you update your working copy directory and receive property changes on a versioned object that clash with your own, Subversion will report that the object is in a conflicted state:

```
$ svn update calc
M  calc/Makefile.in
Conflict for property 'linecount' discovered on 'calc/button.c'.
Select: (p) postpone, (df) diff-full, (e) edit,
        (s) show all options: p
 C calc/button.c
Updated to revision 143.
$
```

Subversion will also create, in the same directory as the conflicted object, a file with a *.prej* extension that contains the details of the conflict. You should examine the contents of this file so you can decide how to resolve the conflict. Until the conflict is resolved, you will see a C in the second column of *svn status* output for that object, and attempts to commit your local modifications will fail:

```
$ svn status calc
 C      calc/button.c
 ?      calc/button.c.prej
$ cat calc/button.c.prej
Trying to change property 'linecount' from '1267' to '1301',
but property has been locally changed from '1267' to '1256'.
$
```

To resolve property conflicts, simply ensure that the conflicting properties contain the values that they should, and then use the *svn resolved* command to alert Subversion that you have manually resolved the problem.

Automatic Property Setting

Properties are a powerful feature of Subversion, acting as key components of many Subversion features discussed elsewhere in this and other chapters: textual diff and merge support, keyword substitution, newline translation, and so on. But to get the full benefit of properties, they must be set on the right files and directories. Unfortunately, that step can be easily forgotten in the routine of things, especially since failing to set a property doesn't usually result in an obvious error (at least compared to, say, failing to add a file to version control). To help your properties get applied to the places that need them, Subversion provides a couple of simple but useful features.

Whenever you introduce a file to version control using the *svn add* or *svn import* commands, Subversion tries to assist by setting some common file properties automatically. First, on operating systems whose filesystems support an execute permission bit, Subversion will automatically set the svn:executable property on newly added or imported files whose execute bit is enabled. (See "File Executability" on page 58 later in this chapter for more about this property.)

Second, Subversion tries to determine the file's MIME type. If you've configured a `mime-types-files` runtime configuration parameter, Subversion will try to find a MIME type mapping in that file for your file's extension. If it finds such a mapping, it will set your file's `svn:mime-type` property to the MIME type it found. If no mapping file is configured, or no mapping for your file's extension could be found, Subversion runs a very basic heuristic to determine whether the file contains nontextual content. If so, it automatically sets the `svn:mime-type` property on that file to `application/octet-stream` (the generic "this is a collection of bytes" MIME type). Of course, if Subversion guesses incorrectly, or if you wish to set the `svn:mime-type` property to something more precise—perhaps `image/png` or `application/x-shockwave-flash`—you can always remove or edit that property. (For more on Subversion's use of MIME types, see "File Content Type" on page 57 later in this chapter.)

Subversion also provides, via its runtime configuration system (see "Runtime Configuration Area" on page 233), a more flexible automatic property setting feature that allows you to create mappings of filename patterns to property names and values. Once again, these mappings affect adds and imports, and can not only override the default MIME type decision made by Subversion during those operations, but can also set additional Subversion or custom properties, too. For example, you might create a mapping that says that anytime you add JPEG files—ones whose names match the pattern `*.jpg`—Subversion should automatically set the `svn:mime-type` property on those files to `image/jpeg`. Or perhaps any files that match `*.cpp` should have `svn:eol-style` set to `native`, and `svn:keywords` set to `Id`. Automatic property support is perhaps the handiest property-related tool in the Subversion toolbox. See "Config" on page 239 for more about configuring that support.

File Portability

Fortunately for Subversion users who routinely find themselves on different computers with different operating systems, Subversion's command-line program behaves almost identically on all those systems. If you know how to wield *svn* on one platform, you know how to wield it everywhere.

However, the same is not always true of other general classes of software or of the actual files you keep in Subversion. For example, on a Windows machine, the definition of a "text file" would be similar to that used on a Linux box, but with a key difference: the character sequences used to mark the ends of the lines of those files. There are other differences, too. Unix platforms have (and Subversion supports) symbolic links; Windows does not. Unix platforms use filesystem permission to determine executability; Windows uses filename extensions.

Because Subversion is in no position to unite the whole world in common definitions and implementations of all of these things, the best it can do is to try to help make your life simpler when you need to work with your versioned files and directories on multiple computers and operating systems. This section describes some of the ways Subversion does this.

File Content Type

Subversion joins the ranks of the many applications that recognize and make use of Multipurpose Internet Mail Extensions (MIME) content types. Besides being a general-purpose storage location for a file's content type, the value of the svn:mime-type file property determines some behavioral characteristics of Subversion itself.

For example, one of the benefits that Subversion typically provides is contextual, line-based merging of changes received from the server during an update into your working file. But for files containing nontextual data, there is often no concept of a "line." So, for versioned files whose svn:mime-type property is set to a nontextual MIME type (generally, something that doesn't begin with text/, though there are exceptions), Subversion does not attempt to perform contextual merges during updates. Instead, any time you have locally modified a binary working copy file that is also being updated, your file is left untouched and Subversion creates two new files. One file has a *.oldrev* extension and contains the BASE revision of the file. The other file has a *.newrev* extension and contains the contents of the updated revision of the file. This behavior is really for the protection of the user against failed attempts at performing contextual merges on files that simply cannot be contextually merged.

 The svn:mime-type property, when set to a value that does not indicate textual file contents, can cause some unexpected behaviors with respect to other properties. For example, since the idea of line endings (and therefore, line-ending conversion) makes no sense when applied to non-textual files, Subversion will prevent you from setting the svn:eol-style property on such files. This is obvious when attempted on a single file target—*svn propset* will error out. But it might not be as clear if you perform a recursive property set, where Subversion will silently skip over files that it deems unsuitable for a given property.

Beginning in Subversion 1.5, users can configure a new mime-types-file runtime configuration parameter, which identifies the location of a MIME types mapping file. Subversion will consult this mapping file to determine the MIME type of newly added and imported files.

Also, if the svn:mime-type property is set, then the Subversion Apache module will use its value to populate the Content-type: HTTP header when responding to GET requests. This gives your web browser a crucial clue about how to display a file when you use it to peruse your Subversion repository's contents.

Identifying File Types

Various programs on most modern operating systems make assumptions about the type and format of the contents of a file by the file's name; specifically, its file extension. For example, files whose names end in *.txt* are generally assumed to be human-readable; that is, able to be understood by simple perusal rather than requiring complex processing to decipher. Files whose names end in *.png*, on the other hand, are assumed to be of the Portable Network Graphics type—not human-readable at all, and sensible only when interpreted by software that understands the PNG format and can render the information in that format as a raster image.

Unfortunately, some of those extensions have changed their meanings over time. When personal computers first appeared, a file named *README.DOC* would have almost certainly been a plain-text file, just like today's *.txt* files. But by the mid-1990s, you could almost bet that a file of that name would not be a plain-text file at all, but instead a Microsoft Word document in a proprietary, non-human-readable format. But this change didn't occur overnight—there was certainly a period of confusion for computer users over what exactly they had in hand when they saw a *.DOC* file.[‡]

The popularity of computer networking cast still more doubt on the mapping between a file's name and its content. With information being served across networks and generated dynamically by server-side scripts, there was often no real file per se, and therefore no filename. Web servers, for example, needed some other way to tell browsers what they were downloading so that the browser could do something intelligent with that information, whether that was to display the data using a program registered to handle that datatype or to prompt the user for where on the client machine it should store the downloaded data.

Eventually, a standard emerged for, among other things, describing the contents of a data stream. In 1996, RFC 2045 was published. It was the first of five RFCs describing MIME. It describes the concept of media types and subtypes and recommends a syntax for the representation of those types. Today, MIME media types—or "MIME types"— are used almost universally across email applications, web servers, and other software as the de facto mechanism for clearing up the file content confusion.

File Executability

On many operating systems, the ability to execute a file as a command is governed by the presence of an execute permission bit. This bit usually defaults to being disabled and must be explicitly enabled by the user for each file that needs it. But it would be a monumental hassle to have to remember exactly which files in a freshly checked-out working copy were supposed to have their executable bits toggled on, and then to have to do that toggling. So, Subversion provides the svn:executable property as a way to

---

[‡] You think that was rough? During that same era, WordPerfect also used *.DOC* for their proprietary file format's preferred extension!

specify that the executable bit for the file on which that property is set should be enabled, and Subversion honors that request when populating working copies with such files.

This property has no effect on filesystems that have no concept of an executable permission bit, such as FAT32 and NTFS.§ Also, although it has no defined values, Subversion will force its value to * when setting this property. Finally, this property is valid only on files, not on directories.

End-of-Line Character Sequences

Unless otherwise noted using a versioned file's `svn:mime-type` property, Subversion assumes the file contains human-readable data. Generally speaking, Subversion uses this knowledge only to determine whether contextual difference reports for that file are possible. Otherwise, to Subversion, bytes are bytes.

This means that, by default, Subversion doesn't pay any attention to the type of *end-of-line (EOL) markers* used in your files. Unfortunately, different operating systems have different conventions about which character sequences represent the end of a line of text in a file. For example, the usual line-ending token used by software on the Windows platform is a pair of ASCII control characters—a carriage return (`CR`) followed by a line feed (`LF`). Unix software, however, just uses the `LF` character to denote the end of a line.

Not all of the various tools on these operating systems understand files that contain line endings in a format that differs from the *native line-ending style* of the operating system on which they are running. So, typically, Unix programs treat the `CR` character present in Windows files as a regular character (usually rendered as `^M`), and Windows programs combine all of the lines of a Unix file into one giant line because no carriage return–line feed (or `CRLF`) character combination was found to denote the ends of the lines.

This sensitivity to foreign EOL markers can be frustrating for folks who share a file across different operating systems. For example, consider a source code file with developers who edit this file on both Windows and Unix systems. If all the developers always use tools that preserve the line-ending style of the file, no problems occur.

But in practice, many common tools either fail to properly read a file with foreign EOL markers, or convert the file's line endings to the native style when the file is saved. If the former is true for a developer, he has to use an external conversion utility (such as *dos2unix* or its companion, *unix2dos*) to prepare the file for editing. The latter case requires no extra preparation. But both cases result in a file that differs from the original quite literally on every line! Prior to committing his changes, the user has two choices. Either he can use a conversion utility to restore the modified file to the same line-ending

---

§ The Windows filesystems use file extensions (such as *.EXE*, *.BAT*, and *.COM*) to denote executable files.

style that it was in before his edits were made, or he can simply commit the file—new EOL markers and all.

The result of scenarios like these include wasted time and unnecessary modifications to committed files. Wasted time is painful enough. But when commits change every line in a file, this complicates the job of determining which of those lines were changed in a nontrivial way. Where was that bug really fixed? On what line was a syntax error introduced?

The solution to this problem is the `svn:eol-style` property. When this property is set to a valid value, Subversion uses it to determine what special processing to perform on the file so that the file's line-ending style isn't flip-flopping with every commit that comes from a different operating system. The valid values are:

native

> This causes the file to contain the EOL markers that are native to the operating system on which Subversion was run. In other words, if a user on a Windows machine checks out a working copy that contains a file with an `svn:eol-style` property set to `native`, that file will contain CRLF EOL markers. A Unix user checking out a working copy that contains the same file will see LF EOL markers in his copy of the file.
>
> Note that Subversion will actually store the file in the repository using normalized LF EOL markers regardless of the operating system. This is basically transparent to the user, though.

CRLF

> This causes the file to contain CRLF sequences for EOL markers, regardless of the operating system in use.

LF

> This causes the file to contain LF characters for EOL markers, regardless of the operating system in use.

CR

> This causes the file to contain CR characters for EOL markers, regardless of the operating system in use. This line-ending style is not very common.

Ignoring Unversioned Items

In any given working copy, there is a good chance that alongside all those versioned files and directories are other files and directories that are neither versioned nor intended to be. Text editors litter directories with backup files. Software compilers generate intermediate—or even final—files that you typically wouldn't bother to version. And users themselves drop various other files and directories wherever they see fit, often in version control working copies.

It's ludicrous to expect Subversion working copies to be somehow impervious to this kind of clutter and impurity. In fact, Subversion counts it as a *feature* that its working copies are just typical directories, just like unversioned trees. But these not-to-be-versioned files and directories can cause some annoyance for Subversion users. For example, because the *svn add* and *svn import* commands act recursively by default and don't know which files in a given tree you do and don't wish to version, it's easy to accidentally add stuff to version control that you didn't mean to. And because *svn status* reports, by default, every item of interest in a working copy—including unversioned files and directories—its output can get quite noisy where many of these things exist.

So Subversion provides two ways for telling it which files you would prefer that it simply disregard. One of the ways involves the use of Subversion's runtime configuration system (see "Runtime Configuration Area" on page 233), and therefore applies to all the Subversion operations that make use of that runtime configuration—generally those performed on a particular computer or by a particular user of a computer. The other way makes use of Subversion's directory property support and is more tightly bound to the versioned tree itself, and therefore affects everyone who has a working copy of that tree. Both of the mechanisms use *file patterns* (strings of literal and special wildcard characters used to match against filenames) to decide which files to ignore.

The Subversion runtime configuration system provides an option, `global-ignores`, whose value is a whitespace-delimited collection of file patterns. The Subversion client checks these patterns against the names of the files that are candidates for addition to version control, as well as to unversioned files that the *svn status* command notices. If any file's name matches one of the patterns, Subversion will basically act as if the file didn't exist at all. This is really useful for the kinds of files that you almost never want to version, such as editor backup files like Emacs' `*~` and `.*~` files.

When found on a versioned directory, the `svn:ignore` property is expected to contain a list of newline-delimited file patterns that Subversion should use to determine ignorable objects in that same directory. These patterns do not override those found in the `global-ignores` runtime configuration option but are instead appended to that list. And it's worth noting again that, unlike the `global-ignores` option, the patterns found in the `svn:ignore` property apply only to the directory on which that property is set, and not to any of its subdirectories. The `svn:ignore` property is a good way to tell Subversion to ignore files that are likely to be present in every user's working copy of that directory, such as compiler output or—to use an example more appropriate to this book—the HTML, PDF, or PostScript files generated as the result of a conversion of some source DocBook XML files to a more legible output format.

File Patterns in Subversion

File patterns (also called *globs* or *shell wildcard patterns*) are strings of characters that are intended to be matched against filenames, typically for the purpose of quickly selecting some subset of similar files from a larger grouping without having to explicitly name each file. The patterns contain two types of characters: regular characters, which are compared explicitly against potential matches, and special wildcard characters, which are interpreted differently for matching purposes.

There are different types of file pattern syntaxes, but Subversion uses the one most commonly found in Unix systems implemented as the fnmatch system function. It supports the following wildcards, described here simply for your convenience:

?

    Matches any single character

*

    Matches any string of characters, including the empty string

[

    Begins a character class definition terminated by], used for matching a subset of characters

You can see this same pattern-matching behavior at a Unix shell prompt. The following are some examples of patterns being used for various things:

```
$ ls    ### the book sources
appa-quickstart.xml              ch06-server-configuration.xml
appb-svn-for-cvs-users.xml       ch07-customizing-svn.xml
appc-webdav.xml                  ch08-embedding-svn.xml
book.xml                         ch09-reference.xml
ch00-preface.xml                 ch10-world-peace-thru-svn.xml
ch01-fundamental-concepts.xml    copyright.xml
ch02-basic-usage.xml             foreword.xml
ch03-advanced-topics.xml         images/
ch04-branching-and-merging.xml   index.xml
ch05-repository-admin.xml        styles.css
$ ls ch*    ### the book chapters
ch00-preface.xml                 ch06-server-configuration.xml
ch01-fundamental-concepts.xml    ch07-customizing-svn.xml
ch02-basic-usage.xml             ch08-embedding-svn.xml
ch03-advanced-topics.xml         ch09-reference.xml
ch04-branching-and-merging.xml   ch10-world-peace-thru-svn.xml
ch05-repository-admin.xml
$ ls ch?0-*    ### the book chapters whose numbers end in zero
ch00-preface.xml  ch10-world-peace-thru-svn.xml
$ ls ch0[3578]-*    ### the book chapters that Mike is responsible for
ch03-advanced-topics.xml    ch07-customizing-svn.xml
ch05-repository-admin.xml    ch08-embedding-svn.xml
$
```

File pattern matching is a bit more complex than what we've described here, but this basic usage level tends to suit the majority of Subversion users.

Subversion's support for ignorable file patterns extends only to the one-time process of adding unversioned files and directories to version control. Once an object is under Subversion's control, the ignore pattern mechanisms no longer apply to it. In other words, don't expect Subversion to avoid committing changes you've made to a versioned file simply because that file's name matches an ignore pattern—Subversion *always* notices all of its versioned objects.

Ignore Patterns for CVS Users

The Subversion `svn:ignore` property is very similar in syntax and function to the CVS *.cvsignore* file. In fact, if you are migrating a CVS working copy to Subversion, you can directly migrate the ignore patterns by using the *.cvsignore* file as input file to the *svn propset* command:

```
$ svn propset svn:ignore -F .cvsignore .
property 'svn:ignore' set on '.'
$
```

There are, however, some differences in the ways that CVS and Subversion handle ignore patterns. The two systems use the ignore patterns at some different times, and there are slight discrepancies in what the ignore patterns apply to. Also, Subversion does not recognize the use of the ! pattern as a reset back to having no ignore patterns at all.

The global list of ignore patterns tends to be more a matter of personal taste and ties more closely to a user's particular toolchain than to the details of any particular working copy's needs. So, the rest of this section will focus on the `svn:ignore` property and its uses.

Say you have the following output from *svn status*:

```
$ svn status calc
 M      calc/button.c
?       calc/calculator
?       calc/data.c
?       calc/debug_log
?       calc/debug_log.1
?       calc/debug_log.2.gz
?       calc/debug_log.3.gz
```

In this example, you have made some property modifications to *button.c*, but in your working copy, you also have some unversioned files: the latest *calculator* program that you've compiled from your source code, a source file named *data.c*, and a set of debugging output logfiles. Now, you know that your build system always results in the *calculator* program being generated.‖ And you know that your test suite always leaves

---

‖ Isn't that the whole point of a build system?

those debugging logfiles lying around. These facts are true for all working copies of this project, not just your own. And you know that you aren't interested in seeing those things every time you run *svn status*, and you are pretty sure that nobody else is interested in them either. So you use `svn propedit svn:ignore calc` to add some ignore patterns to the *calc* directory. For example, you might add this as the new value of the `svn:ignore` property:

```
calculator
debug_log*
```

After you've added this property, you will now have a local property modification on the *calc* directory. But notice what else is different about your *svn status* output:

```
$ svn status
 M     calc
 M     calc/button.c
 ?     calc/data.c
```

Now all that cruft is missing from the output! Your *calculator* compiled program and all those logfiles are still in your working copy; Subversion just isn't constantly reminding you that they are present and unversioned. And now with all the uninteresting noise removed from the display, you are left with more intriguing items—such as that source code file *data.c* that you probably forgot to add to version control.

Of course, this less-verbose report of your working copy status isn't the only one available. If you actually want to see the ignored files as part of the status report, you can pass the `--no-ignore` option to Subversion:

```
$ svn status --no-ignore
 M     calc
 M     calc/button.c
 I     calc/calculator
 ?     calc/data.c
 I     calc/debug_log
 I     calc/debug_log.1
 I     calc/debug_log.2.gz
 I     calc/debug_log.3.gz
```

As mentioned earlier, the list of file patterns to ignore is also used by *svn add* and *svn import*. Both of these operations involve asking Subversion to begin managing some set of files and directories. Rather than force the user to pick and choose which files in a tree she wishes to start versioning, Subversion uses the ignore patterns—both the global and the per-directory lists—to determine which files should not be swept into the version control system as part of a larger recursive addition or import operation. And here again, you can use the `--no-ignore` option to tell Subversion to ignore its ignores list and operate on all the files and directories present.

Even if `svn:ignore` is set, you may run into problems if you use shell wildcards in a command. Shell wildcards are expanded into an explicit list of targets before Subversion operates on them, so running `svn SUBCOMMAND *` is just like running `svn SUBCOMMAND file1 file2 file3 ....` In the case of the *svn add* command, this has an effect similar to passing the `--no-ignore` option. So instead of using a wildcard, use `svn add --force .` to do a bulk scheduling of unversioned things for addition. The explicit target will ensure that the current directory isn't overlooked because of being already under version control, and the `--force` option will cause Subversion to crawl through that directory, adding unversioned files while still honoring the `svn:ignore` property and `global-ignores` runtime configuration variable. Be sure to also provide the `--depth files` option to the *svn add* command if you don't want a fully recursive crawl for things to add.

Keyword Substitution

Subversion has the ability to substitute *keywords*—pieces of useful, dynamic information about a versioned file—into the contents of the file itself. Keywords generally provide information about the last modification made to the file. Because this information changes each time the file changes, and more importantly, just *after* the file changes, it is a hassle for any process except the version control system to keep the data completely up to date. Left to human authors, the information would inevitably grow stale.

For example, say you have a document in which you would like to display the last date on which it was modified. You could burden every author of that document to, just before committing their changes, also tweak the part of the document that describes when it was last changed. But sooner or later, someone would forget to do that. Instead, simply ask Subversion to perform keyword substitution on the `LastChangedDate` keyword. You control where the keyword is inserted into your document by placing a *keyword anchor* at the desired location in the file. This anchor is just a string of text formatted as `$KeywordName$`.

All keywords are case-sensitive where they appear as anchors in files: you must use the correct capitalization for the keyword to be expanded. You should consider the value of the `svn:keywords` property to be case-sensitive, too—certain keyword names will be recognized regardless of case, but this behavior is deprecated.

Subversion defines the list of keywords available for substitution. That list contains the following five keywords, some of which have aliases that you can also use:

Date
> This keyword describes the last time the file was known to have been changed in the repository, and is of the form `$Date: 2006-07-22 21:42:37 -0700 (Sat, 22 Jul 2006) $`. It may also be specified as `LastChangedDate`. Unlike the `Id` keyword, which

uses Coordinated Universal Time (UTC), the `Date` keyword displays dates using the local time zone.

Revision

This keyword describes the last known revision in which this file changed in the repository, and looks something like `$Revision: 144 $`. It may also be specified as `LastChangedRevision` or `Rev`.

Author

This keyword describes the last known user to change this file in the repository, and looks something like `$Author: harry $`. It may also be specified as `LastChangedBy`.

HeadURL

This keyword describes the full URL to the latest version of the file in the repository, and it looks something like `$HeadURL: http://svn.collab.net/repos/trunk/README $`. It may be abbreviated as `URL`.

Id

This keyword is a compressed combination of the other keywords. Its substitution looks something like `$Id: calc.c 148 2006-07-28 21:30:43Z sally $`, and is interpreted to mean that the file *calc.c* was last changed in revision 148 on the evening of July 28, 2006 by the user `sally`. The date displayed by this keyword is in UTC, unlike that of the `Date` keyword (which uses the local time zone).

Several of the preceding descriptions use the phrase "last known" or similar wording. Keep in mind that keyword expansion is a client-side operation, and your client "knows" only about changes that have occurred in the repository when you update your working copy to include those changes. If you never update your working copy, your keywords will never expand to different values, even if those versioned files are being changed regularly in the repository.

Simply adding keyword anchor text to your file does nothing special. Subversion will never attempt to perform textual substitutions on your file contents unless explicitly asked to do so. After all, you might be writing a document# about how to use keywords, and you don't want Subversion to substitute your beautiful examples of unsubstituted keyword anchors!

To tell Subversion whether to substitute keywords on a particular file, we again turn to the property-related subcommands. The `svn:keywords` property, when set on a versioned file, controls which keywords will be substituted on that file. The value is a space-delimited list of keyword names or aliases.

For example, say you have a versioned file named *weather.txt* that looks like this:

```
Here is the latest report from the front lines.
$LastChangedDate$
```

...or maybe even a section of a book....

```
$Rev$
Cumulus clouds are appearing more frequently as summer approaches.
```

With no svn:keywords property set on that file, Subversion will do nothing special. Now, let's enable substitution of the LastChangedDate keyword:

```
$ svn propset svn:keywords "Date Author" weather.txt
property 'svn:keywords' set on 'weather.txt'
$
```

Now you have made a local property modification on the *weather.txt* file. You will see no changes to the file's contents (unless you made some of your own prior to setting the property). Notice that the file contains a keyword anchor for the Rev keyword, yet we do not include that keyword in the property value we set. Subversion will happily ignore requests to substitute keywords that are not present in the file and will not substitute keywords that are not present in the svn:keywords property value.

Where's $GlobalRev$?

New users are often confused by how the Rev keyword works. Since the repository has a single, globally increasing revision number, many people assume that it is this number that is reflected by the Rev keyword's value. But Rev expands to show the last revision in which the file *changed*, not the last revision to which it was updated. Understanding this clears the confusion, but frustration often remains—without the support of a Subversion keyword to do so, how can you automatically get the global revision number into your files?

To do this, you need external processing. Subversion ships with a tool called *svnversion*, which was designed for just this purpose. It crawls your working copy and generates as output the revision(s) it finds. You can use this program, plus some additional tooling, to embed that revision information into your files. For more details, see "svnversion" on page 353.

Immediately after you commit this property change, Subversion will update your working file with the new substitute text. Instead of seeing your keyword anchor $LastChangedDate$, you'll see its substituted result. That result also contains the name of the keyword and continues to be delimited by the dollar sign ($) characters. And as we predicted, the Rev keyword was not substituted because we didn't ask for it to be.

Note also that we set the svn:keywords property to Date Author, yet the keyword anchor used the alias $LastChangedDate$ and still expands correctly:

```
Here is the latest report from the front lines.
$LastChangedDate: 2006-07-22 21:42:37 -0700 (Sat, 22 Jul 2006) $
$Rev$
Cumulus clouds are appearing more frequently as summer approaches.
```

If someone else now commits a change to *weather.txt*, your copy of that file will continue to display the same substituted keyword value as before—until you update your working copy. At that time, the keywords in your *weather.txt* file will be resubstituted with information that reflects the most recent known commit to that file.

Subversion 1.2 introduced a new variant of the keyword syntax, which brought additional, useful—though perhaps atypical—functionality. You can now tell Subversion to maintain a fixed length (in terms of the number of bytes consumed) for the substituted keyword. By using a double colon (::) after the keyword name, followed by a number of space characters, you define that fixed width. When Subversion goes to substitute your keyword for the keyword and its value, it will essentially replace only those space characters, leaving the overall width of the keyword field unchanged. If the substituted value is shorter than the defined field width, there will be extra padding characters (spaces) at the end of the substituted field; if it is too long, it is truncated with a special hash (#) character just before the final dollar sign terminator.

For example, say you have a document in which you have some section of tabular data reflecting the document's Subversion keywords. Using the original Subversion keyword substitution syntax, your file might look something like:

```
$Rev$:     Revision of last commit
$Author$:  Author of last commit
$Date$:    Date of last commit
```

Now, that looks nice and tabular at the start of things. But when you then commit that file (with keyword substitution enabled, of course), you see:

```
$Rev: 12 $:      Revision of last commit
$Author: harry $:  Author of last commit
$Date: 2006-03-15 02:33:03 -0500 (Wed, 15 Mar 2006) $:    Date of last commit
```

The result is not so beautiful. And you might be tempted to then adjust the file after the substitution so that it again looks tabular. But that holds only as long as the keyword values are the same width. If the last committed revision rolls into a new place value (say, from 99 to 100), or if another person with a longer username commits the file, stuff gets all crooked again. However, if you are using Subversion 1.2 or later, you can use the new fixed-length keyword syntax and define some field widths that seem sane, so your file might look like this:

```
$Rev::          $: Revision of last commit
$Author::       $: Author of last commit
$Date::         $: Date of last commit
```

You commit this change to your file. This time, Subversion notices the new fixed-length keyword syntax and maintains the width of the fields as defined by the padding you placed between the double colon and the trailing dollar sign. After substitution, the width of the fields is completely unchanged—the short values for Rev and Author are padded with spaces, and the long Date field is truncated by a hash character:

```
$Rev:: 13         $:  Revision of last commit
$Author:: harry   $:  Author of last commit
$Date:: 2006-03-15 0#$:  Date of last commit
```

The use of fixed-length keywords is especially handy when performing substitutions into complex file formats that themselves use fixed-length fields for data, or for which the stored size of a given data field is overbearingly difficult to modify from outside the format's native application (such as for Microsoft Office documents).

 Be aware that because the width of a keyword field is measured in bytes, the potential for corruption of multibyte values exists. For example, a username that contains some multibyte UTF-8 characters might suffer truncation in the middle of the string of bytes that make up one of those characters. The result will be a mere truncation when viewed at the byte level, but will likely appear as a string with an incorrect or garbled final character when viewed as UTF-8 text. It is conceivable that certain applications, when asked to load the file, would notice the broken UTF-8 text and deem the entire file corrupt, refusing to operate on the file altogether. So, when limiting keywords to a fixed size, choose a size that allows for this type of byte-wise expansion.

Sparse Directories

By default, most Subversion operations on directories act in a recursive manner. For example, *svn checkout* creates a working copy with every file and directory in the specified area of the repository, descending recursively through the repository tree until the entire structure is copied to your local disk. Subversion 1.5 introduces a feature called *sparse directories* (or *shallow checkouts*) that allows you to easily check out a working copy—or a portion of a working copy—more shallowly than full recursion, with the freedom to bring in previously ignored files and subdirectories at a later time.

For example, say we have a repository with a tree of files and directories with names of the members of a human family with pets. (It's an odd example, to be sure, but bear with us.) A regular *svn checkout* operation will give us a working copy of the whole tree:

```
$ svn checkout file:///var/svn/repos mom
A    mom/son
A    mom/son/grandson
A    mom/daughter
A    mom/daughter/granddaughter1
A    mom/daughter/granddaughter1/bunny1.txt
A    mom/daughter/granddaughter1/bunny2.txt
A    mom/daughter/granddaughter2
A    mom/daughter/fishie.txt
A    mom/kitty1.txt
A    mom/doggie1.txt
Checked out revision 1.
$
```

Now, let's check out the same tree again, but this time we'll ask Subversion to give us only the topmost directory with none of its children at all:

```
$ svn checkout file:///var/svn/repos mom-empty --depth empty
Checked out revision 1
$
```

Notice that we added to our original *svn checkout* command line a new --depth option. This option is present on many of Subversion's subcommands and is similar to the --non-recursive (-N) and --recursive (-R) options. In fact, it combines, improves on, supersedes, and ultimately obsoletes these two older options. For starters, it expands the supported degrees of depth specification available to users, adding some previously unsupported (or inconsistently supported) depths. Here are the depth values that you can request for a given Subversion operation:

--depth empty
   Include only the immediate target of the operation, not any of its file or directory children.

--depth files
   Include the immediate target of the operation and any of its immediate file children.

--depth immediates
   Include the immediate target of the operation and any of its immediate file or directory children. The directory children will themselves be empty.

--depth infinity
   Include the immediate target, its file and directory children, its children's children, and so on to full recursion.

Of course, merely combining two existing options into one hardly constitutes a new feature worthy of a whole section in our book. Fortunately, there is more to this story. This idea of depth extends not just to the operations you perform with your Subversion client, but also as a description of a working copy citizen's *ambient depth*, which is the depth persistently recorded by the working copy for that item. Its key strength is this very persistence—the fact that it is *sticky*. The working copy remembers the depth you've selected for each item in it until you later change that depth selection; by default, Subversion commands operate on the working copy citizens present, regardless of their selected depth settings.

You can check the recorded ambient depth of a working copy using the *svn info* command. If the ambient depth is anything other than infinite recursion, *svn info* will display a line describing that depth value:

```
$ svn info mom-immediates | grep '^Depth:'
Depth: immediates
$
```

Our previous examples demonstrated checkouts of infinite depth (the default for *svn checkout*) and empty depth. Let's look now at examples of the other depth values:

```
$ svn checkout file:///var/svn/repos mom-files --depth files
A    mom-files/kitty1.txt
A    mom-files/doggie1.txt
Checked out revision 1.
$ svn checkout file:///var/svn/repos mom-immediates --depth immediates
A    mom-immediates/son
A    mom-immediates/daughter
A    mom-immediates/kitty1.txt
A    mom-immediates/doggie1.txt
Checked out revision 1.
$
```

As described, each of these depths is something more than only the target, but something less than full recursion.

We've used *svn checkout* as an example here, but you'll find the --depth option present on many other Subversion commands, too. In those other commands, depth specification is a way to limit the scope of an operation to some depth, much like the way the older --non-recursive (-N) and --recursive (-R) options behave. This means that when operating on a working copy of some depth, while requesting an operation of a shallower depth, the operation is limited to that shallower depth. In fact, we can make an even more general statement: given a working copy of any arbitrary—even mixed—ambient depth, and a Subversion command with some requested operational depth, the command will maintain the ambient depth of the working copy members while still limiting the scope of the operation to the requested (or default) operational depth.

In addition to the --depth option, the *svn update* and *svn switch* subcommands also accept a second depth-related option: --set-depth. It is with this option that you can change the sticky depth of a working copy item. Watch what happens as we take our empty-depth checkout and gradually telescope it deeper using svn update --set-depth *NEW-DEPTH TARGET*:

```
$ svn update --set-depth files mom-empty
A    mom-empty/kittie1.txt
A    mom-empty/doggie1.txt
Updated to revision 1.
$ svn update --set-depth immediates mom-empty
A    mom-empty/son
A    mom-empty/daughter
Updated to revision 1.
$ svn update --set-depth infinity mom-empty
A    mom-empty/son/grandson
A    mom-empty/daughter/granddaughter1
A    mom-empty/daughter/granddaughter1/bunny1.txt
A    mom-empty/daughter/granddaughter1/bunny2.txt
A    mom-empty/daughter/granddaughter2
A    mom-empty/daughter/fishie1.txt
Updated to revision 1.
$
```

As we gradually increased our depth selection, the repository gave us more pieces of our tree.

In our example, we operated only on the root of our working copy, changing its ambient depth value. But we can independently change the ambient depth value of *any* subdirectory inside the working copy, too. Careful use of this ability allows us to flesh out only certain portions of the working copy tree, leaving other portions absent altogether (hence the "sparse" bit of the feature's name). Here's an example of how we might build out a portion of one branch of our family's tree, enable full recursion on another branch, and keep still other pieces pruned (absent from disk):

```
$ rm -rf mom-empty
$ svn checkout file:///var/svn/repos mom-empty --depth empty
Checked out revision 1.
$ svn update --set-depth empty mom-empty/son
A    mom-empty/son
Updated to revision 1.
$ svn update --set-depth empty mom-empty/daughter
A    mom-empty/daughter
Updated to revision 1.
$ svn update --set-depth infinity mom-empty/daughter/granddaughter1
A    mom-empty/daughter/granddaughter1
A    mom-empty/daughter/granddaughter1/bunny1.txt
A    mom-empty/daughter/granddaughter1/bunny2.txt
Updated to revision 1.
$
```

Fortunately, having a complex collection of ambient depths in a single working copy doesn't complicate the way you interact with that working copy. You can still make, revert, display, and commit local modifications in your working copy without providing any new options (including `--depth` and `--set-depth`) to the relevant subcommands. Even *svn update* works as it does elsewhere when no specific depth is provided—it updates the working copy targets that are present while honoring their sticky depths.

You might at this point be wondering, "So what? When would I use this?" One scenario where this feature finds utility is tied to a particular repository layout, specifically where you have many related or codependent projects or software modules living as siblings in a single repository location (*trunk/project1*, *trunk/project2*, *trunk/project3*, etc.). In such scenarios, it might be the case that you personally care about only a handful of those projects—maybe some primary project and a few other modules on which it depends. You can check out individual working copies of all of these things, but those working copies are disjoint and, as a result, it can be cumbersome to perform operations across several or all of them at the same time. The alternative is to use the sparse directories feature, building out a single working copy that contains only the modules you care about. You'd start with an empty-depth checkout of the common parent directory of the projects, and then update with infinite depth only the items you wish to have, as we demonstrated in the previous example. Think of it as an opt-in system for working copy citizens.

Subversion 1.5's implementation of shallow checkouts is good but does not support a couple of interesting behaviors. First, you cannot de-telescope a working copy item. Running `svn update --set-depth empty` in an infinite-depth working copy will not have the effect of discarding everything but the topmost directory—it will simply error out. Second, there is no depth value to indicate that you wish an item to be explicitly excluded. You have to do implicit exclusion of an item by including everything else.

Locking

Subversion's copy-modify-merge version control model lives and dies on its data merging algorithms—specifically, on how well those algorithms perform when trying to resolve conflicts caused by multiple users modifying the same file concurrently. Subversion itself provides only one such algorithm: a three-way differencing algorithm that is smart enough to handle data at a granularity of a single line of text. Subversion also allows you to supplement its content merge processing with external differencing utilities (as described in "External diff3" on page 248), some of which may do an even better job, perhaps providing granularity of a word or a single character of text. But common among those algorithms is that they generally work only on text files. The landscape starts to look pretty grim when you start talking about content merges of nontextual file formats. And when you can't find a tool that can handle that type of merging, you begin to run into problems with the copy-modify-merge model.

Let's look at a real-life example of where this model runs aground. Harry and Sally are both graphic designers working on the same project, a bit of marketing collateral for an automobile mechanic. Central to the design of a particular poster is an image of a car in need of some bodywork, stored in a file using the PNG image format. The poster's layout is almost finished, and both Harry and Sally are pleased with the particular photo they chose for their damaged car—a baby blue 1967 Ford Mustang with an unfortunate bit of crumpling on the left front fender.

Now, as is common in graphic design work, there's a change in plans, which causes the car's color to be a concern. So Sally updates her working copy to HEAD, fires up her photo-editing software, and sets about tweaking the image so that the car is now cherry red. Meanwhile, Harry, feeling particularly inspired that day, decides that the image would have greater impact if the car appears to have suffered greater impact. He, too, updates to HEAD, and then draws some cracks on the vehicle's windshield. He manages to finish his work before Sally finishes hers, and after admiring the fruits of his undeniable talent, he commits the modified image. Shortly thereafter, Sally is finished with the car's new finish and tries to commit her changes. But, as expected, Subversion fails the commit, informing Sally that her version of the image is now out of date.

Here's where the difficulty sets in. If Harry and Sally were making changes to a text file, Sally would simply update her working copy, receiving Harry's changes in the process. In the worst possible case, they would have modified the same region of the file, and Sally would have to work out by hand the proper resolution to the conflict. But these aren't text files—they are binary images. And while it's a simple matter to describe what one would expect the results of this content merge to be, there is precious little chance that any software exists that is smart enough to examine the common baseline image that each of these graphic artists worked against, the changes that Harry made, and the changes that Sally made, and then spit out an image of a busted-up red Mustang with a cracked windshield!

Of course, things would have gone more smoothly if Harry and Sally had serialized their modifications to the image—if, say, Harry had waited to draw his windshield cracks on Sally's now-red car, or if Sally had tweaked the color of a car whose windshield was already cracked. As is discussed in "The Copy-Modify-Merge Solution" on page 4, most of these types of problems go away entirely where perfect communication between Harry and Sally exists.[*] But as one's version control system is, in fact, one form of communication, it follows that having that software facilitate the serialization of nonparallelizable editing efforts is no bad thing. This is where Subversion's implementation of the lock-modify-unlock model steps into the spotlight. This is where we talk about Subversion's *locking* feature, which is similar to the "reserved checkouts" mechanisms of other version control systems.

Subversion's locking feature exists ultimately to minimize wasted time and effort. By allowing a user to programmatically claim the exclusive right to change a file in the repository, that user can be reasonably confident that any energy he invests on unmergeable changes won't be wasted—his commit of those changes will succeed. Also, because Subversion communicates to other users that serialization is in effect for a particular versioned object, those users can reasonably expect that the object is about to be changed by someone else. They, too, can then avoid wasting their time and energy on unmergeable changes that won't be committable due to eventual out-of-dateness.

When referring to Subversion's locking feature, one is actually talking about a fairly diverse collection of behaviors, which include the ability to lock a versioned file[†] (claiming the exclusive right to modify the file), to unlock that file (yielding that exclusive right to modify), to see reports about which files are locked and by whom, to annotate files for which locking before editing is strongly advised, and so on. In this section, we'll cover all of these facets of the larger locking feature.

---

[*] Communication wouldn't have been such bad medicine for Harry and Sally's Hollywood namesakes, either, for that matter.

[†] Subversion does not currently allow locks on directories.

The Three Meanings of "Lock"

In this section, and almost everywhere in this book, the words "lock" and "locking" describe a mechanism for mutual exclusion between users to avoid clashing commits. Unfortunately, there are two other sorts of "lock" with which Subversion, and therefore this book, sometimes needs to be concerned.

The second is *working copy locks*, used internally by Subversion to prevent clashes between multiple Subversion clients operating on the same working copy. This is the sort of lock indicated by an L in the third column of *svn status* output, and removed by the *svn cleanup* command, as described in "Sometimes You Just Need to Clean Up" on page 43.

Third, there are *database locks*, used internally by the Berkeley DB backend to prevent clashes between multiple programs trying to access the database. This is the sort of lock whose unwanted persistence after an error can cause a repository to be "wedged," as described in "Berkeley DB Recovery" on page 167.

You can generally forget about these other kinds of locks until something goes wrong that requires you to care about them. In this book, "lock" means the first sort unless the contrary is either clear from context or explicitly stated.

Creating Locks

In the Subversion repository, a *lock* is a piece of metadata that grants exclusive access to one user to change a file. This user is said to be the *lock owner*. Each lock also has a unique identifier, typically a long string of characters, known as the *lock token*. The repository manages locks, ultimately handling their creation, enforcement, and removal. If any commit transaction attempts to modify or delete a locked file (or delete one of the parent directories of the file), the repository will demand two pieces of information—that the client performing the commit be authenticated as the lock owner, and that the lock token has been provided as part of the commit process as a form of proof that the client knows which lock it is using.

To demonstrate lock creation, let's refer back to our example of multiple graphic designers working on the same binary image files. Harry has decided to change a JPEG image. To prevent other people from committing changes to the file while he is modifying it (as well as alerting them that he is about to change it), he locks the file in the repository using the *svn lock* command:

```
$ svn lock banana.jpg -m "Editing file for tomorrow's release."
'banana.jpg' locked by user 'harry'.
$
```

The preceding example demonstrates a number of new things. First, notice that Harry passed the --message (-m) option to *svn lock*. Similar to *svn commit*, the *svn lock* command can take comments—via either --message (-m) or --file (-F)—to describe the reason for locking the file. Unlike *svn commit*, however, *svn lock* will not demand a message by launching your preferred text editor. Lock comments are optional, but still recommended to aid communication.

Second, the lock attempt succeeded. This means that the file wasn't already locked, and that Harry had the latest version of the file. If Harry's working copy of the file had been out of date, the repository would have rejected the request, forcing Harry to *svn update* and reattempt the locking command. The locking command would also have failed if the file had already been locked by someone else.

As you can see, the *svn lock* command prints confirmation of the successful lock. At this point, the fact that the file is locked becomes apparent in the output of the *svn status* and *svn info* reporting subcommands:

```
$ svn status
    K banana.jpg

$ svn info banana.jpg
Path: banana.jpg
Name: banana.jpg
URL: http://svn.example.com/repos/project/banana.jpg
Repository UUID: edb2f264-5ef2-0310-a47a-87b0ce17a8ec
Revision: 2198
Node Kind: file
Schedule: normal
Last Changed Author: frank
Last Changed Rev: 1950
Last Changed Date: 2006-03-15 12:43:04 -0600 (Wed, 15 Mar 2006)
Text Last Updated: 2006-06-08 19:23:07 -0500 (Thu, 08 Jun 2006)
Properties Last Updated: 2006-06-08 19:23:07 -0500 (Thu, 08 Jun 2006)
Checksum: 3b110d3b10638f5d1f4fe0f436a5a2a5
Lock Token: opaquelocktoken:0c0f600b-88f9-0310-9e48-355b44d4a58e
Lock Owner: harry
Lock Created: 2006-06-14 17:20:31 -0500 (Wed, 14 Jun 2006)
Lock Comment (1 line):
Editing file for tomorrow's release.

$
```

The fact that the *svn info* command, which does not contact the repository when run against working copy paths, can display the lock token reveals an important piece of information about those tokens: they are cached in the working copy. The presence of the lock token is critical. It gives the working copy authorization to make use of the lock later on. Also, the *svn status* command shows a K next to the file (short for locKed), indicating that the lock token is present.

Now that Harry has locked *banana.jpg*, Sally is unable to change or delete that file:

```
$ svn delete banana.jpg
D         banana.jpg
$ svn commit -m "Delete useless file."
Deleting       banana.jpg
svn: Commit failed (details follow):
svn: Server sent unexpected return value (423 Locked) in response to DELETE\
```

```
request for '/repos/project/!svn/wrk/64bad3a9-96f9-0310-818a-df4224ddc35d/\
banana.jpg'
$
```

But Harry, after touching up the banana's shade of yellow, is able to commit his changes to the file. That's because he authenticates as the lock owner and also because his working copy holds the correct lock token:

```
$ svn status
M     K banana.jpg
$ svn commit -m "Make banana more yellow"
Sending        banana.jpg
Transmitting file data .
Committed revision 2201.
$ svn status
$
```

Regarding Lock Tokens

A lock token isn't an authentication token so much as an *authorization* token. The token isn't a protected secret. In fact, a lock's unique token is discoverable by anyone who runs `svn info URL`. A lock token is special only when it lives inside a working copy. It's proof that the lock was created in that particular working copy and not somewhere else by some other client. Merely authenticating as the lock owner isn't enough to prevent accidents.

For example, suppose you lock a file using a computer at your office, but you leave work for the day before you finish your changes to that file. It should not be possible to accidentally commit changes to that same file from your home computer later that evening simply because you've authenticated as the lock's owner. In other words, the lock token prevents one piece of Subversion-related software from undermining the work of another. (In our example, if you really need to change the file from an alternative working copy, you would need to *break* the lock and relock the file.)

Notice that after the commit is finished, *svn status* shows that the lock token is no longer present in the working copy. This is the standard behavior of *svn commit*—it searches the working copy (or list of targets, if you provide such a list) for local modifications and sends all the lock tokens it encounters during this walk to the server as part of the commit transaction. After the commit completes successfully, all of the repository locks that were mentioned are released—*even on files that weren't committed.* This is meant to discourage users from being sloppy about locking or from holding locks for too long. If Harry haphazardly locks 30 files in a directory named *images* because he's unsure of which files he needs to change, yet changes only four of those files, when he runs `svn commit images`, the process will still release all 30 locks.

This behavior of automatically releasing locks can be overridden with the `--no-unlock` option to *svn commit*. This is best used for those times when you want to commit changes but you still plan to make more changes and thus need to retain existing locks.

You can also make this your default behavior by setting the no-unlock runtime configuration option (see "Runtime Configuration Area" on page 233).

Of course, locking a file doesn't oblige one to commit a change to it. The lock can be released at any time with a simple *svn unlock* command:

```
$ svn unlock banana.c
'banana.c' unlocked.
```

Discovering Locks

When a commit fails due to someone else's locks, it's fairly easy to learn about them. The easiest way is to run svn status --show-updates:

```
$ svn status -u
M              23    bar.c
M      0       32    raisin.jpg
       *       72    foo.h
Status against revision:     105
$
```

In this example, Sally can see not only that her copy of *foo.h* is out of date, but also that one of the two modified files she plans to commit is locked in the repository. The 0 symbol stands for "Other," meaning that a lock exists on the file and was created by somebody else. If she were to attempt a commit, the lock on *raisin.jpg* would prevent it. Sally is left wondering who made the lock, when, and why. Once again, *svn info* has the answers:

```
$ svn info http://svn.example.com/repos/project/raisin.jpg
Path: raisin.jpg
Name: raisin.jpg
URL: http://svn.example.com/repos/project/raisin.jpg
Repository UUID: edb2f264-5ef2-0310-a47a-87b0ce17a8ec
Revision: 105
Node Kind: file
Last Changed Author: sally
Last Changed Rev: 32
Last Changed Date: 2006-01-25 12:43:04 -0600 (Sun, 25 Jan 2006)
Lock Token: opaquelocktoken:fc2b4dee-98f9-0310-abf3-653ff3226e6b
Lock Owner: harry
Lock Created: 2006-02-16 13:29:18 -0500 (Thu, 16 Feb 2006)
Lock Comment (1 line):
Need to make a quick tweak to this image.
$
```

Just as you can use *svn info* to examine objects in the working copy, you can also use it to examine objects in the repository. If the main argument to *svn info* is a working copy path, then all of the working copy's cached information is displayed; any mention of a lock means that the working copy is holding a lock token (if a file is locked by another user or in another working copy, *svn info* on a working copy path will show no lock information at all). If the main argument to *svn info* is a URL, the information reflects the latest version of an object in the repository, and any mention of a lock describes the current lock on the object.

So in this particular example, Sally can see that Harry locked the file on February 16 to "make a quick tweak." It being June, she suspects that he probably forgot all about the lock. She might phone Harry to complain and ask him to release the lock. If he's unavailable, she might try to forcibly break the lock herself or ask an administrator to do so.

Breaking and Stealing Locks

A repository lock isn't sacred—in Subversion's default configuration state, locks can be released not only by the person who created them, but by anyone. When somebody other than the original lock creator destroys a lock, we refer to this as *breaking the lock*.

From the administrator's chair, it's simple to break locks. The *svnlook* and *svnadmin* programs have the ability to display and remove locks directly from the repository. (For more information about these tools, see "An Administrator's Toolkit" on page 159.)

```
$ svnadmin lslocks /var/svn/repos
Path: /project2/images/banana.jpg
UUID Token: opaquelocktoken:c32b4d88-e8fb-2310-abb3-153ff1236923
Owner: frank
Created: 2006-06-15 13:29:18 -0500 (Thu, 15 Jun 2006)
Expires:
Comment (1 line):
Still improving the yellow color.

Path: /project/raisin.jpg
UUID Token: opaquelocktoken:fc2b4dee-98f9-0310-abf3-653ff3226e6b
Owner: harry
Created: 2006-02-16 13:29:18 -0500 (Thu, 16 Feb 2006)
Expires:
Comment (1 line):
Need to make a quick tweak to this image.

$ svnadmin rmlocks /var/svn/repos /project/raisin.jpg
Removed lock on '/project/raisin.jpg'.
$
```

The more interesting option is to allow users to break each other's locks over the network. To do this, Sally simply needs to pass the `--force` to the *svn unlock* command:

```
$ svn status -u
M              23   bar.c
M    0         32   raisin.jpg
     *         72   foo.h
Status against revision:    105
$ svn unlock raisin.jpg
svn: 'raisin.jpg' is not locked in this working copy
$ svn info raisin.jpg | grep URL
URL: http://svn.example.com/repos/project/raisin.jpg
$ svn unlock http://svn.example.com/repos/project/raisin.jpg
```

```
svn: Unlock request failed: 403 Forbidden (http://svn.example.com)
$ svn unlock --force http://svn.example.com/repos/project/raisin.jpg
'raisin.jpg' unlocked.
$
```

Now, Sally's initial attempt to unlock failed because she ran *svn unlock* directly on her working copy of the file, and no lock token was present. To remove the lock directly from the repository, she needs to pass a URL to *svn unlock*. Her first attempt to unlock the URL fails, because she can't authenticate as the lock owner (nor does she have the lock token). But when she passes `--force`, the authentication and authorization requirements are ignored, and the remote lock is broken.

Locking Policies

Different systems have different notions of how strict a lock should be. Some folks argue that locks must be strictly enforced at all costs, releasable only by the original creator or administrator. They argue that if anyone can break a lock, chaos runs rampant and the whole point of locking is defeated. The other side argues that locks are first and foremost a communication tool. If users are constantly breaking each other's locks, it represents a cultural failure within the team and the problem falls outside the scope of software enforcement.

Subversion defaults to the "softer" approach, but still allows administrators to create stricter enforcement policies through the use of hook scripts. In particular, the *pre-lock* and *pre-unlock* hooks allow administrators to decide when lock creation and lock releases are allowed to happen. Depending on whether a lock already exists, these two hooks can decide whether to allow a certain user to break or steal a lock. The *post-lock* and *post-unlock* hooks are also available and can be used to send email after locking actions. To learn more about repository hooks, see "Implementing Repository Hooks" on page 156.

Simply breaking a lock may not be enough. In the running example, Sally may not only want to break Harry's long-forgotten lock, but relock the file for her own use. She can accomplish this by using *svn unlock* with `--force` and then *svn lock* back-to-back, but there's a small chance that somebody else might lock the file between the two commands. The simpler thing to do is to *steal* the lock, which involves breaking and relocking the file all in one atomic step. To do this, Sally passes the `--force` option to *svn lock*:

```
$ svn lock raisin.jpg
svn: Lock request failed: 423 Locked (http://svn.example.com)
$ svn lock --force raisin.jpg
'raisin.jpg' locked by user 'sally'.
$
```

In any case, whether the lock is broken or stolen, Harry may be in for a surprise. Harry's working copy still contains the original lock token, but that lock no longer exists. The lock token is said to be *defunct*. The lock represented by the lock token has either been broken (no longer in the repository) or stolen (replaced with a different lock). Either way, Harry can see this by asking *svn status* to contact the repository:

```
$ svn status
    K raisin.jpg
$ svn status -u
    B         32    raisin.jpg
$ svn update
  B raisin.jpg
$ svn status
$
```

If the repository lock was broken, then `svn status --show-updates` displays a B (Broken) symbol next to the file. If a new lock exists in place of the old one, then a T (sTolen) symbol is shown. Finally, *svn update* notices any defunct lock tokens and removes them from the working copy.

Lock Communication

We've seen how *svn lock* and *svn unlock* can be used to create, release, break, and steal locks. This satisfies the goal of serializing commit access to a file. But what about the larger problem of preventing wasted time?

For example, suppose Harry locks an image file and then begins editing it. Meanwhile, miles away, Sally wants to do the same thing. She doesn't think to run `svn status --show-updates`, so she has no idea that Harry has already locked the file. She spends hours editing the file, and when she tries to commit her change, she discovers that either the file is locked or that it's out of date. Regardless, her changes aren't mergeable with Harry's. One of these two people has to throw away his or her work, and a lot of time has been wasted.

Subversion's solution to this problem is to provide a mechanism to remind users that a file ought to be locked *before* the editing begins. The mechanism is a special property: `svn:needs-lock`. If that property is attached to a file (regardless of its value, which is irrelevant), Subversion will try to use filesystem-level permissions to make the file read-only—unless, of course, the user has explicitly locked the file. When a lock token is present (as a result of using *svn lock*), the file becomes read/write. When the lock is released, the file becomes read-only again.

The theory, then, is that if the image file has this property attached, Sally would immediately notice something is strange when she opens the file for editing: many applications alert users immediately when a read-only file is opened for editing, and nearly all would prevent her from saving changes to the file. This reminds her to lock the file before editing, whereby she discovers the preexisting lock:

```
$ /usr/local/bin/gimp raisin.jpg
gimp: error: file is read-only!
$ ls -l raisin.jpg
-r--r--r--   1 sally    sally    215589 Jun  8 19:23 raisin.jpg
$ svn lock raisin.jpg
```

```
svn: Lock request failed: 423 Locked (http://svn.example.com)
$ svn info http://svn.example.com/repos/project/raisin.jpg | grep Lock
Lock Token: opaquelocktoken:fc2b4dee-98f9-0310-abf3-653ff3226e6b
Lock Owner: harry
Lock Created: 2006-06-08 07:29:18 -0500 (Thu, 08 June 2006)
Lock Comment (1 line):
Making some tweaks.  Locking for the next two hours.
$
```

 Users and administrators alike are encouraged to attach the svn:needs-lock property to any file that cannot be contextually merged. This is the primary technique for encouraging good locking habits and preventing wasted effort.

Note that this property is a communication tool that works independently from the locking system. In other words, any file can be locked, whether or not this property is present. And conversely, the presence of this property doesn't make the repository require a lock when committing.

Unfortunately, the system isn't flawless. It's possible that even when a file has the property, the read-only reminder won't always work. Sometimes applications misbehave and "hijack" the read-only file, silently allowing users to edit and save the file anyway. There's not much that Subversion can do in this situation—at the end of the day, there's simply no substitution for good interpersonal communication.‡

Externals Definitions

Sometimes it is useful to construct a working copy that is made out of a number of different checkouts. For example, you may want different subdirectories to come from different locations in a repository or perhaps from different repositories altogether. You could certainly set up such a scenario by hand—using *svn checkout* to create the sort of nested working copy structure you are trying to achieve. But if this layout is important for everyone who uses your repository, every other user will need to perform the same checkout operations that you did.

Fortunately, Subversion provides support for *externals definitions*. An externals definition is a mapping of a local directory to the URL—and ideally a particular revision—of a versioned directory. In Subversion, you declare externals definitions in groups using the svn:externals property. You can create or modify this property using *svn propset* or *svn propedit* (see "Manipulating Properties" on page 51). It can be set on any versioned directory, and its value describes both the external repository location and the client-side directory to which that location should be checked out.

---

‡ Except, perhaps, a classic Vulcan mind-meld.

The convenience of the `svn:externals` property is that once it is set on a versioned directory, everyone who checks out a working copy with that directory also gets the benefit of the externals definition. In other words, once one person has made the effort to define the nested working copy structure, no one else has to bother—Subversion will, after checking out the original working copy, automatically also check out the external working copies.

 The relative target subdirectories of externals definitions *must not* already exist on your or other users' systems—Subversion will create them when it checks out the external working copy.

You also get in the externals definition design all the regular benefits of Subversion properties. The definitions are versioned. If you need to change an externals definition, you can do so using the regular property modification subcommands. When you commit a change to the `svn:externals` property, Subversion will synchronize the checked-out items against the changed externals definition when you next run *svn update*. The same thing will happen when others update their working copies and receive your changes to the externals definition.

 Because the `svn:externals` property has a multiline value, we strongly recommend that you use *svn propedit* instead of *svn propset*.

Subversion releases prior to 1.5 honor an externals definition format that is a multiline table of subdirectories (relative to the versioned directory on which the property is set), optional revision flags, and fully qualified, absolute Subversion repository URLs. An example of this might looks as follows:

```
$ svn propget svn:externals calc
third-party/sounds           http://svn.example.com/repos/sounds
third-party/skins -r148      http://svn.example.com/skinproj
third-party/skins/toolkit -r21 http://svn.example.com/skin-maker
```

When someone checks out a working copy of the *calc* directory referred to in the previous example, Subversion also continues to check out the items found in its externals definition:

```
$ svn checkout http://svn.example.com/repos/calc
A  calc
A  calc/Makefile
A  calc/integer.c
A  calc/button.c
Checked out revision 148.

Fetching external item into calc/third-party/sounds
A  calc/third-party/sounds/ding.ogg
A  calc/third-party/sounds/dong.ogg
```

```
A  calc/third-party/sounds/clang.ogg
…
A  calc/third-party/sounds/bang.ogg
A  calc/third-party/sounds/twang.ogg
Checked out revision 14.

Fetching external item into calc/third-party/skins
…
```

As of Subversion 1.5, however, a new format of the svn:externals property is supported. Externals definitions are still multiline, but the order and format of the various pieces of information have changed. The new syntax more closely mimics the order of arguments you might pass to *svn checkout*: the optional revision flags come first, then the external Subversion repository URL, and finally the relative local subdirectory. Notice, though, that this time we didn't say "fully qualified, absolute Subversion repository URLs." That's because the new format supports relative URLs and URLs that carry peg revisions. The previous example of an externals definition might, in Subversion 1.5, look like the following:

```
$ svn propget svn:externals calc
        http://svn.example.com/repos/sounds third-party/sounds
-r148 http://svn.example.com/skinproj third-party/skins
-r21  http://svn.example.com/skin-maker third-party/skins/toolkit
```

Or, making use of the peg revision syntax (which we describe in detail in "Peg and Operative Revisions" on page 87), it might appear as:

```
$ svn propget svn:externals calc
http://svn.example.com/repos/sounds third-party/sounds
http://svn.example.com/skinproj@148 third-party/skins
http://svn.example.com/skin-maker@21 third-party/skins/toolkit
```

 You should seriously consider using explicit revision numbers in all of your externals definitions. Doing so means that you get to decide when to pull down a different snapshot of external information, and exactly which snapshot to pull. Besides avoiding the surprise of getting changes to third-party repositories that you might not have any control over, using explicit revision numbers also means that as you backdate your working copy to a previous revision, your externals definitions will also revert to the way they looked in that previous revision, which in turn means that the external working copies will be updated to match the way *they* looked back when your repository was at that previous revision. For software projects, this could be the difference between a successful and a failed build of an older snapshot of your complex codebase.

For most repositories, these three ways of formatting the externals definitions have the same ultimate effect. They all bring the same benefits. Unfortunately, they all bring the same annoyances, too. Since the definitions shown use absolute URLs, moving or copying a directory to which they are attached will not affect what gets checked out as an external (though the relative local target subdirectory will, of course, move with the renamed directory). This can be confusing—even frustrating—in certain situations. For example, say you have a top-level directory named *my-project*, and you've created an externals definition on one of its subdirectories (*my-project/some-dir*) that tracks the latest revision of another of its subdirectories (*my-project/external-dir*):

```
$ svn checkout http://svn.example.com/projects .
A    my-project
A    my-project/some-dir
A    my-project/external-dir
...
Fetching external item into 'my-project/some-dir/subdir'
Checked out external at revision 11.

Checked out revision 11.
$ svn propget svn:externals my-project/some-dir
subdir http://svn.example.com/projects/my-project/external-dir

$
```

Now you use *svn move* to rename the *my-project* directory. At this point, your externals definition will still refer to a path under the *my-project* directory, even though that directory no longer exists:

```
$ svn move -q my-project renamed-project
$ svn commit -m "Rename my-project to renamed-project."
Deleting       my-project
Adding         renamed-project

Committed revision 12.
$ svn update

Fetching external item into 'renamed-project/some-dir/subdir'
svn: Target path does not exist
$
```

Also, absolute URLs can cause problems with repositories that are available via multiple URL schemes. For example, if your Subversion server is configured to allow everyone to check out the repository over http:// or https://, but to allow commits to come in only via https://, you have an interesting problem on your hands. If your externals definitions use the http:// form of the repository URLs, you won't be able to commit anything from the working copies created by those externals. On the other hand, if they use the https:// form of the URLs, anyone who might be checking out via http:// because his client doesn't support https:// will be unable to fetch the external items. Be aware, too, that if you need to reparent your working copy (using *svn switch* with the --relocate option), externals definitions will *not* also be reparented.

Subversion 1.5 takes a huge step forward in relieving these frustrations. As mentioned earlier, the URLs used in the new externals definition format can be relative, and Subversion provides syntax magic for specifying multiple flavors of URL relativity:

../

Relative to the URL of the directory on which the `svn:externals` property is set

^/

Relative to the root of the repository in which the `svn:externals` property is versioned

//

Relative to the scheme of the URL of the directory on which the `svn:externals` property is set

/

Relative to the root URL of the server on which the `svn:externals` property is versioned

So, looking a fourth time at our previous externals definition example, and making use of the new absolute URL syntax in various ways, we might now see:

```
$ svn propget svn:externals calc
^/sounds third-party/sounds
/skinproj@148 third-party/skins
//svn.example.com/skin-maker@21 third-party/skins/toolkit
```

However, the support that exists for externals definitions in Subversion remains less than ideal. An externals definition can point only to directories, not to files. Also, the local subdirectory part of the definition cannot contain `..` parent directory indicators (such as *../../skins/myskin*). Perhaps most disappointingly, the working copies created via the externals definition support are still disconnected from the primary working copy (on whose versioned directories the `svn:externals` property was actually set). And Subversion still truly operates only on nondisjoint working copies. So, for example, if you want to commit changes that you've made in one or more of those external working copies, you must run *svn commit* explicitly on those working copies—committing on the primary working copy will not recurse into any external ones.

We've already mentioned some of the additional shortcomings of the old `svn:externals` format and how the new Subversion 1.5 format improves upon it. But be careful when making use of the new format that you don't inadvertently cause problems for other folks accessing your repository who are using older Subversion clients. While Subversion 1.5 clients will continue to recognize and support the original externals definition format, older clients will *not* be able to correctly parse the new format.

Besides the *svn checkout*, *svn update*, *svn switch*, and *svn export* commands which actually manage the *disjoint* (or disconnected) subdirectories into which externals are checked out, the *svn status* command also recognizes externals definitions. It displays a status code of **X** for the disjoint external subdirectories, and then recurses into those subdirectories to display the status of the external items themselves. You can pass the `--ignore-externals` option to any of these subcommands to disable externals definition processing.

Peg and Operative Revisions

We copy, move, rename, and completely replace files and directories on our computers all the time. And your version control system shouldn't get in the way of your doing these things with your version-controlled files and directories, either. Subversion's file management support is quite liberating, affording almost as much flexibility for versioned files as you'd expect when manipulating your unversioned ones. But that flexibility means that across the lifetime of your repository, a given versioned object might have many paths, and a given path might represent several entirely different versioned objects. This introduces a certain level of complexity to your interactions with those paths and objects.

Subversion is pretty smart about noticing when an object's version history includes such "changes of address." For example, if you ask for the revision history log of a particular file that was renamed last week, Subversion happily provides all those logs—the revision in which the rename itself happened, plus the logs of relevant revisions both before and after that rename. So, most of the time, you don't even have to think about such things. But occasionally, Subversion needs your help to clear up ambiguities.

The simplest example of this occurs when a directory or file is deleted from version control, and then a new directory or file is created with the same name and added to version control. The thing you deleted and the thing you later added aren't the same thing. They merely happen to have had the same path—*/trunk/object*, for example. What, then, does it mean to ask Subversion about the history of */trunk/object*? Are you asking about the thing currently at that location, or the old thing you deleted from that location? Are you asking about the operations that have happened to *all* the objects that have ever lived at that path? Subversion needs a hint about what you really want.

And thanks to moves, versioned object history can get far more twisted than even that. For example, you might have a directory named *concept*, containing some nascent software project you've been toying with. Eventually, though, that project matures to the point that the idea seems to actually have some wings, so you do the unthinkable and decide to give the project a name.[§] Let's say you called your software Frabnaggilywort. At this point, it makes sense to rename the directory to reflect the project's new name, so *concept* is renamed to *frabnaggilywort*. Life goes on, Frabnaggilywort releases a 1.0 version and is downloaded and used daily by hordes of people aiming to improve their lives.

It's a nice story, really, but it doesn't end there. Entrepreneur that you are, you've already got another think in the tank. So you make a new directory, *concept*, and the cycle begins again. In fact, the cycle begins again many times over the years, each time starting with that old *concept* directory, then sometimes seeing that directory renamed

---

[§] "You're not supposed to name it. Once you name it, you start getting attached to it."—Mike Wazowski

as the idea cures, sometimes seeing it deleted when you scrap the idea. Or, to get really sick, maybe you rename *concept* to something else for a while, but later rename the thing back to *concept* for some reason.

In scenarios like these, attempting to instruct Subversion to work with these reused paths can be a little like instructing a motorist in Chicago's West Suburbs to drive east down Roosevelt Road and turn left onto Main Street. In a mere 20 minutes, you can cross "Main Street" in Wheaton, Glen Ellyn, and Lombard. And no, they aren't the same street. Our motorist—and our Subversion—needs a little more detail to do the right thing.

In version 1.1, Subversion introduced a way for you to tell it exactly which Main Street you meant. It's called the *peg revision*, and it is provided to Subversion for the sole purpose of identifying a unique line of history. Because at most, one versioned object may occupy a path at any given time—or, more precisely, in any one revision—the combination of a path and a peg revision is all that is needed to refer to a specific line of history. Peg revisions are specified to the Subversion command-line client using *at syntax*, so called because the syntax involves appending an "at sign" (@) and the peg revision to the end of the path with which the revision is associated.

But what of the `--revision` (`-r`) of which we've spoken so much in this book? That revision (or set of revisions) is called the *operative revision* (or *operative revision range*). Once a particular line of history has been identified using a path and peg revision, Subversion performs the requested operation using the operative revision(s). To map this to our Chicagoland streets analogy, if we are told to go to 606 N. Main Street in Wheaton,[‖] we can think of "Main Street" as our path and "Wheaton" as our peg revision. These two pieces of information identify a unique path that can be traveled (north or south on Main Street), and they keep us from traveling up and down the wrong Main Street in search of our destination. Now we throw in "606 N." as our operative revision of sorts, and we know *exactly* where to go.

The Peg Revision Algorithm

The Subversion command-line client performs the peg revision algorithm any time it needs to resolve possible ambiguities in the paths and revisions provided to it. Here's an example of such an invocation:

```
$ svn command -r OPERATIVE-REV item@PEG-REV
```

If *OPERATIVE-REV* is older than *PEG-REV*, the algorithm is as follows:

1. Locate *item* in the revision identified by *PEG-REV*. There can be only one such object.
2. Trace the object's history backwards (through any possible renames) to its ancestor in the revision *OPERATIVE-REV*.

‖ 606 N. Main Street, Wheaton, Illinois, is the home of the Wheaton *History* Center. It seemed appropriate....

3. Perform the requested action on that ancestor, wherever it is located, or whatever its name might be or might have been at that time.

But what if *OPERATIVE-REV* is *younger* than *PEG-REV*? Well, that adds some complexity to the theoretical problem of locating the path in *OPERATIVE-REV*, because the path's history could have forked multiple times (thanks to copy operations) between *PEG-REV* and *OPERATIVE-REV*. And that's not all—Subversion doesn't store enough information to performantly trace an object's history forward, anyway. So the algorithm is a little different:

1. Locate *item* in the revision identified by *OPERATIVE-REV*. There can be only one such object.

2. Trace the object's history backward (through any possible renames) to its ancestor in the revision *PEG-REV*.

3. Verify that the object's location (path-wise) in *PEG-REV* is the same as it is in *OPERATIVE-REV*. If that's the case, at least the two locations are known to be directly related, so perform the requested action on the location in *OPERATIVE-REV*. Otherwise, relatedness was not established, so error out with a loud complaint that no viable location was found. (Someday, we expect that Subversion will be able to handle this usage scenario with more flexibility and grace.)

Note that even when you don't explicitly supply a peg revision or operative revision, they are still present. For your convenience, the default peg revision is BASE for working copy items and HEAD for repository URLs. And when no operative revision is provided, it defaults to being the same revision as the peg revision.

Say that long ago we created our repository, and in revision 1 we added our first *concept* directory, plus an *IDEA* file in that directory talking about the concept. After several revisions in which real code was added and tweaked, we, in revision 20, renamed this directory to *frabnaggilywort*. By revision 27, we had a new concept, a new *concept* directory to hold it, and a new *IDEA* file to describe it. And then five years and thousands of revisions flew by, just like they would in any good romance story.

Now, years later, we wonder what the *IDEA* file looked like back in revision 1. But Subversion needs to know whether we are asking about how the *current* file looked back in revision 1, or whether we are asking for the contents of whatever file lived at *concepts/IDEA* in revision 1. Certainly those questions have different answers, and because of peg revisions, you can ask those questions. To find out how the current *IDEA* file looked in that old revision, you run:

```
$ svn cat -r 1 concept/IDEA
svn: Unable to find repository location for 'concept/IDEA' in revision 1
```

Of course, in this example, the current *IDEA* file didn't exist yet in revision 1, so Subversion gives an error. The previous command is shorthand for a longer notation that explicitly lists a peg revision. The expanded notation is:

```
$ svn cat -r 1 concept/IDEA@BASE
svn: Unable to find repository location for 'concept/IDEA' in revision 1
```

And when executed, it has the expected results.

The perceptive reader is probably wondering at this point whether the peg revision syntax causes problems for working copy paths or URLs that actually have at signs in them. After all, how does *svn* know whether `news@11` is the name of a directory in my tree or just a syntax for "revision 11 of *news*"? Thankfully, while *svn* will always assume the latter, there is a trivial workaround. You need only append an at sign to the end of the path, such as `news@11@`. *svn* cares only about the last at sign in the argument, and it is not considered illegal to omit a literal peg revision specifier after that at sign. This workaround even applies to paths that end in an at sign—you would use `filename@@` to talk about a file named *filename@*.

Let's ask the other question, then—in revision 1, what were the contents of whatever file occupied the address *concepts/IDEA* at the time? We'll use an explicit peg revision to help us out:

```
$ svn cat concept/IDEA@1
The idea behind this project is to come up with a piece of software
that can frab a naggily wort.  Frabbing naggily worts is tricky
business, and doing it incorrectly can have serious ramifications, so
we need to employ over-the-top input validation and data verification
mechanisms.
```

Notice that we didn't provide an operative revision this time. That's because when no operative revision is specified, Subversion assumes a default operative revision that's the same as the peg revision.

As you can see, the output from our operation appears to be correct. The text even mentions frabbing naggily worts, so this is almost certainly the file that describes the software now called Frabnaggilywort. In fact, we can verify this using the combination of an explicit peg revision and explicit operative revision. We know that in HEAD, the Frabnaggilywort project is located in the *frabnaggilywort* directory. So we specify that we want to see how the line of history identified in HEAD as the path *frabnaggilywort/ IDEA* looked in revision 1:

```
$ svn cat -r 1 frabnaggilywort/IDEA@HEAD
The idea behind this project is to come up with a piece of software
that can frab a naggily wort.  Frabbing naggily worts is tricky
business, and doing it incorrectly can have serious ramifications, so
we need to employ over-the-top input validation and data verification
mechanisms.
```

And the peg and operative revisions need not be so trivial, either. For example, say *frabnaggilywort* had been deleted from HEAD, but we know it existed in revision 20, and we want to see the diffs for its *IDEA* file between revisions 4 and 10. We can use the peg revision 20 in conjunction with the URL that would have held Frabnaggilywort's *IDEA* file in revision 20, and then use 4 and 10 as our operative revision range:

```
$ svn diff -r 4:10 http://svn.red-bean.com/projects/frabnaggilywort/IDEA@20
Index: frabnaggilywort/IDEA
===================================================================
```

```
--- frabnaggilywort/IDEA     (revision 4)
+++ frabnaggilywort/IDEA     (revision 10)
@@ -1,5 +1,5 @@
-The idea behind this project is to come up with a piece of software
-that can frab a naggily wort.  Frabbing naggily worts is tricky
-business, and doing it incorrectly can have serious ramifications, so
-we need to employ over-the-top input validation and data verification
-mechanisms.
+The idea behind this project is to come up with a piece of
+client-server software that can remotely frab a naggily wort.
+Frabbing naggily worts is tricky business, and doing it incorrectly
+can have serious ramifications, so we need to employ over-the-top
+input validation and data verification mechanisms.
```

Fortunately, most folks aren't faced with such complex situations. But when you are, remember that peg revisions are that extra hint Subversion needs to clear up ambiguity.

Changelists

It is commonplace for a developer to find himself working at any given time on multiple distinct changes to a particular bit of source code. This isn't necessarily due to poor planning or some form of digital masochism. A software engineer often spots bugs in his peripheral vision while working on some nearby chunk of source code. Or perhaps he's halfway through some large change when he realizes the solution he's working on is best committed as several smaller logical units. Often, these logical units aren't nicely contained in some module, safely separated from other changes. The units might overlap, modifying different files in the same module, or even modifying different lines in the same file.

Developers can employ various work methodologies to keep these logical changes organized. Some use separate working copies of the same repository to hold each individual change in progress. Others might choose to create short-lived feature branches in the repository and use a single working copy that is constantly switched to point to one such branch or another. Still others use *diff* and *patch* tools to back up and restore uncommitted changes to and from patch files associated with each change. Each of these methods has its pros and cons, and to a large degree, the details of the changes being made heavily influence the methodology used to distinguish them.

Subversion 1.5 brings a new *changelists* feature that adds yet another method to the mix. Changelists are basically arbitrary labels (currently at most one per file) applied to working copy files for the express purpose of associating multiple files together. Users of many of Google's software offerings are familiar with this concept already. For example, Gmail (*http://mail.google.com/*) doesn't provide the traditional folders-based email organization mechanism. In Gmail, you apply arbitrary labels to emails, and multiple emails can be said to be part of the same group if they happen to share a particular label. Viewing only a group of similarly labeled emails then becomes a simple user interface trick. Many other Web 2.0 sites have similar mechanisms—consider the "tags" used by sites such as YouTube (*http://www.youtube.com/*) and Flickr (*http://www .flickr.com/*), "categories" applied to blog posts, and so on. Folks understand today that organization of data is critical, but they also understand that how that data is organized needs to be a flexible concept. The old files-and-folders paradigm is too rigid for some applications.

Subversion's changelist support allows you to create changelists by applying labels to files you want to be associated with that changelist, remove those labels, and limit the scope of the files on which its subcommands operate to only those bearing a particular label. In this section, we'll look in detail at how to do these things.

Creating and Modifying Changelists

You can create, modify, and delete changelists using the *svn changelist* command. More accurately, you use this command to set or unset the changelist association of a particular working copy file. A changelist is effectively created the first time you label a file with that changelist; it is deleted when you remove that label from the last file that had it. Let's examine a usage scenario that demonstrates these concepts.

Harry is fixing some bugs in the calculator application's mathematics logic. His work leads him to change a couple of files:

```
$ svn status
M       integer.c
M       mathops.c
$
```

While testing his bug fix, Harry notices that his changes bring to light a tangentially related bug in the user interface logic found in *button.c*. Harry decides that he'll go ahead and fix that bug, too, as a separate commit from his math fixes. Now, in a small working copy with only a handful of files and few logical changes, Harry can probably keep his two logical change groupings mentally organized without any problem. But today he's going to use Subversion's changelists feature as a special favor to the authors of this book.

Harry first creates a changelist and associates with it the two files he's already changed. He does this by using the *svn changelist* command to assign the same arbitrary changelist name to those files:

```
$ svn changelist math-fixes integer.c mathops.c
Path 'integer.c' is now a member of changelist 'math-fixes'.
Path 'mathops.c' is now a member of changelist 'math-fixes'.
$ svn status

--- Changelist 'math-fixes':
M       integer.c
M       mathops.c
$
```

As you can see, the output of *svn status* reflects this new grouping.

Harry now sets off to fix the secondary UI problem. Since he knows which file he'll be changing, he assigns that path to a changelist, too. Unfortunately, Harry carelessly assigns this third file to the same changelist as the previous two files:

```
$ svn changelist math-fixes button.c
Path 'button.c' is now a member of changelist 'math-fixes'.
$ svn status

--- Changelist 'math-fixes':
        button.c
M       integer.c
M       mathops.c
$
```

Fortunately, Harry catches his mistake. At this point, he has two options. He can remove the changelist association from *button.c*, and then assign a different changelist name:

```
$ svn changelist --remove button.c
Path 'button.c' is no longer a member of a changelist.
$ svn changelist ui-fix button.c
Path 'button.c' is now a member of changelist 'ui-fix'.
$
```

Or, he can skip the removal and just assign a new changelist name. In this case, Subversion will first warn Harry that *button.c* is being removed from the first changelist:

```
$ svn changelist ui-fix button.c
svn: warning: Removing 'button.c' from changelist 'math-fixes'.
Path 'button.c' is now a member of changelist 'ui-fix'.
$ svn status

--- Changelist 'ui-fix':
        button.c

--- Changelist 'math-fixes':
M       integer.c
M       mathops.c
$
```

Harry now has two distinct changelists present in his working copy, and *svn status* will group its output according to these changelist determinations. Notice that even though Harry hasn't yet modified *button.c*, it still shows up in the output of *svn status* as interesting because it has a changelist assignment. Changelists can be added to and removed from files at any time, regardless of whether they contain local modifications.

Harry now fixes the user interface problem in *button.c*:

```
$ svn status

--- Changelist 'ui-fix':
M       button.c

--- Changelist 'math-fixes':
M       integer.c
```

```
M       mathops.c
$
```

Changelists As Operation Filters

The visual grouping that Harry sees in the output of *svn status* as shown in our previous section is nice, but not entirely useful. The *status* command is just one of many operations he might wish to perform on his working copy. Fortunately, many of Subversion's other operations understand how to operate on changelists via the use of the `--changelist` option.

When provided with a `--changelist` option, Subversion commands will limit the scope of their operation to only those files to which a particular changelist name is assigned. If Harry now wants to see the actual changes he's made to the files in his `math-fixes` changelist, he *could* explicitly list only the files that make up that changelist on the *svn diff* command line:

```
$ svn diff integer.c mathops.c
Index: integer.c
===================================================================
--- integer.c      (revision 1157)
+++ integer.c      (working copy)
...
Index: mathops.c
===================================================================
--- mathops.c      (revision 1157)
+++ mathops.c      (working copy)
...
$
```

That works okay for a few files, but what if Harry's change touched 20 or 30 files? That would be an annoyingly long list of explicitly named files. Now that he's using change-lists, though, Harry can avoid explicitly listing the set of files in his changelist from now on, and instead provide just the changelist name:

```
$ svn diff --changelist math-fixes
Index: integer.c
===================================================================
--- integer.c      (revision 1157)
+++ integer.c      (working copy)
...
Index: mathops.c
===================================================================
--- mathops.c      (revision 1157)
+++ mathops.c      (working copy)
...
$
```

And when it's time to commit, Harry can again use the `--changelist` option to limit the scope of the commit to files in a certain changelist. He might commit his user interface fix by doing the following:

```
$ svn ci -m "Fix a UI bug found while working on math logic." \
    --changelist ui-fix
Sending          button.c
Transmitting file data .
Committed revision 1158.
$
```

In fact, the *svn commit* command provides a second changelists-related option: `--keep-changelists`. Normally, changelist assignments are removed from files after they are committed. But if `--keep-changelists` is provided, Subversion will leave the changelist assignment on the committed (and now unmodified) files. In any case, committing files assigned to one changelist leaves other changelists undisturbed:

```
$ svn status

--- Changelist 'math-fixes':
M      integer.c
M      mathops.c
$
```

 The `--changelist` option acts only as a filter for Subversion command targets and will not add targets to an operation. For example, on a commit operation specified as `svn commit /path/to/dir`, the target is the directory */path/to/dir* and its children (to infinite depth). If you then add a changelist specifier to that command, only those files in and under */path/to/dir* that are assigned that changelist name will be considered as targets of the commit—the commit will not include files located elsewhere (such is in */path/to/another-dir*), regardless of their changelist assignment, even if they are part of the same working copy as the operation's target(s).

Even the *svn changelist* command accepts the `--changelist` option. This allows you to quickly and easily rename or remove a changelist:

```
$ svn changelist math-bugs --changelist math-fixes --depth infinity .
svn: warning: Removing 'integer.c' from changelist 'math-fixes'.
Path 'integer.c' is now a member of changelist 'math-bugs'.
svn: warning: Removing 'mathops.c' from changelist 'math-fixes'.
Path 'mathops.c' is now a member of changelist 'math-bugs'.
$ svn changelist --remove --changelist math-bugs --depth infinity .
Path 'integer.c' is no longer a member of a changelist.
Path 'mathops.c' is no longer a member of a changelist.
$
```

Finally, you can specify multiple instances of the `--changelist` option on a single command line. Doing so limits the operation you are performing to files found in any of the specified changesets.

Changelist Limitations

Subversion's changelist feature is a handy tool for grouping working copy files, but it does have a few limitations. Changelists are artifacts of a particular working copy, which means that changelist assignments cannot be propagated to the repository or otherwise shared with other users. Changelists can be assigned only to files—Subversion doesn't currently support the use of changelists with directories. Finally, you can have at most one changelist assignment on a given working copy file. Here is where the blog post category and photo service tag analogies break down—if you find yourself needing to assign a file to multiple changelists, you're out of luck.

Network Model

At some point, you're going to need to understand how your Subversion client communicates with its server. Subversion's networking layer is abstracted, meaning that Subversion clients exhibit the same general behaviors no matter what sort of server they are operating against. Whether speaking the HTTP protocol (http://) with the Apache HTTP Server or speaking the custom Subversion protocol (svn://) with *svnserve*, the basic network model is the same. In this section, we'll explain the basics of that network model, including how Subversion manages authentication and authorization matters.

Requests and Responses

The Subversion client spends most of its time managing working copies. When it needs information from a remote repository, however, it makes a network request, and the server responds with an appropriate answer. The details of the network protocol are hidden from the user—the client attempts to access a URL, and depending on the URL scheme, a particular protocol is used to contact the server (see the sidebar "Repository URLs" on page 8).

 Run svn --version to see which URL schemes and protocols the client knows how to use.

When the server process receives a client request, it often demands that the client identify itself. It issues an authentication challenge to the client, and the client responds by providing *credentials* back to the server. Once authentication is complete, the server responds with the original information that the client asked for. Notice that this system is different from systems such as CVS, where the client preemptively offers credentials ("logs in") to the server before ever making a request. In Subversion, the server "pulls" credentials by challenging the client at the appropriate moment, rather than the client "pushing" them. This makes certain operations more elegant. For example, if a server is configured to allow anyone in the world to read a repository, the server will never issue an authentication challenge when a client attempts to *svn checkout*.

If the particular network requests issued by the client result in a new revision being created in the repository (e.g., *svn commit*), Subversion uses the authenticated user-name associated with those requests as the author of the revision. That is, the authenticated user's name is stored as the value of the `svn:author` property on the new revision (see "Subversion Properties" on page 358). If the client was not authenticated (i.e., if the server never issued an authentication challenge, the revision's never issued an authentication challenge), then the revision's `svn:author` property is empty.

Client Credentials Caching

Many servers are configured to require authentication on every request. This would be a big annoyance to users if they were forced to type their passwords over and over again. Fortunately, the Subversion client has a remedy for this—a built-in system for caching authentication credentials on disk. By default, whenever the command-line client successfully responds to a server's authentication challenge, it saves the credentials in the user's private runtime configuration area (*~/.subversion/auth/* on Unix-like systems or *%APPDATA%/Subversion/auth/* on Windows; see "Runtime Configuration Area" on page 233 for more details about the runtime configuration system). Successful credentials are cached on disk and keyed on a combination of the server's hostname, port, and authentication realm.

When the client receives an authentication challenge, it first looks for the appropriate credentials in the user's disk cache. If seemingly suitable credentials are not present, or if the cached credentials ultimately fail to authenticate, the client will, by default, fall back to prompting the user for the necessary information.

The security-conscious reader will suspect immediately that there is reason for concern here. "Caching passwords on disk? That's terrible! You should never do that!"

The Subversion developers recognize the legitimacy of such concerns, and so Subversion works with available mechanisms provided by the operating system and environment to try to minimize the risk of leaking this information. Here's a breakdown of what this means for users on the most common platforms:

- On Windows 2000 and later, the Subversion client uses standard Windows cryptography services to encrypt the password on disk. Because the encryption key is managed by Windows and is tied to the user's own login credentials, only the user can decrypt the cached password. (Note that if the user's Windows account password is reset by an administrator, all of the cached passwords become undecipherable. The Subversion client will behave as though they don't exist, prompting for passwords when required.)

- Similarly, on Mac OS X, the Subversion client stores all repository passwords in the login keyring (managed by the Keychain service), which is protected by the user's account password. User preference settings can impose additional policies, such as requiring that the user's account password be entered each time the Subversion password is used.

- For other Unix-like operating systems, no standard "keychain" services exist. However, the *auth/* caching area is still permission-protected so that only the user (owner) can read data from it, not the world at large. The operating system's own file permissions protect the passwords.

Of course, for the truly paranoid, none of these mechanisms meets the test of perfection. So, for those folks willing to sacrifice convenience for the ultimate in security, Subversion provides various ways of disabling its credentials caching system altogether.

To disable caching for a single command, pass the `--no-auth-cache` option:

```
$ svn commit -F log_msg.txt --no-auth-cache
Authentication realm: <svn://host.example.com:3690> example realm
Username: joe
Password for 'joe':

Adding          newfile
Transmitting file data .
Committed revision 2324.

# password was not cached, so a second commit still prompts us

$ svn delete newfile
$ svn commit -F new_msg.txt
Authentication realm: <svn://host.example.com:3690> example realm
Username: joe
...
```

Or, if you want to disable credential caching permanently, you can edit the *config* file in your runtime configuration area and set the `store-auth-creds` option to `no`. This will prevent the storing of credentials used in any Subversion interactions you perform on the affected computer. This can be extended to cover all users on the computer, too, by modifying the system-wide runtime configuration area (described in "Configuration Area Layout" on page 233):

```
[auth]
store-auth-creds = no
```

Sometimes users will want to remove specific credentials from the disk cache. To do this, you need to navigate into the *auth/* area and manually delete the appropriate cache file. Credentials are cached in individual files; if you look inside each file, you will see keys and values. The `svn:realmstring` key describes the particular server realm that the file is associated with:

```
$ ls ~/.subversion/auth/svn.simple/
5671adf2865e267db74f09ba6f872c28
3893ed123b39500bca8a0b382839198e
5c3c22968347b390f349ff340196ed39
```

```
$ cat ~/.subversion/auth/svn.simple/5671adf2865e267db74f09ba6f872c28

K 8
username
V 3
joe
K 8
password
V 4
blah
K 15
svn:realmstring
V 45
<https://svn.domain.com:443> Joe's repository
END
```

Once you have located the proper cache file, just delete it.

One last word about *svn*'s authentication behavior, specifically regarding the `--username` and `--password` options. Many client subcommands accept these options, but it is important to understand that using these options does *not* automatically send credentials to the server. As discussed earlier, the server "pulls" credentials from the client when it deems necessary; the client cannot "push" them at will. If a username and/or password are passed as options, they will be presented to the server only if the server requests them. These options are typically used to authenticate as a different user than Subversion would have chosen by default (such as your system login name) or when trying to avoid interactive prompting (such as when calling *svn* from a script).

 A common mistake is to misconfigure a server so that it never issues an authentication challenge. When users pass `--username` and `--password` options to the client, they're surprised to see that they're never used; that is, new revisions still appear to have been committed anonymously!

Here is a final summary that describes how a Subversion client behaves when it receives an authentication challenge:

1. First, the client checks whether the user specified any credentials as command-line options (`--username` and/or `--password`). If so, the client will try to use those credentials to authenticate against the server.

2. If no command-line credentials were provided, or the provided ones were invalid, the client looks up the server's hostname, port, and realm in the runtime configuration's *auth/* area, to see whether appropriate credentials are cached there. If so, it attempts to use those credentials to authenticate.

3. Finally, if the previous mechanisms failed to successfully authenticate the user against the server, the client resorts to interactively prompting the user for valid credentials (unless instructed not to do so via the `--non-interactive` option or its client-specific equivalents).

If the client successfully authenticates by any of these methods, it will attempt to cache the credentials on disk (unless the user has disabled this behavior, as mentioned earlier).

Summary

After reading this chapter, you should have a firm grasp on some of Subversion's features that, while perhaps not used *every* time you interact with your version control system, are certainly handy to know about. But don't stop here! Read on to the following chapter, where you'll learn about branches, tags, and merging. Then you'll have nearly full mastery of the Subversion client. Though our lawyers won't allow us to promise you anything, this additional knowledge could make you measurably more cool.#

No purchase necessary. Certain terms and conditions apply. No guarantee of coolness—implicit or otherwise—exists. Mileage may vary.

## CHAPTER 4

Branching and Merging

"君子务本 (It is upon the Trunk that a gentleman works.)"

—Confucius

Branching, tagging, and merging are concepts common to almost all version control systems. If you're not familiar with these ideas, we provide a good introduction in this chapter. If you are familiar, hopefully you'll find it interesting to see how Subversion implements them.

Branching is a fundamental part of version control. If you're going to allow Subversion to manage your data, this is a feature you'll eventually come to depend on. This chapter assumes that you're already familiar with Subversion's basic concepts (see Chapter 1).

What's a Branch?

Suppose it's your job to maintain a document for a division in your company—a handbook of some sort. One day a different division asks you for the same handbook, but with a few parts "tweaked" for them, since they do things slightly differently.

What do you do in this situation? You do the obvious: make a copy of your document and begin maintaining the two copies separately. As each department asks you to make small changes, you incorporate them into one copy or the other.

You often want to make the same change to both copies. For example, if you discover a typo in the first copy, it's very likely that the same typo exists in the second copy. The two documents are almost the same, after all; they differ only in small, specific ways.

This is the basic concept of a *branch*—namely, a line of development that exists independently of another line, yet still shares a common history if you look far enough back in time. A branch always begins life as a copy of something, and moves on from there, generating its own history (see Figure 4-1).

Subversion has commands to help you maintain parallel branches of your files and directories. It allows you to create branches by copying your data, and it remembers that the copies are related to one another. It also helps you duplicate changes from one

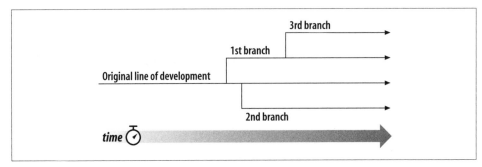

Figure 4-1. Branches of development

branch to another. Finally, it can make portions of your working copy reflect different branches so that you can "mix and match" different lines of development in your daily work.

Using Branches

At this point, you should understand how each commit creates an entirely new filesystem tree (called a "revision") in the repository. If you don't, go back and read about revisions in "Revisions" on page 11.

For this chapter, we'll go back to the same example from Chapter 1. Remember that you and your collaborator, Sally, are sharing a repository that contains two projects, *paint* and *calc*. Notice that in Figure 4-2, however, each project directory now contains subdirectories named *trunk* and *branches*. The reason for this will soon become clear.

As before, assume that Sally and you both have working copies of the "calc" project. Specifically, you each have a working copy of */calc/trunk*. All the files for the project are in this subdirectory rather than in */calc* itself, because your team has decided that */calc/trunk* is where the "main line" of development is going to take place.

Let's say that you've been given the task of implementing a large software feature. It will take a long time to write, and it will affect all the files in the project. The immediate problem is that you don't want to interfere with Sally, who is in the process of fixing small bugs here and there. She's depending on the fact that the latest version of the project (in */calc/trunk*) is always usable. If you start committing your changes bit by bit, you'll surely break things for Sally (and other team members as well).

One strategy is to crawl into a hole: you and Sally can stop sharing information for a week or two. That is, start gutting and reorganizing all the files in your working copy, but don't commit or update until you're completely finished with the task. There are a number of problems with this, though. First, it's not very safe. Most people like to save their work to the repository frequently, should something bad accidentally happen to their working copy. Second, it's not very flexible. If you do your work on different computers (perhaps you have a working copy of */calc/trunk* on two different machines),

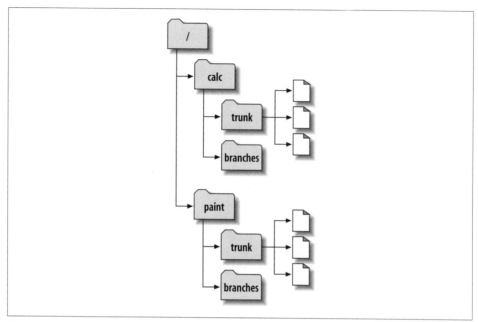

Figure 4-2. Starting repository layout

you'll need to manually copy your changes back and forth or just do all the work on a single computer. By that same token, it's difficult to share your changes in progress with anyone else. A common software development "best practice" is to allow your peers to review your work as you go. If nobody sees your intermediate commits, you lose potential feedback and may end up going down the wrong path for weeks before another person on your team notices. Finally, when you're finished with all your changes, you might find it very difficult to remerge your final work with the rest of the company's main body of code. Sally (or others) may have made many other changes in the repository that are difficult to incorporate into your working copy—especially if you run *svn update* after weeks of isolation.

The better solution is to create your own branch, or line of development, in the repository. This allows you to save your half-broken work frequently without interfering with others, yet you can still selectively share information with your collaborators. You'll see exactly how this works as we go.

Creating a Branch

Creating a branch is very simple—you make a copy of the project in the repository using the *svn copy* command. Subversion is able to copy not only single files but whole directories as well. In this case, you want to make a copy of the */calc/trunk* directory. Where should the new copy live? Wherever you wish—it's a matter of project policy.

Let's say that your team has a policy of creating branches in the */calc/branches* area of the repository, and you want to name your branch *my-calc-branch*. You'll want to create a new directory, */calc/branches/my-calc-branch*, which begins its life as a copy of */calc/trunk*.

You may already have seen *svn copy* used to copy one file to another within a working copy. But it can also be used to do a "remote" copy entirely within the repository. Just copy one URL to another:

```
$ svn copy http://svn.example.com/repos/calc/trunk \
           http://svn.example.com/repos/calc/branches/my-calc-branch \
       -m "Creating a private branch of /calc/trunk."

Committed revision 341.
```

This command causes a near-instantaneous commit in the repository, creating a new directory in revision 341. The new directory is a copy of */calc/trunk*, as shown in Figure 4-3.* While it's possible to create a branch by using *svn copy* to duplicate a directory within the working copy, this technique isn't recommended. It can be quite slow, in fact! Copying a directory on the client side is a linear-time operation, in that it actually has to duplicate every file and subdirectory on the local disk. Copying a directory on the server, however, is a constant-time operation, and it's the way most people create branches.

Cheap Copies

Subversion's repository has a special design. When you copy a directory, you don't need to worry about the repository growing huge—Subversion doesn't actually duplicate any data. Instead, it creates a new directory entry that points to an *existing* tree. If you're an experienced Unix user, you'll recognize this as the same concept behind a hard link. As further changes are made to files and directories beneath the copied directory, Subversion continues to employ this hard link concept where it can. It duplicates data only when it is necessary to disambiguate different versions of objects.

This is why you'll often hear Subversion users talk about "cheap copies." It doesn't matter how large the directory is—it takes a very tiny, constant amount of time and space to make a copy of it. In fact, this feature is the basis of how commits work in Subversion: each revision is a "cheap copy" of the previous revision, with a few items lazily changed within. (To read more about this, visit Subversion's web site and read about the "bubble up" method in Subversion's design documents.)

Of course, these internal mechanics of copying and sharing data are hidden from the user, who simply sees copies of trees. The point is that copies are cheap, both in time and in space. If you create a branch entirely within the repository (by running svn copy URL1 URL2), it's a quick, constant-time operation. Make branches as often as you want.

---

* Subversion does not support copying between different repositories. When using URLs with *svn copy* or *svn move*, you can only copy items within the same repository.

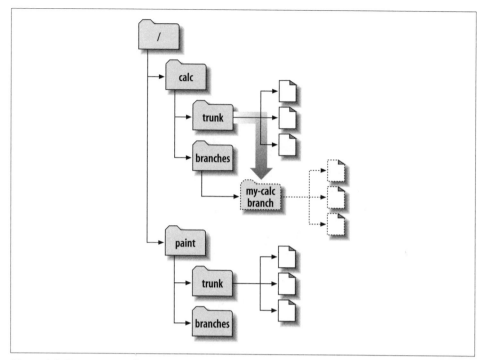

Figure 4-3. Repository with new copy

Working with Your Branch

Now that you've created a branch of the project, you can check out a new working copy to start using it:

```
$ svn checkout http://svn.example.com/repos/calc/branches/my-calc-branch
A  my-calc-branch/Makefile
A  my-calc-branch/integer.c
A  my-calc-branch/button.c
Checked out revision 341.
```

There's nothing special about this working copy; it simply mirrors a different directory in the repository. When you commit changes, however, Sally won't see them when she updates, because her working copy is of */calc/trunk*. (Be sure to read "Traversing Branches" on page 130; the *svn switch* command is an alternative way of creating a working copy of a branch.)

Let's pretend that a week goes by, and the following commits happen:

- You make a change to */calc/branches/my-calc-branch/button.c*, which creates revision 342.

- You make a change to */calc/branches/my-calc-branch/integer.c*, which creates revision 343.

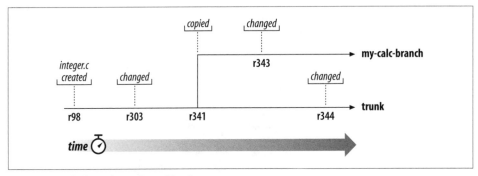

Figure 4-4. The branching of one file's history

- Sally makes a change to */calc/trunk/integer.c*, which creates revision 344.

Now, two independent lines of development (shown in Figure 4-4) are happening on *integer.c*. Things get interesting when you look at the history of changes made to your copy of *integer.c*:

```
$ pwd
/home/user/my-calc-branch

$ svn log -v integer.c
------------------------------------------------------------------------
r343 | user | 2002-11-07 15:27:56 -0600 (Thu, 07 Nov 2002) | 2 lines
Changed paths:
   M /calc/branches/my-calc-branch/integer.c

* integer.c:  frozzled the wazjub.

------------------------------------------------------------------------
r341 | user | 2002-11-03 15:27:56 -0600 (Thu, 07 Nov 2002) | 2 lines
Changed paths:
   A /calc/branches/my-calc-branch (from /calc/trunk:340)

Creating a private branch of /calc/trunk.

------------------------------------------------------------------------
r303 | sally | 2002-10-29 21:14:35 -0600 (Tue, 29 Oct 2002) | 2 lines
Changed paths:
   M /calc/trunk/integer.c

* integer.c:  changed a docstring.

------------------------------------------------------------------------
r98 | sally | 2002-02-22 15:35:29 -0600 (Fri, 22 Feb 2002) | 2 lines
Changed paths:
   A /calc/trunk/integer.c

* integer.c:  adding this file to the project.

------------------------------------------------------------------------
```

Notice that Subversion is tracing the history of your branch's *integer.c* all the way back through time, even traversing the point where it was copied. It shows the creation of the branch as an event in the history, because *integer.c* was implicitly copied when all of */calc/trunk/* was copied. Now look at what happens when Sally runs the same command on her copy of the file:

```
$ pwd
/home/sally/calc

$ svn log -v integer.c
------------------------------------------------------------------------
r344 | sally | 2002-11-07 15:27:56 -0600 (Thu, 07 Nov 2002) | 2 lines
Changed paths:
   M /calc/trunk/integer.c

* integer.c:  fix a bunch of spelling errors.

------------------------------------------------------------------------
r303 | sally | 2002-10-29 21:14:35 -0600 (Tue, 29 Oct 2002) | 2 lines
Changed paths:
   M /calc/trunk/integer.c

* integer.c:  changed a docstring.

------------------------------------------------------------------------
r98 | sally | 2002-02-22 15:35:29 -0600 (Fri, 22 Feb 2002) | 2 lines
Changed paths:
   A /calc/trunk/integer.c

* integer.c:  adding this file to the project.

------------------------------------------------------------------------
```

Sally sees her own revision 344 change, but not the change you made in revision 343. As far as Subversion is concerned, these two commits affected different files in different repository locations. However, Subversion *does* show that the two files share a common history. Before the branch copy was made in revision 341, the files used to be the same file. That's why you and Sally both see the changes made in revisions 303 and 98.

The Key Concepts Behind Branching

You should remember two important lessons from this section. First, Subversion has no internal concept of a branch—it knows only how to make copies. When you copy a directory, the resultant directory is only a "branch" because *you* attach that meaning to it. You may think of the directory differently, or treat it differently, but to Subversion it's just an ordinary directory that happens to carry some extra historical information.

Second, because of this copy mechanism, Subversion's branches exist as *normal file-system directories* in the repository. This is different from other version control systems, where branches are typically defined by adding extra-dimensional "labels" to collections of files. The location of your branch directory doesn't matter to Subversion. Most teams follow a convention of putting all branches into a */branches* directory, but you're free to invent any policy you wish.

Basic Merging

Now you and Sally are working on parallel branches of the project: you're working on a private branch, and Sally is working on the *trunk*, or main line of development.

For projects that have a large number of contributors, it's common for most people to have working copies of the trunk. Whenever someone needs to make a long-running change that is likely to disrupt the trunk, a standard procedure is to create a private branch and commit changes there until all the work is complete.

So, the good news is that you and Sally aren't interfering with each other. The bad news is that it's very easy to drift *too* far apart. Remember that one of the problems with the "crawl in a hole" strategy is that by the time you're finished with your branch, it may be near-impossible to merge your changes back into the trunk without a huge number of conflicts.

Instead, you and Sally might continue to share changes as you work. It's up to you to decide which changes are worth sharing; Subversion gives you the ability to selectively "copy" changes between branches. And when you're completely finished with your branch, your entire set of branch changes can be copied back into the trunk. In Subversion terminology, the general act of replicating changes from one branch to another is called *merging*, and it is performed using various invocations of the *svn merge* command.

In the examples that follow, we're assuming that both your Subversion client and server are running Subversion 1.5 (or later). If either client or server is older than version 1.5, things are more complicated: the system won't track changes automatically, and you'll have to use painful manual methods to achieve similar results. That is, you'll always need to use the detailed merge syntax to specify ranges of revisions to replicate (see "Merge Syntax: Full Disclosure" on page 121), and take special care to keep track of what's already been merged and what hasn't. For this reason, we *strongly* recommend that you make sure your client and server are at least at version 1.5.

Changesets

Before we proceed further, we should warn you that there's going to be a lot of discussion of "changes" in the pages ahead. A lot of people experienced with version control systems use the terms "change" and "changeset" interchangeably, and we should clarify what Subversion understands as a *changeset*.

Everyone seems to have a slightly different definition of changeset, or at least a different expectation of what it means for a version control system to have one. For our purposes, let's say that a changeset is just a collection of changes with a unique name. The changes might include textual edits to file contents, modifications to tree structure, or tweaks to metadata. In more common speak, a changeset is just a patch with a name you can refer to.

In Subversion, a global revision number N names a tree in the repository: it's the way the repository looked after the Nth commit. It's also the name of an implicit changeset: if you compare tree N with tree N–1, you can derive the exact patch that was committed. For this reason, it's easy to think of revision N as not just a tree, but a changeset as well. If you use an issue tracker to manage bugs, you can use the revision numbers to refer to particular patches that fix bugs—for example, "this issue was fixed by r9238." Somebody can then run `svn log -r 9238` to read about the exact changeset that fixed the bug, and can run `svn diff -c 9238` to see the patch itself. And (as you'll see shortly) Subversion's *svn merge* command is able to use revision numbers. You can merge specific changesets from one branch to another by naming them in the merge arguments: passing `-c 9238` to *svn merge* would merge changeset r9238 into your working copy.

Keeping a Branch in Sync

Continuing with our running example, let's suppose that a week has passed since you started working on your private branch. Your new feature isn't finished yet, but at the same time you know that other people on your team have continued to make important changes in the project's */trunk*. It's in your best interest to replicate those changes to your own branch, just to make sure they mesh well with your changes. In fact, this is a best practice: frequently keeping your branch in sync with the main development line helps prevent "surprise" conflicts when it comes time for you to fold your changes back into the trunk.

Subversion is aware of the history of your branch and knows when it divided away from the trunk. To replicate the latest, greatest trunk changes to your branch, first make sure your working copy of the branch is "clean"—that it has no local modifications reported by *svn status*. Then simply run:

```
$ pwd
/home/user/my-calc-branch

$ svn merge http://svn.example.com/repos/calc/trunk
--- Merging r345 through r356 into '.':
U    button.c
U    integer.c
```

This basic syntax—`svn merge URL`—tells Subversion to merge all recent changes from the URL to the current working directory (which is typically the root of your working copy). After running the prior example, your branch working copy now contains new local modifications, and these edits are duplications of all of the changes that have happened on the trunk since you first created your branch:

```
$ svn status
 M     .
```

```
M      button.c
M      integer.c
```

At this point, the wise thing to do is look at the changes carefully with *svn diff*, and then build and test your branch. Notice that the current working directory (".") has also been modified; the *svn diff* will show that its `svn:mergeinfo` property has been either created or modified. This is important merge-related metadata that you should *not* touch, since it will be needed by future *svn merge* commands. (We'll learn more about this metadata later in the chapter.)

After performing the merge, you might also need to resolve some conflicts (just as you do with *svn update*) or possibly make some small edits to get things working properly. (Remember, just because there are no *syntactic* conflicts doesn't mean there aren't any *semantic* conflicts!) If you encounter serious problems, you can always abort the local changes by running `svn revert . -R` (which will undo all local modifications) and start a long "what's going on?" discussion with your collaborators. If things look good, however, you can submit these changes into the repository:

```
$ svn commit -m "Merged latest trunk changes to my-calc-branch."
Sending        .
Sending        button.c
Sending        integer.c
Transmitting file data ..
Committed revision 357.
```

At this point, your private branch is now "in sync" with the trunk, so you can rest easier knowing that as you continue to work in isolation, you're not drifting too far away from what everyone else is doing.

Why Not Use Patches Instead?

A question may be on your mind, especially if you're a Unix user: why bother to use *svn merge* at all? Why not simply use the operating system's *patch* command to accomplish the same job? For example:

```
$ cd my-calc-branch
$ svn diff -r 341:HEAD http://svn.example.com/repos/calc/trunk > patchfile
$ patch -p0 < patchfile
Patching file integer.c using Plan A...
Hunk #1 succeeded at 147.
Hunk #2 succeeded at 164.
Hunk #3 succeeded at 241.
Hunk #4 succeeded at 249.
done
```

In this particular example, there really isn't much difference. But *svn merge* has special abilities that surpass the *patch* program. The file format used by *patch* is quite limited; it's able to tweak file contents only. There's no way to represent changes to *trees*, such as the addition, removal, or renaming of files and directories. Nor can the *patch* program notice changes to properties. If Sally's change had, say, added a new directory, the output of *svn diff* wouldn't have mentioned it at all. *svn diff* outputs only the limited patch format, so there are some ideas it simply can't express.

The *svn merge* command, however, can express changes in tree structure and properties by directly applying them to your working copy. Even more important, this command records the changes that have been duplicated to your branch so that Subversion is aware of exactly which changes exist in each location (see "Mergeinfo and Previews" on page 113.) This is a critical feature that makes branch management usable; without it, users would have to manually keep notes on which sets of changes have or haven't been merged yet.

Suppose that another week has passed. You've committed more changes to your branch, and your comrades have continued to improve the trunk as well. Once again, you'd like to replicate the latest trunk changes to your branch and bring yourself in sync. Just run the same merge command again!

```
$ svn merge http://svn.example.com/repos/calc/trunk
--- Merging r357 through r380 into '.':
U    integer.c
U    Makefile
A    README
```

Subversion knows which trunk changes you've already replicated to your branch, so it carefully replicates only those changes you don't yet have. Once again, you'll have to build, test, and *svn commit* the local modifications to your branch.

What happens when you finally finish your work, though? Your new feature is done, and you're ready to merge your branch changes back to the trunk (so your team can enjoy the bounty of your labor). The process is simple. First, bring your branch in sync with the trunk again, just as you've been doing all along:

```
$ svn merge http://svn.example.com/repos/calc/trunk
--- Merging r381 through r385 into '.':
U    button.c
U    README

$ # build, test, ...

$ svn commit -m "Final merge of trunk changes to my-calc-branch."
Sending        .
Sending        button.c
Sending        README
Transmitting file data ..
Committed revision 390.
```

Now, you use *svn merge* to replicate your branch changes back into the trunk. You'll need an up-to-date working copy of */trunk*. You can do this by either doing an *svn checkout*, dredging up an old trunk working copy from somewhere on your disk, or using *svn switch* (see "Traversing Branches" on page 130). However you get a trunk working copy, remember that it's a best practice to do your merge into a working copy that has *no* local edits and has been recently updated (i.e., is not a mixture of local revisions). If your working copy isn't "clean" in these ways, you can run into some unnecessary conflict-related headaches and *svn merge* will likely return an error.

Once you have a clean working copy of the trunk, you're ready to merge your branch back into it:

```
$ pwd
/home/user/calc-trunk

$ svn update  # (make sure the working copy is up to date)
At revision 390.

$ svn merge --reintegrate http://svn.example.com/repos/calc/branches/my-calc-branch
--- Merging differences between repository URLs into '.':
U    button.c
U    integer.c
U    Makefile
 U   .

$ # build, test, verify, ...

$ svn commit -m "Merge my-calc-branch back into trunk!"
Sending        .
Sending        button.c
Sending        integer.c
Sending        Makefile
Transmitting file data ..
Committed revision 391.
```

Congratulations—your branch has now been remerged back into the main line of development. Notice our use of the --reintegrate option this time around. The option is critical for reintegrating changes from a branch back into its original line of development—don't forget it! It's needed because this sort of "merge back" is a different sort of work than what you've been doing up until now. Previously, we had been asking *svn merge* to grab the "next set" of changes from one line of development (the trunk) and duplicate them to another (your branch). This is fairly straightforward, and each time Subversion knows how to pick up where it left off. In our prior examples, you can see that first it merges the ranges 345:356 from trunk to branch; later on, it continues by merging the next contiguously available range, 356:380. When doing the final sync, it merges the range 380:385.

When merging your branch back to the trunk, however, the underlying mathematics is quite different. Your feature branch is now a mishmash of both duplicated trunk changes and private branch changes, so there's no simple contiguous range of revisions to copy over. By specifying the --reintegrate option, you're asking Subversion to carefully replicate *only* those changes unique to your branch. (And in fact, it does this by comparing the latest trunk tree with the latest branch tree: the resulting difference is exactly your branch changes!)

Now that your private branch is merged to trunk, you may wish to remove it from the repository:

```
$ svn delete http://svn.example.com/repos/calc/branches/my-calc-branch \
      -m "Remove my-calc-branch."
Committed revision 392.
```

But wait! Isn't the history of that branch valuable? What if somebody wants to audit the evolution of your feature someday and look at all of your branch changes? No need to worry. Remember that even though your branch is no longer visible in the */branches* directory, its existence is still an immutable part of the repository's history. A simple *svn log* command on the */branches* URL will show the entire history of your branch. Your branch can even be resurrected at some point, should you desire it (see "Resurrecting Deleted Items" on page 116).

In Subversion 1.5, once a `--reintegrate` merge is done from branch to trunk, the branch is no longer usable for further work. It's not able to correctly absorb new trunk changes, nor can it be properly reintegrated to trunk again. For this reason, if you want to keep working on your feature branch, we recommend destroying it and then re-creating it from the trunk:

```
$ svn delete http://svn.example.com/repos/calc/branches/my-calc-branch \
      -m "Remove my-calc-branch."
Committed revision 392.

$ svn copy http://svn.example.com/repos/calc/trunk \
           http://svn.example.com/repos/calc/branches/new-branch
      -m "Create a new branch from trunk."
Committed revision 393.

$ cd my-calc-branch

$ svn switch http://svn.example.com/repos/calc/branches/new-branch
Updated to revision 393.
```

The final command in the prior example—*svn switch*—is a way of updating an existing working copy to reflect a different repository directory. We'll discuss this more in "Traversing Branches" on page 130.

Mergeinfo and Previews

The basic mechanism Subversion uses to track changesets—that is, which changes have been merged to which branches—is by recording data in properties. Specifically, merge data is tracked in the `svn:mergeinfo` property attached to files and directories. (If you're not familiar with Subversion properties, now is the time to skim "Properties" on page 48.)

You can examine the property, just like any other:

```
$ cd my-calc-branch
$ svn propget svn:mergeinfo .
/trunk:341-390
```

It is *not* recommended that you change the value of this property yourself, unless you really know what you're doing. This property is automatically maintained by Subversion whenever you run *svn merge*. Its value indicates which changes (at a given path) have been replicated into the directory in question. In this case, the path is */trunk* and the directory which has received the specific changes is */branches/my-calc-branch*.

There's also a subcommand, *svn mergeinfo*, which can be helpful in seeing not only which changesets a directory has absorbed, but also which changesets it's still eligible to receive. This gives a sort of preview of the next set of changes that *svn merge* will replicate to your branch:

```
$ cd my-calc-branch

# Which changes have already been merged from trunk to branch?
$ svn mergeinfo http://svn.example.com/repos/calc/trunk
r341
r342
r343
...
r388
r389
r390

# Which changes are still eligible to merge from trunk to branch?
$ svn mergeinfo http://svn.example.com/repos/calc/trunk --show-revs eligible
r391
r392
r393
r394
r395
```

The *svn mergeinfo* command requires a "source" URL (where the changes would be coming from), and takes an optional "target" URL (where the changes would be merged to). If no target URL is given, it assumes that the current working directory is the target. In the prior example, because we're querying our branch working copy, the command assumes we're interested in receiving changes to */branches/mybranch* from the specified trunk URL.

Another way to get a more precise preview of a merge operation is to use the **--dry-run** option:

```
$ svn merge http://svn.example.com/repos/calc/trunk --dry-run
U    integer.c

$ svn status
# nothing printed, working copy is still unchanged.
```

The --dry-run option doesn't actually apply any local changes to the working copy. It shows only status codes that *would* be printed in a real merge. It's useful for getting a "high-level" preview of the potential merge, for those times when running *svn diff* gives too much detail.

After performing a merge operation, but before committing the results of the merge, you can use `svn diff --depth=empty /path/to/merge/target` to see only the changes to the immediate target of your merge. If your merge target was a directory, only property differences will be displayed. This is a handy way to see the changes to the `svn:mergeinfo` property recorded by the merge operation, which will remind you about what you've just merged.

Of course, the best way to preview a merge operation is to just do it! Remember, running *svn merge* isn't an inherently risky thing (unless you've made local modifications to your working copy—but we've already stressed that you shouldn't be merging into such an environment). If you don't like the results of the merge, simply run `svn revert . -R` to revert the changes from your working copy and retry the command with different options. The merge isn't final until you actually *svn commit* the results.

While it's perfectly fine to experiment with merges by running *svn merge* and *svn revert* over and over, you may run into some annoying (but easily bypassed) roadblocks. For example, if the merge operation adds a new file (i.e., schedules it for addition), *svn revert* won't actually remove the file; it simply unschedules the addition. You're left with an unversioned file. If you then attempt to run the merge again, you may get conflicts due to the unversioned file "being in the way." Solution? After performing a revert, be sure to clean up the working copy and remove unversioned files and directories. The output of *svn status* should be as clean as possible, ideally showing no output.

Undoing Changes

An extremely common use for *svn merge* is to roll back a change that has already been committed. Suppose you're working away happily on a working copy of */calc/trunk*, and you discover that the change made way back in revision 303, which changed *integer.c*, is completely wrong. It never should have been committed. You can use *svn merge* to "undo" the change in your working copy, and then commit the local modification to the repository. All you need to do is to specify a *reverse* difference. (You can do this by specifying `--revision 303:302`, or by an equivalent `--change -303`.)

```
$ svn merge -c -303 http://svn.example.com/repos/calc/trunk
--- Reverse-merging r303 into 'integer.c':
U    integer.c

$ svn status
 M   .
M    integer.c

$ svn diff
...
# verify that the change is removed
...
```

```
$ svn commit -m "Undoing change committed in r303."
Sending        integer.c
Transmitting file data .
Committed revision 350.
```

As we mentioned earlier, one way to think about a repository revision is as a specific changeset. By using the -r option, you can ask *svn merge* to apply a changeset, or a whole range of changesets, to your working copy. In our case of undoing a change, we're asking *svn merge* to apply changeset #303 to our working copy *backward*.

Keep in mind that rolling back a change like this is just like any other *svn merge* operation, so you should use *svn status* and *svn diff* to confirm that your work is in the state you want it to be in, and then use *svn commit* to send the final version to the repository. After committing, this particular changeset is no longer reflected in the HEAD revision.

Again, you may be thinking: well, that really didn't undo the commit, did it? The change still exists in revision 303. If somebody checks out a version of the *calc* project between revisions 303 and 349, she'll still see the bad change, right?

Yes, that's true. When we talk about "removing" a change, we're really talking about removing it from the HEAD revision. The original change still exists in the repository's history. For most situations, this is good enough. Most people are only interested in tracking the HEAD of a project anyway. There are special cases, however, where you really might want to destroy all evidence of the commit. (Perhaps somebody accidentally committed a confidential document.) This isn't so easy, it turns out, because Subversion was deliberately designed to never lose information. Revisions are immutable trees that build upon one another. Removing a revision from history would cause a domino effect, creating chaos in all subsequent revisions and possibly invalidating all working copies.[†]

Resurrecting Deleted Items

The great thing about version control systems is that information is never lost. Even when you delete a file or directory, it may be gone from the HEAD revision, but the object still exists in earlier revisions. One of the most common questions new users ask is, "How do I get my old file or directory back?"

The first step is to define exactly *which* item you're trying to resurrect. Here's a useful metaphor: you can think of every object in the repository as existing in a sort of two-dimensional coordinate system. The first coordinate is a particular revision tree, and the second coordinate is a path within that tree. So, every version of your file or directory can be defined by a specific coordinate pair. (Remember the "peg revision" syntax—*foo.c@224*—mentioned back in "Peg and Operative Revisions" on page 87.)

[†] The Subversion project has plans, however, to someday implement a command that would accomplish the task of permanently deleting information. In the meantime, see "svndumpfilter" on page 161 for a possible workaround.

First, you might need to use *svn log* to discover the exact coordinate pair you wish to resurrect. A good strategy is to run `svn log --verbose` in a directory that used to contain your deleted item. The `--verbose (-v)` option shows a list of all changed items in each revision; all you need to do is find the revision in which you deleted the file or directory. You can do this visually, or by using another tool to examine the log output (via *grep*, or perhaps via an incremental search in an editor):

```
$ cd parent-dir
$ svn log -v
...
------------------------------------------------------------------------
r808 | joe | 2003-12-26 14:29:40 -0600 (Fri, 26 Dec 2003) | 3 lines
Changed paths:
   D /calc/trunk/real.c
   M /calc/trunk/integer.c

Added fast fourier transform functions to integer.c.
Removed real.c because code now in double.c.
...
```

In the example, we're assuming that you're looking for a deleted file *real.c*. By looking through the logs of a parent directory, you've spotted that this file was deleted in revision 808. Therefore, the last version of the file to exist was in the revision right before that. Conclusion: you want to resurrect the path */calc/trunk/real.c* from revision 807.

That was the hard part—the research. Now that you know what you want to restore, you have two different choices.

One option is to use *svn merge* to apply revision 808 "in reverse." (We already discussed how to undo changes in "Undoing Changes" on page 115.) This would have the effect of re-adding *real.c* as a local modification. The file would be scheduled for addition, and after a commit, the file would again exist in HEAD.

In this particular example, however, this is probably not the best strategy. Reverse-applying revision 808 would not only schedule *real.c* for addition, but the log message indicates that it would also undo certain changes to *integer.c*, which you don't want. Certainly, you could reverse-merge revision 808 and then *svn revert* the local modifications to *integer.c*, but this technique doesn't scale well. What if 90 files were changed in revision 808?

A second, more targeted strategy is not to use *svn merge* at all, but rather to use the *svn copy* command. Simply copy the exact revision and path "coordinate pair" from the repository to your working copy:

```
$ svn copy http://svn.example.com/repos/calc/trunk/real.c@807 ./real.c

$ svn status
A  +   real.c

$ svn commit -m "Resurrected real.c from revision 807, /calc/trunk/real.c."
Adding         real.c
```

```
Transmitting file data .
Committed revision 1390.
```

The plus sign in the status output indicates that the item isn't merely scheduled for addition, but scheduled for addition "with history." Subversion remembers where it was copied from. In the future, running *svn log* on this file will traverse back through the file's resurrection and through all the history it had prior to revision 807. In other words, this new *real.c* isn't really new; it's a direct descendant of the original, deleted file. This is usually considered a good and useful thing. If, however, you wanted to resurrect the file *without* maintaining a historical link to the old file, this technique works just as well:

```
$ svn cat http://svn.example.com/repos/calc/trunk/real.c@807 > ./real.c

$ svn add real.c
A         real.c

$ svn commit -m "Re-created real.c from revision 807."
Adding         real.c
Transmitting file data .
Committed revision 1390.
```

Although our example shows us resurrecting a file, note that these same techniques work just as well for resurrecting deleted directories. Also note that a resurrection doesn't have to happen in your working copy—it can happen entirely in the repository:

```
$ svn copy http://svn.example.com/repos/calc/trunk/real.c@807 \
           http://svn.example.com/repos/calc/trunk/ \
       -m "Resurrect real.c from revision 807."
Committed revision 1390.

$ svn update
A    real.c
Updated to revision 1390.
```

Advanced Merging

Here ends the automated magic. Sooner or later, once you get the hang of branching and merging, you're going to have to ask Subversion to merge *specific* changes from one place to another. To do this, you're going to have to start passing more complicated arguments to *svn merge*. The next section describes the fully expanded syntax of the command and discusses a number of common scenarios that require it.

Cherrypicking

Just as the term "changeset" is often used in version control systems, so is the term *cherrypicking*. This word refers to the act of choosing *one* specific changeset from a branch and replicating it to another. Cherrypicking may also refer to the act of duplicating a particular set of (not necessarily contiguous!) changesets from one branch to another. This is in contrast to more typical merging scenarios, where the "next" contiguous range of revisions is duplicated automatically.

Why would people want to replicate just a single change? It comes up more often than you'd think. For example, let's go back in time and imagine that you haven't yet merged your private feature branch back to the trunk. At the water cooler, you get word that Sally made an interesting change to *integer.c* on the trunk. Looking over the history of commits to the trunk, you see that in revision 355 she fixed a critical bug that directly affects the feature you're working on. You might not be ready to merge all the trunk changes to your branch just yet, but you certainly need that particular bug fix in order to continue your work:

```
$ svn diff -c 355 http://svn.example.com/repos/calc/trunk

Index: integer.c
===================================================================
--- integer.c    (revision 354)
+++ integer.c    (revision 355)
@@ -147,7 +147,7 @@
    case 6:  sprintf(info->operating_system, "HPFS (OS/2 or NT)"); break;
    case 7:  sprintf(info->operating_system, "Macintosh"); break;
    case 8:  sprintf(info->operating_system, "Z-System"); break;
-   case 9:  sprintf(info->operating_system, "CP/MM");
+   case 9:  sprintf(info->operating_system, "CP/M"); break;
    case 10: sprintf(info->operating_system, "TOPS-20"); break;
    case 11: sprintf(info->operating_system, "NTFS (Windows NT)"); break;
    case 12: sprintf(info->operating_system, "QDOS"); break;
```

Just as you used *svn diff* in the prior example to examine revision 355, you can pass the same option to *svn merge*:

```
$ svn merge -c 355 http://svn.example.com/repos/calc/trunk
U    integer.c

$ svn status
M       integer.c
```

You can now go through the usual testing procedures before committing this change to your branch. After the commit, Subversion marks r355 as having been merged to the branch so that future "magic" merges that synchronize your branch with the trunk know to skip over r355. (Merging the same change to the same branch almost always results in a conflict!)

```
$ cd my-calc-branch

$ svn propget svn:mergeinfo .
/trunk:341-349,355

# Notice that r355 isn't listed as "eligible" to merge, because
# it's already been merged.
$ svn mergeinfo http://svn.example.com/repos/calc/trunk --show-revs eligible
r350
r351
```

```
r352
r353
r354
r356
r357
r358
r359
r360

$ svn merge http://svn.example.com/repos/calc/trunk
--- Merging r350 through r354 into '.':
 U   .
U    integer.c
U    Makefile
--- Merging r356 through r360 into '.':
 U   .
U    integer.c
U    button.c
```

This use case of replicating (or *backporting*) bug fixes from one branch to another is perhaps the most popular reason for cherrypicking changes; it comes up all the time, for example, when a team is maintaining a "release branch" of software. (We discuss this pattern in "Release Branches" on page 136.)

 Did you notice how, in the last example, the merge invocation caused two distinct ranges of merges to be applied? The *svn merge* command applied two independent patches to your working copy to skip over changeset 355, which your branch already contained. There's nothing inherently wrong with this, except that it has the potential to make conflict resolution trickier. If the first range of changes creates conflicts, you *must* resolve them interactively for the merge process to continue and apply the second range of changes. If you postpone a conflict from the first wave of changes, the whole merge command will bail out with an error message.[‡]

A word of warning: while *svn diff* and *svn merge* are very similar in concept, they do have different syntax in many cases. Be sure to read about them in Chapter 9 for details, or ask *svn help*. For example, *svn merge* requires a working copy path as a target, that is, a place where it should apply the generated patch. If the target isn't specified, it assumes you are trying to perform one of the following common operations:

- You want to merge directory changes into your current working directory.
- You want to merge the changes in a specific file into a file by the same name that exists in your current working directory.

[‡] At least, this is true in Subversion 1.5 at the time of this writing. This behavior may improve in future versions of Subversion.

If you are merging a directory and haven't specified a target path, *svn merge* assumes the first case and tries to apply the changes into your current directory. If you are merging a file, and that file (or a file by the same name) exists in your current working directory, *svn merge* assumes the second case and tries to apply the changes to a local file with the same name.

Merge Syntax: Full Disclosure

You've now seen some examples of the *svn merge* command, and you're about to see several more. If you're feeling confused about exactly how merging works, you're not alone. Many users (especially those new to version control) are initially perplexed about the proper syntax of the command and about how and when the feature should be used. But fear not, this command is actually much simpler than you think! There's a very easy technique for understanding exactly how *svn merge* behaves.

The main source of confusion is the *name* of the command. The term "merge" somehow denotes that branches are combined together, or that some sort of mysterious blending of data is going on. That's not the case. A better name for the command might have been *svn diff-and-apply*, because that's all that happens: two repository trees are compared, and the differences are applied to a working copy.

If you're using *svn merge* to do basic copying of changes between branches, it will generally do the right thing automatically. For example, a command such as the following:

```
$ svn merge http://svn.example.com/repos/calc/some-branch
```

will attempt to duplicate any changes made on *some-branch* into your current working directory, which is presumably a working copy that shares some historical connection to the branch. The command is smart enough to duplicate only changes that your working copy doesn't yet have. If you repeat this command once a week, it will duplicate only the "newest" branch changes that happened since you last merged.

If you choose to use the *svn merge* command in all its full glory by giving it specific revision ranges to duplicate, the command takes three main arguments:

1. An initial repository tree (often called the *left side* of the comparison)
2. A final repository tree (often called the *right side* of the comparison)
3. A working copy to accept the differences as local changes (often called the *target* of the merge)

Once these three arguments are specified, the two trees are compared, and the differences are applied to the target working copy as local modifications. When the command is done, the results are no different than if you had hand-edited the files or run various *svn add* or *svn delete* commands yourself. If you like the results, you can commit them. If you don't like the results, you can simply *svn revert* all of the changes.

The syntax of *svn merge* allows you to specify the three necessary arguments rather flexibly. Here are some examples:

```
$ svn merge http://svn.example.com/repos/branch1@150 \
            http://svn.example.com/repos/branch2@212 \
            my-working-copy

$ svn merge -r 100:200 http://svn.example.com/repos/trunk my-working-copy

$ svn merge -r 100:200 http://svn.example.com/repos/trunk
```

The first syntax lays out all three arguments explicitly, naming each tree in the form *URL@REV* and naming the working copy target. The second syntax can be used as a shorthand for situations when you're comparing two different revisions of the same URL. The last syntax shows how the working copy argument is optional; if omitted, it defaults to the current directory.

While the first example shows the "full" syntax of *svn merge*, it needs to be used very carefully; it can result in merges that do not record any `svn:mergeinfo` metadata at all. The next section talks a little more about this.

Merges Without Mergeinfo

Subversion tries to generate merge metadata whenever it can, to make future invocations of *svn merge* smarter. There are still situations, however, where `svn:mergeinfo` data is not created or changed. Remember to be a bit wary of these scenarios:

Merging unrelated sources

> If you ask *svn merge* to compare two URLs that aren't related to each other, a patch will still be generated and applied to your working copy, but no merging metadata will be created. There's no common history between the two sources, and future "smart" merges depend on that common history.

Merging from foreign repositories

> While it's possible to run a command such as `svn merge -r 100:200` *http:// svn.foreignproject.com/repos/trunk*, the resultant patch will also lack any historical merge metadata. At time of this writing, Subversion has no way of representing different repository URLs within the `svn:mergeinfo` property.

Using `--ignore-ancestry`

> If this option is passed to *svn merge*, it causes the merging logic to mindlessly generate differences the same way that *svn diff* does, ignoring any historical relationships. We discuss this later in the chapter in "Noticing or Ignoring Ancestry" on page 127.

Applying reverse merges to a target's natural history

> Earlier in this chapter ("Undoing Changes" on page 115), we discussed how to use *svn merge* to apply a "reverse patch" as a way of rolling back changes. If this technique is used to undo a change to an object's personal history (e.g., commit r5 to

the trunk, then immediately roll back r5 using `svn merge . -c -5`), this sort of merge doesn't affect the recorded mergeinfo.§

More on Merge Conflicts

Just like the *svn update* command, *svn merge* applies changes to your working copy. And therefore it's also capable of creating conflicts. The conflicts produced by *svn merge*, however, are sometimes different, and this section explains those differences.

To begin with, assume that your working copy has no local edits. When you *svn update* to a particular revision, the changes sent by the server will always apply "cleanly" to your working copy. The server produces the delta by comparing two trees: a virtual snapshot of your working copy, and the revision tree you're interested in. Because the left hand side of the comparison is exactly equal to what you already have, the delta is guaranteed to correctly convert your working copy into the righthand tree.

But *svn merge* has no such guarantees and can be much more chaotic: the advanced user can ask the server to compare *any* two trees at all, even ones that are unrelated to the working copy! This means there's large potential for human error. Users will sometimes compare the wrong two trees, creating a delta that doesn't apply cleanly. *svn merge* will do its best to apply as much of the delta as possible, but some parts may be impossible. Just as the Unix *patch* command sometimes complains about "failed hunks," *svn merge* will similarly complain about "skipped targets":

```
$ svn merge -r 1288:1351 http://svn.example.com/repos/branch
U    foo.c
U    bar.c
Skipped missing target: 'baz.c'
U    glub.c
U    sputter.h

Conflict discovered in 'glorb.h'.
Select: (p) postpone, (df) diff-full, (e) edit,
        (h) help for more options:
```

In the preceding example, it might be the case that *baz.c* exists in both snapshots of the branch being compared, and the resultant delta wants to change the file's contents, but the file doesn't exist in the working copy. Whatever the case, the "skipped" message means that the user is most likely comparing the wrong two trees; it's the classic sign of user error. When this happens, it's easy to recursively revert all the changes created by the merge (`svn revert . --recursive`), delete any unversioned files or directories left behind after the revert, and rerun *svn merge* with different arguments.

Also notice that the preceding example shows a conflict happening on *glorb.h*. We already stated that the working copy has no local edits: how can a conflict possibly

§ Interestingly, after rolling back a revision like this, we wouldn't be able to reapply the revision using `svn merge . -c 5`, since the mergeinfo would already list r5 as being applied. We would have to use the `--ignore-ancestry` option to make the merge command ignore the existing mergeinfo!

happen? Again, because the user can use *svn merge* to define and apply any old delta to the working copy, that delta may contain textual changes that don't cleanly apply to a working file, even if the file has no local modifications.

Another small difference between *svn update* and *svn merge* is the names of the full-text files created when a conflict happens. In "Resolve Conflicts (Merging Others' Changes)" on page 30, we saw that an update produces files named *filename.mine*, *filename.rOLDREV*, and *filename.rNEWREV*. When *svn merge* produces a conflict, however, it creates three files that are named *filename.working*, *filename.left*, and *filename.right*. In this case, the terms "left" and "right" are describing which side of the double-tree comparison the file came from. In any case, these differing names will help you distinguish between conflicts that happened as a result of an update and ones that happened as a result of a merge.

Blocking Changes

Sometimes there's a particular changeset that you don't want to be automatically merged. For example, perhaps your team's policy is to do new development work on */trunk*, but to be more conservative about backporting changes to a stable branch you use for releasing to the public. On one extreme, you can manually cherrypick single changesets from the trunk to the branch—just the changes that are stable enough to pass muster. Maybe things aren't quite that strict, though; perhaps most of the time you'd like to just let *svn merge* automatically merge most changes from trunk to branch. In this case, you'd like a way to mask a few specific changes out, that is, prevent them from ever being automatically merged.

In Subversion 1.5, the only way to block a changeset is to make the system believe that the change has *already* been merged. To do this, one can invoke a merge command with the `--record-only` option:

```
$ cd my-calc-branch

$ svn propget svn:mergeinfo .
/trunk:1680-3305

# Let's make the metadata list r3328 as already merged.
$ svn merge -c 3328 --record-only http://svn.example.com/repos/calc/trunk

$ svn status
M       .

$ svn propget svn:mergeinfo .
/trunk:1680-3305,3328

$ svn commit -m "Block r3328 from being merged to the branch."
...
```

This technique works, but it's also a little bit dangerous. The main problem is that we're not clearly differentiating between the ideas of "I don't want this change" and

"I already have this change." We're effectively lying to the system, making it think that the change was previously merged. This puts the responsibility on you, the user, to remember that the change wasn't actually merged—it just wasn't wanted. There's no way to ask Subversion for a list of "blocked changelists." If you want to track them (so that you can unblock them someday). you'll need to record them in a text file somewhere, or perhaps in an invented property. In Subversion 1.5, unfortunately, this is the only way to manage blocked revisions; the plans are to make a better interface for this in future versions.

Merge-Sensitive Logs and Annotations

One of the main features of any version control system is keeping track of who changed what and when they did it. The *svn log* and *svn blame* commands are just the tools for this: when invoked on individual files, they show not only the history of changesets that affected the file, but also exactly which user wrote which line of code and when.

When changes start getting replicated between branches, however, things start to get complicated. For example, if you were to ask *svn log* about the history of your feature branch, it would show exactly every revision that ever affected the branch:

```
$ cd my-calc-branch
$ svn log -q
------------------------------------------------------------------------
r390 | user | 2002-11-22 11:01:57 -0600 (Fri, 22 Nov 2002) | 1 line
------------------------------------------------------------------------
r388 | user | 2002-11-21 05:20:00 -0600 (Thu, 21 Nov 2002) | 2 lines
------------------------------------------------------------------------
r381 | user | 2002-11-20 15:07:06 -0600 (Wed, 20 Nov 2002) | 2 lines
------------------------------------------------------------------------
r359 | user | 2002-11-19 19:19:20 -0600 (Tue, 19 Nov 2002) | 2 lines
------------------------------------------------------------------------
r357 | user | 2002-11-15 14:29:52 -0600 (Fri, 15 Nov 2002) | 2 lines
------------------------------------------------------------------------
r343 | user | 2002-11-07 13:50:10 -0600 (Thu, 07 Nov 2002) | 2 lines
------------------------------------------------------------------------
r341 | user | 2002-11-03 07:17:16 -0600 (Sun, 03 Nov 2002) | 2 lines
------------------------------------------------------------------------
r303 | sally | 2002-10-29 21:14:35 -0600 (Tue, 29 Oct 2002) | 2 lines
------------------------------------------------------------------------
r98 | sally | 2002-02-22 15:35:29 -0600 (Fri, 22 Feb 2002) | 2 lines
------------------------------------------------------------------------
```

But is this really an accurate picture of all the changes that happened on the branch? What's being left out here is the fact that revisions 390, 381, and 357 were actually the results of merging changes from the trunk. If you look at one of these logs in detail, the multiple trunk changesets that comprised the branch change are nowhere to be seen:

```
$ svn log -v -r 390
------------------------------------------------------------------------
r390 | user | 2002-11-22 11:01:57 -0600 (Fri, 22 Nov 2002) | 1 line
Changed paths:
```

```
M /branches/my-calc-branch/button.c
M /branches/my-calc-branch/README

    Final merge of trunk changes to my-calc-branch.
```

We happen to know that this merge to the branch was nothing but a merge of trunk changes. How can we see those trunk changes as well? The answer is to use the `--use-merge-history` (-g) option. This option expands those "child" changes that were part of the merge:

```
$ svn log -v -r 390 -g
------------------------------------------------------------------------
r390 | user | 2002-11-22 11:01:57 -0600 (Fri, 22 Nov 2002) | 1 line
Changed paths:
   M /branches/my-calc-branch/button.c
   M /branches/my-calc-branch/README

    Final merge of trunk changes to my-calc-branch.
------------------------------------------------------------------------
r383 | sally | 2002-11-21 03:19:00 -0600 (Thu, 21 Nov 2002) | 2 lines
Changed paths:
   M /branches/my-calc-branch/button.c
Merged via: r390

    Fix inverse graphic error on button.
------------------------------------------------------------------------
r382 | sally | 2002-11-20 16:57:06 -0600 (Wed, 20 Nov 2002) | 2 lines
Changed paths:
   M /branches/my-calc-branch/README
Merged via: r390

    Document my last fix in README.
```

By making the log operation use merge history, we see not just the revision we queried (r390), but also the two revisions that came along for the ride with it—a couple of changes made by Sally to the trunk. This is a much more complete picture of history!

The *svn blame* command also takes the `--use-merge-history` (-g) option. If this option is neglected, somebody looking at a line-by-line annotation of *button.c* may get the mistaken impression that you were responsible for the lines that fixed a certain error:

```
$ svn blame button.c
...
  390   user    retval = inverse_func(button, path);
  390   user    return retval;
  390   user    }
...
```

And while it's true that you did actually commit those three lines in revision 390, two of them were actually written by Sally back in revision 383:

```
$ svn blame button.c -g
...
G    383   sally    retval = inverse_func(button, path);
G    383   sally    return retval;
```

```
    390    user    }
...
```

Now we know who to *really* blame for those two lines of code!

Noticing or Ignoring Ancestry

When conversing with a Subversion developer, you might very likely hear reference to the term *ancestry*. This word is used to describe the relationship between two objects in a repository: if they're related to each other, one object is said to be an ancestor of the other.

For example, suppose you commit revision 100, which includes a change to a file *foo.c*. Then *foo.c@99* is an "ancestor" of *foo.c@100*. On the other hand, suppose you commit the deletion of *foo.c* in revision 101, and then you add a new file by the same name in revision 102. In this case, *foo.c@99* and *foo.c@102* may appear to be related (they have the same path), but in fact they are completely different objects in the repository. They share no history or "ancestry."

The reason for bringing this up is to point out an important difference between *svn diff* and *svn merge*. The former command ignores ancestry, whereas the latter command is quite sensitive to it. For example, if you asked *svn diff* to compare revisions 99 and 102 of *foo.c*, you would see line-based diffs; the *diff* command is blindly comparing two paths. But if you asked *svn merge* to compare the same two objects, it would notice that they're unrelated and first attempt to delete the old file, then add the new file; the output would indicate a deletion followed by an add:

```
    D    foo.c
    A    foo.c
```

Most merges involve comparing trees that are ancestrally related to one another; therefore, *svn merge* defaults to this behavior. Occasionally, however, you may want the *merge* command to compare two unrelated trees. For example, you may have imported two source-code trees representing different vendor releases of a software project (see "Vendor Branches" on page 138). If you ask *svn merge* to compare the two trees, you'd see the entire first tree being deleted, followed by an add of the entire second tree! In these situations, you'll want *svn merge* to do a path-based comparison only, ignoring any relations between files and directories. Add the `--ignore-ancestry` option to your *merge* command, and it will behave just like *svn diff*. (And conversely, the `--notice-ancestry` option will cause *svn diff* to behave like the *svn merge* command.)

Merges and Moves

A common desire is to refactor source code, especially in Java-based software projects. Files and directories are shuffled around and renamed, often causing great disruption to everyone working on the project. Sounds like a perfect case to use a branch, doesn't it? Just create a branch, shuffle things around, and then merge the branch back to the trunk, right?

Alas, this scenario doesn't work so well right now and is considered one of Subversion's current weak spots. The problem is that Subversion's *svn update* command isn't as robust as it should be, particularly when dealing with copy and move operations.

When you use *svn copy* to duplicate a file, the repository remembers where the new file came from, but it fails to transmit that information to the client that is running *svn update* or *svn merge*. Instead of telling the client, "Copy that file you already have to this new location," it sends down an entirely new file. This can lead to problems, especially because the same thing happens with renamed files. A lesser-known fact about Subversion is that it lacks "true renames"—the *svn move* command is nothing more than an aggregation of *svn copy* and *svn delete*.

For example, suppose that while working on your private branch, you rename *integer.c* to *whole.c*. Effectively you've created a new file in your branch that is a copy of the original file, and you've deleted the original file. Meanwhile, back on *trunk*, Sally has committed some improvements to *integer.c*. Now you decide to merge your branch to the trunk:

```
$ cd calc/trunk

$ svn merge --reintegrate http://svn.example.com/repos/calc/branches/my-calc-branch
--- Merging differences between repository URLs into '.':
D    integer.c
A    whole.c
U    .
```

This doesn't look so bad at first glance, but it's probably not what you or Sally expected. The merge operation has deleted the latest version of the *integer.c* file (the one containing Sally's latest changes) and blindly added your new *whole.c* file—which is a duplicate of the *older* version of *integer.c*. The net effect is that merging your "rename" to the branch has removed Sally's recent changes from the latest revision!

This isn't true data loss. Sally's changes are still in the repository's history, but it may not be immediately obvious that this has happened. The moral of this story is that until Subversion improves, be very careful about merging copies and renames from one branch to another.

Blocking Merge-Unaware Clients

If you've just upgraded your server to Subversion 1.5 or later, there's a significant risk that pre-1.5 Subversion clients can mess up your automated merge tracking. Why is this? When a pre-1.5 Subversion client performs *svn merge*, it doesn't modify the value of the svn:mergeinfo property at all. So the subsequent commit, despite being the result of a merge, doesn't tell the repository about the duplicated changes—that information is lost. Later on, when "merge-aware" clients attempt automatic merging, they're likely to run into all sorts of conflicts resulting from repeated merges.

If you and your team are relying on the merge-tracking features of Subversion, you may want to configure your repository to prevent older clients from committing changes. The easy way to do this is by inspecting the "capabilities" parameter in the start-commit hook script. If the client reports itself as having mergeinfo capabilities, the hook script can allow the commit to start. If the client doesn't report that capability, have the hook deny the commit. We'll learn more about hook scripts in the next chapter; see "Implementing Repository Hooks" on page 156 and "start-commit" in Chapter 9 for details.

The Final Word on Merge Tracking

The bottom line is that Subversion's merge-tracking feature has an extremely complex internal implementation, and the svn:mergeinfo property is the only window the user has into the machinery. Because the feature is relatively new, a numbers of edge cases and possible unexpected behaviors may pop up.

For example, sometimes mergeinfo will be generated when running a simple *svn copy* or *svn move* command. Sometimes mergeinfo will appear on files that you didn't expect to be touched by an operation. Sometimes mergeinfo won't be generated at all, when you expect it to. Furthermore, the management of mergeinfo metadata has a whole set of taxonomies and behaviors around it, such as "explicit" versus "implicit" mergeinfo, "operative" versus "inoperative" revisions, specific mechanisms of mergeinfo "elision," and even "inheritance" from parent to child directories.

We've chosen not to cover these detailed topics in this book for a couple of reasons. First, the level of detail is absolutely overwhelming for a typical user. Second, as Subversion continues to improve, we feel that a typical user *shouldn't* have to understand these concepts; they'll eventually fade into the background as pesky implementation details. All that said, if you enjoy this sort of thing, you can get a fantastic overview in a paper posted at CollabNet's web site: *http://www.collab.net/community/subversion/articles/merge-info.html*.

For now, if you want to steer clear of bugs and odd behaviors in automatic merging, the CollabNet article recommends that you stick to these simple best practices:

- For short-term feature branches, follow the simple procedure described throughout "Basic Merging" on page 108.
- For long-lived release branches (as described in "Common Branching Patterns" on page 136), perform merges only on the root of the branch, not on subdirectories.
- Never merge into working copies with a mixture of working revision numbers, or with "switched" subdirectories (as described next in "Traversing Branches" on page 130). A merge target should be a working copy that represents a *single* location in the repository at a single point in time.

- Don't ever edit the `svn:mergeinfo` property directly; use *svn merge* with the `--record-only` option to effect a desired change to the metadata (as demonstrated in "Blocking Changes" on page 124).
- Always make sure you have complete read access to all of your merge sources, and that your target working copy has no sparse directories.

Traversing Branches

The *svn switch* command transforms an existing working copy to reflect a different branch. While this command isn't strictly necessary for working with branches, it provides a nice shortcut. In our earlier example, after creating your private branch, you checked out a fresh working copy of the new repository directory. Instead, you can simply ask Subversion to change your working copy of */calc/trunk* to mirror the new branch location:

```
$ cd calc

$ svn info | grep URL
URL: http://svn.example.com/repos/calc/trunk

$ svn switch http://svn.example.com/repos/calc/branches/my-calc-branch
U    integer.c
U    button.c
U    Makefile
Updated to revision 341.

$ svn info | grep URL
URL: http://svn.example.com/repos/calc/branches/my-calc-branch
```

"Switching" a working copy that has no local modifications to a different branch results in the working copy looking just as it would if you'd done a fresh checkout of the directory. It's usually more efficient to use this command, because often branches differ by only a small degree. The server sends only the minimal set of changes necessary to make your working copy reflect the branch directory.

The *svn switch* command also takes a `--revision` (`-r`) option, so you need not always move your working copy to the HEAD of the branch.

Of course, most projects are more complicated than our *calc* example and contain multiple subdirectories. Subversion users often follow a specific algorithm when using branches:

1. Copy the project's entire "trunk" to a new branch directory
2. Switch only *part* of the trunk working copy to mirror the branch

In other words, if a user knows that the branch work needs to happen on only a specific subdirectory, she uses *svn switch* to move only that subdirectory to the branch. (Or sometimes users will switch just a single working file to the branch!) That way, the user can continue to receive normal "trunk" updates to most of her working copy, but the switched portions will remain immune (unless someone commits a change to her branch). This feature adds a whole new dimension to the concept of a "mixed working copy"—not only can working copies contain a mixture of working revisions, but they can also contain a mixture of repository locations.

If your working copy contains a number of switched subtrees from different repository locations, it continues to function as normal. When you update, you'll receive patches to each subtree as appropriate. When you commit, your local changes will still be applied as a single, atomic change to the repository.

Note that while it's okay for your working copy to reflect a mixture of repository locations, these locations must all be within the *same* repository. Subversion repositories aren't yet able to communicate with one another; that feature is planned for the future.‖

Switches and Updates

Have you noticed that the output of *svn switch* and *svn update* looks the same? The switch command is actually a superset of the update command.

When you run *svn update*, you're asking the repository to compare two trees. The repository does so, and then sends a description of the differences back to the client. The only difference between *svn switch* and *svn update* is that the latter command always compares two identical repository paths.

That is, if your working copy is a mirror of */calc/trunk*, *svn update* will automatically compare your working copy of */calc/trunk* to */calc/trunk* in the HEAD revision. If you're switching your working copy to a branch, *svn switch* will compare your working copy of */calc/trunk* to some *other* branch directory in the HEAD revision.

In other words, an update moves your working copy through time. A switch moves your working copy through time *and* space.

Because *svn switch* is essentially a variant of *svn update*, it shares the same behaviors; any local modifications in your working copy are preserved when new data arrives from the repository.

 Have you ever found yourself making some complex edits (in your */trunk* working copy) when you suddenly realized, "Hey, these changes ought to be in their own branch?" A great technique to do this can be summarized in two steps:

```
$ svn copy http://svn.example.com/repos/calc/trunk \
           http://svn.example.com/repos/calc/branches/newbranch \
```

‖ You *can*, however, use *svn switch* with the `--relocate` option if the URL of your server changes and you don't want to abandon an existing working copy. See "svn switch" in Chapter 9 for more information and an example.

```
            -m "Create branch 'newbranch'."
Committed revision 353.
$ svn switch http://svn.example.com/repos/calc/branches/newbranch
At revision 353.
```

The *svn switch* command, like *svn update*, preserves your local edits. At this point, your working copy is now a reflection of the newly created branch, and your next *svn commit* invocation will send your changes there.

Tags

Another common version control concept is a *tag*. A tag is just a "snapshot" of a project in time. In Subversion, this idea already seems to be everywhere. Each repository revision is exactly that—a snapshot of the filesystem after each commit.

However, people often want to give more human-friendly names to tags, such as `release-1.0`. And they want to make snapshots of smaller subdirectories of the filesystem. After all, it's not so easy to remember that release 1.0 of a piece of software is a particular subdirectory of revision 4822.

Creating a Simple Tag

Once again, *svn copy* comes to the rescue. If you want to create a snapshot of */calc/ trunk* exactly as it looks in the HEAD revision, make a copy of it:

```
$ svn copy http://svn.example.com/repos/calc/trunk \
           http://svn.example.com/repos/calc/tags/release-1.0 \
      -m "Tagging the 1.0 release of the 'calc' project."

Committed revision 902.
```

This example assumes that a */calc/tags* directory already exists. (If it doesn't, you can create it using *svn mkdir*.) After the copy completes, the new *release-1.0* directory is forever a snapshot of how the */trunk* directory looked in the HEAD revision at the time you made the copy. Of course, you might want to be more precise about exactly which revision you copy, in case somebody else may have committed changes to the project when you weren't looking. So if you know that revision 901 of */calc/trunk* is exactly the snapshot you want, you can specify it by passing `-r 901` to the *svn copy* command.

But wait a moment: isn't this tag creation procedure the same procedure we used to create a branch? Yes, in fact, it is. In Subversion, there's no difference between a tag and a branch. Both are just ordinary directories that are created by copying. Just as with branches, the only reason a copied directory is a "tag" is because *humans* have decided to treat it that way: as long as nobody ever commits to the directory, it forever remains a snapshot. If people start committing to it, it becomes a branch.

If you are administering a repository, there are two approaches you can take to managing tags. The first approach is "hands off": as a matter of project policy, decide where your tags will live, and make sure all users know how to treat the directories they copy. (That is, make sure they know not to commit to them.) The second approach is more paranoid: you can use one of the access control scripts provided with Subversion to prevent anyone from doing anything but creating new copies in the tags area (see Chapter 6). The paranoid approach, however, isn't usually necessary. If a user accidentally commits a change to a tag directory, you can simply undo the change as discussed in the previous section. This is version control, after all!

Creating a Complex Tag

Sometimes you may want your "snapshot" to be more complicated than a single directory at a single revision.

For example, pretend your project is much larger than our *calc* example; suppose it contains a number of subdirectories and many more files. In the course of your work, you may decide that you need to create a working copy that is designed to have specific features and bug fixes. You can accomplish this by selectively backdating files or directories to particular revisions (using *svn update* with the -r option liberally), by switching files and directories to particular branches (making use of *svn switch*), or even just by making a bunch of local changes. When you're done, your working copy is a hodgepodge of repository locations from different revisions. But after testing, you know it's the precise combination of data you need to tag.

Time to make a snapshot. Copying one URL to another won't work here. In this case, you want to make a snapshot of your exact working copy arrangement and store it in the repository. Luckily, *svn copy* actually has four different uses (which you can read about in Chapter 9), including the ability to copy a working copy tree to the repository:

```
$ ls
my-working-copy/

$ svn copy my-working-copy \
           http://svn.example.com/repos/calc/tags/mytag \
           -m "Tag my existing working copy state."

Committed revision 940.
```

Now there is a new directory in the repository, */calc/tags/mytag*, which is an exact snapshot of your working copy—mixed revisions, URLs, local changes, and all.

Other users have found interesting uses for this feature. Sometimes there are situations where you have a bunch of local changes made to your working copy and you'd like a collaborator to see them. Instead of running *svn diff* and sending a patch file (which won't capture directory, symlink, or property changes), you can use *svn copy* to "upload" your working copy to a private area of the repository. Your collaborator can then either check out a verbatim copy of your working copy or use *svn merge* to receive your exact changes.

While this is a nice method for uploading a quick snapshot of your working copy, note that this is *not* a good way to initially create a branch. Branch creation should be an event unto itself, and this method conflates the creation of a branch with extra changes to files, all within a single revision. This makes it very difficult (later on) to identify a single revision number as a branch point.

Branch Maintenance

You may have noticed by now that Subversion is extremely flexible. Because it implements branches and tags with the same underlying mechanism (directory copies), and because branches and tags appear in normal filesystem space, many people find Subversion intimidating. It's almost *too* flexible. In this section, we'll offer some suggestions for arranging and managing your data over time.

Repository Layout

There are some standard, recommended ways to organize a repository. Most people create a *trunk* directory to hold the "main line" of development, a *branches* directory to contain branch copies, and a *tags* directory to contain tag copies. If a repository holds only one project, often people create these top-level directories:

```
/trunk
/branches
/tags
```

If a repository contains multiple projects, admins typically index their layout by project (see "Planning Your Repository Organization" on page 147 to read more about "project roots"):

```
/paint/trunk
/paint/branches
/paint/tags
/calc/trunk
/calc/branches
/calc/tags
```

Of course, you're free to ignore these common layouts. You can create any sort of variation, whatever works best for you or your team. Remember that whatever you choose, it's not a permanent commitment. You can reorganize your repository at any time. Because branches and tags are ordinary directories, the *svn move* command can move or rename them however you wish. Switching from one layout to another is just a matter of issuing a series of server-side moves; if you don't like the way things are organized in the repository, just juggle the directories around.

Remember, though, that while moving directories may be easy to do, you need to be considerate of your users as well. Your juggling can be disorienting to users with existing working copies. If a user has a working copy of a particular repository directory, your *svn move* operation might remove the path from the latest revision. When the user next runs *svn update*, she will be told that her working copy represents a path that no longer exists, and the user will be forced to *svn switch* to the new location.

Data Lifetimes

Another nice feature of Subversion's model is that branches and tags can have finite lifetimes, just like any other versioned item. For example, suppose you eventually finish all your work on your personal branch of the *calc* project. After merging all of your changes back into */calc/trunk*, there's no need for your private branch directory to stick around anymore:

```
$ svn delete http://svn.example.com/repos/calc/branches/my-calc-branch \
          -m "Removing obsolete branch of calc project."

Committed revision 375.
```

And now your branch is gone. Of course, it's not really gone: the directory is simply missing from the HEAD revision, no longer distracting anyone. If you use *svn checkout*, *svn switch*, or *svn list* to examine an earlier revision, you'll still be able to see your old branch.

If browsing your deleted directory isn't enough, you can always bring it back. Resurrecting data is very easy in Subversion. If there's a deleted directory (or file) that you'd like to bring back into HEAD, simply use *svn copy* to copy it from the old revision:

```
$ svn copy http://svn.example.com/repos/calc/branches/my-calc-branch@374 \
          http://svn.example.com/repos/calc/branches/my-calc-branch \
          -m "Restore my-calc-branch."

Committed revision 376.
```

In our example, your personal branch had a relatively short lifetime; you may have created it to fix a bug or implement a new feature. When your task is done, so is the branch. In software development, though, it's also common to have two "main" branches running side by side for very long periods. For example, suppose it's time to release a stable version of the *calc* project to the public, and you know it's going to take a couple of months to shake bugs out of the software. You don't want people to add new features to the project, but you don't want to tell all developers to stop programming either. So instead, you create a "stable" branch of the software that won't change much:

```
$ svn copy http://svn.example.com/repos/calc/trunk \
          http://svn.example.com/repos/calc/branches/stable-1.0 \
          -m "Creating stable branch of calc project."

Committed revision 377.
```

And now developers are free to continue adding cutting-edge (or experimental) features to */calc/trunk*, and you can declare a project policy that only bug fixes are to be committed to */calc/branches/stable-1.0*. That is, as people continue to work on the trunk, a human selectively ports bug fixes over to the stable branch. Even after the stable branch has shipped, you'll probably continue to maintain the branch for a long time—that is, as long as you continue to support that release for customers. We'll discuss this more in the next section.

Common Branching Patterns

There are many different uses for branching and *svn merge*, and this section describes the most common ones.

Version control is most often used for software development, so here's a quick peek at two of the most common branching/merging patterns used by teams of programmers. If you're not using Subversion for software development, feel free to skip this section. If you're a software developer using version control for the first time, pay close attention, as these patterns are often considered best practices by experienced folk. These processes aren't specific to Subversion; they're applicable to any version control system. Still, it may help to see them described in Subversion terms.

Release Branches

Most software has a typical life cycle: code, test, release, repeat. There are two problems with this process. First, developers need to keep writing new features while quality assurance teams take time to test supposedly stable versions of the software. New work cannot halt while the software is tested. Second, the team almost always needs to support older, released versions of software; if a bug is discovered in the latest code, it most likely exists in released versions as well, and customers will want to get that bug fix without having to wait for a major new release.

Here's where version control can help. The typical procedure looks like this:

1. *Developers commit all new work to the trunk.* Day-to-day changes are committed to */trunk*: new features, bug fixes, and so on.

2. *The trunk is copied to a "release" branch.* When the team thinks the software is ready for release (say, a 1.0 release), */trunk* might be copied to */branches/1.0*.

3. *Teams continue to work in parallel.* One team begins rigorous testing of the release branch, while another team continues new work (say, for version 2.0) on */trunk*. If bugs are discovered in either location, fixes are ported back and forth as necessary. At some point, however, even that process stops. The branch is "frozen" for final testing right before a release.

4. *The branch is tagged and released.* When testing is complete, */branches/1.0* is copied to */tags/1.0.0* as a reference snapshot. The tag is packaged and released to customers.

5. *The branch is maintained over time.* While work continues on */trunk* for version 2.0, bug fixes continue to be ported from */trunk* to */branches/1.0*. When enough

bug fixes have accumulated, management may decide to do a 1.0.1 release: */branches/1.0* is copied to */tags/1.0.1*, and the tag is packaged and released.

This entire process repeats as the software matures: when the 2.0 work is complete, a new 2.0 release branch is created, tested, tagged, and eventually released. After some years, the repository ends up with a number of release branches in "maintenance" mode and a number of tags representing final shipped versions.

Feature Branches

A *feature branch* is the sort of branch that's been the dominant example in this chapter (the one you've been working on while Sally continues to work on */trunk*). It's a temporary branch created to work on a complex change without interfering with the stability of */trunk*. Unlike release branches (which may need to be supported forever), feature branches are born, used for a while, merged back to the trunk, and then ultimately deleted. They have a finite span of usefulness.

Again, project policies vary widely concerning exactly when it's appropriate to create a feature branch. Some projects never use feature branches at all: commits to */trunk* are a free-for-all. The advantage to this system is that it's simple—nobody needs to learn about branching or merging. The disadvantage is that the trunk code is often unstable or unusable. Other projects use branches to an extreme: no change is *ever* committed to the trunk directly. Even the most trivial changes are created on a short-lived branch, carefully reviewed, and merged to the trunk. Then the branch is deleted. This system guarantees an exceptionally stable and usable trunk at all times, but at the cost of tremendous process overhead.

Most projects take a middle-of-the-road approach. They commonly insist that */trunk* compile and pass regression tests at all times. A feature branch is required only when a change requires a large number of destabilizing commits. A good rule of thumb is to ask this question: if the developer worked for days in isolation and then committed the large change all at once (so that */trunk* were never destabilized), would it be too large a change to review? If the answer to that question is "yes," the change should be developed on a feature branch. As the developer commits incremental changes to the branch, they can be easily reviewed by peers.

Finally, there's the issue of how to best keep a feature branch in "sync" with the trunk as work progresses. As we mentioned earlier, there's a great risk to working on a branch for weeks or months; trunk changes may continue to pour in, to the point where the two lines of development differ so greatly that it may become a nightmare trying to merge the branch back to the trunk.

This situation is best avoided by regularly merging trunk changes to the branch. Make up a policy: once a week, merge the last week's worth of trunk changes to the branch.

At some point, you'll be ready to merge the "synchronized" feature branch back to the trunk. To do this, begin by doing a final merge of the latest trunk changes to the branch.

When that's done, the latest versions of branch and trunk will be absolutely identical except for your branch changes. You would then merge back with the `--reintegrate` option:

```
$ cd trunk-working-copy

$ svn update
At revision 1910.

$ svn merge --reintegrate http://svn.example.com/repos/calc/branches/mybranch
--- Merging differences between repository URLs into '.':
U    real.c
U    integer.c
A    newdirectory
A    newdirectory/newfile
 U   .
...
```

Another way to think about this pattern is that your weekly sync of trunk to branch is analogous to running *svn update* in a working copy, whereas the final merge step is analogous to running *svn commit* from a working copy. After all, what else *is* a working copy but a very shallow private branch? It's a branch that's capable of storing only one change at a time.

Vendor Branches

As is especially the case when developing software, the data that you maintain under version control is often closely related to, or perhaps dependent upon, someone else's data. Generally, the needs of your project will dictate that you stay as up to date as possible with the data provided by that external entity without sacrificing the stability of your own project. This scenario plays itself out all the time—anywhere that the information generated by one group of people has a direct effect on that which is generated by another group.

For example, software developers might be working on an application that makes use of a third-party library. Subversion has just such a relationship with the Apache Portable Runtime (APR) library (see "The Apache Portable Runtime Library" on page 261). The Subversion source code depends on the APR library for all its portability needs. In earlier stages of Subversion's development, the project closely tracked APR's changing API, always sticking to the "bleeding edge" of the library's code churn. Now that both APR and Subversion have matured, Subversion attempts to synchronize with APR's library API only at well-tested, stable release points.

Now, if your project depends on someone else's information, you could attempt to synchronize that information with your own in several ways. Most painfully, you could issue oral or written instructions to all the contributors of your project, telling them to make sure they have the specific versions of that third-party information that your project needs. If the third-party information is maintained in a Subversion repository, you could also use Subversion's externals definitions to effectively "pin down" specific versions of that information to some location in your own working copy directory (see "Externals Definitions" on page 82).

But sometimes you want to maintain custom modifications to third-party code in your own version control system. Returning to the software development example, programmers might need to make modifications to that third-party library for their own purposes. These modifications might include new functionality or bug fixes, maintained internally only until they become part of an official release of the third-party library. Or the changes might never be relayed back to the library maintainers, existing solely as custom tweaks to make the library further suit the needs of the software developers.

Now you face an interesting situation. Your project could house its custom modifications to the third-party data in some disjointed fashion, such as using patch files or full-fledged alternative versions of files and directories. But these quickly become maintenance headaches, requiring some mechanism by which to apply your custom changes to the third-party code and necessitating regeneration of those changes with each successive version of the third-party code that you track.

The solution to this problem is to use *vendor branches*. A vendor branch is a directory tree in your own version control system that contains information provided by a third-party entity, or vendor. Each version of the vendor's data that you decide to absorb into your project is called a *vendor drop*.

Vendor branches provide two benefits. First, by storing the currently supported vendor drop in your own version control system, you ensure that the members of your project never need to question whether they have the right version of the vendor's data. They simply receive that correct version as part of their regular working copy updates. Second, because the data lives in your own Subversion repository, you can store your custom changes to it in place—you have no more need of an automated (or worse, manual) method for swapping in your customizations.

General Vendor Branch Management Procedure

Managing vendor branches generally works like this: first, you create a top-level directory (such as /vendor) to hold the vendor branches. Then, you import the third-party code into a subdirectory of that top-level directory. You then copy that subdirectory into your main development branch (e.g., /trunk) at the appropriate location. You always make your local changes in the main development branch. With each new release of the code you are tracking, you bring it into the vendor branch and merge the changes into /trunk, resolving whatever conflicts occur between your local changes and the upstream changes.

An example will help clarify this algorithm. We'll use a scenario where your development team is creating a calculator program that links against a third-party complex number arithmetic library, libcomplex. We'll begin with the initial creation of the vendor branch and the import of the first vendor drop. We'll call our vendor branch directory *libcomplex*, and our code drops will go into a subdirectory of our vendor branch called *current*. And since *svn import* creates all the intermediate parent directories it needs, we can actually accomplish both of these steps with a single command:

```
$ svn import /path/to/libcomplex-1.0 \
            http://svn.example.com/repos/vendor/libcomplex/current \
            -m 'importing initial 1.0 vendor drop'
…
```

We now have the current version of the libcomplex source code in */vendor/libcomplex/current*. Now, we tag that version (see "Tags" on page 132) and then copy it into the main development branch. Our copy will create a new directory called *libcomplex* in our existing *calc* project directory. It is in this copied version of the vendor data that we will make our customizations:

```
$ svn copy http://svn.example.com/repos/vendor/libcomplex/current  \
            http://svn.example.com/repos/vendor/libcomplex/1.0      \
            -m 'tagging libcomplex-1.0'
…
$ svn copy http://svn.example.com/repos/vendor/libcomplex/1.0 \
            http://svn.example.com/repos/calc/libcomplex       \
            -m 'bringing libcomplex-1.0 into the main branch'
…
```

We check out our project's main branch—which now includes a copy of the first vendor drop—and we get to work customizing the libcomplex code. Before we know it, our modified version of libcomplex is now completely integrated into our calculator program.[#]

A few weeks later, the developers of libcomplex release a new version of their library—version 1.1—which contains some features and functionality that we really want. We'd like to upgrade to this new version, but without losing the customizations we made to the existing version. What we essentially would like to do is to replace our current baseline version of libcomplex 1.0 with a copy of libcomplex 1.1, and then re-apply the custom modifications we previously made to that library to the new version. But we actually approach the problem from the other direction, applying the changes made to libcomplex between versions 1.0 and 1.1 to our modified copy of it.

To perform this upgrade, we check out a copy of our vendor branch and replace the code in the *current* directory with the new libcomplex 1.1 source code. We quite literally copy new files on top of existing files, perhaps exploding the libcomplex 1.1 release tarball atop our existing files and directories. The goal here is to make our *current* directory contain only the libcomplex 1.1 code and to ensure that all that code is under version control. Oh, and we want to do this with as little version control history disturbance as possible.

[#] And is entirely bug-free, of course!

After replacing the 1.0 code with 1.1 code, *svn status* will show files with local modifications as well as, perhaps, some unversioned files. If we did what we were supposed to do, the unversioned files are only those new files introduced in the 1.1 release of libcomplex—we run *svn add* on those to get them under version control. If the 1.1 code no longer has certain files that were in the 1.0 tree, it may be hard to notice them; you'd have to compare the two trees with some external tool and then *svn delete* any files present in 1.0 but not in 1.1. (Although it might also be just fine to let these same files live on in unused obscurity!) Finally, once our *current* working copy contains only the libcomplex 1.1 code, we commit the changes we made to get it looking that way.

Our *current* branch now contains the new vendor drop. We tag the new version as 1.1 (in the same way we previously tagged the version 1.0 vendor drop), and then merge the differences between the tag of the previous version and the new current version into our main development branch:

```
$ cd working-copies/calc
$ svn merge http://svn.example.com/repos/vendor/libcomplex/1.0      \
            http://svn.example.com/repos/vendor/libcomplex/current  \
            libcomplex
... # resolve all the conflicts between their changes and our changes
$ svn commit -m 'merging libcomplex-1.1 into the main branch'
...
```

In the trivial use case, the new version of our third-party tool would look, from a files-and-directories point of view, just like the previous version. None of the libcomplex source files would have been deleted, renamed, or moved to different locations—the new version would contain only textual modifications against the previous one. In a perfect world, our modifications would apply cleanly to the new version of the library, with absolutely no complications or conflicts.

But things aren't always that simple, and in fact it is quite common for source files to get moved around between releases of software. This complicates the process of ensuring that our modifications are still valid for the new version of code, and things can quickly degrade into a situation where we have to manually re-create our customizations in the new version. Once Subversion knows about the history of a given source file—including all its previous locations—the process of merging in the new version of the library is pretty simple. But we are responsible for telling Subversion how the source file layout changed from vendor drop to vendor drop.

svn_load_dirs.pl

Vendor drops that contain more than a few deletes, additions, and moves complicate the process of upgrading to each successive version of the third-party data. So Subversion supplies the *svn_load_dirs.pl* script to assist with this process. This script automates the importing steps we mentioned in the general vendor branch management procedure to make sure mistakes are minimized. You will still be responsible for using the merge commands to merge the new versions of the third-party data into your main development branch, but *svn_load_dirs.pl* can help you more quickly and easily arrive at that stage.

In short, *svn_load_dirs.pl* is an enhancement to *svn import* that has several important characteristics:

- It can be run at any point in time to bring an existing directory in the repository to exactly match an external directory, performing all the necessary adds and deletes, and optionally performing moves, too.
- It takes care of a complicated series of operations between which Subversion requires an intermediate commit—such as before renaming a file or directory twice.
- It will optionally tag the newly imported directory.
- It will optionally add arbitrary properties to files and directories that match a regular expression.

svn_load_dirs.pl takes three mandatory arguments. The first argument is the URL to the base Subversion directory to work in. This argument is followed by the URL—relative to the first argument—into which the current vendor drop will be imported. Finally, the third argument is the local directory to import. Using our previous example, a typical run of *svn_load_dirs.pl* might look like this:

```
$ svn_load_dirs.pl http://svn.example.com/repos/vendor/libcomplex \
                   current                                        \
                   /path/to/libcomplex-1.1
...
```

You can indicate that you'd like *svn_load_dirs.pl* to tag the new vendor drop by passing the -t command-line option and specifying a tag name. This tag is another URL relative to the first program argument:

```
$ svn_load_dirs.pl -t libcomplex-1.1                              \
                   http://svn.example.com/repos/vendor/libcomplex \
                   current                                        \
                   /path/to/libcomplex-1.1
...
```

When you run *svn_load_dirs.pl*, it examines the contents of your existing "current" vendor drop and compares them with the proposed new vendor drop. In the trivial case, no files will be in one version and not the other, and the script will perform the new import without incident. If, however, there are discrepancies in the file layouts between versions, *svn_load_dirs.pl* will ask you how to resolve those differences. For example, you will have the opportunity to tell the script that you know that the file *math.c* in version 1.0 of libcomplex was renamed to *arithmetic.c* in libcomplex 1.1. Any discrepancies not explained by moves are treated as regular additions and deletions.

The script also accepts a separate configuration file for setting properties on files and directories matching a regular expression that are *added* to the repository. This configuration file is specified to *svn_load_dirs.pl* using the -p command-line option. Each line of the configuration file is a whitespace-delimited set of two or four values: a

Perl-style regular expression against which to match the added path, a control keyword (either break or cont), and then optionally a property name and value:

```
\.png$          break    svn:mime-type   image/png
\.jpe?g$        break    svn:mime-type   image/jpeg
\.m3u$          cont     svn:mime-type   audio/x-mpegurl
\.m3u$          break    svn:eol-style   LF
.*              break    svn:eol-style   native
```

For each added path, the configured property changes whose regular expression matches the path are applied in order, unless the control specification is break (which means that no more property changes should be applied to that path). If the control specification is cont—an abbreviation of continue—matching will continue with the next line of the configuration file.

Any whitespace in the regular expression, property name, or property value must be surrounded by either single or double quotes. You can escape quotes that are not used for wrapping whitespace by preceding them with a backslash (\) character. The backslash escapes only quotes when parsing the configuration file, so do not protect any other characters beyond what is necessary for the regular expression.

Summary

We covered a lot of ground in this chapter. We discussed the concepts of tags and branches and demonstrated how Subversion implements these concepts by copying directories with the *svn copy* command. We showed how to use *svn merge* to copy changes from one branch to another or roll back bad changes. We went over the use of *svn switch* to create mixed-location working copies. And we talked about how one might manage the organization and lifetimes of branches in a repository.

Remember the Subversion mantra: branches and tags are cheap. So don't be afraid to use them when needed!

As a helpful reminder of all the operations we discussed, Table 4-1 is handy reference table you can consult as you begin to make use of branches.

Table 4-1. Branching and merging commands

Action	Command
Create a branch or tag	svn copy *URL1 URL2*
Switch a working copy to a branch or tag	svn switch *URL*
Synchronize a branch with trunk	svn merge *trunkURL*; svn commit
See merge history or eligible changesets	svn mergeinfo target --from-source=*URL*
Merge a branch back into trunk	svn merge --reintegrate *branchURL*; svn commit
Merge one specific change	svn merge -c *REV URL*; svn commit
Merge a range of changes	svn merge -r *REV1:REV2 URL*; svn commit

Action	Command
Block a change from automatic merging	`svn merge -c REV --record-only URL; svn commit`
Preview a merge	`svn merge URL --dry-run`
Abandon merge results	`svn revert -R .`
Resurrect something from history	`svn copy URL@REV localPATH`
Undo a committed change	`svn merge -c -REV URL; svn commit`
Examine merge-sensitive history	`svn log -g; svn blame -g`
Create a tag from a working copy	`svn copy . tagURL`
Rearrange a branch or tag	`svn mv URL1 URL2`
Remove a branch or tag	`svn rm URL`

## CHAPTER 5

Repository Administration

The Subversion repository is the central storehouse of all your versioned data. As such, it becomes an obvious candidate for all the love and attention an administrator can offer. While the repository is generally a low-maintenance item, it is important to understand how to properly configure and care for it so that potential problems are avoided and so actual problems are safely resolved.

In this chapter, we'll discuss how to create and configure a Subversion repository. We'll also talk about repository maintenance, providing examples of how and when to use the *svnlook* and *svnadmin* tools provided with Subversion. We'll address some common questions and mistakes and give some suggestions for how to arrange the data in the repository.

If you plan to access a Subversion repository only in the role of a user whose data is under version control (i.e., via a Subversion client), you can skip this chapter altogether. However, if you are, or wish to become, a Subversion repository administrator,* this chapter is for you.

The Subversion Repository, Defined

Before jumping into the broader topic of repository administration, let's further define what a repository is. How does it look? How does it feel? Does it take its tea hot or iced, sweetened, and with lemon? As an administrator, you'll be expected to understand the composition of a repository both from a literal, OS-level perspective—how a repository looks and acts with respect to non-Subversion tools—and from a logical perspective—dealing with how data is represented *inside* the repository.

Seen through the eyes of a typical file browser application (such as Windows Explorer) or command-line-based filesystem navigation tools, the Subversion repository is just another directory full of stuff. There are some subdirectories with human-readable

---

* This may sound really prestigious and lofty, but we're just talking about anyone who is interested in that mysterious realm beyond the working copy where everyone's data hangs out.

configuration files in them, some subdirectories with some not-so-human-readable data files, and so on. As in other areas of the Subversion design, modularity is given high regard, and hierarchical organization is preferred to cluttered chaos. So, a shallow glance into a typical repository from a nuts-and-bolts perspective is sufficient to reveal the basic components of the repository:

```
$ ls repos
conf/  dav/  db/  format  hooks/  locks/  README.txt
```

Here's a quick fly-by overview of what exactly you're seeing in this directory listing. (Don't get bogged down in the terminology—detailed coverage of these components exists elsewhere in this and other chapters.)

conf
> A directory containing configuration files

dav
> A directory provided to *mod_dav_svn* for its private housekeeping data

db
> The data store for all of your versioned data

format
> A file that contains a single integer that indicates the version number of the repository layout

hooks
> A directory full of hook script templates (and hook scripts themselves, once you've installed some)

locks
> A directory for Subversion's repository lock files, used for tracking accessors to the repository

README.txt
> A file whose contents merely inform its readers that they are looking at a Subversion repository

Of course, when accessed via the Subversion libraries, this otherwise unremarkable collection of files and directories suddenly becomes an implementation of a virtual, versioned filesystem, complete with customizable event triggers. This filesystem has its own notions of directories and files, very similar to the notions of such things held by real filesystems (such as NTFS, FAT32, ext3, etc.). But this is a special filesystem—it hangs these directories and files from revisions, keeping all the changes you've ever made to them safely stored and forever accessible. This is where the entirety of your versioned data lives.

Strategies for Repository Deployment

Due largely to the simplicity of the overall design of the Subversion repository and the technologies on which it relies, creating and configuring a repository are fairly straightforward tasks. There are a few preliminary decisions you'll want to make, but the actual work involved in any given setup of a Subversion repository is pretty basic, tending toward mindless repetition if you find yourself setting up multiples of these things.

Some things you'll want to consider beforehand, though, are:

- What data do you expect to live in your repository (or repositories), and how will that data be organized?
- Where will your repository live, and how will it be accessed?
- What types of access control and repository event reporting do you need?
- Which of the available types of data store do you want to use?

In this section, we'll try to help you answer those questions.

Planning Your Repository Organization

While Subversion allows you to move around versioned files and directories without any loss of information—and even provides ways of moving whole sets of versioned history from one repository to another—doing so can greatly disrupt the workflow of those who access the repository often and come to expect things to be at certain locations. So before creating a new repository, try to peer into the future a bit; plan ahead before placing your data under version control. By conscientiously "laying out" your repository or repositories and their versioned contents ahead of time, you can prevent many future headaches.

Let's assume that as repository administrator, you will be responsible for supporting the version control system for several projects. Your first decision is whether to use a single repository for multiple projects, whether to give each project its own repository, or some compromise of these two.

There are benefits to using a single repository for multiple projects, most obviously the lack of duplicated maintenance. A single repository means that there is one set of hook programs, one thing to routinely back up, one thing to dump and load if Subversion releases an incompatible new version, and so on. Also, you can move data between projects easily, without losing any historical versioning information.

The downside of using a single repository is that different projects may have different requirements in terms of the repository event triggers, such as needing to send commit notification emails to different mailing lists or having different definitions about what does and does not constitute a legitimate commit. These aren't insurmountable problems, of course—it just means that all of your hook scripts have to be sensitive to the layout of your repository rather than assuming that the whole repository is associated with a single group of people. Also, remember that Subversion uses repository-global revision numbers. While those numbers don't have any particular magical powers, some folks still don't like the fact that even though no changes have been made to their project lately, the youngest revision number for the repository keeps climbing because other projects are actively adding new revisions.[†]

A middle-ground approach can be taken, too. For example, projects can be grouped by how well they relate to each other. You might have a few repositories with a handful of projects in each repository. That way, projects that are likely to want to share data can do so easily, and as new revisions are added to the repository, at least the developers know that those new revisions are remotely related to everyone who uses that repository.

After deciding how to organize your projects with respect to repositories, you'll probably want to think about directory hierarchies within the repositories themselves. Because Subversion uses regular directory copies for branching and tagging (see Chapter 4), the Subversion community recommends that you choose a repository location for each *project root*—the "topmost" directory that contains data related to that project—and then create three subdirectories beneath that root: *trunk*, meaning the directory under which the main project development occurs; *branches*, which is a directory in which to create various named branches of the main development line; and *tags*, which is a collection of tree snapshots that are created, and perhaps destroyed, but never changed.[‡]

For example, your repository might look like this:

```
/
    calc/
        trunk/
        tags/
        branches/
    calendar/
        trunk/
        tags/
        branches/
    spreadsheet/
        trunk/
        tags/
        branches/
    ...
```

Note that it doesn't matter where in your repository each project root is. If you have only one project per repository, the logical place to put each project root is at the root of that project's respective repository. If you have multiple projects, you might want to

---

[†] Whether founded in ignorance or in poorly considered concepts about how to derive legitimate software development metrics, global revision numbers are a silly thing to fear, and *not* the kind of thing you should weigh when deciding how to arrange your projects and repositories.

[‡] The *trunk*, *tags*, and *branches* trio is sometimes referred to as "the TTB directories."

arrange them in groups inside the repository, perhaps putting projects with similar goals or shared code in the same subdirectory, or maybe just grouping them alphabetically. Such an arrangement might look like this:

```
/
    utils/
        calc/
            trunk/
            tags/
            branches/
        calendar/
            trunk/
            tags/
            branches/
        ...
    office/
        spreadsheet/
            trunk/
            tags/
            branches/
        ...
```

Lay out your repository in whatever way you see fit. Subversion does not expect or enforce a particular layout—in its eyes, a directory is a directory is a directory. Ultimately, you should choose the repository arrangement that meets the needs of the people who work on the projects that live there.

In the name of full disclosure, though, we'll mention another very common layout. In this layout, the *trunk*, *tags*, and *branches* directories live in the root directory of your repository, and your projects are in subdirectories beneath those, like so:

```
/
    trunk/
        calc/
        calendar/
        spreadsheet/
        ...
    tags/
        calc/
        calendar/
        spreadsheet/
        ...
    branches/
        calc/
        calendar/
        spreadsheet/
        ...
```

There's nothing particularly incorrect about such a layout, but it may or may not seem as intuitive for your users. Especially in large, multiproject situations with many users, those users may tend to be familiar with only one or two of the projects in the repository. But the projects-as-branch-siblings approach tends to deemphasize project individuality and focus on the entire set of projects as a single entity. That's a social issue,

---

though. We like our originally suggested arrangement for purely practical reasons: it's easier to ask about (or modify, or migrate elsewhere) the entire history of a single project when there's a single repository path that holds the entire history—past, present, tagged, and branched—for that project and that project alone.

Deciding Where and How to Host Your Repository

Before creating your Subversion repository, an obvious question you'll need to answer is where the thing is going to live. This is strongly connected to myriad other questions involving how the repository will be accessed (via a Subversion server or directly), by whom (users behind your corporate firewall or the whole world out on the open Internet), what other services you'll be providing around Subversion (repository browsing interfaces, email-based commit notification, etc.), your data backup strategy, and so on.

We cover server choice and configuration in Chapter 6, but the point we'd like to briefly make here is simply that the answers to some of these other questions might have implications that force your hand when deciding where your repository will live. For example, certain deployment scenarios might require accessing the repository via a remote filesystem from multiple computers, in which case (as you'll read in the next section) your choice of a repository backend data store turns out not to be a choice at all because only one of the available backends will work in this scenario.

Addressing each possible way to deploy Subversion is both impossible and outside the scope of this book. We simply encourage you to evaluate your options using these pages and other sources as your reference material and to plan ahead.

Choosing a Data Store

As of version 1.1, Subversion provides two options for the type of underlying data store—often referred to as "the backend" or, somewhat confusingly, "the (versioned) filesystem"—that each repository uses. One type of data store keeps everything in a Berkeley DB (or BDB) database environment; repositories that use this type are often referred to as being "BDB-backed." The other type stores data in ordinary flat files, using a custom format. Subversion developers have adopted the habit of referring to this latter data storage mechanism as *FSFS*§—a versioned filesystem implementation that uses the native OS filesystem directly, rather than via a database library or some other abstraction layer, to store data.

Table 5-1 gives a comparative overview of Berkeley DB and FSFS repositories.

---

§ Often pronounced "fuzz-fuzz," if Jack Repenning has anything to say about it. (This book, however, assumes that the reader is thinking "eff-ess-eff-ess.")

Table 5-1. Repository data store comparison

Category	Feature	Berkeley DB	FSFS
Reliability	Data integrity	When properly deployed, extremely reliable; Berkeley DB 4.4 brings autorecovery	Older versions had some rarely demonstrated but data-destroying bugs
	Sensitivity to interruptions	Very; crashes and permission problems can leave the database "wedged," requiring journaled recovery procedures	Quite insensitive
Accessibility	Usable from a read-only mount	No	Yes
	Platform-independent storage	No	Yes
	Usable over network filesystems	Generally, no	Yes
	Group permissions handling	Sensitive to user umask problems; best if accessed by only one user	Works around umask problems
Scalability	Repository disk usage	Larger (especially if logfiles aren't purged)	Smaller
	Number of revision trees	Database; no problems	Some older native filesystems don't scale well with thousands of entries in a single directory
	Directories with many files	Slower	Faster
Performance	Checking out latest revision	No meaningful difference	No meaningful difference
	Large commits	Slower overall, but cost is amortized across the lifetime of the commit	Faster overall, but finalization delay may cause client timeouts

Each of these two backend types has advantages and disadvantages. Neither one is more "official" than the other, though the newer FSFS is the default data store as of Subversion 1.2. Both are reliable enough to trust with your versioned data. But as you can see in Table 5-1, the FSFS backend provides quite a bit more flexibility in terms of its supported deployment scenarios. More flexibility means you have to work a little harder to find ways to deploy it incorrectly. Those reasons—plus the fact that not using Berkeley DB means there's one fewer component in the system—largely explain why today almost everyone uses the FSFS backend when creating new repositories.

Fortunately, most programs that access Subversion repositories are blissfully ignorant of which backend data store is in use. And you aren't even necessarily stuck with your first choice of a data store—in the event that you change your mind later, Subversion provides ways of migrating your repository's data into another repository that uses a different backend data store. We talk more about that later in this chapter.

The following subsections provide a more detailed look at the available backend data store types.

Berkeley DB

When the initial design phase of Subversion was in progress, the developers decided to use Berkeley DB for a variety of reasons, including its open source license, transaction support, reliability, performance, API simplicity, thread safety, support for cursors, and so on.

Berkeley DB provides real transaction support—perhaps its most powerful feature. Multiple processes accessing your Subversion repositories don't have to worry about accidentally clobbering each other's data. The isolation provided by the transaction system is such that for any given operation, the Subversion repository code sees a static view of the database—not a database that is constantly changing at the hand of some other process—and can make decisions based on that view. If the decision made happens to conflict with what another process is doing, the entire operation is rolled back as though it never happened, and Subversion gracefully retries the operation against a new, updated (and yet still static) view of the database.

Another great feature of Berkeley DB is *hot backups*—the ability to back up the database environment without taking it "offline." We'll discuss how to back up your repository later in this chapter (in "Repository Backup" on page 184), but the benefits of being able to make fully functional copies of your repositories without any downtime should be obvious.

Berkeley DB is also a very reliable database system when properly used. Subversion uses Berkeley DB's logging facilities, which means that the database first writes to on-disk logfiles a description of any modifications it is about to make, and then it makes the modification itself. This is to ensure that if anything goes wrong, the database system can back up to a previous *checkpoint*—a location in the logfiles known not to be corrupt—and replay transactions until the data is restored to a usable state. See "Managing Disk Space" on page 164 for more about Berkeley DB logfiles.

But every rose has its thorn, and so we must note some known limitations of Berkeley DB. First, Berkeley DB environments are not portable. You cannot simply copy a Subversion repository that was created on a Unix system onto a Windows system and expect it to work. While much of the Berkeley DB database format is architecture-independent, other aspects of the environment are not. Second, Subversion uses Berkeley DB in a way that will not operate on Windows 95/98 systems—if you need to house a BDB-backed repository on a Windows machine, stick with Windows 2000 or later.

While Berkeley DB promises to behave correctly on network shares that meet a particular set of specifications,‖ most networked filesystem types and appliances do *not* actually meet those requirements. And in no case can you allow a BDB-backed repository that resides on a network share to be accessed by multiple clients of that share

---

‖ Berkeley DB requires that the underlying filesystem implement strict POSIX locking semantics and, more importantly, the ability to map files directly into process memory.

at once (which quite often is the whole point of having the repository live on a network share in the first place).

 If you attempt to use Berkeley DB on a noncompliant remote filesystem, the results are unpredictable—you may see mysterious errors right away, or it may be months before you discover that your repository database is subtly corrupted. You should strongly consider using the FSFS data store for repositories that need to live on a network share.

Finally, because Berkeley DB is a library linked directly into Subversion, it's more sensitive to interruptions than a typical relational database system. Most SQL systems, for example, have a dedicated server process that mediates all access to tables. If a program accessing the database crashes for some reason, the database daemon notices the lost connection and cleans up any mess left behind. And because the database daemon is the only process accessing the tables, applications don't need to worry about permission conflicts. These things are not the case with Berkeley DB, however. Subversion (and programs using Subversion libraries) access the database tables directly, which means that a program crash can leave the database in a temporarily inconsistent, inaccessible state. When this happens, an administrator needs to ask Berkeley DB to restore to a checkpoint, which is a bit of an annoyance. Other things can cause a repository to "wedge" besides crashed processes, such as programs conflicting over ownership and permissions on the database files.

 Berkeley DB 4.4 brings (to Subversion 1.4 and later) the ability for Subversion to automatically and transparently recover Berkeley DB environments in need of such recovery. When a Subversion process attaches to a repository's Berkeley DB environment, it uses some process accounting mechanisms to detect any unclean disconnections by previous processes, performs any necessary recovery, and then continues on as though nothing happened. This doesn't completely eliminate instances of repository wedging, but it does drastically reduce the amount of human interaction required to recover from them.

So, while a Berkeley DB repository is quite fast and scalable, it's best used by a single server process running as one user—such as Apache's *httpd* or *svnserve* (see Chapter 6)—rather than accessing it as many different users via file:// or svn+ssh:// URLs. If you're accessing a Berkeley DB repository directly as multiple users, be sure to read "Supporting Multiple Repository Access Methods" on page 230 later in this chapter.

FSFS

In mid-2004, a second type of repository storage system—one that doesn't use a database at all—came into being. An FSFS repository stores the changes associated with a revision in a single file, and so all of a repository's revisions can be found in a single subdirectory full of numbered files. Transactions are created in separate subdirectories as individual files. When complete, the transaction file is renamed and moved into the revisions directory, thus guaranteeing that commits are atomic. And because a revision file is permanent and unchanging, the repository also can be backed up while "hot," just like a BDB-backed repository.

The FSFS revision files describe a revision's directory structure, file contents, and deltas against files in other revision trees. Unlike a Berkeley DB database, this storage format is portable across different operating systems and isn't sensitive to CPU architecture. Because no journaling or shared-memory files are being used, the repository can be safely accessed over a network filesystem and examined in a read-only environment. The lack of database overhead also means the overall repository size is a bit smaller.

FSFS has different performance characteristics, too. When committing a directory with a huge number of files, FSFS is able to more quickly append directory entries. On the other hand, FSFS writes the latest version of a file as a delta against an earlier version, which means that checking out the latest tree is a bit slower than fetching the full-texts stored in a Berkeley DB HEAD revision. FSFS also has a longer delay when finalizing a commit, which could in extreme cases cause clients to time out while waiting for a response.

The most important distinction, however, is FSFS's imperviousness to wedging when something goes wrong. If a process using a Berkeley DB database runs into a permissions problem or suddenly crashes, the database can be left in an unusable state until an administrator recovers it. If the same scenarios happen to a process using an FSFS repository, the repository isn't affected at all. At worst, some transaction data is left behind.

The only real argument against FSFS is its relative immaturity compared to Berkeley DB. Unlike Berkeley DB, which has years of history, its own dedicated development team, and now, Oracle's mighty name attached to it,[#] FSFS is a newer bit of engineering. Prior to Subversion 1.4, it was still shaking out some pretty serious data integrity bugs, which, while triggered in only very rare cases, nonetheless did occur. That said, FSFS has quickly become the backend of choice for some of the largest public and private Subversion repositories, and it promises a lower barrier to entry for Subversion across the board.

Creating and Configuring Your Repository

Earlier in this chapter (in "Strategies for Repository Deployment" on page 147), we looked at some of the important decisions that should be made before creating and configuring your Subversion repository. Now, we finally get to get our hands dirty! In

---

[#] Oracle bought Sleepycat and its flagship software, Berkeley DB, on Valentine's Day in 2006.

this section, we'll see how to actually create a Subversion repository and configure it to perform custom actions when special repository events occur.

Creating the Repository

Subversion repository creation is an incredibly simple task. The *svnadmin* utility that comes with Subversion provides a subcommand (*svnadmin create*) for doing just that.

```
$ # Create a repository
$ svnadmin create /var/svn/repos
$
```

This creates a new repository in the directory */var/svn/repos* and with the default filesystem data store. Prior to Subversion 1.2, the default was Berkeley DB; the default is now FSFS. You can explicitly choose the filesystem type using the `--fs-type` argument, which accepts as a parameter either `fsfs` or `bdb`:

```
$ # Create an FSFS-backed repository
$ svnadmin create --fs-type fsfs /var/svn/repos
$

# Create a Berkeley-DB-backed repository
$ svnadmin create --fs-type bdb /var/svn/repos
$
```

After running this simple command, you have a Subversion repository.

The path argument to *svnadmin* is just a regular filesystem path and not a URL such as the *svn* client program uses when referring to repositories. Both *svnadmin* and *svnlook* are considered server-side utilities—they are used on the machine where the repository resides to examine or modify aspects of the repository, and they are in fact unable to perform tasks across a network. A common mistake made by Subversion newcomers is trying to pass URLs (even "local" `file://` ones) to these two programs.

Present in the *db/* subdirectory of your repository is the implementation of the versioned filesystem. Your new repository's versioned filesystem begins life at revision 0, which is defined to consist of nothing but the top-level root (*/*) directory. Initially, revision 0 also has a single revision property, `svn:date`, set to the time at which the repository was created.

Now that you have a repository, it's time to customize it.

While some parts of a Subversion repository—such as the configuration files and hook scripts—are meant to be examined and modified manually, you shouldn't (and shouldn't need to) tamper with the other parts of the repository "by hand." The *svnadmin* tool should be sufficient for any changes necessary to your repository, or you can look to third-party tools (such as Berkeley DB's tool suite) for tweaking relevant subsections of the repository. Do *not* attempt manual manipulation of your version control history by poking and prodding around in your repository's data store files!

Implementing Repository Hooks

A *hook* is a program triggered by some repository event, such as the creation of a new revision or the modification of an unversioned property. Some hooks (the so-called "pre hooks") run in advance of a repository operation and provide a means by which to both report what is about to happen and to prevent it from happening at all. Other hooks (the "post hooks") run after the completion of a repository event and are useful for performing tasks that examine—but don't modify—the repository. Each hook is handed enough information to tell what that event is (or was), the specific repository changes proposed (or completed), and the username of the person who triggered the event.

The *hooks* subdirectory is, by default, filled with templates for various repository hooks:

```
$ ls repos/hooks/
post-commit.tmpl          post-unlock.tmpl     pre-revprop-change.tmpl
post-lock.tmpl            pre-commit.tmpl      pre-unlock.tmpl
post-revprop-change.tmpl  pre-lock.tmpl        start-commit.tmpl
$
```

There is one template for each hook that the Subversion repository supports; by examining the contents of those template scripts, you can see what triggers each script to run and what data is passed to that script. Also present in many of these templates are examples of how one might use that script, in conjunction with other Subversion-supplied programs, to perform common useful tasks. To actually install a working hook, you need only place some executable program or script into the *repos/hooks* directory, which can be executed as the name (such as *start-commit* or *post-commit*) of the hook.

On Unix platforms, this means supplying a script or program (which could be a shell script, a Python program, a compiled C binary, or any number of other things) named exactly like the name of the hook. Of course, the template files are present for more than just informational purposes—the easiest way to install a hook on Unix platforms is simply to copy the appropriate template file to a new file that lacks the *.tmpl* extension, customize the hook's contents, and ensure that the script is executable. Windows, however, uses file extensions to determine whether a program is executable, so you would need to supply a program whose basename is the name of the hook and whose extension is one of the special extensions recognized by Windows for executable programs, such as *.exe* for programs and *.bat* for batch files.

 For security reasons, the Subversion repository executes hook programs with an empty environment—that is, no environment variables are set at all, not even $PATH (or %PATH%, under Windows). Because of this, many administrators are baffled when their hook program runs fine by hand but doesn't work when run by Subversion. Be sure to explicitly set any necessary environment variables in your hook program and/or use absolute paths to programs.

Subversion executes hooks as the same user who owns the process that is accessing the Subversion repository. In most cases, the repository is being accessed via a Subversion server, so this user is the same user as whom the server runs on the system. The hooks themselves will need to be configured with OS-level permissions that allow that user to execute them. Also, this means that any programs or files (including the Subversion repository) accessed directly or indirectly by the hook will be accessed as the same user. In other words, be alert to potential permission-related problems that could prevent the hook from performing the tasks it is designed to perform.

There are several hooks implemented by the Subversion repository, and you can get details about each of them in "Repository Hooks" on page 360. As a repository administrator, you'll need to decide which hooks you wish to implement (by way of providing an appropriately named and permissioned hook program) and how. When you make this decision, keep in mind the big picture of how your repository is deployed. For example, if you are using server configuration to determine which users are permitted to commit changes to your repository, you don't need to do this sort of access control via the hook system.

There is no shortage of Subversion hook programs and scripts that are freely available either from the Subversion community itself or elsewhere. These scripts cover a wide range of utility—basic access control, policy adherence checking, issue tracker integration, email- or syndication-based commit notification, and beyond. Or, if you wish to write your own, see Chapter 8.

While hook scripts can do almost anything, there is one dimension in which hook script authors should show restraint: do *not* modify a commit transaction using hook scripts. Although it might be tempting to use hook scripts to automatically correct errors, shortcomings, or policy violations present in the files being committed, doing so can cause problems. Subversion keeps client-side caches of certain bits of repository data, and if you change a commit transaction in this way, those caches become undetectably stale. This inconsistency can lead to surprising and unexpected behavior. Instead of modifying the transaction, you should simply *validate* the transaction in the `pre-commit` hook and reject the commit if it does not meet the desired requirements. As a bonus, your users will learn the value of careful, compliance-minded work habits.

Berkeley DB Configuration

A Berkeley DB environment is an encapsulation of one or more databases, logfiles, region files, and configuration files. The Berkeley DB environment has its own set of default configuration values for things such as the number of database locks allowed to be taken out at any given time, the maximum size of the journaling logfiles, and so on. Subversion's filesystem logic additionally chooses default values for some of the Berkeley DB configuration options. However, sometimes your particular repository, with its unique collection of data and access patterns, might require a different set of configuration option values.

The producers of Berkeley DB understand that different applications and database environments have different requirements, so they have provided a mechanism for overriding at runtime many of the configuration values for the Berkeley DB environment. BDB checks for the presence of a file named *DB_CONFIG* in the environment directory (namely, the repository's *db* subdirectory) and parses the options found in that file. Subversion itself creates this file when it creates the rest of the repository. The file initially contains some default options, as well as pointers to the Berkeley DB online documentation so that you can read about what those options do. Of course, you are free to add any of the supported Berkeley DB options to your *DB_CONFIG* file. Just be aware that while Subversion never attempts to read or interpret the contents of the file and makes no direct use of the option settings in it, you'll want to avoid any configuration changes that may cause Berkeley DB to behave in a fashion that is at odds with what Subversion might expect. Also, changes made to *DB_CONFIG* won't take effect until you recover the database environment (using *svnadmin recover*).

Repository Maintenance

Maintaining a Subversion repository can be daunting, mostly due to the complexities inherent in systems that have a database backend. Doing the task well is all about knowing the tools—what they are, when to use them, and how. This section will

---

introduce you to the repository administration tools provided by Subversion and discuss how to wield them to accomplish tasks such as repository data migration, upgrades, backups, and cleanups.

An Administrator's Toolkit

Subversion provides a handful of utilities useful for creating, inspecting, modifying, and repairing your repository. Let's look more closely at each of those tools. Afterward, we'll briefly examine some of the utilities included in the Berkeley DB distribution that provide functionality specific to your repository's database backend not otherwise provided by Subversion's own tools.

svnadmin

The *svnadmin* program is the repository administrator's best friend. Besides providing the ability to create Subversion repositories, this program allows you to perform several maintenance operations on those repositories. The syntax of *svnadmin* is similar to that of other Subversion command-line programs:

```
$ svnadmin help
general usage: svnadmin SUBCOMMAND REPOS_PATH  [ARGS & OPTIONS ...]
Type 'svnadmin help <subcommand>' for help on a specific subcommand.
Type 'svnadmin --version' to see the program version and FS modules.

Available subcommands:
   crashtest
   create
   deltify
...
```

Earlier in this chapter (in "Creating the Repository" on page 155), we introduced the *svnadmin create* subcommand. Most of the other *svnadmin* subcommands we will cover later in this chapter, and you can consult "svnadmin" on page 325 for a full rundown of subcommands and what each of them offers.

svnlook

svnlook is a tool provided by Subversion for examining the various revisions and *transactions* (which are revisions in the making) in a repository. No part of this program attempts to change the repository. *svnlook* is typically used by the repository hooks for reporting the changes that are about to be committed (in the case of the `pre-commit` hook) or that were just committed (in the case of the `post-commit` hook) to the repository. A repository administrator may use this tool for diagnostic purposes.

svnlook has a straightforward syntax:

```
$ svnlook help
general usage: svnlook SUBCOMMAND REPOS_PATH [ARGS & OPTIONS ...]
Note: any subcommand which takes the '--revision' and '--transaction'
      options will, if invoked without one of those options, act on
```

```
          the repository's youngest revision.
Type 'svnlook help <subcommand>' for help on a specific subcommand.
Type 'svnlook --version' to see the program version and FS modules.
...
```

Most of *svnlook*'s subcommands can operate on either a revision or a transaction tree, printing information about the tree itself or about how it differs from the previous revision of the repository. You use the `--revision` (`-r`) and `--transaction` (`-t`) options to specify which revision or transaction, respectively, to examine. In the absence of both the `--revision` (`-r`) and `--transaction` (`-t`) options, *svnlook* will examine the youngest (or HEAD) revision in the repository. So the following two commands do exactly the same thing when 19 is the youngest revision in the repository located at */var/svn/ repos*:

```
$ svnlook info /var/svn/repos
$ svnlook info /var/svn/repos -r 19
```

One exception to these rules about subcommands is the *svnlook youngest* subcommand, which takes no options and simply prints out the repository's youngest revision number:

```
$ svnlook youngest /var/svn/repos
19
$
```

Keep in mind that the only transactions you can browse are uncommitted ones. Most repositories will have no such transactions because transactions are usually either committed (in which case, you should access them as revisions with the `--revision` (`-r`) option) or aborted and removed.

Output from *svnlook* is designed to be both human- and machine-parsable. Take, as an example, the output of the *svnlook info* subcommand:

```
$ svnlook info /var/svn/repos
sally
2002-11-04 09:29:13 -0600 (Mon, 04 Nov 2002)
27
Added the usual
Greek tree.
$
```

The output of *svnlook info* consists of the following, in the order given:

1. The author, followed by a newline

2. The date, followed by a newline

3. The number of characters in the log message, followed by a newline

4. The log message itself, followed by a newline

This output is human-readable, meaning items such as the datestamp are displayed using a textual representation instead of something more obscure (such as the number of nanoseconds since the Tastee Freez guy drove by). But the output is also machine-parsable; because the log message can contain multiple lines and be unbounded in length, *svnlook* provides the length of that message before the message itself. This allows scripts and other wrappers around this command to make intelligent decisions about the log message, such as how much memory to allocate for the message, or at least how many bytes to skip in the event that this output is not the last bit of data in the stream.

svnlook can perform a variety of other queries: displaying subsets of bits of information we've mentioned previously, recursively listing versioned directory trees, reporting which paths were modified in a given revision or transaction, showing textual and property differences made to files and directories, and so on. See "svnlook" on page 336 for a full reference of *svnlook*'s features.

svndumpfilter

While it won't be the most commonly used tool at the administrator's disposal, *svndumpfilter* provides a very particular brand of useful functionality—the ability to quickly and easily modify streams of Subversion repository history data by acting as a path-based filter.

The syntax of *svndumpfilter* is as follows:

```
$ svndumpfilter help
general usage: svndumpfilter SUBCOMMAND [ARGS & OPTIONS ...]
Type "svndumpfilter help <subcommand>" for help on a specific subcommand.
Type 'svndumpfilter --version' to see the program version.

Available subcommands:
   exclude
   include
   help (?, h)
```

There are only two interesting subcommands: *svndumpfilter exclude* and *svndumpfilter include*. They allow you to make the choice between implicit or explicit inclusion of paths in the stream. You can learn more about these subcommands and *svndumpfilter*'s unique purpose later in this chapter, in "Filtering Repository History" on page 173.

svnsync

The *svnsync* program, which is new to the 1.4 release of Subversion, provides all the functionality required for maintaining a read-only mirror of a Subversion repository. The program really has one job—to transfer one repository's versioned history into another repository. And while there are few ways to do that, its primary strength is that it can operate remotely—the "source" and "sink"* repositories may be on different computers from each other and from *svnsync* itself.

As you might expect, *svnsync* has a syntax that looks very much like every other program we've mentioned in this chapter:

```
$ svnsync help
general usage: svnsync SUBCOMMAND DEST_URL  [ARGS & OPTIONS ...]
Type 'svnsync help <subcommand>' for help on a specific subcommand.
Type 'svnsync --version' to see the program version and RA modules.

Available subcommands:
   initialize (init)
   synchronize (sync)
   copy-revprops
   help (?, h)
$
```

We talk more about replicating repositories with *svnsync* later in this chapter (see "Repository Replication" on page 177).

fsfs-reshard.py

While not an official member of the Subversion toolchain, the *fsfs-reshard.py* script (found in the *tools/server-side* directory of the Subversion source distribution) is a useful performance tuning tool for administrators of FSFS-backed Subversion repositories. FSFS repositories contain files that describe the changes made in a single revision, and files that contain the revision properties associated with a single revision. Repositories created in versions of Subversion prior to 1.5 keep these files in two directories—one for each type of file. As new revisions are committed to the repository, Subversion drops more files into these two directories—over time, the number of these files in each directory can grow to be quite large. This has been observed to cause performance problems on certain network-based filesystems.

Subversion 1.5 creates FSFS-backed repositories using a slightly modified layout in which the contents of these two directories are *sharded*, or scattered across several subdirectories. This can greatly reduce the time it takes the system to locate any one of these files, and therefore increases the overall performance of Subversion when reading from the repository. The number of subdirectories used to house these files is configurable, though, and that's where *fsfs-reshard.py* comes in. This script reshuffles the repository's file structure into a new arrangement that reflects the requested number of sharding subdirectories. This is especially useful for converting an older Subversion repository into the new Subversion 1.5 sharded layout (which Subversion will not automatically do for you) or for fine-tuning an already sharded repository.

---

* Or is that, the "sync"?

Berkeley DB utilities

If you're using a Berkeley DB repository, all of your versioned filesystem's structure and data live in a set of database tables within the *db/* subdirectory of your repository. This subdirectory is a regular Berkeley DB environment directory and can therefore be used in conjunction with any of the Berkeley database tools, typically provided as part of the Berkeley DB distribution.

For day-to-day Subversion use, these tools are unnecessary. Most of the functionality typically needed for Subversion repositories has been duplicated in the *svnadmin* tool. For example, *svnadmin list-unused-dblogs* and *svnadmin list-dblogs* perform a subset of what is provided by the Berkeley *db_archive* utility, and *svnadmin recover* reflects the common use cases of the *db_recover* utility.

However, there are still a few Berkeley DB utilities that you might find useful. The *db_dump* and *db_load* programs write and read, respectively, a custom file format that describes the keys and values in a Berkeley DB database. Since Berkeley databases are not portable across machine architectures, this format is a useful way to transfer those databases from machine to machine, irrespective of architecture or operating system. As we describe later in this chapter, you can also use *svnadmin dump* and *svnadmin load* for similar purposes, but *db_dump* and *db_load* can do certain jobs just as well and much faster. They can also be useful if the experienced Berkeley DB hacker needs to do in-place tweaking of the data in a BDB-backed repository for some reason, which is something Subversion's utilities won't allow. Also, the *db_stat* utility can provide useful information about the status of your Berkeley DB environment, including detailed statistics about the locking and storage subsystems.

For more information on the Berkeley DB toolchain, visit the documentation section of the Berkeley DB section of Oracle's web site at *http://www.oracle.com/technology/documentation/berkeley-db/db/*.

Commit Log Message Correction

Sometimes a user will have an error in her log message (a misspelling or some misinformation, perhaps). If the repository is configured (using the `pre-revprop-change` hook; see "Implementing Repository Hooks" on page 156) to accept changes to this log message after the commit is finished, the user can "fix" her log message remotely using *svn propset* (see "svn propset" in Chapter 9). However, because of the potential to lose information forever, Subversion repositories are not, by default, configured to allow changes to unversioned properties—except by an administrator.

If a log message needs to be changed by an administrator, this can be done using *svnadmin setlog*. This command changes the log message (the `svn:log` property) on a given revision of a repository, reading the new value from a provided file:

```
$ echo "Here is the new, correct log message" > newlog.txt
$ svnadmin setlog myrepos newlog.txt -r 388
```

The *svnadmin setlog* command, by default, is still bound by the same protections against modifying unversioned properties as a remote client—the `pre-` and `post-revprop-change` hooks are still triggered and therefore must be set up to accept changes of this nature. But an administrator can get around these protections by passing the `--bypass-hooks` option to the *svnadmin setlog* command.

> Remember, though, that by bypassing the hooks, you are likely avoiding such things as email notifications of property changes, backup systems that track unversioned property changes, and so on. In other words, be very careful about what you are changing and how you change it.

Managing Disk Space

While the cost of storage has dropped incredibly in the past few years, disk usage is still a valid concern for administrators seeking to version large amounts of data. Every bit of version history information stored in the live repository needs to be backed up elsewhere, perhaps multiple times as part of rotating backup schedules. It is useful to know which pieces of Subversion's repository data need to remain on the live site, which need to be backed up, and which can be safely removed.

How Subversion saves disk space

To keep the repository small, Subversion uses *deltification* (or deltified storage) within the repository itself. Deltification involves encoding the representation of a chunk of data as a collection of differences against some other chunk of data. If the two pieces of data are very similar, this deltification results in storage savings for the deltified chunk—rather than taking up space equal to the size of the original data, it takes up only enough space to say, "I look just like this other piece of data over here, except for the following couple of changes." The result is that most of the repository data that tends to be bulky—namely, the contents of versioned files—is stored at a much smaller size than the original full-text representation of that data. And for repositories created with Subversion 1.4 or later, the space savings are even better—now those full-text representations of file contents are themselves compressed.

> Because all of the data that is subject to deltification in a BDB-backed repository is stored in a single Berkeley DB database file, reducing the size of the stored values will not immediately reduce the size of the database file itself. Berkeley DB will, however, keep internal records of unused areas of the database file and consume those areas first before growing the size of the database file. So, while deltification doesn't produce immediate space savings, it can drastically slow future growth of the database.

Removing dead transactions

Though they are uncommon, there are circumstances in which a Subversion commit process might fail, leaving behind in the repository the remnants of the revision-to-be that wasn't—an uncommitted transaction and all the file and directory changes associated with it. This could happen for several reasons: perhaps the client operation was inelegantly terminated by the user, or a network failure occurred in the middle of an operation. Regardless of the reason, dead transactions can happen. They don't do any real harm, other than consuming disk space. A fastidious administrator may nonetheless wish to remove them.

You can use the *svnadmin lstxns* command to list the names of the currently outstanding transactions:

```
$ svnadmin lstxns myrepos
19
3a1
a45
$
```

Each item in the resultant output can then be used with *svnlook* (and its --transaction (-t) option) to determine who created the transaction, when it was created, what types of changes were made in the transaction—information that is helpful in determining whether the transaction is a safe candidate for removal! If you do indeed want to remove a transaction, its name can be passed to *svnadmin rmtxns*, which will perform the cleanup of the transaction. In fact, *svnadmin rmtxns* can take its input directly from the output of *svnadmin lstxns*!

```
$ svnadmin rmtxns myrepos 'svnadmin lstxns myrepos'
$
```

If you use these two subcommands like this, you should consider making your repository temporarily inaccessible to clients. That way, no one can begin a legitimate transaction before you start your cleanup. Example 5-1 contains a bit of shell-scripting that can quickly generate information about each outstanding transaction in your repository.

Example 5-1. txn-info.sh (reporting outstanding transactions)

```
#!/bin/sh

### Generate informational output for all outstanding transactions in
### a Subversion repository.

REPOS="${1}"
if [ "x$REPOS" = x ] ; then
  echo "usage: $0 REPOS_PATH"
  exit
fi
```

```
for TXN in 'svnadmin lstxns ${REPOS}'; do
  echo "---[ Transaction ${TXN} ]----------------------------------------"
  svnlook info "${REPOS}" -t "${TXN}"
done
```

The output of the script is basically a concatenation of several chunks of *svnlook info*
output (see "svnlook" on page 159) and will look something like this:

```
$ txn-info.sh myrepos
---[ Transaction 19 ]-------------------------------------
sally
2001-09-04 11:57:19 -0500 (Tue, 04 Sep 2001)
0
---[ Transaction 3a1 ]-------------------------------------
harry
2001-09-10 16:50:30 -0500 (Mon, 10 Sep 2001)
39
Trying to commit over a faulty network.
---[ Transaction a45 ]-------------------------------------
sally
2001-09-12 11:09:28 -0500 (Wed, 12 Sep 2001)
0
$
```

A long-abandoned transaction usually represents some sort of failed or interrupted
commit. A transaction's datestamp can provide interesting information—for example,
how likely is it that an operation begun nine months ago is still active?

In short, transaction cleanup decisions need not be made unwisely. Various sources of
information—including Apache's error and access logs, Subversion's operational logs,
Subversion revision history, and so on—can be employed in the decision-making process. And of course, an administrator can often simply communicate with a seemingly
dead transaction's owner (e.g., via email) to verify that the transaction is, in fact, in a
zombie state.

Purging unused Berkeley DB logfiles

Until recently, the largest offender of disk space usage with respect to BDB-backed
Subversion repositories were the logfiles in which Berkeley DB performs its prewrites
before modifying the actual database files. These files capture all the actions taken along
the route of changing the database from one state to another—while the database files,
at any given time, reflect a particular state, the logfiles contain all of the many changes
along the way *between* states. Thus, they can grow and accumulate quite rapidly.

Fortunately, beginning with the 4.2 release of Berkeley DB, the database environment
has the ability to remove its own unused logfiles automatically. Any repositories created
using *svnadmin* when compiled against Berkeley DB version 4.2 or later will be configured for this automatic logfile removal. If you don't want this feature enabled, simply
pass the --bdb-log-keep option to the *svnadmin create* command. If you forget to do
this or change your mind at a later time, simply edit the *DB_CONFIG* file found in

your repository's *db* directory, comment out the line that contains the `set_flags DB_LOG_AUTOREMOVE` directive, and then run *svnadmin recover* on your repository to force the configuration changes to take effect. See "Berkeley DB Configuration" on page 158 for more information about database configuration.

Without some sort of automatic logfile removal in place, logfiles will accumulate as you use your repository. This is actually something of a feature of the database system— you should be able to recreate your entire database using nothing but the logfiles, so these files can be useful for catastrophic database recovery. But typically, you'll want to archive the logfiles that are no longer in use by Berkeley DB and then remove them from disk to conserve space. Use the *svnadmin list-unused-dblogs* command to list the unused logfiles:

```
$ svnadmin list-unused-dblogs /var/svn/repos
/var/svn/repos/log.0000000031
/var/svn/repos/log.0000000032
/var/svn/repos/log.0000000033
...
$ rm 'svnadmin list-unused-dblogs /var/svn/repos'
## disk space reclaimed!
```

BDB-backed repositories whose logfiles are used as part of a backup or disaster recovery plan should *not* make use of the logfile autoremoval feature. Reconstruction of a repository's data from logfiles can only be accomplished only when *all* the logfiles are available. If some of the logfiles are removed from disk before the backup system has a chance to copy them elsewhere, the incomplete set of backed-up logfiles is essentially useless.

Berkeley DB Recovery

As mentioned in "Berkeley DB" on page 152, a Berkeley DB repository can sometimes be left in a frozen state if not closed properly. When this happens, an administrator needs to rewind the database back into a consistent state. This is unique to BDB-backed repositories, though—if you are using FSFS-backed ones instead, this won't apply to you. And for those of you using Subversion 1.4 with Berkeley DB 4.4 or later, you should find that Subversion has become much more resilient in these types of situations. Still, wedged Berkeley DB repositories do occur, and an administrator needs to know how to safely deal with this circumstance.

To protect the data in your repository, Berkeley DB uses a locking mechanism. This mechanism ensures that portions of the database are not simultaneously modified by multiple database accessors, and that each process sees the data in the correct state when that data is being read from the database. When a process needs to change something in the database, it first checks for the existence of a lock on the target data. If the data is not locked, the process locks the data, makes the change it wants to make, and then unlocks the data. Other processes are forced to wait until that lock is removed before they are permitted to continue accessing that section of the database. (This has nothing to do with the locks that you, as a user, can apply to versioned files within the repository; we try to clear up the confusion caused by this terminology collision in the sidebar "The Three Meanings of "Lock"" on page 75.)

In the course of using your Subversion repository, fatal errors or interruptions can prevent a process from having the chance to remove the locks it has placed in the database. The result is that the backend database system gets "wedged." When this happens, any attempts to access the repository hang indefinitely (since each new accessor is waiting for a lock to go away—which isn't going to happen).

If this happens to your repository, don't panic. The Berkeley DB filesystem takes advantage of database transactions, checkpoints, and prewrite journaling to ensure that only the most catastrophic of events[†] can permanently destroy a database environment. A sufficiently paranoid repository administrator will have made off-site backups of the repository data in some fashion, but don't head off to the tape backup storage closet just yet.

Instead, use the following recipe to attempt to "unwedge" your repository:

1. Make sure no processes are accessing (or attempting to access) the repository. For networked repositories, this also means shutting down the Apache HTTP Server or svnserve daemon.

2. Become the user who owns and manages the repository. This is important, as recovering a repository while running as the wrong user can tweak the permissions of the repository's files in such a way that your repository will still be inaccessible even after it is "unwedged."

3. Run the command svnadmin recover /var/svn/repos. You should see output such as this:

   ```
   Repository lock acquired.
   Please wait; recovering the repository may take some time...

   Recovery completed.
   The latest repos revision is 19.
   ```

   This command may take many minutes to complete.

4. Restart the server process.

This procedure fixes almost every case of repository wedging. Make sure that you run this command as the user who owns and manages the database, not just as root. Part of the recovery process might involve re-creating from scratch various database files (e.g., shared memory regions). Recovering as root will create those files such that they are owned by root, which means that even after you restore connectivity to your repository, regular users will be unable to access it.

[†] For example, hard drive + huge electromagnet = disaster.

If the procedure just shown, for some reason, does not successfully unwedge your repository, you should do two things. First, move your broken repository directory aside (perhaps by renaming it to something like *repos.BROKEN*) and then restore your latest backup of it. Then, send an email to the Subversion users mailing list (at *users@subversion.tigris.org*) describing your problem in detail. Data integrity is an extremely high priority to the Subversion developers.

Migrating Repository Data Elsewhere

A Subversion filesystem has its data spread throughout files in the repository, in a fashion generally understood by (and of interest to) only the Subversion developers themselves. However, circumstances may arise that call for all, or some subset, of that data to be copied or moved into another repository.

Subversion provides such functionality by way of *repository dump streams*. A repository dump stream (often referred to as a "dump file" when stored as a file on disk) is a portable, flat file format that describes the various revisions in your repository—what was changed, by whom, when, and so on. This dump stream is the primary mechanism used to marshal versioned history—in whole or in part, with or without modification—between repositories. And Subversion provides the tools necessary for creating and loading these dump streams: the *svnadmin dump* and *svnadmin load* subcommands, respectively.

While the Subversion repository dump format contains human-readable portions and a familiar structure (it resembles an RFC 822 format, the same type of format used for most email), it is *not* a plain-text file format. It is a binary file format, highly sensitive to meddling. For example, many text editors will corrupt the file by automatically converting line endings.

There are many reasons for dumping and loading Subversion repository data. Early in Subversion's life, the most common reason was due to the evolution of Subversion itself. As Subversion matured, there were times when changes made to the backend database schema caused compatibility issues with previous versions of the repository, so users had to dump their repository data using the previous version of Subversion and load it into a freshly created repository with the new version of Subversion. Now, these types of schema changes haven't occurred since Subversion's 1.0 release, and the Subversion developers promise not to force users to dump and load their repositories when upgrading between minor versions (such as from 1.3 to 1.4) of Subversion. But there are still other reasons for dumping and loading, including re-deploying a Berkeley DB repository on a new OS or CPU architecture, switching between the Berkeley DB and FSFS backends, or (as we'll cover later in "Filtering Repository History" on page 173) purging versioned data from repository history.

The Subversion repository dump format describes versioned repository changes only. It will not carry any information about uncommitted transactions, user locks on filesystem paths, repository or server configuration customizations (including hook scripts), and so on.

Whatever your reason for migrating repository history, using the *svnadmin dump* and *svnadmin load* subcommands is straightforward. *svnadmin dump* will output a range of repository revisions that are formatted using Subversion's custom filesystem dump format. The dump format is printed to the standard output stream, while informative messages are printed to the standard error stream. This allows you to redirect the output stream to a file while watching the status output in your terminal window. For example:

```
$ svnlook youngest myrepos
26
$ svnadmin dump myrepos > dumpfile
* Dumped revision 0.
* Dumped revision 1.
* Dumped revision 2.
...
* Dumped revision 25.
* Dumped revision 26.
```

At the end of the process, you will have a single file (*dumpfile* in the previous example) that contains all the data stored in your repository in the requested range of revisions. Note that *svnadmin dump* is reading revision trees from the repository just like any other "reader" process would (e.g., *svn checkout*), so it's safe to run this command at any time.

The other subcommand in the pair, *svnadmin load*, parses the standard input stream as a Subversion repository dump file and effectively replays those dumped revisions into the target repository for that operation. It also gives informative feedback, this time using the standard output stream:

```
$ svnadmin load newrepos < dumpfile
<<< Started new txn, based on original revision 1
     * adding path : A ... done.
     * adding path : A/B ... done.
     ...
------- Committed new rev 1 (loaded from original rev 1) >>>

<<< Started new txn, based on original revision 2
     * editing path : A/mu ... done.
     * editing path : A/D/G/rho ... done.

------- Committed new rev 2 (loaded from original rev 2) >>>

...

<<< Started new txn, based on original revision 25
     * editing path : A/D/gamma ... done.
```

```
------- Committed new rev 25 (loaded from original rev 25) >>>

<<< Started new txn, based on original revision 26
    * adding path : A/Z/zeta ... done.
    * editing path : A/mu ... done.

------- Committed new rev 26 (loaded from original rev 26) >>>
```

The result of a load is new revisions added to a repository—the same thing you get by making commits against that repository from a regular Subversion client. Just as in a commit, you can use hook programs to perform actions before and after each of the commits made during a load process. By passing the `--use-pre-commit-hook` and `--use-post-commit-hook` options to *svnadmin load*, you can instruct Subversion to execute the `pre-commit` and `post-commit` hook programs, respectively, for each loaded revision. You might use these, for example, to ensure that loaded revisions pass through the same validation steps that regular commits pass through. Of course, you should use these options with care; if your `post-commit` hook sends emails to a mailing list for each new commit, you might not want to spew hundreds or thousands of commit emails in rapid succession at that list! You can read more about the use of hook scripts in "Implementing Repository Hooks" on page 156.

Note that because *svnadmin* uses standard input and output streams for the repository dump and load processes, people who are feeling especially saucy can try things such as this (perhaps even using different versions of *svnadmin* on each side of the pipe):

```
$ svnadmin create newrepos
$ svnadmin dump oldrepos | svnadmin load newrepos
```

By default, the dump file will be quite large—much larger than the repository itself. That's because by default every version of every file is expressed as a full text in the dump file. This is the fastest and simplest behavior, and it's nice if you're piping the dump data directly into some other process (such as a compression program, filtering program, or loading process). But if you're creating a dump file for longer-term storage, you'll likely want to save disk space by using the `--deltas` option. With this option, successive revisions of files will be output as compressed, binary differences—just as file revisions are stored in a repository. This option is slower, but it results in a dump file much closer in size to the original repository.

We mentioned previously that *svnadmin dump* outputs a range of revisions. Use the `--revision` (`-r`) option to specify a single revision, or a range of revisions, to dump. If you omit this option, all the existing repository revisions will be dumped:

```
$ svnadmin dump myrepos -r 23 > rev-23.dumpfile
$ svnadmin dump myrepos -r 100:200 > revs-100-200.dumpfile
```

As Subversion dumps each new revision, it outputs only enough information to allow a future loader to re-create that revision based on the previous one. In other words, for any given revision in the dump file, only the items that were changed in that revision will appear in the dump. The only exception to this rule is the first revision that is dumped with the current *svnadmin dump* command.

By default, Subversion will not express the first dumped revision as merely differences to be applied to the previous revision. For one thing, there is no previous revision in the dump file! And second, Subversion cannot know the state of the repository into which the dump data will be loaded (if it ever is). To ensure that the output of each execution of *svnadmin dump* is self-sufficient, the first dumped revision is, by default, a full representation of every directory, file, and property in that revision of the repository.

However, you can change this default behavior. If you add the `--incremental` option when you dump your repository, *svnadmin* will compare the first dumped revision against the previous revision in the repository—the same way it treats every other revision that gets dumped. It will then output the first revision exactly as it does the rest of the revisions in the dump range—mentioning only the changes that occurred in that revision. The benefit of this is that you can create several small dump files that can be loaded in succession, instead of one large one, like so:

```
$ svnadmin dump myrepos -r 0:1000 > dumpfile1
$ svnadmin dump myrepos -r 1001:2000 --incremental > dumpfile2
$ svnadmin dump myrepos -r 2001:3000 --incremental > dumpfile3
```

These dump files could be loaded into a new repository with the following command sequence:

```
$ svnadmin load newrepos < dumpfile1
$ svnadmin load newrepos < dumpfile2
$ svnadmin load newrepos < dumpfile3
```

Another neat trick you can perform with this `--incremental` option involves appending to an existing dump file a new range of dumped revisions. For example, you might have a `post-commit` hook that simply appends the repository dump of the single revision that triggered the hook. Or you might have a script that runs nightly to append dump file data for all the revisions that were added to the repository since the last time the script ran. Used like this, *svnadmin dump* can be one way to back up changes to your repository over time in case of a system crash or some other catastrophic event.

The dump format can also be used to merge the contents of several different repositories into a single repository. By using the `--parent-dir` option of *svnadmin load*, you can specify a new virtual root directory for the load process. That means if you have dump files for three repositories—say *calc-dumpfile*, *cal-dumpfile*, and *ss-dumpfile*—you can first create a new repository to hold them all:

```
$ svnadmin create /var/svn/projects
$
```

Then, make new directories in the repository that will encapsulate the contents of each of the three previous repositories:

```
$ svn mkdir -m "Initial project roots" \
      file:///var/svn/projects/calc \
      file:///var/svn/projects/calendar \
      file:///var/svn/projects/spreadsheet
Committed revision 1.
$
```

Lastly, load the individual dump files into their respective locations in the new repository:

```
$ svnadmin load /var/svn/projects --parent-dir calc < calc-dumpfile
…
$ svnadmin load /var/svn/projects --parent-dir calendar < cal-dumpfile
…
$ svnadmin load /var/svn/projects --parent-dir spreadsheet < ss-dumpfile
…
$
```

We'll mention one final way to use the Subversion repository dump format—conversion from a different storage mechanism or version control system altogether. Because the dump file format is, for the most part, human-readable, it should be relatively easy to describe generic sets of changes—each of which should be treated as a new revision— using this file format. In fact, the *cvs2svn* utility (see "Converting a Repository from CVS to Subversion" on page 375) uses the dump format to represent the contents of a CVS repository so that those contents can be copied into a Subversion repository.

Filtering Repository History

Since Subversion stores your versioned history using, at the very least, binary differencing algorithms and data compression (optionally in a completely opaque database system), attempting manual tweaks is unwise, if not quite difficult, and at any rate is strongly discouraged. And once data has been stored in your repository, Subversion generally doesn't provide an easy way to remove that data.[‡] But inevitably, there will be times when you would like to manipulate the history of your repository. You might need to strip out all instances of a file that was accidentally added to the repository (and shouldn't be there for whatever reason).[§] Or perhaps you have multiple projects sharing a single repository, and you decide to split them up into their own repositories. To accomplish tasks such as these, administrators need a more manageable and malleable representation of the data in their repositories—the Subversion repository dump format.

As we described earlier in "Migrating Repository Data Elsewhere" on page 169, the Subversion repository dump format is a human-readable representation of the changes

---

[‡] That's rather the reason you use version control at all, right?

[§] Conscious, cautious removal of certain bits of versioned data is actually supported by real use cases. That's why an "obliterate" feature has been one of the most highly requested Subversion features, and one that the Subversion developers hope to soon provide.

that you've made to your versioned data over time. Use the *svnadmin dump* command to generate the dump data, and use *svnadmin load* to populate a new repository with it. The great thing about the human-readability aspect of the dump format is that, if you aren't careless about it, you can manually inspect and modify it. Of course, the downside is that if you have three years' worth of repository activity encapsulated in what is likely to be a very large dump file, it could take you a long, long time to manually inspect and modify it.

That's where *svndumpfilter* becomes useful. This program acts as a path-based filter for repository dump streams. Simply give it either a list of paths you wish to keep or a list of paths you wish not to keep, and then pipe your repository dump data through this filter. The result will be a modified stream of dump data that contains only the versioned paths you (explicitly or implicitly) requested.

Let's look at a realistic example of how you might use this program. Earlier in this chapter (see "Planning Your Repository Organization" on page 147), we discussed the process of deciding how to choose a layout for the data in your repositories—using one repository per project or combining them, arranging stuff within your repository, and so on. But sometimes after new revisions start flying in, you rethink your layout and would like to make some changes. A common change is the decision to move multiple projects that are sharing a single repository into separate repositories for each project.

Our imaginary repository contains three projects: calc, calendar, and spreadsheet. They have been living side-by-side in a layout like this:

```
/
    calc/
        trunk/
        branches/
        tags/
    calendar/
        trunk/
        branches/
        tags/
    spreadsheet/
        trunk/
        branches/
        tags/
```

To get these three projects into their own repositories, we first dump the whole repository:

```
$ svnadmin dump /var/svn/repos > repos-dumpfile
* Dumped revision 0.
* Dumped revision 1.
* Dumped revision 2.
* Dumped revision 3.
...
$
```

Next, run that dump file through the filter, each time including only one of our top-level directories. This results in three new dump files:

```
$ svndumpfilter include calc < repos-dumpfile > calc-dumpfile
...
$ svndumpfilter include calendar < repos-dumpfile > cal-dumpfile
...
$ svndumpfilter include spreadsheet < repos-dumpfile > ss-dumpfile
...
$
```

At this point, you have to make a decision. Each of your dump files will create a valid repository, but they will preserve the paths exactly as they were in the original repository. This means that even though you would have a repository solely for your calc project, that repository would still have a top-level directory named *calc*. If you want your *trunk*, *tags*, and *branches* directories to live in the root of your repository, you might wish to edit your dump files, tweaking the Node-path and Node-copyfrom-path headers so that they no longer have that first *calc/* path component. Also, you'll want to remove the section of dump data that creates the *calc* directory. It will look something like the following:

```
Node-path: calc
Node-action: add
Node-kind: dir
Content-length: 0
```

 If you do plan on manually editing the dump file to remove a top-level directory, make sure your editor is not set to automatically convert end-of-line characters to the native format (e.g., \r\n to \n), as the content will then not agree with the metadata. This will render the dump file useless.

All that remains now is to create your three new repositories, and load each dump file into the right repository, ignoring the Universal Unique Identifier (UUID) found in the dump stream:

```
$ svnadmin create calc
$ svnadmin load --ignore-uuid calc < calc-dumpfile
<<< Started new transaction, based on original revision 1
     * adding path : Makefile ... done.
     * adding path : button.c ... done.
...
$ svnadmin create calendar
$ svnadmin load --ignore-uuid calendar < cal-dumpfile
<<< Started new transaction, based on original revision 1
     * adding path : Makefile ... done.
     * adding path : cal.c ... done.
...
$ svnadmin create spreadsheet
$ svnadmin load --ignore-uuid spreadsheet < ss-dumpfile
<<< Started new transaction, based on original revision 1
```

```
    * adding path : Makefile ... done.
    * adding path : ss.c ... done.
  ...
  $
```

Both of *svndumpfilter*'s subcommands accept options for deciding how to deal with "empty" revisions. If a given revision contains only changes to paths that were filtered out, that now-empty revision could be considered uninteresting or even unwanted. So to give the user control over what to do with those revisions, *svndumpfilter* provides the following command-line options:

--drop-empty-revs

    Do not generate empty revisions at all—just omit them.

--renumber-revs

    If empty revisions are dropped (using the **--drop-empty-revs** option), change the revision numbers of the remaining revisions so that there are no gaps in the numeric sequence.

--preserve-revprops

    If empty revisions are not dropped, preserve the revision properties (log message, author, date, custom properties, etc.) for those empty revisions. Otherwise, empty revisions will contain only the original datestamp and a generated log message that indicates that this revision was emptied by *svndumpfilter*.

While *svndumpfilter* can be very useful and a huge timesaver, there are unfortunately a couple of gotchas. First, this utility is overly sensitive to path semantics. Pay attention to whether paths in your dump file are specified with or without leading slashes. You'll want to look at the Node-path and Node-copyfrom-path headers:

```
...
Node-path: spreadsheet/Makefile
...
```

If the paths have leading slashes, you should include leading slashes in the paths you pass to *svndumpfilter include* and *svndumpfilter exclude* (and if they don't, you shouldn't). Further, if your dump file has an inconsistent usage of leading slashes for some reason,[||] you should probably normalize those paths so that they all have, or all lack, leading slashes.

Also, copied paths can give you some trouble. Subversion supports copy operations in the repository, where a new path is created by copying some already existing path. It is possible that at some point in the lifetime of your repository, you might have copied a file or directory from some location that *svndumpfilter* is excluding to a location that it is including. To make the dump data self-sufficient, *svndumpfilter* needs to still show the addition of the new path—including the contents of any files created by the copy— and not represent that addition as a copy from a source that won't exist in your filtered

---

[||] While *svnadmin dump* has a consistent leading slash policy (to not include them), other programs that generate dump data might not be so consistent.

dump data stream. But because the Subversion repository dump format shows only what was changed in each revision, the contents of the copy source might not be readily available. If you suspect that you have any copies of this sort in your repository, you might want to rethink your set of included/excluded paths, perhaps including the paths that served as sources of your troublesome copy operations, too.

Finally, *svndumpfilter* takes path filtering quite literally. If you are trying to copy the history of a project rooted at *trunk/my-project* and move it into a repository of its own, you would, of course, use the *svndumpfilter include* command to keep all the changes in and under *trunk/my-project*. But the resultant dump file makes no assumptions about the repository into which you plan to load this data. Specifically, the dump data might begin with the revision that added the *trunk/my-project* directory, but it will *not* contain directives that would create the *trunk* directory itself (because *trunk* doesn't match the include filter). You'll need to make sure that any directories that the new dump stream expects to exist actually do exist in the target repository before trying to load the stream into that repository.

Repository Replication

There are several scenarios in which it is quite handy to have a Subversion repository whose version history is exactly the same as some other repository's. Perhaps the most obvious one is the maintenance of a simple backup repository, used when the primary repository has become inaccessible due to a hardware failure, network outage, or other such annoyance. Other scenarios include deploying mirror repositories to distribute heavy Subversion load across multiple servers, use as a soft-upgrade mechanism, and so on.

As of version 1.4, Subversion provides a program for managing scenarios such as these: *svnsync*. This works by essentially asking the Subversion server to "replay" revisions, one at a time. It then uses that revision information to mimic a commit of the same to another repository. Neither repository needs to be locally accessible to the machine on which *svnsync* is running—its parameters are repository URLs, and it does all its work through Subversion's Repository Access (RA) interfaces. All it requires is read access to the source repository and read/write access to the destination repository.

 When using *svnsync* against a remote source repository, the Subversion server for that repository must be running Subversion version 1.4 or later.

Assuming you already have a source repository that you'd like to mirror, the next thing you need is an empty target repository that will actually serve as that mirror. This target repository can use either of the available filesystem data-store backends (see "Choosing a Data Store" on page 150), but it must not yet have any version history in it. The protocol that *svnsync* uses to communicate revision information is highly sensitive to mismatches between the versioned histories contained in the source and target repositories. For this reason, while *svnsync* cannot *demand* that the target repository be read-only,[#] allowing the revision history in the target repository to change by any mechanism other than the mirroring process is a recipe for disaster.

 Do *not* modify a mirror repository in such a way as to cause its version history to deviate from that of the repository it mirrors. The only commits and revision property modifications that ever occur on that mirror repository should be those performed by the *svnsync* tool.

Another requirement of the target repository is that the *svnsync* process be allowed to modify revision properties. Because *svnsync* works within the framework of that repository's hook system, the default state of the repository (which is to disallow revision property changes; see "pre-revprop-change" in Chapter 9) is insufficient. You'll need to explicitly implement the `pre-revprop-change` hook, and your script must allow *svnsync* to set and change revision properties. With those provisions in place, you are ready to start mirroring repository revisions.

 It's a good idea to implement authorization measures that allow your repository replication process to perform its tasks while preventing other users from modifying the contents of your mirror repository at all.

Let's walk through the use of *svnsync* in a somewhat typical mirroring scenario. We'll pepper this discourse with practical recommendations, which you are free to disregard if they aren't required by or suitable for your environment.

As a service to the fine developers of our favorite version control system, we will be mirroring the public Subversion source code repository and exposing that mirror publicly on the Internet, hosted on a different machine from the one on which the original Subversion source code repository lives. This remote host has a global configuration that permits anonymous users to read the contents of repositories on the host, but requires users to authenticate to modify those repositories. (Please forgive us for glossing over the details of Subversion server configuration for the moment—those are covered thoroughly in Chapter 6.) And for no other reason than that it makes for a more interesting example, we'll be driving the replication process from a third machine—the one that we currently find ourselves using.

First, we'll create the repository that will be our mirror. This and the next couple of steps do require shell access to the machine on which the mirror repository will live. Once the repository is all configured, though, we shouldn't need to touch it directly again:

[#] In fact, it can't truly be read-only, or *svnsync* itself would have a tough time copying revision history into it.

```
$ ssh admin@svn.example.com \
    "svnadmin create /var/svn/svn-mirror"
admin@svn.example.com's password: ********
$
```

At this point, we have our repository, and due to our server's configuration, that repository is now "live" on the Internet. Now, because we don't want anything modifying the repository except our replication process, we need a way to distinguish that process from other would-be committers. To do so, we use a dedicated username for our process. Only commits and revision property modifications performed by the special username syncuser will be allowed.

We'll use the repository's hook system both to allow the replication process to do what it needs to do and to enforce that only it is doing those things. We accomplish this by implementing two of the repository event hooks—pre-revprop-change and start-commit. Our pre-revprop-change hook script is found in Example 5-2, and it basically verifies that the user attempting the property changes is our syncuser user. If so, the change is allowed; otherwise, it is denied.

Example 5-2. Mirror repository's pre-revprop-change hook script

```
#!/bin/sh

USER="$3"

if [ "$USER" = "syncuser" ]; then exit 0; fi

echo "Only the syncuser user may change revision properties" >&2
exit 1
```

That covers revision property changes. Now we need to ensure that only the syncuser user is permitted to commit new revisions to the repository. We do this using a start-commit hook scripts such as the one in Example 5-3.

Example 5-3. Mirror repository's start-commit hook script

```
#!/bin/sh

USER="$2"

if [ "$USER" = "syncuser" ]; then exit 0; fi

echo "Only the syncuser user may commit new revisions" >&2
exit 1
```

After installing our hook scripts and ensuring that they are executable by the Subversion server, we're finished with the setup of the mirror repository. Now, we get to actually do the mirroring.

The first thing we need to do with *svnsync* is to register in our target repository the fact that it will be a mirror of the source repository. We do this using the *svnsync initialize* subcommand. The URLs we provide point to the root directories of the target and source repositories, respectively. In Subversion 1.4, this is required—only full mirroring of repositories is permitted. In Subversion 1.5, though, you can use *svnsync* to mirror only some subtree of the repository, too:

```
$ svnsync help init
initialize (init): usage: svnsync initialize DEST_URL SOURCE_URL

Initialize a destination repository for synchronization from
another repository.
...
$ svnsync initialize http://svn.example.com/svn-mirror \
                     http://svn.collab.net/repos/svn \
                     --sync-username syncuser --sync-password syncpass
Copied properties for revision 0.
$
```

Our target repository will now remember that it is a mirror of the public Subversion source code repository. Notice that we provided a username and password as arguments to *svnsync*—that was required by the `pre-revprop-change` hook on our mirror repository.

 In Subversion 1.4, the values given to *svnsync*'s `--username` and `--password` command-line options were used for authentication against both the source and destination repositories. This caused problems when a user's credentials weren't exactly the same for both repositories, especially when running in noninteractive mode (with the `--non-interactive` option).

This has been fixed in Subversion 1.5 with the introduction of two new pairs of options. Use `--source-username` and `--source-password` to provide authentication credentials for the source repository; use `--sync-username` and `--sync-password` to provide credentials for the destination repository. (The old `--username` and `--password` options still exist for compatibility, but we advise against using them.)

And now comes the fun part. With a single subcommand, we can tell *svnsync* to copy all the as-yet-unmirrored revisions from the source repository to the target.[*] The *svnsync synchronize* subcommand will peek into the special revision properties previously stored on the target repository, and it will determine which repository it is mirroring as well as the fact that the most recently mirrored revision was revision 0. Then it will query the source repository and determine what the latest revision in that repository is. Finally, it asks the source repository's server to start replaying all the revisions between 0 and that latest revision. As *svnsync* get the resultant response from the source

---

[*] Be forewarned that although it will take only a few seconds for the average reader to parse this paragraph and the sample output that follows it, the actual time required to complete such a mirroring operation is, shall we say, quite a bit longer.

repository's server, it begins forwarding those revisions to the target repository's server as new commits:

```
$ svnsync help synchronize
synchronize (sync): usage: svnsync synchronize DEST_URL

Transfer all pending revisions to the destination from the source
with which it was initialized.
...
$ svnsync synchronize http://svn.example.com/svn-mirror
Transmitting file data .......................................
Committed revision 1.
Copied properties for revision 1.
Transmitting file data ..
Committed revision 2.
Copied properties for revision 2.
Transmitting file data .....
Committed revision 3.
Copied properties for revision 3.
...
Transmitting file data ..
Committed revision 23406.
Copied properties for revision 23406.
Transmitting file data .
Committed revision 23407.
Copied properties for revision 23407.
Transmitting file data ....
Committed revision 23408.
Copied properties for revision 23408.
$
```

Of particular interest here is that for each mirrored revision, there is first a commit of that revision to the target repository, and then property changes follow. This is because the initial commit is performed by (and attributed to) the user syncuser, and it is datestamped with the time as of that revision's creation. Also, Subversion's underlying repository access interfaces don't provide a mechanism for setting arbitrary revision properties as part of a commit. So *svnsync* follows up with an immediate series of property modifications that copy into the target repository all the revision properties found for that revision in the source repository. This also has the effect of fixing the author and datestamp of the revision to match that of the source repository.

Also noteworthy is that *svnsync* performs careful bookkeeping that allows it to be safely interrupted and restarted without ruining the integrity of the mirrored data. If a network glitch occurs while mirroring a repository, simply repeat the *svnsync synchronize* command and it will happily pick up right where it left off. In fact, as new revisions appear in the source repository, this is exactly what you to do to keep your mirror up to date.

svnsync Bookkeeping

svnsync needs to be able to set and modify revision properties on the mirror repository because those properties are part of the data it is tasked with mirroring. As those properties change in the source repository, those changes need to be reflected in the mirror repository, too. But *svnsync* also uses a set of custom revision properties—stored in revision 0 of the mirror repository—for its own internal bookkeeping. These properties contain information such as the URL and UUID of the source repository, plus some additional state-tracking information.

One of those pieces of state-tracking information is a flag that essentially just means "there's a synchronization in progress right now." This is used to prevent multiple *svnsync* processes from colliding with each other while trying to mirror data to the same destination repository. Now, generally you won't need to pay any attention whatsoever to *any* of these special properties (all of which begin with the prefix `svn:sync-`). Occasionally, though, if a synchronization fails unexpectedly, Subversion never has a chance to remove this particular state flag. This causes all future synchronization attempts to fail because it appears that a synchronization is still in progress when, in fact, none is. Fortunately, recovering from this situation is as simple as removing the `svn:sync-lock` property that serves as this flag from revision 0 of the mirror repository:

```
$ svn propdel --revprop -r0 svn:sync-lock http://svn.example.com/svn-mirror
property 'svn:sync-lock' deleted from repository revision 0
$
```

That *svnsync* stores the source repository URL in a bookkeeping property on the mirror repository is the reason why you have to specify that URL only once, during *svnsync init*. Future synchronization operations against that mirror simply consult the special `svn:sync-from-url` property stored on the mirror itself to know where to synchronize from. This value is used literally by the synchronization process, though. So while from within *CollabNet*'s network you can perhaps access our example source URL as `http://svn/repos/svn` (because that first `svn` magically gets `.collab.net` appended to it by DNS voodoo), if you later need to update that mirror from another machine outside CollabNet's network, the synchronization might fail (because the hostname `svn` is ambiguous). For this reason, it's best to use fully qualified source repository URLs when initializing a mirror repository rather than those that refer to only hostnames or IP addresses (which can change over time). But here again, if you need an existing mirror to start referring to a different URL for the same source repository, you can change the bookkeeping property that houses that information:

```
$ svn propset --revprop -r0 svn:sync-from-url NEW-SOURCE-URL \
    http://svn.example.com/svn-mirror
property 'svn:sync-from-url' set on repository revision 0
$
```

Another interesting thing about these special bookkeeping properties is that *svnsync* will not attempt to mirror any of those properties when they are found in the source repository. The reason is probably obvious, but it basically boils down to *svnsync* not being able to distinguish the special properties it has merely copied from the source repository from those it needs to consult and maintain for its own bookkeeping needs.

This situation could occur if, for example, you were maintaining a mirror of a mirror of a third repository. When *svnsync* sees its own special properties in revision 0 of the source repository, it simply ignores them.

There is, however, one bit of inelegance in the process. Because Subversion revision properties can be changed at any time throughout the lifetime of the repository, and because they don't leave an audit trail that indicates when they were changed, replication processes have to pay special attention to them. If you've already mirrored the first 15 revisions of a repository, and someone then changes a revision property on revision 12, *svnsync* won't know to go back and patch up its copy of revision 12. You'll need to tell it to do so manually by using (or with some additional tooling around) the *svnsync copy-revprops* subcommand, which simply rereplicates all the revision properties for a particular revision or range thereof:

```
$ svnsync help copy-revprops
copy-revprops: usage: svnsync copy-revprops DEST_URL [REV[:REV2]]

Copy the revision properties in a given range of revisions to the
destination from the source with which it was initialized.
...
$ svnsync copy-revprops http://svn.example.com/svn-mirror 12
Copied properties for revision 12.
$
```

That's repository replication in a nutshell. You'll likely want some automation around such a process. For example, while our example was a pull-and-push setup, you might wish to have your primary repository push changes to one or more blessed mirrors as part of its `post-commit` and `post-revprop-change` hook implementations. This would enable the mirror to be up to date in as near to real time as is likely possible.

Also, while it isn't very commonplace to do so, *svnsync* does gracefully mirror repositories in which the user as whom it authenticates has only partial read access. It simply copies only the bits of the repository that it is permitted to see. Obviously, such a mirror is not useful as a backup solution.

In Subversion 1.5, *svnsync* gained the ability to also mirror a subset of a repository rather than the whole thing. The process of setting up and maintaining such a mirror is exactly the same as when mirroring a whole repository, except that instead of specifying the source repository's root URL when running *svnsync init*, you specify the URL of some subdirectory within that repository. Synchronization to that mirror will now copy only the bits that changed under that source repository subdirectory. There are some limitations to this support, though. First, you can't mirror multiple disjoint subdirectories of the source repository into a single mirror repository—you'd need to instead mirror some parent directory that is common to both. Second, the filtering logic is entirely path-based, so if the subdirectory you are mirroring was renamed at some point in the past, your mirror would contain only the revisions since the directory appeared at the URL you specified. And likewise, if the source subdirectory is renamed in the future, your synchronization processes will stop mirroring data at the point that the source URL you specified is no longer valid.

As far as user interaction with repositories and mirrors goes, it *is* possible to have a single working copy that interacts with both, but you'll have to jump through some hoops to make it happen. First, you need to ensure that both the primary and mirror repositories have the same repository UUID (which is not the case by default). See "Managing Repository UUIDs" on page 187 later in this chapter for more about this.

Once the two repositories have the same UUID, you can use *svn switch* with the `--relocate` option to point your working copy to whichever of the repositories you wish to operate against, a process that is described in "svn switch" in Chapter 9. There is a possible danger here, though: if the primary and mirror repositories aren't in close synchronization, a working copy up to date with and pointing to the primary repository will, if relocated to point to an out-of-date mirror, become confused about the apparent sudden loss of revisions it fully expects to be present, and it will throw errors to that effect. If this occurs, you can relocate your working copy back to the primary repository and then either wait until the mirror repository is up to date, or backdate your working copy to a revision you know is present in the sync repository, and then retry the relocation.

Finally, be aware that the revision-based replication provided by *svnsync* is only that—replication of revisions. Only information carried by the Subversion repository dump file format is available for replication. As such, *svnsync* has the same sorts of limitations that the repository dump stream has, and it does not include such things as the hook implementations, repository or server configuration data, uncommitted transactions, or information about user locks on repository paths.

Repository Backup

Despite numerous advances in technology since the birth of the modern computer, one thing unfortunately rings true with crystalline clarity—sometimes things go very, very awry. Power outages, network connectivity dropouts, corrupt RAM, and crashed hard drives are but a taste of the evil that Fate is poised to unleash on even the most conscientious administrator. And so we arrive at a very important topic: how to make backup copies of your repository data.

Two types of backup methods are available for Subversion repository administrators: full and incremental. A full backup of the repository involves squirreling away in one sweeping action all the information required to fully reconstruct that repository in the event of a catastrophe. Usually, it means, quite literally, the duplication of the entire repository directory (which includes either a Berkeley DB or FSFS environment). Incremental backups are lesser things: backups of only the portion of the repository data that has changed since the previous backup.

As far as full backups go, the naïve approach might seem like a sane one, but unless you temporarily disable all other access to your repository, simply doing a recursive directory copy runs the risk of generating a faulty backup. In the case of Berkeley DB, the documentation describes a certain order in which database files can be copied that will guarantee a valid backup copy. A similar ordering exists for FSFS data. But you don't have to implement these algorithms yourself, because the Subversion development team has already done so. The *svnadmin hotcopy* command takes care of the minutia involved in making a hot backup of your repository. And its invocation is as trivial as the Unix *cp* or Windows *copy* operations:

```
$ svnadmin hotcopy /var/svn/repos /var/svn/repos-backup
```

The resultant backup is a fully functional Subversion repository, able to be dropped in as a replacement for your live repository should something go horribly wrong.

When making copies of a Berkeley DB repository, you can even instruct *svnadmin hotcopy* to purge any unused Berkeley DB logfiles (see "Purging unused Berkeley DB logfiles" on page 166) from the original repository upon completion of the copy. Simply provide the `--clean-logs` option on the command line:

```
$ svnadmin hotcopy --clean-logs /var/svn/bdb-repos /var/svn/bdb-repos-backup
```

Additional tooling around this command is available, too. The *tools/backup/* directory of the Subversion source distribution holds the *hot-backup.py* script. This script adds a bit of backup management atop *svnadmin hotcopy*, allowing you to keep only the most recent configured number of backups of each repository. It will automatically manage the names of the backed-up repository directories to avoid collisions with previous backups and will "rotate off" older backups, deleting them so that only the most recent ones remain. Even if you also have an incremental backup, you might want to run this program on a regular basis. For example, you might consider using *hot-backup.py* from a program scheduler (such as *cron* on Unix systems), which can cause it to run nightly (or at whatever granularity of time you deem safe).

Some administrators use a different backup mechanism built around generating and storing repository dump data. We described in "Migrating Repository Data Elsewhere" on page 169 how to use *svnadmin dump* with the `--incremental` option to perform an incremental backup of a given revision or range of revisions. And of course, you can achieve a full backup variation of this by omitting the `--incremental` option to that command. There is some value in these methods, in that the format of your backed-up information is flexible—it's not tied to a particular platform, versioned filesystem type, or release of Subversion or Berkeley DB. But that flexibility comes at a cost, namely that restoring that data can take a long time—longer with each new revision committed to your repository. Also, as is the case with so many of the various backup methods, revision property changes that are made to already backed-up revisions won't get picked up by a nonoverlapping, incremental dump generation. For these reasons, we recommend against relying solely on dump-based backup approaches.

As you can see, each of the various backup types and methods has its advantages and disadvantages. The easiest is by far the full hot backup, which will always result in a perfect working replica of your repository. Should something bad happen to your live repository, you can restore from the backup with a simple recursive directory copy. Unfortunately, if you are maintaining multiple backups of your repository, these full copies will each eat up just as much disk space as your live repository. Incremental backups, by contrast, tend to be quicker to generate and smaller to store. But the restoration process can be a pain, often involving applying multiple incremental backups. And other methods have their own peculiarities. Administrators need to find the balance between the cost of making the backup and the cost of restoring it.

The *svnsync* program (see "Repository Replication" on page 177) actually provides a rather handy middle-ground approach. If you are regularly synchronizing a read-only mirror with your main repository, in a pinch your read-only mirror is probably a good candidate for replacing that main repository if it falls over. The primary disadvantage of this method is that only the versioned repository data gets synchronized—repository configuration files, user-specified repository path locks, and other items that might live in the physical repository directory but not *inside* the repository's virtual versioned filesystem are not handled by *svnsync*.

In any backup scenario, repository administrators need to be aware of how modifications to unversioned revision properties affect their backups. Since these changes do not themselves generate new revisions, they will not trigger `post-commit` hooks, and may not even trigger the `pre-revprop-change` and `post-revprop-change` hooks.[†] And since you can change revision properties without respect to chronological order—you can change any revision's properties at any time—an incremental backup of the latest few revisions might not catch a property modification to a revision that was included as part of a previous backup.

Generally speaking, only the truly paranoid would need to back up their entire repository, say, every time a commit occurred. However, assuming that a given repository has some other redundancy mechanism in place with relatively fine granularity (such as per-commit emails or incremental dumps), a hot backup of the database might be something that a repository administrator would want to include as part of a system-wide nightly backup. It's your data—protect it as much as you'd like.

Often, the best approach to repository backups is a diversified one that leverages combinations of the methods described here. The Subversion developers, for example, back up the Subversion source code repository nightly using *hot-backup.py* and an off-site *rsync* of those full backups; keep multiple archives of all the commit and property change notification emails; and have repository mirrors maintained by various volunteers using *svnsync*. Your solution might be similar, but it should be catered to your needs and that delicate balance of convenience and paranoia. And whatever you do,

---

[†] *svnadmin setlog* can be called in a way that bypasses the hook interface altogether.

validate your backups from time to time—what good is a spare tire that has a hole in it? While all of this might not save your hardware from the iron fist of Fate,[‡] it should certainly help you recover from those trying times.

Managing Repository UUIDs

Subversion repositories have a Universally Unique Identifier (UUID) associated with them. This is used by Subversion clients to verify the identity of a repository when other forms of verification aren't good enough (such as checking the repository URL, which can change over time). Most Subversion repository administrators rarely, if ever, need to think about repository UUIDs as anything more than a trivial implementation detail of Subversion. Sometimes, however, there is cause for attention to this detail.

As a general rule, you want the UUIDs of your live repositories to be unique. That is, after all, the point of having UUIDs. But there are times when you want the repository UUIDs of two repositories to be exactly the same. For example, if you make a copy of a repository for backup purposes, you want the backup to be a perfect replica of the original so that, in the event that you have to restore that backup and replace the live repository, users don't suddenly see what looks like a different repository. When dumping and loading repository history (as described earlier in "Migrating Repository Data Elsewhere" on page 169), you get to decide whether to apply the UUID encapsulated in the data dump stream to the repository in which you are loading the data. The particular circumstance will dictate the correct behavior.

There are a couple of ways to set (or reset) a repository's UUID, should you need to. As of Subversion 1.5, this is as simple as using the *svnadmin setuuid* command. If you provide this subcommand with an explicit UUID, it will validate that the UUID is well-formed and then set the repository UUID to that value. If you omit the UUID, a brand-new UUID will be generated for your repository:

```
$ svnlook uuid /var/svn/repos
cf2b9d22-acb5-11dc-bc8c-05e83ce5dbec
$ svnadmin setuuid /var/svn/repos    # generate a new UUID
$ svnlook uuid /var/svn/repos
3c3c38fe-acc0-11dc-acbc-1b37ff1c8e7c
$ svnadmin setuuid /var/svn/repos \
          cf2b9d22-acb5-11dc-bc8c-05e83ce5dbec  # restore the old UUID
$ svnlook uuid /var/svn/repos
cf2b9d22-acb5-11dc-bc8c-05e83ce5dbec
$
```

For folks using versions of Subversion earlier than 1.5, these tasks are a little more complicated. You can explicitly set a repository's UUID by piping a repository dump file stub that carries the new UUID specification through svnadmin load --force-uuid *REPOS-PATH*:

[‡] You know—the collective term for all of her "fickle fingers."

```
$ svnadmin load --force-uuid /var/svn/repos <<EOF
SVN-fs-dump-format-version: 2

UUID: cf2b9d22-acb5-11dc-bc8c-05e83ce5dbec
EOF
$ svnlook uuid /var/svn/repos
cf2b9d22-acb5-11dc-bc8c-05e83ce5dbec
$
```

Having older versions of Subversion generate a brand-new UUID is not quite as simple to do, though. Your best bet here is to find some other way to generate a UUID, and then explicitly set the repository's UUID to that value.

Moving and Removing Repositories

Subversion repository data is wholly contained within the repository directory. As such, you can move a Subversion repository to some other location on disk, rename a repository, copy a repository, or delete a repository altogether using the tools provided by your operating system for manipulating directories—*mv*, *cp -a*, and *rm -r* on Unix platforms; *copy*, *move*, and *rmdir /s /q* on Windows; vast numbers of mouse and menu gyrations in various graphical file explorer applications; and so on.

Of course, there's often still more to be done when trying to cleanly effect changes such as this. For example, you might need to update your Subversion server configuration to point to the new location of a relocated repository or to remove configuration bits for a now-deleted repository. If you have automated processes that publish information from or about your repositories, they may need to be updated. Hook scripts might need to be reconfigured. Users may need to be notified. The list can go on indefinitely, or at least to the extent that you've built processes and procedures around your Subversion repository.

In the case of a copied repository, you should also consider the fact that Subversion uses repository UUIDs to distinguish repositories. If you copy a Subversion repository using a typical shell recursive copy command, you'll wind up with two repositories that are identical in every way—including their UUIDs. In some circumstances, this might be desirable. But in the instances where it is not, you'll need to generate a new UUID for one of these identical repositories. See "Managing Repository UUIDs" on page 187 for more about managing repository UUIDs.

Summary

By now, you should have a basic understanding of how to create, configure, and maintain Subversion repositories. We introduced you to the various tools that will assist you with this task. Throughout the chapter, we noted common administration pitfalls and offered suggestions for avoiding them.

All that remains is for you to decide what exciting data to store in your repository, and finally, how to make it available over a network. The next chapter is all about networking.

## CHAPTER 6

Server Configuration

A Subversion repository can be accessed simultaneously by clients running on the same machine on which the repository resides using the `file://` method. But the typical Subversion setup involves a single server machine being accessed from clients on computers all over the office—or, perhaps, all over the world.

This chapter describes how to get your Subversion repository exposed outside its host machine for use by remote clients. We will cover Subversion's currently available server mechanisms, discussing the configuration and use of each. After reading this chapter, you should be able to decide which networking setup is right for your needs as well as understand how to enable such a setup on your host computer.

Overview

Subversion was designed with an abstract network layer. This means that a repository can be programmatically accessed by any sort of server process, and the client "repository access" API allows programmers to write plug-ins that speak relevant network protocols. In theory, Subversion can use an infinite number of network implementations. In practice, there are only two servers at the time of this writing.

Apache is an extremely popular web server; using the *mod_dav_svn* module, Apache can access a repository and make it available to clients via the WebDAV/DeltaV protocol, which is an extension of HTTP. Because Apache is an extremely extensible server, it provides a number of features "for free," such as encrypted SSL communication, logging, integration with a number of third-party authentication systems, and limited built-in web browsing of repositories.

In the other corner is *svnserve*: a small, lightweight server program that speaks a custom protocol with clients. Because its protocol is explicitly designed for Subversion and is stateful (unlike HTTP), it provides significantly faster network operations—but at the cost of some features. While it can use SASL to provide a variety of authentication and encryption options, it has no logging or built-in web browsing. It is, however, extremely easy to set up and is often the best option for small teams just starting out with Subversion.

A third option is to use *svnserve* tunneled over an SSH connection. Even though this scenario still uses *svnserve*, it differs quite a bit in features from a traditional *svnserve* deployment. SSH is used to encrypt all communication. SSH is also used exclusively to authenticate, so real system accounts are required on the server host (unlike vanilla *svnserve*, which has its own private user accounts). Finally, because this setup requires that each user spawn a private, temporary *svnserve* process, it's equivalent (from a permissions point of view) to allowing a group of local users all to access the repository via `file://` URLs. Path-based access control has no meaning, since each user is accessing the repository database files directly.

Table 6-1 provides a quick summary of the three typical server deployments.

Table 6-1. Comparison of subversion server options

Feature	Apache + mod_dav_svn	svnserve	svnserve over SSH
Authentication options	HTTP(S) basic auth, X.509 certificates, LDAP, NTLM, or any other mechanism available to Apache httpd	CRAM-MD5 by default; LDAP, NTLM, or any other mechanism available to SASL	SSH
User account options	Private "users" file, or other mechanisms available to Apache httpd (LDAP, SQL, etc.)	Private "users" file, or other mechanisms available to SASL (LDAP, SQL, etc.)	System accounts
Authorization options	Read/write access can be granted over the whole repository or specified per path	Read/write access can be granted over the whole repository or specified per path	Read/write access only grantable over the whole repository
Encryption	Available via optional SSL	Available via optional SASL features	Inherent in SSH connection
Logging	Full Apache logs of each HTTP request, with optional "high-level" logging of general client operations	No logging	No logging
Interoperability	Accessible by other WebDAV clients	Talks only to svn clients	Talks only to svn clients
Web viewing	Limited built-in support, or via third-party tools such as ViewVC	Only via third-party tools such as ViewVC	Only via third-party tools such as ViewVC
Master-slave server replication	Transparent write-proxying available from slave to master	Can create only read-only slave servers	Can create only read-only slave servers
Speed	Somewhat slower	Somewhat faster	Somewhat faster
Initial setup	Somewhat complex	Extremely simple	Moderately simple

Choosing a Server Configuration

So, which server should you use? Which is best?

Obviously, there's no one answer to that question. Every team has different needs, and the different servers all represent different sets of trade-offs. The Subversion project itself doesn't endorse one server over another or consider either server more "official."

Here are some reasons why you might choose one deployment over another, as well as reasons you might *not* choose one.

The svnserve Server

Why you might want to use it:

- Quick and easy to set up.
- Network protocol is stateful and noticeably faster than WebDAV.
- No need to create system accounts on the server.
- Password is not passed over the network.

Why you might want to avoid it:

- By default, only one authentication method is available, the network protocol is not encrypted, and the server stores clear text passwords. (All these things can be changed by configuring SASL, but it's a bit more work to do.)
- No logging of any kind, not even errors.
- No built-in web browsing. (You'd have to install a separate web server and repository browsing software to add this.)

svnserve over SSH

Why you might want to use it:

- The network protocol is stateful and noticeably faster than WebDAV.
- You can take advantage of existing SSH accounts and user infrastructure.
- All network traffic is encrypted.

Why you might want to avoid it:

- Only one choice of authentication method is available.
- There is no logging of any kind, not even errors.
- It requires users to be in the same system group, or use a shared SSH key.
- If used improperly, it can lead to file permission problems.

The Apache HTTP Server

Why you might want to use it:

- It allows Subversion to use any of the numerous authentication systems already integrated with Apache.
- There is no need to create system accounts on the server.
- Full Apache logging is available.
- Network traffic can be encrypted via SSL.
- HTTP(S) can usually go through corporate firewalls.
- Built-in repository browsing is available via web browser.
- The repository can be mounted as a network drive for transparent version control (see "Autoversioning" on page 378).

Why you might want to avoid it:

- Noticeably slower than *svnserve*, because HTTP is a stateless protocol and requires more network turnarounds.
- Initial setup can be complex.

Recommendations

In general, the authors of this book recommend a vanilla *svnserve* installation for small teams just trying to get started with a Subversion server; it's the simplest to set up and has the fewest maintenance issues. You can always switch to a more complex server deployment as your needs change.

Here are some general recommendations and tips, based on years of supporting users:

- If you're trying to set up the simplest possible server for your group, a vanilla *svnserve* installation is the easiest, fastest route. Note, however, that your repository data will be transmitted in the clear over the network. If your deployment is entirely within your company's LAN or VPN, this isn't an issue. If the repository is exposed to the wide-open Internet, you might want to make sure that either the repository's contents aren't sensitive (e.g., it contains only open source code), or that you go the extra mile in configuring SASL to encrypt network communications.
- If you need to integrate with existing legacy identity systems (LDAP, Active Directory, NTLM, X.509, etc.), you must use either the Apache-based server or *svnserve* configured with SASL. If you absolutely need server-side logs of either server errors or client activities, an Apache-based server is your only option.
- If you've decided to use either Apache or stock *svnserve*, create a single *svn* user on your system and run the server process as that user. Be sure to make the repository directory wholly owned by the *svn* user as well. From a security point of view, this

keeps the repository data nicely siloed and protected by operating system filesystem permissions, changeable by only the Subversion server process itself.

- If you have an existing infrastructure that is heavily based on SSH accounts, and if your users already have system accounts on your server machine, it makes sense to deploy an *svnserve*-over-SSH solution. Otherwise, we don't widely recommend this option to the public. It's generally considered safer to have your users access the repository via (imaginary) accounts managed by *svnserve* or Apache, rather than by full-blown system accounts. If your deep desire for encrypted communication still draws you to this option, we recommend using Apache with SSL or *svnserve* with SASL encryption instead.

- Do *not* be seduced by the simple idea of having all of your users access a repository directly via `file://` URLs. Even if the repository is readily available to everyone via a network share, this is a bad idea. It removes any layers of protection between the users and the repository: users can accidentally (or intentionally) corrupt the repository database, it becomes hard to take the repository offline for inspection or upgrade, and it can lead to a mess of file permission problems (see "Supporting Multiple Repository Access Methods" on page 230). Note that this is also one of the reasons we warn against accessing repositories via `svn+ssh://` URLs—from a security standpoint, it's effectively the same as local users accessing via `file://`, and it can entail all the same problems if the administrator isn't careful.

svnserve, a Custom Server

The *svnserve* program is a lightweight server, capable of speaking to clients over TCP/IP using a custom, stateful protocol. Clients contact an *svnserve* server by using URLs that begin with the `svn://` or `svn+ssh://` scheme. This section will explain the different ways of running *svnserve*, how clients authenticate themselves to the server, and how to configure appropriate access control to your repositories.

Invoking the Server

There are a few different ways to run the *svnserve* program:

- Run *svnserve* as a standalone daemon, listening for requests.
- Have the Unix *inetd* daemon temporarily spawn *svnserve* whenever a request comes in on a certain port.
- Have SSH invoke a temporary *svnserve* over an encrypted tunnel.
- Run *svnserve* as a Microsoft Windows service.

svnserve as daemon

The easiest option is to run *svnserve* as a standalone "daemon" process. Use the `-d` option for this:

```
$ svnserve -d
$                 # svnserve is now running, listening on port 3690
```

When running *svnserve* in daemon mode, you can use the `--listen-port` and `--listen-host` options to customize the exact port and hostname to "bind" to.

Once we successfully start *svnserve* as explained previously, it makes every repository on your system available to the network. A client needs to specify an *absolute* path in the repository URL. For example, if a repository is located at */var/svn/project1*, a client would reach it via *svn://host.example.com/var/svn/project1*. To increase security, you can pass the `-r` option to *svnserve*, which restricts it to exporting only repositories below that path. For example:

```
$ svnserve -d -r /var/svn
...
```

Using the `-r` option effectively modifies the location that the program treats as the root of the remote filesystem space. Clients then use URLs that have that path portion removed from them, leaving much shorter (and much less revealing) URLs:

```
$ svn checkout svn://host.example.com/project1
...
```

svnserve via inetd

If you want *inetd* to launch the process, you need to pass the `-i` (`--inetd`) option. In the following example, we've shown the output from running `svnserve -i` at the command line, but note that this isn't how you actually start the daemon; see the paragraphs following the example for details on how to configure *inetd* to start *svnserve*:

```
$ svnserve -i
( success ( 1 2 ( ANONYMOUS ) ( edit-pipeline ) ) )
```

When invoked with the `--inetd` option, *svnserve* attempts to speak with a Subversion client via *stdin* and *stdout* using a custom protocol. This is the standard behavior for a program being run via *inetd*. The Internet Assigned Numbers Authority (IANA) has reserved port 3690 for the Subversion protocol, so on a Unix-like system you can add lines to */etc/services* such as these (if they don't already exist):

```
svn          3690/tcp   # Subversion
svn          3690/udp   # Subversion
```

If your system is using a classic Unix-like *inetd* daemon, you can add this line to */etc/inetd.conf*:

```
svn stream tcp nowait svnowner /usr/bin/svnserve svnserve -i
```

Make sure "svnowner" is a user that has appropriate permissions to access your repositories. Now, when a client connection comes into your server on port 3690, *inetd* will spawn an *svnserve* process to service it. Of course, you may also want to add -r to the configuration line as well, to restrict which repositories are exported.

svnserve over a tunnel

A third way to invoke *svnserve* is in tunnel mode, using the -t option. This mode assumes that a remote-service program such as *rsh* or *ssh* has successfully authenticated a user and is now invoking a private *svnserve* process *as that user*. (Note that you, the user, will rarely, if ever, have reason to invoke *svnserve* with the -t at the command line; instead, the SSH daemon does so for you.) The *svnserve* program behaves normally (communicating via *stdin* and *stdout*) and assumes that the traffic is being automatically redirected over some sort of tunnel back to the client. When *svnserve* is invoked by a tunnel agent like this, be sure that the authenticated user has full read and write access to the repository database files. It's essentially the same as a local user accessing the repository via file:// URLs.

This option is described in much more detail later in this chapter in "Tunneling over SSH" on page 203.

svnserve as Windows service

If your Windows system is a descendant of Windows NT (2000, 2003, XP, or Vista), you can run *svnserve* as a standard Windows service. This is typically a much nicer experience than running it as a standalone daemon with the --daemon (-d) option. Using daemon mode requires launching a console, typing a command, and then leaving the console window running indefinitely. A Windows service, however, runs in the background, can start at boot time automatically, and can be started and stopped using the same consistent administration interface as other Windows services.

You'll need to define the new service using the command-line tool *SC.EXE*. Much like the *inetd* configuration line, you must specify an exact invocation of *svnserve* for Windows to run at startup time:

```
C:\> sc create svn
        binpath= "C:\svn\bin\svnserve.exe --service -r C:\repos"
        displayname= "Subversion Server"
        depend= Tcpip
        start= auto
```

This defines a new Windows service named "svn," which executes a particular *svnserve.exe* command when started (in this case, rooted at *C:\repos*). However, there are a number of caveats in the prior example.

First, notice that the *svnserve.exe* program must always be invoked with the --service option. Any other options to *svnserve* must then be specified on the same line, but you cannot add conflicting options such as --daemon (-d), --tunnel, or --inetd (-i). Options such as -r or --listen-port are fine, though. Second, be careful about spaces when invoking the *SC.EXE* command: the key= value patterns must have no spaces between key= and must have exactly one space before the value. Lastly, be careful about spaces in your command line to be invoked. If a directory name contains spaces (or other characters that need escaping), place the entire inner value of binpath in double quotes, by escaping them:

```
C:\> sc create svn
        binpath= "\"C:\program files\svn\bin\svnserve.exe\" --service -r C:\repos"
        displayname= "Subversion Server"
        depend= Tcpip
        start= auto
```

Also note that the word binpath is misleading—its value is a *command line*, not the path to an executable. That's why you need to surround it with quotes if it contains embedded spaces.

Once the service is defined, it can be stopped, started, or queried using standard GUI tools (the Services administrative control panel) or at the command line:

```
C:\> net stop svn
C:\> net start svn
```

The service can also be uninstalled (i.e., undefined) by deleting its definition: sc delete svn. Just be sure to stop the service first! The *SC.EXE* program has many other sub-commands and options; run sc /? to learn more about it.

Built-in Authentication and Authorization

When a client connects to an *svnserve* process, the following things happen:

- The client selects a specific repository.
- The server processes the repository's *conf/svnserve.conf* file and begins to enforce any authentication and authorization policies it describes.
- Depending on the defined policies, one of the following may occur:
  —The client may be allowed to make requests anonymously, without ever receiving an authentication challenge.
  —The client may be challenged for authentication at any time.
  —If operating in tunnel mode, the client will declare itself to be already externally authenticated (typically by SSH).

The *svnserve* server, by default, knows only how to send a CRAM-MD5[*] authentication challenge. In essence, the server sends a small amount of data to the client. The client uses the MD5 hash algorithm to create a fingerprint of the data and password combined, and then sends the fingerprint as a response. The server performs the same computation with the stored password to verify that the result is identical. *At no point does the actual password travel over the network.*

---

[*] See RFC 2195.

If your *svnserve* server was built with SASL support, it not only knows how to send CRAM-MD5 challenges, but also likely knows a whole host of other authentication mechanisms. See "Using svnserve with SASL" on page 201 to learn how to configure SASL authentication and encryption.

It's also possible, of course, for the client to be externally authenticated via a tunnel agent, such as *ssh*. In that case, the server simply examines the user it's running as and uses this name as the authenticated username. For more on this, see "Tunneling over SSH" on page 203.

As you've already guessed, a repository's *svnserve.conf* file is the central mechanism for controlling authentication and authorization policies. The file has the same format as other configuration files (see "Runtime Configuration Area" on page 233): section names are marked by square brackets ([and]), comments begin with hashes (#), and each section contains specific variables that can be set (`variable = value`). Let's walk through these files and learn how to use them.

Create a users file and realm

For now, the [general] section of *svnserve.conf* has all the variables you need. Begin by changing the values of those variables—choose a name for a file that will contain your usernames and passwords, and choose an authentication realm:

```
[general]
password-db = userfile
realm = example realm
```

The `realm` is a name that you define. It tells clients which sort of "authentication namespace" they're connecting to; the Subversion client displays it in the authentication prompt and uses it as a key (along with the server's hostname and port) for caching credentials on disk (see "Client Credentials Caching" on page 97). The `password-db` variable points to a separate file that contains a list of usernames and passwords, using the same familiar format. For example:

```
[users]
harry = foopassword
sally = barpassword
```

The value of `password-db` can be an absolute or relative path to the users file. For many admins, it's easy to keep the file right in the *conf/* area of the repository, alongside *svnserve.conf*. On the other hand, it's possible you may want to have two or more repositories share the same users file; in that case, the file should probably live in a more public place. The repositories sharing the users file should also be configured to have the same realm, since the list of users essentially defines an authentication realm. Wherever the file lives, be sure to set the file's read and write permissions appropriately. If you know which user(s) *svnserve* will run as, restrict read access to the users file as necessary.

Set access controls

There are two more variables to set in the *svnserve.conf* file: they determine what unauthenticated (anonymous) and authenticated users are allowed to do. The variables `anon-access` and `auth-access` can be set to the value `none`, `read`, or `write`. Setting the value to `none` prohibits both reading and writing; `read` allows read-only access to the repository, and `write` allows complete read/write access to the repository. For example:

```
[general]
password-db = userfile
realm = example realm

# anonymous users can only read the repository
anon-access = read

# authenticated users can both read and write
auth-access = write
```

The example settings are, in fact, the default values of the variables, should you forget to define them. If you want to be even more conservative, you can block anonymous access completely:

```
[general]
password-db = userfile
realm = example realm

# anonymous users aren't allowed
anon-access = none

# authenticated users can both read and write
auth-access = write
```

The server process understands not only these "blanket" access controls to the repository, but also finer-grained access restrictions placed on specific files and directories within the repository. To make use of this feature, you need to define a file containing more detailed rules, and then set the `authz-db` variable to point to it:

```
[general]
password-db = userfile
realm = example realm

# Specific access rules for specific locations
authz-db = authzfile
```

We discuss the syntax of the *authzfile* file in detail later in "Path-Based Authorization" on page 226. Note that the `authz-db` variable isn't mutually exclusive with the `anon-access` and `auth-access` variables; if all the variables are defined at once, *all* of the rules must be satisfied before access is allowed.

Using svnserve with SASL

For many teams, the built-in CRAM-MD5 authentication is all they need from *svnserve*. However, if your server (and your Subversion clients) were built with the Cyrus Simple Authentication and Security Layer (SASL) library, you have a number of authentication and encryption options available to you.

What Is SASL?

The Cyrus Simple Authentication and Security Layer is open source software written by Carnegie Mellon University. It adds generic authentication and encryption capabilities to any network protocol, and as of Subversion 1.5, both the *svnserve* server and *svn* client know how to make use of this library. It may or may not be available to you: if you're building Subversion yourself, you'll need to have at least version 2.1 of SASL installed on your system, and you'll need to make sure that it's detected during Subversion's build process. If you're using a prebuilt Subversion binary package, you'll have to check with the package maintainer as to whether SASL support was compiled in. SASL comes with a number of pluggable modules that represent different authentication systems: Kerberos (GSSAPI), NTLM, One-Time-Passwords (OTP), DIGEST-MD5, LDAP, Secure-Remote-Password (SRP), and others. Certain mechanisms may or may not be available to you; be sure to check which modules are provided.

You can download Cyrus SASL (both code and documentation) from *http://asg.web.cmu.edu/sasl/sasl-library.html*.

Normally, when a subversion client connects to *svnserve*, the server sends a greeting that advertises a list of the capabilities it supports, and the client responds with a similar list of capabilities. If the server is configured to require authentication, it then sends a challenge that lists the authentication mechanisms available; the client responds by choosing one of the mechanisms, and then authentication is carried out in some number of round-trip messages. Even when SASL capabilities aren't present, the client and server inherently know how to use the CRAM-MD5 and ANONYMOUS mechanisms (see "Built-in Authentication and Authorization" on page 198). If server and client were linked against SASL, a number of other authentication mechanisms may also be available. However, you'll need to explicitly configure SASL on the server side to advertise them.

Authenticating with SASL

To activate specific SASL mechanisms on the server, you'll need to do two things. First, create a [sasl] section in your repository's *svnserve.conf* file with an initial key-value pair:

```
[sasl]
use-sasl = true
```

Second, create a main SASL configuration file called *svn.conf* in a place where the SASL library can find it—typically in the directory where SASL plug-ins are located. You'll have to locate the plug-in directory on your particular system, such as */usr/lib/sasl2/* or */etc/sasl2/*. (Note that this is *not* the *svnserve.conf* file that lives within a repository!)

On a Windows server, you'll also have to edit the system registry (using a tool such as *regedit*) to tell SASL where to find things. Create a registry key named [HKEY_LOCAL_MACHINE\SOFTWARE\Carnegie Mellon\Project Cyrus\SASL Library], and place two keys inside it: a key called SearchPath (whose value is a path to the directory containing the SASL *sasl*.dll* plug-in libraries), and a key called ConfFile (whose value is a path to the parent directory containing the *svn.conf* file you created).

Because SASL provides so many different kinds of authentication mechanisms, it would be foolish (and far beyond the scope of this book) to try to describe every possible server-side configuration. Instead, we recommend that you read the documentation supplied in the *doc/* subdirectory of the SASL source code. It goes into great detail about every mechanism and how to configure the server appropriately for each. For the purposes of this discussion, we'll just demonstrate a simple example of configuring the DIGEST-MD5 mechanism. For example, if your *subversion.conf* (or *svn.conf*) file contains the following:

```
pwcheck_method: auxprop
auxprop_plugin: sasldb
sasldb_path: /etc/my_sasldb
mech_list: DIGEST-MD5
```

you've told SASL to advertise the DIGEST-MD5 mechanism to clients and to check user passwords against a private password database located at */etc/my_sasldb*. A system administrator can then use the *saslpasswd2* program to add or modify usernames and passwords in the database:

```
$ saslpasswd2 -c -f /etc/my_sasldb -u realm username
```

A few words of warning: first, make sure the "realm" argument to *saslpasswd2* matches the same realm you've defined in your repository's *svnserve.conf* file; if they don't match, authentication will fail. Also, due to a shortcoming in SASL, the common realm must be a string with no space characters. Finally, if you decide to go with the standard SASL password database, make sure the *svnserve* program has read access to the file (and possibly write access as well, if you're using a mechanism such as OTP).

This is just one simple way of configuring SASL. Many other authentication mechanisms are available, and passwords can be stored in other places such as in LDAP or a SQL database. Consult the full SASL documentation for details.

Remember that if you configure your server to allow only certain SASL authentication mechanisms, this forces all connecting clients to have SASL support as well. Any Subversion client built without SASL support (which includes all pre-1.5 clients) will be unable to authenticate. On the one hand, this sort of restriction may be exactly what you want ("My clients must all use Kerberos!"). However, if you still want non-SASL clients to be able to authenticate, be sure to advertise the CRAM-MD5 mechanism as an option. All clients are able to use CRAM-MD5, whether they have SASL capabilities or not.

SASL encryption

SASL is also able to perform data encryption if a particular mechanism supports it. The built-in CRAM-MD5 mechanism doesn't support encryption, but DIGEST-MD5 does, and mechanisms such as SRP actually require use of the OpenSSL library. To enable or disable different levels of encryption, you can set two values in your repository's *svnserve.conf* file:

```
[sasl]
use-sasl = true
min-encryption = 128
max-encryption = 256
```

The `min-encryption` and `max-encryption` variables control the level of encryption demanded by the server. To disable encryption completely, set both values to 0. To enable simple checksumming of data (i.e., prevent tampering and guarantee data integrity without encryption), set both values to 1. If you wish to allow—but not require—encryption, set the minimum value to 0, and the maximum value to some bit length. To require encryption unconditionally, set both values to numbers greater than 1. In our previous example, we require clients to do at least 128-bit encryption but no more than 256-bit encryption.

Tunneling over SSH

svnserve's built-in authentication (and SASL support) can be very handy because it avoids the need to create real system accounts. However, some administrators already have well-established SSH authentication frameworks in place. In these situations, all of the project's users already have system accounts and the ability to "SSH into" the server machine.

It's easy to use SSH in conjunction with *svnserve*. The client simply uses the **svn +ssh://** URL scheme to connect:

```
$ whoami
harry

$ svn list svn+ssh://host.example.com/repos/project
harryssh@host.example.com's password:  *****

foo
bar
baz
...
```

In this example, the Subversion client is invoking a local *ssh* process, connecting to host.example.com, authenticating as the user harryssh (according to SSH user configuration), and then spawning a private *svnserve* process on the remote machine running as the user harryssh. The *svnserve* command is being invoked in tunnel mode (-t), and its network protocol is being "tunneled" over the encrypted connection by *ssh*, the tunnel agent. If the client performs a commit, the authenticated username harryssh will be used as the author of the new revision.

The important thing to understand here is that the Subversion client is *not* connecting to a running *svnserve* daemon. This method of access doesn't require a daemon, nor does it notice one if present. It relies wholly on the ability of *ssh* to spawn a temporary *svnserve* process, which then terminates when the network connection is closed.

When using svn+ssh:// URLs to access a repository, remember that it's the *ssh* program prompting for authentication, *not* the *svn* client program. That means there's no automatic password-caching going on (see "Client Credentials Caching" on page 97). The Subversion client often makes multiple connections to the repository, though users don't normally notice this due to the password-caching feature. When using svn+ssh:// URLs, however, users may be annoyed by *ssh* repeatedly asking for a password for every outbound connection. The solution is to use a separate SSH password-caching tool such as *ssh-agent* on a Unix-like system, or *pageant* on Windows.

When running over a tunnel, authorization is primarily controlled by operating system permissions to the repository's database files; it's very much the same as if Harry were accessing the repository directly via a file:// URL. If multiple system users are going to be accessing the repository directly, you may want to place them into a common group, and you'll need to be careful about umasks (be sure to read "Supporting Multiple Repository Access Methods" on page 230 later in this chapter). But even in the case of tunneling, you can still use the *svnserve.conf* file to block access, simply by setting auth-access = read or auth-access = none.[†]

You'd think that the story of SSH tunneling would end here, but it doesn't. Subversion allows you to create custom tunnel behaviors in your runtime *config* file (see "Runtime Configuration Area" on page 233). For example, suppose you want to use RSH instead of SSH.[‡] In the [tunnels] section of your *config* file, simply define it like this:

```
[tunnels]
rsh = rsh
```

And now, you can use this new tunnel definition by using a URL scheme that matches the name of your new variable: svn+rsh://host/path. When using the new URL scheme, the Subversion client will actually be running the command rsh host svnserve -t behind the scenes. If you include a username in the URL (for example,

---

[†] Note that using any sort of *svnserve*-enforced access control at all is a bit pointless; the user already has direct access to the repository database.

[‡] We don't actually recommend this, since RSH is notably less secure than SSH.

svn+rsh://username@host/path), the client will also include that in its command (rsh username@host svnserve -t). But you can define new tunneling schemes to be much more clever than that:

```
[tunnels]
joessh = $JOESSH /opt/alternate/ssh -p 29934
```

This example demonstrates a couple of things. First, it shows how to make the Subversion client launch a very specific tunneling binary (the one located at */opt/alternate/ ssh*) with specific options. In this case, accessing an svn+joessh:// URL would invoke the particular SSH binary with -p 29934 as arguments—useful if you want the tunnel program to connect to a nonstandard port.

Second, it shows how to define a custom environment variable that can override the name of the tunneling program. Setting the SVN_SSH environment variable is a convenient way to override the default SSH tunnel agent. But if you need to have several different overrides for different servers, each perhaps contacting a different port or passing a different set of options to SSH, you can use the mechanism demonstrated in this example. Now if we were to set the JOESSH environment variable, its value would override the entire value of the tunnel variable—*$JOESSH* would be executed instead of /opt/alternate/ssh -p 29934.

SSH configuration tricks

It's possible to control not only the way in which the client invokes *ssh*, but also the behavior of *sshd* on your server machine. In this section, we'll show how to control the exact *svnserve* command executed by *sshd*, as well as how to have multiple users share a single system account.

Initial setup

To begin, locate the home directory of the account you'll be using to launch *svnserve*. Make sure that the account has an SSH public/private keypair installed and that the user can log in via public-key authentication. Password authentication will not work, since all of the following SSH tricks revolve around using the SSH *authorized_keys* file.

If it doesn't already exist, create the *authorized_keys* file (on Unix, typically ~/.ssh/ *authorized_keys*). Each line in this file describes a public key that is allowed to connect. The lines are typically of the form:

```
ssh-dsa AAAABtce9euch... user@example.com
```

The first field describes the type of key, the second field is the base64-encoded key itself, and the third field is a comment. However, it's a lesser known fact that the entire line can be preceded by a command field:

```
command="program" ssh-dsa AAAABtce9euch... user@example.com
```

When the `command` field is set, the SSH daemon will run the named program instead of the typical tunnel-mode *svnserve* invocation that the Subversion client asks for. This opens the door to a number of server-side tricks. In the following examples, we abbreviate the lines of the file as:

```
command="program" TYPE KEY COMMENT
```

Controlling the invoked command

Because we can specify the executed server-side command, it's easy to name a specific *svnserve* binary to run and to pass it extra arguments:

```
command="/path/to/svnserve -t -r /virtual/root" TYPE KEY COMMENT
```

In this example, */path/to/svnserve* might be a custom wrapper script around *svnserve* that sets the umask (see "Supporting Multiple Repository Access Methods" on page 230). It also shows how to anchor *svnserve* in a virtual root directory, just as one often does when running *svnserve* as a daemon process. This might be done either to restrict access to parts of the system, or simply to relieve the user of having to type an absolute path in the `svn+ssh://` URL.

It's also possible to have multiple users share a single account. Instead of creating a separate system account for each user, generate a public/private key pair for each person. Then place each public key into the *authorized_users* file, one per line, and use the `--tunnel-user` option:

```
command="svnserve -t --tunnel-user=harry" TYPE1 KEY1 harry@example.com
command="svnserve -t --tunnel-user=sally" TYPE2 KEY2 sally@example.com
```

This example allows both Harry and Sally to connect to the same account via public key authentication. Each of them has a custom command that will be executed; the `--tunnel-user` option tells *svnserve* to assume that the named argument is the authenticated user. Without `--tunnel-user`, it would appear as though all commits were coming from the one shared system account.

A final word of caution: giving a user access to the server via a public key in a shared account might still allow other forms of SSH access, even if you've set the `command` value in *authorized_keys*. For example, the user may still get shell access through SSH or be able to perform X11 or general port forwarding through your server. To give the user as little permission as possible, you may want to specify a number of restrictive options immediately after the `command`:

```
command="svnserve -t --tunnel-user=harry",no-port-forwarding,no-agent-forw
arding,no-X11-forwarding,no-pty TYPE1 KEY1 harry@example.com
```

Note that this all must be on one line—truly on one line—since SSH *authorized_keys* files do not even allow the conventional backslash character (\) for line continuation. The only reason we've shown it with a line break is to fit it on the physical page of a book.

httpd, the Apache HTTP Server

The Apache HTTP Server is a "heavy-duty" network server that Subversion can leverage. Via a custom module, *httpd* makes Subversion repositories available to clients via the WebDAV/DeltaV protocol, which is an extension to HTTP 1.1 (go to *http://www.webdav.org/* for more information). This protocol takes the ubiquitous HTTP protocol that is the core of the World Wide Web, and adds writing—specifically, versioned writing—capabilities. The result is a standardized, robust system that is conveniently packaged as part of the Apache 2.0 software, supported by numerous operating systems and third-party products, and doesn't require network administrators to open up yet another custom port.§ While an Apache-Subversion server has more features than *svnserve*, it's also a bit more difficult to set up. With flexibility often comes more complexity.

Much of the following discussion includes references to Apache configuration directives. While some examples are given of the use of these directives, describing them in full is outside the scope of this chapter. The Apache team maintains excellent documentation, publicly available on their web site at *http://httpd.apache.org*. For example, a general reference for the configuration directives is located at *http://httpd.apache.org/docs-2.0/mod/directives.html*.

Why Apache 2?

If you're a system administrator, it's very likely that you're already running the Apache web server and have some prior experience with it. At the time of this writing, Apache 1.3 is the more popular version of Apache. The world has been somewhat slow to upgrade to the Apache 2.x series for various reasons: some people fear change, especially changing something as critical as a web server. Other people depend on plug-in modules that work only against the Apache 1.3 API, and they are waiting for a 2.x port. Whatever the reason, many people begin to worry when they first discover that Subversion's Apache module is written specifically for the Apache 2 API.

The proper response to this problem is: don't worry about it. It's easy to run Apache 1.3 and Apache 2 side by side; simply install them to separate places and use Apache 2 as a dedicated Subversion server that runs on a port other than 80. Clients can access the repository by placing the port number into the URL:

```
$ svn checkout http://host.example.com:7382/repos/project
```

Also, as you make changes to your Apache setup, it is likely that somewhere along the way a mistake will be made. If you are not already familiar with Apache's logging subsystem, you should become aware of it. In your *httpd.conf* file are directives that specify the on-disk locations of the access and error logs generated by Apache (the

---

§ They really hate doing that.

CustomLog and ErrorLog directives, respectively). Subversion's *mod_dav_svn* uses Apache's error logging interface as well. You can always browse the contents of those files for information that might reveal the source of a problem that is not clearly noticeable otherwise.

Prerequisites

To network your repository over HTTP, you basically need four components, available in two packages. You'll need Apache *httpd* 2.0, the *mod_dav* DAV module that comes with it, Subversion, and the *mod_dav_svn* filesystem provider module distributed with Subversion. Once you have all of those components, the process of networking your repository is as simple as:

- Getting httpd 2.0 up and running with the *mod_dav* module
- Installing the *mod_dav_svn* backend to *mod_dav*, which uses Subversion's libraries to access the repository
- Configuring your *httpd.conf* file to export (or expose) the repository

You can accomplish the first two items either by compiling *httpd* and Subversion from source code or by installing prebuilt binary packages of them on your system. For the most up-to-date information on how to compile Subversion for use with the Apache HTTP Server, as well as how to compile and configure Apache itself for this purpose, see the *INSTALL* file in the top level of the Subversion source code tree.

Basic Apache Configuration

Once you have all the necessary components installed on your system, all that remains is the configuration of Apache via its *httpd.conf* file. Instruct Apache to load the *mod_dav_svn* module using the LoadModule directive. This directive must precede any other Subversion-related configuration items. If your Apache was installed using the default layout, your *mod_dav_svn* module should have been installed in the *modules* subdirectory of the Apache install location (often */usr/local/apache2*). The LoadModule directive has a simple syntax, mapping a named module to the location of a shared library on disk:

```
LoadModule dav_svn_module    modules/mod_dav_svn.so
```

Note that if *mod_dav* was compiled as a shared object (instead of statically linked directly to the *httpd* binary), you'll need a similar LoadModule statement for it, too. Be sure that it comes before the *mod_dav_svn* line:

```
LoadModule dav_module        modules/mod_dav.so
LoadModule dav_svn_module    modules/mod_dav_svn.so
```

At a later location in your configuration file, you now need to tell Apache where you keep your Subversion repository (or repositories). The `Location` directive has an XML-like notation, starting with an opening tag and ending with a closing tag, with various other configuration directives in the middle. The purpose of the `Location` directive is to instruct Apache to do something special when handling requests that are directed at a given URL or one of its children. In the case of Subversion, you want Apache to simply hand off support for URLs that point at versioned resources to the DAV layer. You can instruct Apache to delegate the handling of all URLs whose path portions (the part of the URL that follows the server's name and the optional port number) begin with */repos/* to a DAV provider whose repository is located at */var/svn/repository* using the following *httpd.conf* syntax:

```
<Location /repos>
  DAV svn
  SVNPath /var/svn/repository
</Location>
```

If you plan to support multiple Subversion repositories that will reside in the same parent directory on your local disk, you can use an alternative directive—`SVNParent Path` —to indicate that common parent directory. For example, if you know you will be creating multiple Subversion repositories in a directory */var/svn* that would be accessed via URLs such as *http://my.server.com/svn/repos1*, *http://my.server.com/svn/repos2*, and so on, you could use the *httpd.conf* configuration syntax in the following example:

```
<Location /svn>
  DAV svn

  # any "/svn/foo" URL will map to a repository /var/svn/foo
  SVNParentPath /var/svn
</Location>
```

Using the previous syntax, Apache will delegate the handling of all URLs whose path portions begin with */svn/* to the Subversion DAV provider, which will then assume that any items in the directory specified by the `SVNParentPath` directive are actually Subversion repositories. This is a particularly convenient syntax in that, unlike the use of the `SVNPath` directive, you don't have to restart Apache to create and network new repositories.

Be sure that when you define your new `Location`, it doesn't overlap with other exported locations. For example, if your main `DocumentRoot` is exported to */www*, do not export a Subversion repository in `<Location /www/repos>`. If a request comes in for the URI */www/repos/foo.c*, Apache won't know whether to look for a file *repos/foo.c* in the `DocumentRoot`, or whether to delegate *mod_dav_svn* to return *foo.c* from the Subversion repository. The result is often an error from the server of the form `301 Moved Permanently`.

Server Names and the COPY Request

Subversion makes use of the COPY request type to perform server-side copies of files and directories. As part of the sanity checking done by the Apache modules, the source of the copy is expected to be located on the same machine as the destination of the copy. To satisfy this requirement, you might need to tell *mod_dav* the name you use as the hostname of your server. Generally, you can use the ServerName directive in *httpd.conf* to accomplish this:

```
ServerName svn.example.com
```

If you are using Apache's virtual hosting support via the NameVirtualHost directive, you may need to use the ServerAlias directive to specify additional names by which your server is known. Again, refer to the Apache documentation for full details.

At this stage, you should strongly consider the question of permissions. If you've been running Apache for some time now as your regular web server, you probably already have a collection of content—web pages, scripts, and such. These items have already been configured with a set of permissions that allows them to work with Apache, or more appropriately, that allows Apache to work with those files. Apache, when used as a Subversion server, will also need the correct permissions to read and write to your Subversion repository.

You will need to determine a permission system setup that satisfies Subversion's requirements without messing up any previously existing web page or script installations. This might mean changing the permissions on your Subversion repository to match those in use by other things that Apache serves for you, or it could mean using the User and Group directives in *httpd.conf* to specify that Apache should run as the user and group that owns your Subversion repository. There is no single correct way to set up your permissions, and each administrator will have different reasons for doing things a certain way. Just be aware that permission-related problems are perhaps the most common oversight when configuring a Subversion repository for use with Apache.

Authentication Options

At this point, if you configured *httpd.conf* to contain something such as the following:

```
<Location /svn>
  DAV svn
  SVNParentPath /var/svn
</Location>
```

your repository is "anonymously" accessible to the world. Until you configure some authentication and authorization policies, the Subversion repositories that you make available via the Location directive will be generally accessible to everyone. In other words:

- Anyone can use a Subversion client to check out a working copy of a repository URL (or any of its subdirectories).

- Anyone can interactively browse the repository's latest revision simply by pointing a web browser to the repository URL.

- Anyone can commit to the repository.

Of course, you might have already set up a pre-commit hook script to prevent commits (see "Implementing Repository Hooks" on page 156). But as you read on, you'll see that it's also possible to use Apache's built-in methods to restrict access in specific ways.

Setting up HTTP authentication

The easiest way to authenticate a client is via the HTTP Basic authentication mechanism, which simply uses a username and password to verify that a user is who she says she is. Apache provides an *htpasswd* utility for managing the list of acceptable usernames and passwords. Let's grant commit access to Sally and Harry. First, we need to add them to the password file:

```
$ ### First time: use -c to create the file
$ ### Use -m to use MD5 encryption of the password, which is more secure
$ htpasswd -cm /etc/svn-auth-file harry
New password: *****
Re-type new password: *****
Adding password for user harry
$ htpasswd -m /etc/svn-auth-file sally
New password: *******
Re-type new password: *******
Adding password for user sally
```

Next, you need to add some more *httpd.conf* directives inside your <Location> block to tell Apache what to do with your new password file. The AuthType directive specifies the type of authentication system to use. In this case, we want to specify the Basic authentication system. AuthName is an arbitrary name that you give for the authentication domain. Most browsers will display this name in the pop-up dialog box when the browser queries the user for her name and password. Finally, use the AuthUserFile directive to specify the location of the password file you created using *htpasswd*.

After adding these three directives, your <Location> block should look like this:

```
<Location /svn>
  DAV svn
  SVNParentPath /var/svn
  AuthType Basic
  AuthName "Subversion repository"
  AuthUserFile /etc/svn-auth-file
</Location>
```

This <Location> block is not yet complete, and it will not do anything useful. It's merely telling Apache that whenever authorization is required, Apache should harvest a username and password from the Subversion client. What's missing here, however, are directives that tell Apache *which* sorts of client requests require authorization. Wherever authorization is required, Apache will demand authentication as well. The simplest thing to do is protect all requests. Adding `Require valid-user` tells Apache that all requests require an authenticated user:

```
<Location /svn>
  DAV svn
  SVNParentPath /var/svn
  AuthType Basic
  AuthName "Subversion repository"
  AuthUserFile /etc/svn-auth-file
  Require valid-user
</Location>
```

Be sure to read the next section ("Authorization Options" on page 214) for more details on the `Require` directive and other ways to set authorization policies.

One word of warning: HTTP Basic Auth passwords pass in very nearly plain text over the network, and thus are extremely insecure.

Another option is to use Digest authentication instead of Basic. Digest authentication allows the server to verify the client's identity *without* passing the plain-text password over the network. Assuming that the client and server both know the user's password, they can verify that the password is the same by using it to apply a hashing function to a one-time bit of information. The server sends a small random-ish string to the client; the client uses the user's password to hash the string; the server then looks to see whether the hashed value is what it expected.

Configuring Apache for Digest authentication is also fairly easy and only a small variation on our prior example. Be sure to consult Apache's documentation for full details:

```
<Location /svn>
  DAV svn
  SVNParentPath /var/svn
  AuthType Digest
  AuthName "Subversion repository"
  AuthDigestDomain /svn/
  AuthUserFile /etc/svn-auth-file
  Require valid-user
</Location>
```

If you're looking for maximum security, public key cryptography is the best solution. It may be best to use some sort of SSL encryption, so that clients authenticate via `https://` instead of `http://`. At a bare minimum, you can configure Apache to use a self-signed server certificate.‖ Consult Apache's documentation (and OpenSSL documentation) about how to do that.

‖ Although self-signed server certificates are still vulnerable to a "man-in-the-middle" attack, such an attack is much more difficult for a casual observer to pull off, compared to sniffing unprotected passwords.

SSL certificate management

Businesses that need to expose their repositories for access outside the company firewall should be conscious of the possibility that unauthorized parties could be "sniffing" their network traffic. SSL makes that kind of unwanted attention less likely to result in sensitive data leaks.

If a Subversion client is compiled to use OpenSSL, it gains the ability to speak to an Apache server via `https://` URLs. The Neon library used by the Subversion client is not only able to verify server certificates, but it can also supply client certificates when challenged. When the client and server have exchanged SSL certificates and successfully authenticated one another, all further communication is encrypted via a session key.

It's beyond the scope of this book to describe how to generate client and server certificates and how to configure Apache to use them. Many other books, including Apache's own documentation, describe this task. But what we *can* cover here is how to manage server and client certificates from an ordinary Subversion client.

When speaking to Apache via `https://`, a Subversion client can receive two different types of information:

- A server certificate
- A demand for a client certificate

If the client receives a server certificate, it needs to verify that it trusts the certificate: is the server really who it claims to be? The OpenSSL library does this by examining the signer of the server certificate, or *certificate authority* (CA). If OpenSSL is unable to automatically trust the CA, or if some other problem occurs (such as an expired certificate or hostname mismatch), the Subversion command-line client will ask you whether you want to trust the server certificate anyway:

```
$ svn list https://host.example.com/repos/project

Error validating server certificate for 'https://host.example.com:443':
 - The certificate is not issued by a trusted authority. Use the
   fingerprint to validate the certificate manually!
Certificate information:
 - Hostname: host.example.com
 - Valid: from Jan 30 19:23:56 2004 GMT until Jan 30 19:23:56 2006 GMT
 - Issuer: CA, example.com, Sometown, California, US
 - Fingerprint: 7d:e1:a9:34:33:39:ba:6a:e9:a5:c4:22:98:7b:76:5c:92:a0:9c:7b

(R)eject, accept (t)emporarily or accept (p)ermanently?
```

This dialogue should look familiar; it's essentially the same question you've probably seen coming from your web browser (which is just another HTTP client like Subversion). If you choose the (p)ermanent option, the server certificate will be cached in your private runtime *auth/* area in just the same way your username and password are cached (see "Client Credentials Caching" on page 97). If cached, Subversion will automatically trust this certificate in future negotiations.

Your runtime *servers* file also gives you the ability to make your Subversion client automatically trust specific CAs, either globally or on a per-host basis. Simply set the `ssl-authority-files` variable to a semicolon-separated list of PEM-encoded CA certificates:

```
[global]
ssl-authority-files = /path/to/CAcert1.pem;/path/to/CAcert2.pem
```

Many OpenSSL installations also have a predefined set of "default" CAs that are nearly universally trusted. To make the Subversion client automatically trust these standard authorities, set the `ssl-trust-default-ca` variable to `true`.

When talking to Apache, a Subversion client might also receive a challenge for a client certificate. Apache is asking the client to identify itself: is the client really who it says it is? If all goes correctly, the Subversion client sends back a private certificate signed by a CA that Apache trusts. A client certificate is usually stored on disk in encrypted format, protected by a local password. When Subversion receives this challenge, it will ask you for a path to the certificate and the password that protects it:

```
$ svn list https://host.example.com/repos/project

Authentication realm: https://host.example.com:443
Client certificate filename: /path/to/my/cert.p12
Passphrase for '/path/to/my/cert.p12':  ********
...
```

Notice that the client certificate is a "p12" file. To use a client certificate with Subversion, it must be in PKCS#12 format, which is a portable standard. Most web browsers are already able to import and export certificates in that format. Another option is to use the OpenSSL command-line tools to convert existing certificates into PKCS#12.

Again, the runtime *servers* file allows you to automate this challenge on a per-host basis. Either or both pieces of information can be described in runtime variables:

```
[groups]
examplehost = host.example.com

[examplehost]
ssl-client-cert-file = /path/to/my/cert.p12
ssl-client-cert-password = somepassword
```

Once you've set the `ssl-client-cert-file` and `ssl-client-cert-password` variables, the Subversion client can automatically respond to a client certificate challenge without prompting you.#

Authorization Options

At this point, you've configured authentication, but not authorization. Apache is able to challenge clients and confirm identities, but it has not been told how to allow or

---

More security-conscious folk might not want to store the client certificate password in the runtime *servers* file.

restrict access to the clients bearing those identities. This section describes two strategies for controlling access to your repositories.

Blanket access control

The simplest form of access control is to authorize certain users for either read-only access to a repository or read/write access to a repository.

You can restrict access on all repository operations by adding the `Require valid-user` directive to your `<Location>` block. Using our previous example, this would mean that only clients that claimed to be either `harry` or `sally` and that provided the correct password for their respective username would be allowed to do anything with the Subversion repository:

```
<Location /svn>
  DAV svn
  SVNParentPath /var/svn

  # how to authenticate a user
  AuthType Basic
  AuthName "Subversion repository"
  AuthUserFile /path/to/users/file

  # only authenticated users may access the repository
  Require valid-user
</Location>
```

Sometimes you don't need to run such a tight ship. For example, Subversion's own source code repository at *http://svn.collab.net/repos/svn* allows anyone in the world to perform read-only repository tasks (such as checking out working copies and browsing the repository with a web browser), but it restricts all write operations to authenticated users. To do this type of selective restriction, you can use the `Limit` and `LimitExcept` configuration directives. Like the `Location` directive, these blocks have starting and ending tags, and you would nest them inside your `<Location>` block.

The parameters present on the `Limit` and `LimitExcept` directives are HTTP request types that are affected by that block. For example, if you wanted to disallow all access to your repository except the currently supported read-only operations, you would use the `LimitExcept` directive, passing the `GET`, `PROPFIND`, `OPTIONS`, and `REPORT` request type parameters. Then the previously mentioned `Require valid-user` directive would be placed inside the `<LimitExcept>` block instead of just inside the `<Location>` block:

```
<Location /svn>
  DAV svn
  SVNParentPath /var/svn

  # how to authenticate a user
  AuthType Basic
  AuthName "Subversion repository"
  AuthUserFile /path/to/users/file
```

```
# For any operations other than these, require an authenticated user.
<LimitExcept GET PROPFIND OPTIONS REPORT>
  Require valid-user
</LimitExcept>
</Location>
```

These are only a few simple examples. For more in-depth information about Apache access control and the `Require` directive, take a look at the `Security` section of the Apache documentation's tutorials collection at *http://httpd.apache.org/docs-2.0/misc/tutorials.html*.

Per-directory access control

It's possible to set up finer-grained permissions using a second Apache httpd module, *mod_authz_svn*. This module grabs the various opaque URLs passing from client to server, asks *mod_dav_svn* to decode them, and then possibly vetoes requests based on access policies defined in a configuration file.

If you've built Subversion from source code, *mod_authz_svn* is automatically built and installed alongside *mod_dav_svn*. Many binary distributions install it automatically as well. To verify that it's installed correctly, make sure it comes right after *mod_dav_svn*'s `LoadModule` directive in *httpd.conf*:

```
LoadModule dav_module          modules/mod_dav.so
LoadModule dav_svn_module      modules/mod_dav_svn.so
LoadModule authz_svn_module    modules/mod_authz_svn.so
```

To activate this module, you need to configure your `Location` block to use the `AuthzSVNAccessFile` directive, which specifies a file containing the permissions policy for paths within your repositories. (In a moment, we'll discuss the format of that file.)

Apache is flexible, so you have the option to configure your block in one of three general patterns. To begin, choose one of these basic configuration patterns. (The following examples are very simple; look at Apache's own documentation for much more detail on Apache authentication and authorization options.)

The simplest block is to allow open access to everyone. In this scenario, Apache never sends authentication challenges, so all users are treated as "anonymous." See Example 6-1.

Example 6-1. A sample configuration for anonymous access

```
<Location /repos>
  DAV svn
  SVNParentPath /var/svn

  # our access control policy
  AuthzSVNAccessFile /path/to/access/file
</Location>
```

On the opposite end of the paranoia scale, you can configure your block to demand authentication from everyone. All clients must supply credentials to identify

---

themselves. Your block unconditionally requires authentication via the `Require valid-user` directive, and it defines a means to authenticate. See Example 6-2.

Example 6-2. A sample configuration for authenticated access

```
<Location /repos>
  DAV svn
  SVNParentPath /var/svn

  # our access control policy
  AuthzSVNAccessFile /path/to/access/file

  # only authenticated users may access the repository
  Require valid-user

  # how to authenticate a user
  AuthType Basic
  AuthName "Subversion repository"
  AuthUserFile /path/to/users/file
</Location>
```

A third very popular pattern is to allow a combination of authenticated and anonymous access. For example, many administrators want to allow anonymous users to read certain repository directories, but they want only authenticated users to read (or write to) more sensitive areas. In this setup, all users start out accessing the repository anonymously. If your access control policy demands a real username at any point, Apache will demand authentication from the client. To do this, use both the `Satisfy Any` and `Require valid-user` directives together. See Example 6-3.

Example 6-3. A sample configuration for mixed authenticated/anonymous access

```
<Location /repos>
  DAV svn
  SVNParentPath /var/svn

  # our access control policy
  AuthzSVNAccessFile /path/to/access/file

  # try anonymous access first, resort to real
  # authentication if necessary.
  Satisfy Any
  Require valid-user

  # how to authenticate a user
  AuthType Basic
  AuthName "Subversion repository"
  AuthUserFile /path/to/users/file
</Location>
```

Once you've settled on one of these three basic *httpd.conf* templates, you need to create your file containing access rules for particular paths within the repository. We describe this later in "Path-Based Authorization" on page 226.

Disabling path-based checks

The *mod_dav_svn* module goes through a lot of work to make sure that data you've marked "unreadable" doesn't get accidentally leaked. This means it needs to closely monitor all of the paths and file contents returned by commands such as *svn checkout* and *svn update*. If these commands encounter a path that isn't readable according to some authorization policy, the path is typically omitted altogether. In the case of history or rename tracing—for example, running a command such as `svn cat -r OLD foo.c` on a file that was renamed long ago—the rename tracking will simply halt if one of the object's former names is determined to be read-restricted.

All of this path checking can be quite expensive, especially in the case of *svn log*. When retrieving a list of revisions, the server looks at every changed path in each revision and checks it for readability. If an unreadable path is discovered, it's omitted from the list of the revision's changed paths (normally seen with the `--verbose` option), and the whole log message is suppressed. Needless to say, this can be time-consuming on revisions that affect a large number of files. This is the cost of security: even if you haven't configured a module such as *mod_authz_svn* at all, the *mod_dav_svn* module is still asking Apache *httpd* to run authorization checks on every path. The *mod_dav_svn* module has no idea what authorization modules have been installed, so all it can do is ask Apache to invoke whatever might be present.

On the other hand, there's also an escape hatch of sorts, which allows you to trade security features for speed. If you're not enforcing any sort of per-directory authorization (i.e., not using *mod_authz_svn* or similar module), you can disable all of this path checking. In your *httpd.conf* file, use the `SVNPathAuthz` directive as shown in Example 6-4.

Example 6-4. Disabling path checks altogether

```
<Location /repos>
  DAV svn
  SVNParentPath /var/svn

  SVNPathAuthz off
</Location>
```

The `SVNPathAuthz` directive is "on" by default. When set to "off," all path-based authorization checking is disabled; *mod_dav_svn* stops invoking authorization checks on every path it discovers.

Extra Goodies

We've covered most of the authentication and authorization options for Apache and *mod_dav_svn*. But Apache provides a few other nice features.

Repository browsing

One of the most useful benefits of an Apache/WebDAV configuration for your Subversion repository is that the youngest revisions of your versioned files and directories are immediately available for viewing via a regular web browser. Since Subversion uses URLs to identify versioned resources, those URLs used for HTTP-based repository access can be typed directly into a web browser. Your browser will issue an HTTP GET request for that URL; based on whether that URL represents a versioned directory or file, *mod_dav_svn* will respond with a directory listing or with file contents.

Since the URLs do not contain any information about which version of the resource you wish to see, *mod_dav_svn* will always answer with the youngest version. This functionality has the wonderful side effect that you can pass around Subversion URLs to your peers as references to documents, and those URLs will always point at the latest manifestation of that document. Of course, you can even use the URLs as hyperlinks from other web sites, too.

Can I View Older Revisions?

With an ordinary web browser? In one word: nope. At least, not with *mod_dav_svn* as your only tool.

Your web browser speaks ordinary HTTP only. That means it knows only how to GET public URLs, which represent the latest versions of files and directories. According to the WebDAV/DeltaV specification, each server defines a private URL syntax for older versions of resources, and that syntax is opaque to clients. To find an older version of a file, a client must follow a specific procedure to "discover" the proper URL; the procedure involves issuing a series of WebDAV PROPFIND requests and understanding DeltaV concepts. This is something your web browser simply can't do.

So, to answer the question, one obvious way to see older revisions of files and directories is by passing the `--revision` (`-r`) argument to the *svn list* and *svn cat* commands. To browse old revisions with your web browser, however, you can use third-party software. A good example of this is ViewVC (*http://viewvc.tigris.org/*). ViewVC was originally written to display CVS repositories through the Web,[*] and the latest releases are able to understand Subversion repositories as well.

Proper MIME type. When browsing a Subversion repository, the web browser gets a clue about how to render a file's contents by looking at the Content-Type: header returned in Apache's response to the HTTP GET request. The value of this header is some sort of MIME type. By default, Apache will tell the web browsers that all repository files are of the "default" MIME type, typically text/plain. This can be frustrating, however, if a user wishes repository files to render as something more meaningful—for example, it might be nice to have a *foo.html* file in the repository actually render as HTML when browsing.

---

[*] Back then, it was called ViewCVS.

To make this happen, you need only make sure that your files have the proper svn:mime-type set. We discuss this in more detail in "File Content Type" on page 57, and you can even configure your client to automatically attach proper svn:mime-type properties to files entering the repository for the first time; see "Automatic Property Setting" on page 55.

So, in our example, if one were to set the svn:mime-type property to text/html on file *foo.html*, Apache would properly tell your web browser to render the file as HTML. One could also attach proper image/* MIME-type properties to image files and ultimately get an entire web site to be viewable directly from a repository! There's generally no problem with this, as long as the web site doesn't contain any dynamically generated content.

Customizing the look. You generally will get more use out of URLs to versioned files—after all, that's where the interesting content tends to lie. But you might have occasion to browse a Subversion directory listing, where you'll quickly note that the generated HTML used to display that listing is very basic, and certainly not intended to be aesthetically pleasing (or even interesting). To enable customization of these directory displays, Subversion provides an XML index feature. A single SVNIndexXSLT directive in your repository's Location block of *httpd.conf* will instruct *mod_dav_svn* to generate XML output when displaying a directory listing, and to reference the XSLT stylesheet of your choice:

```
<Location /svn>
  DAV svn
  SVNParentPath /var/svn
  SVNIndexXSLT "/svnindex.xsl"
  ...
</Location>
```

Using the SVNIndexXSLT directive and a creative XSLT stylesheet, you can make your directory listings match the color schemes and imagery used in other parts of your web site. Or, if you'd prefer, you can use the sample stylesheets provided in the Subversion source distribution's *tools/xslt/* directory. Keep in mind that the path provided to the SVNIndexXSLT directory is actually a URL path—browsers need to be able to read your stylesheets to make use of them!

Listing repositories. If you're serving a collection of repositories from a single URL via the SVNParentPath directive, then it's also possible to have Apache display all available repositories to a web browser. Just activate the SVNListParentPath directive:

```
<Location /svn>
  DAV svn
  SVNParentPath /var/svn
  SVNListParentPath on
  ...
</Location>
```

If a user now points her web browser to the URL http://host.example.com/svn/, she'll see a list of all Subversion repositories sitting in */var/svn*. Obviously, this can be a security problem, so this feature is turned off by default.

Apache logging

Because Apache is an HTTP server at heart, it contains fantastically flexible logging features. It's beyond the scope of this book to discuss all of the ways logging can be configured, but we should point out that even the most generic *httpd.conf* file will cause Apache to produce two logs: *error_log* and *access_log*. These logs may appear in different places, but they are typically created in the logging area of your Apache installation. (On Unix, they often live in */usr/local/apache2/logs/*.)

The *error_log* describes any internal errors that Apache runs into as it works. The *access_log* file records every incoming HTTP request received by Apache. This makes it easy to see, for example, which IP addresses Subversion clients are coming from, how often particular clients use the server, which users are authenticating properly, and which requests succeed or fail.

Unfortunately, because HTTP is a stateless protocol, even the simplest Subversion client operation generates multiple network requests. It's very difficult to look at the *access_log* and deduce what the client was doing—most operations look like a series of cryptic PROPPATCH, GET, PUT, and REPORT requests. To make things worse, many client operations send nearly identical series of requests, so it's even harder to tell them apart.

mod_dav_svn, however, can come to your aid. By activating an "operational logging" feature, you can ask *mod_dav_svn* to create a separate logfile describing what sort of high-level operations your clients are performing.

To do this, you need to make use of Apache's CustomLog directive (which is explained in more detail in Apache's own documentation). Be sure to invoke this directive *outside* your Subversion Location block:

```
<Location /svn>
  DAV svn
  ...
</Location>

CustomLog logs/svn_logfile "%t %u %{SVN-ACTION}e" env=SVN-ACTION
```

In this example, we're asking Apache to create a special logfile, *svn_logfile*, in the standard Apache *logs* directory. The %t and %u variables are replaced by the time and username of the request, respectively. The really important parts are the two instances of SVN-ACTION. When Apache sees that variable, it substitutes the value of the SVN-ACTION environment variable, which is automatically set by *mod_dav_svn* whenever it detects a high-level client action.

So, instead of having to interpret a traditional *access_log* like this:

```
[26/Jan/2007:22:25:29 -0600] "PROPFIND /svn/calc/!svn/vcc/default HTTP/1.1" 207 398
[26/Jan/2007:22:25:29 -0600] "PROPFIND /svn/calc/!svn/bln/59 HTTP/1.1" 207 449
[26/Jan/2007:22:25:29 -0600] "PROPFIND /svn/calc HTTP/1.1" 207 647
[26/Jan/2007:22:25:29 -0600] "REPORT /svn/calc/!svn/vcc/default HTTP/1.1" 200 607
[26/Jan/2007:22:25:31 -0600] "OPTIONS /svn/calc HTTP/1.1" 200 188
[26/Jan/2007:22:25:31 -0600] "MKACTIVITY /svn/calc/!svn/act/\
    e6035ef7-5df0-4ac0-b811-4be7c823f998 HTTP/1.1" 201 227
...
```

you can peruse a much more intelligible *svn_logfile* like this:

```
[26/Jan/2007:22:24:20 -0600] - get-dir /tags r1729 props
[26/Jan/2007:22:24:27 -0600] - update /trunk r1729 depth=infinity send-copyfrom-args
[26/Jan/2007:22:25:29 -0600] - status /trunk/foo r1729 depth=infinity
[26/Jan/2007:22:25:31 -0600] sally commit r1730
```

For an exhaustive list of all actions logged, see "High-Level Logging" on page 357.

Write-through proxying

One of the nice advantages of using Apache as a Subversion server is that it can be set up for simple replication. For example, suppose that your team is distributed across four offices around the globe. The Subversion repository can exist only in one of those offices, which means the other three offices will not enjoy accessing it—they're likely to experience significantly slower traffic and response times when updating and committing code. A powerful solution is to set up a system consisting of one *master* Apache server and several *slave* Apache servers. If you place a slave server in each office, users can check out a working copy from whichever slave is closest to them. All read requests go to their local slave. Write requests get automatically routed to the single master server. When the commit completes, the master then automatically "pushes" the new revision to each slave server using the *svnsync* replication tool.

This configuration creates a huge perceptual speed increase for your users, because Subversion client traffic is typically 80–90% read requests. And if those requests are coming from a *local* server, it's a huge win.

In this section, we'll walk you through a standard setup of this single-master/multiple-slave system. However, keep in mind that your servers must be running at least Apache 2.2.0 (with *mod_proxy* loaded) and Subversion 1.5 (*mod_dav_svn*).

Configure the servers. First, configure your master server's *httpd.conf* file in the usual way. Make the repository available at a certain URI location, and configure authentication and authorization however you'd like. After that's done, configure each of your "slave" servers in the exact same way, but add the special SVNMasterURI directive to the block:

```
<Location /svn>
  DAV svn
  SVNPath /var/svn/repos
  SVNMasterURI http://master.example.com/svn
```

```
    ...
  </Location>
```

This new directive tells a slave server to redirect all write requests to the master. (This is done automatically via Apache's *mod_proxy* module.) Ordinary read requests, however, are still serviced by the slaves. Be sure that your master and slave servers all have matching authentication and authorization configurations; if they fall out of sync, it can lead to big headaches.

Next, we need to deal with the problem of infinite recursion. With the current configuration, imagine what will happen when a Subversion client performs a commit to the master server. After the commit completes, the server uses *svnsync* to replicate the new revision to each slave. But because *svnsync* appears to be just another Subversion client performing a commit, the slave will immediately attempt to proxy the incoming write request back to the master! Hilarity ensues.

The solution to this problem is to have the master push revisions to a different Location on the slaves. This location is configured to *not* proxy write requests at all, but to accept normal commits from (and only from) the master's IP address:

```
  <Location /svn-proxy-sync>
    DAV svn
    SVNPath /var/svn/repos
    Order deny,allow
    Deny from all
    # Only let the server's IP address access this Location:
    Allow from 10.20.30.40
    ...
  </Location>
```

Set up replication. Now that you've configured your Location blocks on master and slaves, you need to configure the master to replicate to the slaves. This is done the usual way—using *svnsync*. If you're not familiar with this tool, see "Repository Replication" on page 177 for details.

First, make sure that each slave repository has a pre-revprop-change hook script that allows remote revision property changes. (This is standard procedure for being on the receiving end of *svnsync*.) Then, log into the master server and configure each of the slave repository URIs to receive data from the master repository on the local disk:

```
$ svnsync init http://slave1.example.com/svn-proxy-sync file:///var/svn/repos
Copied properties for revision 0.
$ svnsync init http://slave2.example.com/svn-proxy-sync file:///var/svn/repos
Copied properties for revision 0.
$ svnsync init http://slave3.example.com/svn-proxy-sync file:///var/svn/repos
Copied properties for revision 0.

# Perform the initial replication

$ svnsync sync http://slave1.example.com/svn-proxy-sync
Transmitting file data ....
Committed revision 1.
```

```
Copied properties for revision 1.
Transmitting file data .......
Committed revision 2.
Copied properties for revision 2.
...

$ svnsync sync http://slave2.example.com/svn-proxy-sync
Transmitting file data ....
Committed revision 1.
Copied properties for revision 1.
Transmitting file data .......
Committed revision 2.
Copied properties for revision 2.
...

$ svnsync sync http://slave3.example.com/svn-proxy-sync
Transmitting file data ....
Committed revision 1.
Copied properties for revision 1.
Transmitting file data .......
Committed revision 2.
Copied properties for revision 2.
...
```

After this is done, configure the master server's **post-commit** hook script to invoke *svnsync* on each slave server:

```
#!/bin/sh
# Post-commit script to replicate newly committed revision to slaves

svnsync sync http://slave1.example.com/svn-proxy-sync > /dev/null 2>&1
svnsync sync http://slave2.example.com/svn-proxy-sync > /dev/null 2>&1
svnsync sync http://slave3.example.com/svn-proxy-sync > /dev/null 2>&1
```

The extra bits on the end of each line aren't necessary, but they're a sneaky way to allow the sync commands to run in the background so that the Subversion client isn't left waiting forever for the commit to finish. In addition to this **post-commit** hook, you'll need a **post-revprop-change** hook as well so that when a user, say, modifies a log message, the slave servers get that change also:

```
#!/bin/sh
# Post-revprop-change script to replicate revprop-changes to slaves

REV=${2}
svnsync copy-revprops http://slave1.example.com/svn-proxy-sync ${REV} > /dev/null 2>&1
svnsync copy-revprops http://slave2.example.com/svn-proxy-sync ${REV} > /dev/null 2>&1
svnsync copy-revprops http://slave3.example.com/svn-proxy-sync ${REV} > /dev/null 2>&1
```

The only thing we've left out here is what to do about locks. Because locks are strictly enforced by the master server (the only place where commits happen), we don't technically need to do anything. Many teams don't use Subversion's locking features at all, so it may be a nonissue for you. However, if lock changes aren't replicated from master to slaves, it means that clients won't be able to query the status of locks (e.g., **svn status -u** will show no information about repository locks). If this bothers you, you can write post-lock and post-unlock hook scripts that run *svn lock* and *svn unlock* on each slave machine, presumably through a remote shell method such as SSH. That's left as an exercise for the reader!

Caveats. Your master/slave replication system should now be ready to use. However, a couple of words of warning are in order. Remember that this replication isn't entirely robust in the face of computer or network crashes. For example, if one of the automated *svnsync* commands fails to complete for some reason, the slaves will begin to fall behind. For example, your remote users will see that they've committed revision 100, but then when they run *svn update*, their local server will tell them that revision 100 doesn't yet exist! Of course, the problem will be automatically fixed the next time another commit happens and the subsequent *svnsync* is successful—the sync will replicate all waiting revisions. But still, you may want to set up some sort of out-of-band monitoring to notice synchronization failures and force *svnsync* to run when things go wrong.

Can We Set Up Replication with svnserve?

If you're using *svnserve* instead of Apache as your server, you can certainly configure your repository's hook scripts to invoke *svnsync* as we've shown here, thereby causing automatic replication from master to slaves. Unfortunately, at the time of this writing there is no way to make slave *svnserve* servers automatically proxy write requests back to the master server. This means your users would only be able to check out read-only working copies from the slave servers. You'd have to configure your slave servers to disallow write access completely. This might be useful for creating read-only "mirrors" of popular open source projects, but it's not a transparent proxying system.

Other Apache features

Several of the features already provided by Apache in its role as a robust web server can be leveraged for increased functionality or security in Subversion as well. The Subversion client is able to use SSL (the Secure Sockets Layer, discussed earlier). If your Subversion client is built to support SSL, it can access your Apache server using https:// and enjoy a high-quality encrypted network session.

Equally useful are other features of the Apache and Subversion relationship, such as the ability to specify a custom port (instead of the default HTTP port 80) or a virtual domain name by which the Subversion repository should be accessed, or the ability to access the repository through an HTTP proxy.

Finally, because *mod_dav_svn* is speaking a subset of the WebDAV/DeltaV protocol, it's possible to access the repository via third-party DAV clients. Most modern operating systems (Win32, OS X, and Linux) have the built-in ability to mount a DAV server as a standard network "shared folder." This is a complicated topic, but also wondrous when implemented. For details, read Appendix C.

Note that there are a number of other small tweaks one can make to *mod_dav_svn* that are too obscure to mention in this chapter. For a complete list of all *httpd.conf* directives that *mod_dav_svn* responds to, see "Directives" on page 355.

Path-Based Authorization

Both Apache and *svnserve* are capable of granting (or denying) permissions to users. Typically this is done over the entire repository: a user can read the repository (or not), and she can write to the repository (or not). It's also possible, however, to define finer-grained access rules. One set of users may have permission to write to a certain directory in the repository, but not others; another directory might not even be readable by all but a few special people.

Both servers use a common file format to describe these path-based access rules. In the case of Apache, one needs to load the *mod_authz_svn* module and then add the `AuthzSVNAccessFile` directive (within the *httpd.conf* file) pointing to your own rules file. (For a full explanation, see "Per-directory access control" on page 216.) If you're using *svnserve*, you need to make the `authz-db` variable (within *svnserve.conf*) point to your rules file.

> ## Do You Really Need Path-Based Access Control?
>
> A lot of administrators setting up Subversion for the first time tend to jump into path-based access control without giving it a lot of thought. The administrator usually knows which teams of people are working on which projects, so it's easy to jump in and grant certain teams access to certain directories and not others. It seems like a natural thing, and it appeases the administrator's desire to maintain tight control of the repository.
>
> Note, though, that there are often invisible (and visible!) costs associated with this feature. In the visible category, the server needs to do a lot more work to ensure that the user has the right to read or write each specific path; in certain situations, there's very noticeable performance loss. In the invisible category, consider the culture you're creating. Most of the time, while certain users *shouldn't* be committing changes to certain parts of the repository, that social contract doesn't need to be technologically enforced. Teams can sometimes spontaneously collaborate with each other; someone may want to help someone else out by committing to an area she doesn't normally work on. By preventing this sort of thing at the server level, you're setting up barriers to unexpected collaboration. You're also creating a bunch of rules that need to be maintained as projects develop, new users are added, and so on. It's a bunch of extra work to maintain.
>
> Remember that this is a version control system! Even if somebody accidentally commits a change to something she shouldn't, it's easy to undo the change. And if a user commits to the wrong place with deliberate malice, it's a social problem anyway, and that problem needs to be dealt with outside Subversion.
>
> So, before you begin restricting users' access rights, ask yourself whether there's a real, honest need for this, or whether it's just something that "sounds good" to an

administrator. Decide whether it's worth sacrificing some server speed, and remember that there's very little risk involved; it's bad to become dependent on technology as a crutch for social problems.†

As an example to ponder, consider that the Subversion project itself has always had a notion of who is allowed to commit where, but it's always been enforced socially. This is a good model of community trust, especially for open source projects. Of course, sometimes there *are* truly legitimate needs for path-based access control; within corporations, for example, certain types of data really can be sensitive, and access needs to be genuinely restricted to small groups of people.

Once your server knows where to find your rules file, it's time to define the rules.

The syntax of the file is the same familiar one used by *svnserve.conf* and the runtime configuration files. Lines that start with a hash (#) are ignored. In its simplest form, each section names a repository and path within it, as well as the authenticated user-names are the option names within each section. The value of each option describes the user's level of access to the repository path: either **r** (read-only) or **rw** (read/write). If the user is not mentioned at all, no access is allowed.

To be more specific: the value of the section names is either of the form [`repos-name:path`] or of the form [`path`]. If you're using the `SVNParentPath` directive, it's important to specify the repository names in your sections. If you omit them, a section such as [`/some/dir`] will match the path */some/dir* in *every* repository. If you're using the `SVNPath` directive, however, it's fine to only define paths in your sections—after all, there's only one repository:

```
[calc:/branches/calc/bug-142]
harry = rw
sally = r
```

In this first example, the user **harry** has full read and write access on the */branches/calc/bug-142* directory in the **calc** repository, but the user **sally** has read-only access. Any other users are blocked from accessing this directory.

Of course, permissions are inherited from parent to child directory. That means we can specify a subdirectory with a different access policy for Sally:

```
[calc:/branches/calc/bug-142]
harry = rw
sally = r

# give sally write access only to the 'testing' subdir
[calc:/branches/calc/bug-142/testing]
sally = rw
```

† A common theme in this book!

Now Sally can write to the *testing* subdirectory of the branch, but she can still only read other parts. Harry, meanwhile, continues to have complete read/write access to the whole branch.

It's also possible to explicitly deny permission to someone via inheritance rules, by setting the username variable to nothing:

```
[calc:/branches/calc/bug-142]
harry = rw
sally = r

[calc:/branches/calc/bug-142/secret]
harry =
```

In this example, Harry has read/write access to the entire *bug-142* tree, but he has absolutely no access at all to the *secret* subdirectory within it.

> The thing to remember is that the most specific path always matches first. The server tries to match the path itself, and then the parent of the path, and then the parent of that, and so on. The net effect is that mentioning a specific path in the access file will always override any permissions inherited from parent directories.

By default, nobody has any access to the repository at all. That means that if you're starting with an empty file, you'll probably want to give at least read permission to all users at the root of the repository. You can do this by using the asterisk variable (*), which means "all users":

```
[/]
* = r
```

This is a common setup; notice that no repository name is mentioned in the section name. This makes all repositories world-readable to all users. Once all users have read access to the repositories, you can give explicit rw permission to certain users on specific subdirectories within specific repositories.

The asterisk variable (*) is also worth special mention because it's the *only* pattern that matches an anonymous user. If you've configured your server block to allow a mixture of anonymous and authenticated access, all users start out accessing anonymously. The server looks for a * value defined for the path being accessed; if it can't find one, it demands real authentication from the client.

The access file also allows you to define whole groups of users, much like the Unix */etc/group* file:

```
[groups]
calc-developers = harry, sally, joe
paint-developers = frank, sally, jane
everyone = harry, sally, joe, frank, sally, jane
```

Groups can be granted access control just like users. Distinguish them with an "at" (@) prefix:

```
[calc:/projects/calc]
@calc-developers = rw

[paint:/projects/paint]
jane = r
@paint-developers = rw
```

Another important fact is that the *first* matching rule is the one that gets applied to a user. In the prior example, even though Jane is a member of the `paint-developers` group (which has read/write access), the `jane = r` rule will be discovered and matched before the group rule, thus denying Jane write access.

Groups can also be defined to contain other groups:

```
[groups]
calc-developers = harry, sally, joe
paint-developers = frank, sally, jane
everyone = @calc-developers, @paint-developers
```

Subversion 1.5 brings another useful feature to the access file syntax: username aliases. Some authentication systems expect and carry relatively short usernames of the sorts we've been describing here—`harry`, `sally`, `joe`, and so on. But other authentication systems—such as those that use LDAP stores or SSL client certificates—may carry much more complex usernames. For example, Harry's username in an LDAP-protected system might be `CN=Harold Hacker,OU=Engineers,DC=red-bean,DC=com`. With usernames like that, the access file can become quite bloated with long or obscure usernames that are easy to mistype. Fortunately, username aliases allow you to have to type the correct complex username only once, in a statement which assigns to it a more easily digestible alias:

```
[aliases]
harry = CN=Harold Hacker,OU=Engineers,DC=red-bean,DC=com
sally = CN=Sally Swatterbug,OU=Engineers,DC=red-bean,DC=com
joe = CN=Gerald I. Joseph,OU=Engineers,DC=red-bean,DC=com
...
```

Once you've defined a set of aliases, you can refer to the users elsewhere in the access file via their aliases in all the same places you could have instead used their actual usernames. Simply prepend an ampersand to the alias to distinguish it from a regular username:

```
[groups]
calc-developers = &harry, &sally, &joe
paint-developers = &frank, &sally, &jane
everyone = @calc-developers, @paint-developers
```

You might also choose to use aliases if your users' usernames change frequently. Doing so allows you to need to update only the aliases table when these username changes occur, instead of doing global-search-and-replace operations on the whole access file.

Partial Readability and Checkouts

If you're using Apache as your Subversion server and have made certain subdirectories of your repository unreadable to certain users, you need to be aware of a possible non-optimal behavior with *svn checkout*.

When the client requests a checkout or update over HTTP, it makes a single server request and receives a single (often large) server response. When the server receives the request, that is the *only* opportunity Apache has to demand user authentication. This has some odd side effects. For example, if a certain subdirectory of the repository is readable only by user Sally, and user Harry checks out a parent directory, his client will respond to the initial authentication challenge as Harry. As the server generates the large response, there's no way it can resend an authentication challenge when it reaches the special subdirectory; thus the subdirectory is skipped altogether, rather than asking the user to reauthenticate as Sally at the right moment. In a similar way, if the root of the repository is anonymously world-readable, the entire checkout will be done without authentication—again, skipping the unreadable directory, rather than asking for authentication partway through.

Supporting Multiple Repository Access Methods

You've seen how a repository can be accessed in many different ways. But is it possible—or safe—for your repository to be accessed by multiple methods simultaneously? The answer is yes, provided you use a bit of foresight.

At any given time, these processes may require read and write access to your repository:

- Regular system users using a Subversion client (as themselves) to access the repository directly via `file://` URLs
- Regular system users connecting to SSH-spawned private *svnserve* processes (running as themselves), which access the repository
- An *svnserve* process—either a daemon or one launched by *inetd*—running as a particular fixed user
- An Apache *httpd* process, running as a particular fixed user

The most common problem administrators run into is repository ownership and permissions. Does every process (or user) in the preceding list have the rights to read and write the repository's underlying data files? Assuming you have a Unix-like operating system, a straightforward approach might be to place every potential repository user into a new `svn` group, and then make the repository wholly owned by that group. But even that's not enough, because a process may write to the database files using an unfriendly umask—one that prevents access by other users.

So, the next step beyond setting up a common group for repository users is to force every repository-accessing process to use a sane umask. For users accessing the repository directly, you can make the *svn* program into a wrapper script that first runs umask 002 and then runs the real *svn* client program. You can write a similar wrapper script for the *svnserve* program and add a umask 002 command to Apache's own startup script, *apachectl*. For example:

```
$ cat /usr/bin/svn

#!/bin/sh

umask 002
/usr/bin/svn-real "$@"
```

Another common problem is often encountered on Unix-like systems. If your repository is backed by Berkeley DB, for example, it occasionally creates new logfiles to journal its actions. Even if the Berkeley DB repository is wholly owned by the *svn* group, these newly created logfiles won't necessarily be owned by that same group, which then creates more permissions problems for your users. A good workaround is to set the group SUID bit on the repository's *db* directory. This causes all newly created logfiles to have the same group owner as the parent directory.

Once you've jumped through these hoops, your repository should be accessible by all the necessary processes. It may seem a bit messy and complicated, but the problems of having multiple users sharing write access to common files are classic ones that are not often elegantly solved.

Fortunately, most repository administrators will never *need* to have such a complex configuration. Users who wish to access repositories that live on the same machine are not limited to using file:// access URLs—they can typically contact the Apache HTTP server or *svnserve* using localhost for the server name in their http:// or svn:// URL. And maintaining multiple server processes for your Subversion repositories is likely to be more of a headache than necessary. We recommend that you choose a single server that best meets your needs and stick with it!

The svn+ssh:// Server Checklist

It can be quite tricky to get a bunch of users with existing SSH accounts to share a repository without permissions problems. If you're confused about all the things that you (as an administrator) need to do on a Unix-like system, here's a quick checklist that resummarizes some of the topics discussed in this section:

- All of your SSH users need to be able to read and write to the repository, so put all the SSH users into a single group.
- Make the repository wholly owned by that group.
- Set the group permissions to read/write.

## CHAPTER 7

Customizing Your Subversion Experience

Version control can be a complex subject, as much art as science, that offers myriad ways of getting stuff done. Throughout this book, you've read of the various Subversion command-line client subcommands and the options that modify their behavior. In this chapter, we'll look into still more ways to customize the way Subversion works for you—setting up the Subversion runtime configuration, using external helper applications, Subversion's interaction with the operating system's configured locale, and so on.

Runtime Configuration Area

Subversion provides many optional behaviors that the user can control. Many of these options are of the kind that a user would wish to apply to all Subversion operations. So, rather than forcing users to remember command-line arguments for specifying these options and to use them for every operation they perform, Subversion uses configuration files, segregated into a Subversion configuration area.

The Subversion *configuration area* is a two-tiered hierarchy of option names and their values. Usually, this boils down to a special directory that contains *configuration files* (the first tier), which are just text files in standard INI format (with "sections" providing the second tier). You can easily edit these files using your favorite text editor (such as Emacs or vi), and they contain directives read by the client to determine which of several optional behaviors the user prefers.

Configuration Area Layout

The first time the *svn* command-line client is executed, it creates a per-user configuration area. On Unix-like systems, this area appears as a directory named *.subversion* in the user's home directory. On Win32 systems, Subversion creates a folder named *Subversion*, typically inside the *Application Data* area of the user's profile directory (which, by the way, is usually a hidden directory). However, on this platform, the exact location differs from system to system and is dictated by the Windows Registry.* We will refer to the per-user configuration area using its Unix name, *.subversion*.

In addition to the per-user configuration area, Subversion also recognizes the existence of a system-wide configuration area. This gives system administrators the ability to establish defaults for all users on a given machine. Note that the system-wide configuration area alone does not dictate mandatory policy—the settings in the per-user configuration area override those in the system-wide one, and command-line arguments supplied to the *svn* program have the final word on behavior. On Unix-like platforms, the system-wide configuration area is expected to be the */etc/subversion* directory; on Windows machines, it looks for a *Subversion* directory inside the common *Application Data* location (again, as specified by the Windows Registry). Unlike the per-user case, the *svn* program does not attempt to create the system-wide configuration area.

The per-user configuration area currently contains three files—two configuration files (*config* and *servers*), and a *README.txt* file, which describes the INI format. At the time of their creation, the files contain default values for each of the supported Subversion options, mostly commented out and grouped with textual descriptions about how the values for the key affect Subversion's behavior. To change a certain behavior, you need only load the appropriate configuration file into a text editor and modify the desired option's value. If at any time you wish to have the default configuration settings restored, you can simply remove (or rename) your configuration directory and then run some innocuous *svn* command, such as `svn --version`. A new configuration directory with the default contents will be created.

The per-user configuration area also contains a cache of authentication data. The *auth* directory holds a set of subdirectories that contain pieces of cached information used by Subversion's various supported authentication methods. This directory is created in such a way that only the user himself has permission to read its contents.

Configuration and the Windows Registry

In addition to the usual INI-based configuration area, Subversion clients running on Windows platforms may also use the Windows Registry to hold the configuration data. The option names and their values are the same as in the INI files. The "file/section" hierarchy is preserved as well, though addressed in a slightly different fashion—in this schema, files and sections are just levels in the Registry key tree.

---

* The APPDATA environment variable points to the *Application Data* area, so you can always refer to this folder as *%APPDATA%\Subversion*.

Subversion looks for system-wide configuration values under the `HKEY_LOCAL_MACHINE\Software\Tigris.org\Subversion` key. For example, the `global-ignores` option, which is in the `miscellany` section of the *config* file, would be found at `HKEY_LOCAL_MACHINE\Software\Tigris.org\Subversion\Config\Miscellany\global-ignores`. Per-user configuration values should be stored under `HKEY_CURRENT_USER\Software\Tigris.org\Subversion`.

Registry-based configuration options are parsed *before* their file-based counterparts, so they are overridden by values found in the configuration files. In other words, Subversion looks for configuration information in the following locations on a Windows system; lower-numbered locations take precedence over higher-numbered locations:

1. Command-line options
2. The per-user INI files
3. The per-user Registry values
4. The system-wide INI files
5. The system-wide Registry values

Also, the Windows Registry doesn't really support the notion of something being "commented out." However, Subversion will ignore any option key whose name begins with a hash (#) character. This allows you to effectively comment out a Subversion option without deleting the entire key from the Registry, obviously simplifying the process of restoring that option.

The *svn* command-line client never attempts to write to the Windows Registry and will not attempt to create a default configuration area there. You can create the keys you need using the *REGEDIT* program. Alternatively, you can create a *.reg* file (such as the one in Example 7-1), and then double-click on that file's icon in the Explorer shell, which will cause the data to be merged into your Registry.

Example 7-1. Sample registration entries (.reg) file

```
REGEDIT4

[HKEY_LOCAL_MACHINE\Software\Tigris.org\Subversion\Servers\groups]

[HKEY_LOCAL_MACHINE\Software\Tigris.org\Subversion\Servers\global]
"#http-proxy-host"=""
"#http-proxy-port"=""
"#http-proxy-username"=""
"#http-proxy-password"=""
"#http-proxy-exceptions"=""
"#http-timeout"="0"
"#http-compression"="yes"
"#neon-debug-mask"=""
"#ssl-authority-files"=""
"#ssl-trust-default-ca"=""
"#ssl-client-cert-file"=""
"#ssl-client-cert-password"=""
```

```
[HKEY_CURRENT_USER\Software\Tigris.org\Subversion\Config\auth]
"#store-passwords"="yes"
"#store-auth-creds"="yes"

[HKEY_CURRENT_USER\Software\Tigris.org\Subversion\Config\helpers]
"#editor-cmd"="notepad"
"#diff-cmd"=""
"#diff3-cmd"=""
"#diff3-has-program-arg"=""

[HKEY_CURRENT_USER\Software\Tigris.org\Subversion\Config\tunnels]

[HKEY_CURRENT_USER\Software\Tigris.org\Subversion\Config\miscellany]
"#global-ignores"="*.o *.lo *.la #*# .*.rej *.rej .*~ *~ .#* .DS_Store"
"#log-encoding"=""
"#use-commit-times"=""
"#no-unlock"=""
"#enable-auto-props"=""

[HKEY_CURRENT_USER\Software\Tigris.org\Subversion\Config\auto-props]
```

The preceding example shows the contents of a *.reg* file, which contains some of the
most commonly used configuration options and their default values. Note the presence
of both system-wide (for network proxy-related options) and per-user settings (editor
programs and password storage, among others). Also note that all the options are
effectively commented out. You need only remove the hash (#) character from the
beginning of the option names and set the values as you desire.

Configuration Options

In this section, we will discuss the specific runtime configuration options that Subversion currently supports.

Servers

The *servers* file contains Subversion configuration options related to the network layers.
There are two special section names in this file—groups and global. The groups section
is essentially a cross-reference table. The keys in this section are the names of other
sections in the file; their values are *globs*—textual tokens that possibly contain wildcard
characters—that are compared against the hostnames of the machine to which Subversion requests are sent:

```
[groups]
beanie-babies = *.red-bean.com
collabnet = svn.collab.net

[beanie-babies]
...
```

```
[collabnet]
...
```

When Subversion is used over a network, it attempts to match the name of the server it is trying to reach with a group name under the **groups** section. If a match is made, Subversion then looks for a section in the *servers* file whose name is the matched group's name. From that section, it reads the actual network configuration settings.

The **global** section contains the settings that are meant for all of the servers not matched by one of the globs under the **groups** section. The options available in this section are exactly the same as those that are valid for the other server sections in the file (except, of course, the special **groups** section), and are as follows:

http-proxy-exceptions
> This specifies a comma-separated list of patterns for repository hostnames that should be accessed directly, without using the proxy machine. The pattern syntax is the same as is used in the Unix shell for filenames. A repository hostname matching any of these patterns will not be proxied.

http-proxy-host
> This specifies the hostname of the proxy computer through which your HTTP-based Subversion requests must pass. It defaults to an empty value, which means that Subversion will not attempt to route HTTP requests through a proxy computer and will instead attempt to contact the destination machine directly.

http-proxy-port
> This specifies the port number on the proxy host to use. It defaults to an empty value.

http-proxy-username
> This specifies the username to supply to the proxy machine. It defaults to an empty value.

http-proxy-password
> This specifies the password to supply to the proxy machine. It defaults to an empty value.

http-timeout
> This specifies the amount of time, in seconds, to wait for a server response. If you experience problems with a slow network connection causing Subversion operations to time out, you should increase the value of this option. The default value is **0**, which instructs the underlying HTTP library, Neon, to use its default timeout setting.

http-compression
> This specifies whether Subversion should attempt to compress network requests made to DAV-ready servers. The default value is **yes** (though compression will occur only if that capability is compiled into the network layer). Set this to **no** to disable compression, such as when debugging network transmissions.

http-library

Subversion provides a pair of repository access modules that understand its Web-DAV network protocol. The original one, which shipped with Subversion 1.0, is `libsvn_ra_neon` (though back then it was called `libsvn_ra_dav`). Newer Subversion versions also provide `libsvn_ra_serf`, which uses a different underlying implementation and aims to support some of the newer HTTP concepts.

At this point, `libsvn_ra_serf` is still considered experimental, though it appears to work in the common cases quite well. To encourage experimentation, Subversion provides the `http-library` runtime configuration option to allow users to specify (generally, or in a per-server-group fashion) which WebDAV access module they'd prefer to use—neon or serf.

http-auth-types

This option is a semicolon-delimited list of authentication types supported by the Neon-based WebDAV repository access modules. Valid members of this list are `basic`, `digest`, and `negotiate`.

neon-debug-mask

This is an integer mask that the underlying HTTP library, Neon, uses for choosing what type of debugging output to yield. The default value is 0, which will silence all debugging output. For more information about how Subversion makes use of Neon, see Chapter 8.

ssl-authority-files

This is a semicolon-delimited list of paths to files containing certificates of the certificate authorities (or CAs) that are accepted by the Subversion client when accessing the repository over HTTPS.

ssl-trust-default-ca

Set this variable to yes if you want Subversion to automatically trust the set of default CAs that ship with OpenSSL.

ssl-client-cert-file

If a host (or set of hosts) requires an SSL client certificate, you'll normally be prompted for a path to your certificate. By setting this variable to that same path, Subversion will be able to find your client certificate automatically without prompting you. There's no standard place to store your certificate on disk; Subversion will grab it from any path you specify.

ssl-client-cert-password

If your SSL client certificate file is encrypted by a passphrase, Subversion will prompt you for the passphrase whenever the certificate is used. If you find this annoying (and don't mind storing the password in the *servers* file), you can set this variable to the certificate's passphrase. You won't be prompted anymore.

Config

The *config* file contains the rest of the currently available Subversion runtime options—those not related to networking. Only a few options are in use as of this writing, but they are again grouped into sections in expectation of future additions.

The `auth` section contains settings related to Subversion's authentication and authorization against the repository. It contains the following:

store-passwords

This instructs Subversion to cache, or not to cache, passwords that are supplied by the user in response to server authentication challenges. The default value is yes. Set this to no to disable this on-disk password caching. You can override this option for a single instance of the *svn* command using the `--no-auth-cache` command-line parameter (for those subcommands that support it). For more information, see "Client Credentials Caching" on page 97.

store-auth-creds

This setting is the same as `store-passwords`, except that it enables or disables on-disk caching of *all* authentication information: usernames, passwords, server certificates, and any other types of cacheable credentials.

The `helpers` section controls which external applications Subversion uses to accomplish its tasks. Valid options in this section are:

editor-cmd

This specifies the program that Subversion will use to query the user for certain types of textual metadata or when interactively resolving conflicts. See "Using External Editors" on page 244 for more details on using external text editors with Subversion.

diff-cmd

This specifies the absolute path of a differencing program, used when Subversion generates "diff" output (such as when using the *svn diff* command). By default, Subversion uses an internal differencing library—setting this option will cause it to perform this task using an external program. See "Using External Differencing and Merge Tools" on page 245 for more details on using such programs.

diff3-cmd

This specifies the absolute path of a three-way differencing program. Subversion uses this program to merge changes made by the user with those received from the repository. By default, Subversion uses an internal differencing library—setting this option will cause it to perform this task using an external program. See "Using External Differencing and Merge Tools" on page 245 for more details on using such programs.

diff3-has-program-arg

This flag should be set to true if the program specified by the `diff3-cmd` option accepts a `--diff-program` command-line parameter.

merge-tool-cmd

This specifies the program that Subversion will use to perform three-way merge operations on your versioned files. See "Using External Differencing and Merge Tools" on page 245 for more details on using such programs.

The tunnels section allows you to define new tunnel schemes for use with *svnserve* and svn:// client connections. For more details, see "Tunneling over SSH" on page 203.

The miscellany section is where everything that doesn't belong elsewhere winds up.[†] In this section, you can find:

global-ignores

When running the *svn status* command, Subversion lists unversioned files and directories along with the versioned ones, annotating them with a ? character (see "See an overview of your changes" on page 26). Sometimes, it can be annoying to see uninteresting, unversioned items—for example, object files that result from a program's compilation—in this display. The global-ignores option is a list of whitespace-delimited globs that describe the names of files and directories that Subversion should not display unless they are versioned. The default value is *.o *.lo *.la #*# .*.rej *.rej .*~ *~ .#* .DS_Store.

As well as *svn status*, the *svn add* and *svn import* commands also ignore files that match the list when they are scanning a directory. You can override this behavior for a single instance of any of these commands by explicitly specifying the filename, or by using the --no-ignore command-line flag.

For information on finer-grained control of ignored items, see "Ignoring Unversioned Items" on page 60.

enable-auto-props

This instructs Subversion to automatically set properties on newly added or imported files. The default value is no, so set this to yes to enable this feature. The auto-props section of this file specifies which properties are to be set on which files.

log-encoding

This variable sets the default character set encoding for commit log messages. It's a permanent form of the --encoding option (see "svn Options" on page 271). The Subversion repository stores log messages in UTF-8 and assumes that your log message is written using your operating system's native locale. You should specify a different encoding if your commit messages are written in any other encoding.

use-commit-times

Normally your working copy files have timestamps that reflect the last time they were touched by any process, whether your own editor or some *svn* subcommand. This is generally convenient for people developing software, because build systems often look at timestamps as a way of deciding which files need to be recompiled.

[†] Anyone for potluck dinner?

In other situations, however, it's sometimes nice for the working copy files to have timestamps that reflect the last time they were changed in the repository. The *svn export* command always places these "last-commit timestamps" on trees that it produces. By setting this config variable to **yes**, the *svn checkout*, *svn update*, *svn switch*, and *svn revert* commands will also set last-commit timestamps on files that they touch.

`mime-types-file`

This option, new to Subversion 1.5, specifies the path of a MIME types mapping file, such as the *mime.types* file provided by the Apache HTTP Server. Subversion uses this file to assign MIME types to newly added or imported files. See "Automatic Property Setting" on page 55 and "File Content Type" on page 57 for more about Subversion's detection and use of file content types.

`preserved-conflict-file-exts`

The value of this option is a space-delimited list of file extensions that Subversion should preserve when generating conflict filenames. By default, the list is empty. This option is new to Subversion 1.5.

When Subversion detects conflicting file content changes, it defers resolution of those conflicts to the user. To assist in the resolution, Subversion keeps pristine copies of the various competing versions of the file in the working copy. By default, those conflict files have names constructed by appending to the original filename a custom extension such as *.mine* or *.REV* (where *REV* is a revision number). A mild annoyance with this naming scheme is that on operating systems where a file's extension determines the default application used to open and edit that file, appending a custom extension prevents the file from being easily opened by its native application. For example, if the file *ReleaseNotes.pdf* was conflicted, the conflict files might be named *ReleaseNotes.pdf.mine* or *ReleaseNotes.pdf.r4231*. While your system might be configured to use Adobe's Acrobat Reader to open files whose extensions are *.pdf*, there probably isn't an application configured on your system to open all files whose extensions are *.r4231*.

You can fix this annoyance by using this configuration option, though. For files with one of the specified extensions, Subversion will append to the conflict file names the custom extension just as before, but then also reappend the file's original extension. Using the previous example, and assuming that `pdf` is one of the extensions configured in this list thereof, the conflict files generated for *ReleaseNotes.pdf* would instead be named *ReleaseNotes.pdf.mine.pdf* and *ReleaseNotes.pdf.r4231.pdf*. Because each file ends in *.pdf*, the correct default application will be used to view them.

`interactive-conflicts`

This is a Boolean option that specifies whether Subversion should try to resolve conflicts interactively. If its value is **yes** (the default value), Subversion will prompt the user for how to handle conflicts in the manner demonstrated in the section "Resolve Conflicts (Merging Others' Changes)" on page 30. Otherwise, it will simply flag the conflict and continue its operation, postponing resolution to a later time.

no-unlock

> This Boolean option corresponds to *svn commit*'s `--no-unlock` option, which tells Subversion not to release locks on files you've just committed. If this runtime option is set to yes, Subversion will never release locks automatically, leaving you to run *svn unlock* explicitly. It defaults to no.

The `auto-props` section controls the Subversion client's ability to automatically set properties on files when they are added or imported. It contains any number of key-value pairs in the format `PATTERN = PROPNAME=VALUE[;PROPNAME=VALUE ...]`, where `PATTERN` is a file pattern that matches one or more filenames and the rest of the line is a semicolon-delimited set of property assignments. Multiple matches on a file will result in multiple propsets for that file; however, there is no guarantee that auto-props will be applied in the order in which they are listed in the config file, so you can't have one rule "override" another. You can find several examples of auto-props usage in the *config* file. Lastly, don't forget to set `enable-auto-props` to yes in the `miscellany` section if you want to enable auto-props.

Localization

Localization is the act of making programs behave in a region-specific way. When a program formats numbers or dates in a way specific to your part of the world or prints messages (or accepts input) in your native language, the program is said to be *localized*. This section describes steps Subversion has made toward localization.

Understanding Locales

Most modern operating systems have a notion of the "current locale"—that is, the region or country whose localization conventions are honored. These conventions, typically chosen by some runtime configuration mechanism on the computer, affect the way in which programs present data to the user, as well as the way in which they accept user input.

On most Unix-like systems, you can check the values of the locale-related runtime configuration options by running the *locale* command:

```
$ locale
LANG=
LC_COLLATE="C"
LC_CTYPE="C"
LC_MESSAGES="C"
LC_MONETARY="C"
LC_NUMERIC="C"
LC_TIME="C"
LC_ALL="C"
$
```

The output is a list of locale-related environment variables and their current values. In this example, the variables are all set to the default C locale, but users can set these variables to specific country/language code combinations. For example, if one were to set the LC_TIME variable to fr_CA, programs would know to present time and date information formatted according to a French-speaking Canadian's expectations. And if one were to set the LC_MESSAGES variable to zh_TW, programs would know to present human-readable messages in traditional Chinese. Setting the LC_ALL variable has the effect of changing every locale variable to the same value. The value of LANG is used as a default value for any locale variable that is unset. To see the list of available locales on a Unix system, run the command locale -a.

On Windows, locale configuration is done via the "Regional and Language Options" control panel item. There, you can view and select the values of individual settings from the available locales, and even customize (at a sickening level of detail) several of the display formatting conventions.

Subversion's Use of Locales

The Subversion client, *svn*, honors the current locale configuration in two ways. First, it notices the value of the LC_MESSAGES variable and attempts to print all messages in the specified language. For example:

```
$ export LC_MESSAGES=de_DE
$ svn help cat
cat: Gibt den Inhalt der angegebenen Dateien oder URLs aus.
Aufruf: cat ZIEL[@REV]...
...
```

This behavior works identically on both Unix and Windows systems. Note, though, that while your operating system might have support for a certain locale, the Subversion client still may not be able to speak the particular language. In order to produce localized messages, human volunteers must provide translations for each language. The translations are written using the GNU gettext package, which results in translation modules that end with the *.mo* filename extension. For example, the German translation file is named *de.mo*. These translation files are installed somewhere on your system. On Unix, they typically live in */usr/share/locale/*, whereas on Windows they're often found in the *\share\locale* folder in Subversion's installation area. Once installed, a module is named after the program for which it provides translations. For example, the *de.mo* file may ultimately end up installed as */usr/share/locale/de/LC_MESSAGES/subversion.mo*. By browsing the installed *.mo* files, you can see which languages the Subversion client is able to speak.

The second way in which the locale is honored involves how *svn* interprets your input. The repository stores all paths, filenames, and log messages in Unicode, encoded as UTF-8. In that sense, the repository is *internationalized*—that is, the repository is ready to accept input in any human language. This means, however, that the Subversion client is responsible for sending only UTF-8 filenames and log messages into the repository. To do this, it must convert the data from the native locale into UTF-8.

For example, suppose you create a file named *caffè.txt*, and then when committing the file, you write the log message as "Adesso il caffè è più forte." Both the filename and the log message contain non-ASCII characters, but because your locale is set to it_IT, the Subversion client knows to interpret them as Italian. It uses an Italian character set to convert the data to UTF-8 before sending it off to the repository.

Note that although the repository demands UTF-8 filenames and log messages, it *does not* pay attention to file contents. Subversion treats file contents as opaque strings of bytes, and neither client nor server makes an attempt to understand the character set or encoding of the contents.

Character Set Conversion Errors

While using Subversion, you might get hit with an error related to character set conversions:

```
svn: Can't convert string from native encoding to 'UTF-8':
...
svn: Can't convert string from 'UTF-8' to native encoding:
...
```

Errors such as this typically occur when the Subversion client has received a UTF-8 string from the repository but not all of the characters in that string can be represented using the encoding of the current locale. For example, if your locale is en_US but a collaborator has committed a Japanese filename, you're likely to see this error when you receive the file during an *svn update*.

The solution is either to set your locale to something that *can* represent the incoming UTF-8 data, or to change the filename or log message in the repository. (And don't forget to slap your collaborator's hand—projects should decide on common languages ahead of time so that all participants are using the same locale.)

Using External Editors

The most obvious way to get data into Subversion is through the addition of files to version control, committing changes to those files, and so on. But other pieces of information besides merely versioned file data live in your Subversion repository. Some of these bits of information—commit log messages, lock comments, and some property values—tend to be textual in nature and are provided explicitly by users. Most of this information can be provided to the Subversion command-line client using the --message (-m) and --file (-F) options with the appropriate subcommands.

Each of these options has its pros and cons. For example, when performing a commit, --file (-F) works well if you've already prepared a text file that holds your commit log message. If you didn't, though, you can use --message (-m) to provide a log message on the command line. Unfortunately, it can be tricky to compose anything more than a simple one-line message on the command line. Users want more flexibility—multiline, free-form log message editing on demand.

Subversion supports this by allowing you to specify an external text editor that it will launch as necessary to give you a more powerful input mechanism for this textual metadata. There are several ways to tell Subversion which editor you'd like use. Subversion checks the following things, in the order specified, when it wants to launch such an editor:

1. `--editor-cmd` command-line option
2. `SVN_EDITOR` environment variable
3. `editor-cmd` runtime configuration option
4. `VISUAL` environment variable
5. `EDITOR` environment variable
6. Possibly, a fallback value built into the Subversion libraries (not present in the official builds)

The value of any of these options or variables is the beginning of a command line to be executed by the shell. Subversion appends to that command line a space and the pathname of a temporary file to be edited. So, to be used with Subversion, the configured or specified editor needs to support an invocation in which its last command-line parameter is a file to be edited, and it should be able to save the file in place and return a zero exit code to indicate success.

As noted, external editors can be used to provide commit log messages to any of the committing subcommands (such as *svn commit* or *import*, *svn mkdir* or *delete* when provided a URL target, etc.), and Subversion will try to launch the editor automatically if you don't specify either of the `--message` (`-m`) or `--file` (`-F`) options. The *svn propedit* command is built almost entirely around the use of an external editor. And beginning in version 1.5, Subversion will also use the configured external text editor when the user asks it to launch an editor during interactive conflict resolution. Oddly, there doesn't appear to be a way to use external editors to interactively provide lock comments.

Using External Differencing and Merge Tools

The interface between Subversion and external two- and three-way differencing tools hearkens back to a time when Subversion's only contextual differencing capabilities were built around invocations of the GNU diffutils toolchain, specifically the *diff* and *diff3* utilities. To get the kind of behavior Subversion needed, it called these utilities with more than a handful of options and parameters, most of which were quite specific to the utilities. Some time later, Subversion grew its own internal differencing library, and as a failover mechanism, the `--diff-cmd` and `--diff3-cmd` options were added to the Subversion command-line client so that users could more easily indicate that they preferred to use the GNU diff and diff3 utilities instead of the newfangled internal diff library. If those options were used, Subversion would simply ignore the internal diff library and would fall back to running those external programs, lengthy argument lists and all. And that's where things remain today.

It didn't take long for folks to realize that having such easy configuration mechanisms for specifying that Subversion should use the external GNU diff and diff3 utilities located at a particular place on the system could be applied toward the use of other differencing tools, too. After all, Subversion didn't actually verify that the things it was being told to run were members of the GNU diffutils toolchain. But the only configurable aspect of using those external tools is their location on the system—not the option set, parameter order, and so on. Subversion continues to throw all those GNU utility options at your external diff tool regardless of whether that program can understand those options. And that's where things get unintuitive for most users.

The key to using external two- and three-way differencing tools (other than GNU diff and diff3, of course) with Subversion is to use wrapper scripts, which convert the input from Subversion into something that your differencing tool can understand, and then to convert the output of your tool back into a format that Subversion expects—the format that the GNU tools would have used. The following sections cover the specifics of those expectations.

 The decision of when to fire off a contextual two- or three-way diff as part of a larger Subversion operation is made entirely by Subversion and is affected by, among other things, whether the files being operated on are human-readable as determined by their `svn:mime-type` property. This means, for example, that even if you had the niftiest Microsoft Word-aware differencing or merging tool in the universe, it would never be invoked by Subversion as long as your versioned Word documents had a configured MIME type that denoted that they were not human-readable (such as `application/msword`). For more about MIME type settings, see "File Content Type" on page 57.

Subversion 1.5 introduces interactive resolution of conflicts—described in "Resolve Conflicts (Merging Others' Changes)" on page 30—and one of the options provided to users is the ability to launch a third-party merge tool. If this action is taken, Subversion will consult the `merge-tool-cmd` runtime configuration option to find the name of an external merge tool and, upon finding one, will launch that tool with the appropriate input files. This differs from the configurable three-way differencing tool in a couple of ways. First, the differencing tool is always used to handle three-way differences, whereas the merge tool is employed only when three-way difference application has detected a conflict. Second, the interface is much cleaner—your configured merge tool need only accept as command-line parameters four path specifications: the base file, the "theirs" file (which contains upstream changes), the "mine" file (which contains

local modifications), and the path of the file where the final resolved contents should be stored.

External diff

Subversion calls external diff programs with parameters suitable for the GNU diff utility, and it expects only that the external program will return with a successful error code. For most alternative diff programs, only the sixth and seventh arguments—the paths of the files that represent the left and right sides of the diff, respectively—are of interest. Note that Subversion runs the diff program once per modified file covered by the Subversion operation, so if your program runs in an asynchronous fashion (or is "backgrounded"), you might have several instances of it all running simultaneously. Finally, Subversion expects that your program will return an error code of 1 if your program detected differences, or 0 if it did not—any other error code is considered a fatal error.[‡]

Examples 7-2 and 7-3 are templates for external diff tool wrappers in the Python and Windows batch scripting languages, respectively.

Example 7-2. diffwrap.py

```
#!/usr/bin/env python
import sys
import os

# Configure your favorite diff program here.
DIFF = "/usr/local/bin/my-diff-tool"

# Subversion provides the paths we need as the last two parameters.
LEFT  = sys.argv[-2]
RIGHT = sys.argv[-1]

# Call the diff command (change the following line to make sense for
# your diff program).
cmd = [DIFF, '--left', LEFT, '--right', RIGHT]
os.execv(cmd[0], cmd)

# Return an errorcode of 0 if no differences were detected, 1 if some were.
# Any other errorcode will be treated as fatal.
```

Example 7-3. diffwrap.bat

```
@ECHO OFF

REM Configure your favorite diff program here.
SET DIFF="C:\Program Files\Funky Stuff\My Diff Tool.exe"

REM Subversion provides the paths we need as the last two parameters.
```

[‡] The GNU diff manual page puts it this way: "An exit status of 0 means no differences were found, 1 means some differences were found, and 2 means trouble."

```
REM These are parameters 6 and 7 (unless you use svn diff -x, in
REM which case, all bets are off).
SET LEFT=%6
SET RIGHT=%7

REM Call the diff command (change the following line to make sense for
REM your diff program).
%DIFF% --left %LEFT% --right %RIGHT%

REM Return an errorcode of 0 if no differences were detected, 1 if some were.
REM Any other errorcode will be treated as fatal.
```

External diff3

Subversion calls external merge programs with parameters suitable for the GNU diff3
utility, expecting that the external program will return with a successful error code and
that the full file contents that result from the completed merge operation are printed
on the standard output stream (so that Subversion can redirect them into the appropriate version-controlled file). For most alternative merge programs, only the 9th, 10th,
and 11th arguments, the paths of the files which represent the "mine," "older," and
"yours" inputs, respectively, are of interest. Note that because Subversion depends on
the output of your merge program, your wrapper script must not exit before that output
has been delivered to Subversion. When it finally does exit, it should return an error
code of 0 if the merge was successful or 1 if unresolved conflicts remain in the output
—any other error code is considered a fatal error.

Examples 7-4 and 7-5 are templates for external merge tool wrappers in the Python and
Windows batch scripting languages, respectively.

Example 7-4. diff3wrap.py

```
#!/usr/bin/env python
import sys
import os

# Configure your favorite diff program here.
DIFF3 = "/usr/local/bin/my-merge-tool"

# Subversion provides the paths we need as the last three parameters.
MINE  = sys.argv[-3]
OLDER = sys.argv[-2]
YOURS = sys.argv[-1]

# Call the merge command (change the following line to make sense for
# your merge program).
cmd = [DIFF3, '--older', OLDER, '--mine', MINE, '--yours', YOURS]
os.execv(cmd[0], cmd)

# After performing the merge, this script needs to print the contents
# of the merged file to stdout.  Do that in whatever way you see fit.
# Return an errorcode of 0 on successful merge, 1 if unresolved conflicts
# remain in the result.  Any other errorcode will be treated as fatal.
```

Example 7-5. diff3wrap.bat

```
@ECHO OFF

REM Configure your favorite diff3/merge program here.
SET DIFF3="C:\Program Files\Funky Stuff\My Merge Tool.exe"

REM Subversion provides the paths we need as the last three parameters.
REM These are parameters 9, 10, and 11.  But we have access to only
REM nine parameters at a time, so we shift our nine-parameter window
REM twice to let us get to what we need.
SHIFT
SHIFT
SET MINE=%7
SET OLDER=%8
SET YOURS=%9

REM Call the merge command (change the following line to make sense for
REM your merge program).
%DIFF3% --older %OLDER% --mine %MINE% --yours %YOURS%

REM After performing the merge, this script needs to print the contents
REM of the merged file to stdout.  Do that in whatever way you see fit.
REM Return an errorcode of 0 on successful merge, 1 if unresolved conflicts
REM remain in the result.  Any other errorcode will be treated as fatal.
```

Summary

Sometimes there's a single right way to do things; sometimes there are many. Subversion's developers understand that while the majority of its exact behaviors are acceptable to most of its users, there are some corners of its functionality where such a universally pleasing approach doesn't exist. In those places, Subversion offers users the opportunity to tell it how *they* want it to behave.

In this chapter, we explored Subversion's runtime configuration system and other mechanisms by which users can control those configurable behaviors. If you are a developer, though, the next chapter will take you one step further. It describes how you can further customize your Subversion experience by writing your own software against Subversion's libraries.

## CHAPTER 8

Embedding Subversion

Subversion has a modular design: it's implemented as a collection of libraries written in C. Each library has a well-defined purpose and application programming interface (API), and that interface is available not only for Subversion itself to use but for any software that wishes to embed or otherwise programmatically control Subversion. Additionally, Subversion's API is available not only to other C programs, but also to programs written in higher-level languages such as Python, Perl, Java, and Ruby.

This chapter is for those who wish to interact with Subversion through its public API or its various language bindings. If you wish to write robust wrapper scripts around Subversion functionality to simplify your own life, if you are trying to develop more complex integrations between Subversion and other pieces of software, or if you just have an interest in Subversion's various library modules and what they offer, this chapter is for you. If, however, you don't foresee yourself participating with Subversion at such a level, feel free to skip this chapter with the confidence that your experience as a Subversion user will not be affected.

Layered Library Design

Each of Subversion's core libraries can be said to exist in one of three main layers—the Repository layer, the Repository Access (RA) layer, or the Client layer (see Figure P-1 in the Preface). We will examine these layers shortly, but first, let's briefly summarize Subversion's various libraries. For the sake of consistency, we will refer to the libraries by their extensionless Unix library names (*libsvn_fs*, *libsvn_wc*, *mod_dav_svn*, etc.):

libsvn_client
> Primary interface for client programs

libsvn_delta
> Tree and byte-stream differencing routines

libsvn_diff
> Contextual differencing and merging routines

libsvn_fs
> Filesystem commons and module loader

libsvn_fs_base
> The Berkeley DB filesystem backend

libsvn_fs_fs
> The native filesystem (FSFS) backend

libsvn_ra
> Repository Access commons and module loader

libsvn_ra_local
> The local Repository Access module

libsvn_ra_neon
> The WebDAV Repository Access module

libsvn_ra_serf
> Another (experimental) WebDAV Repository Access module

libsvn_ra_svn
> The custom protocol Repository Access module

libsvn_repos
> Repository interface

libsvn_subr
> Miscellaneous helpful subroutines

libsvn_wc
> The working copy management library

mod_authz_svn
> Apache authorization module for Subversion repositories access via WebDAV

mod_dav_svn
> Apache module for mapping WebDAV operations to Subversion ones

The fact that the word "miscellaneous" appears only once in the previous list is a good sign. The Subversion development team is serious about making sure that functionality lives in the right layer and libraries. Perhaps the greatest advantage of the modular design is its lack of complexity from a developer's point of view. As a developer, you can quickly formulate that kind of "big picture" that allows you to pinpoint the location of certain pieces of functionality with relative ease.

Another benefit of modularity is the ability to replace a given module with a whole new library that implements the same API without affecting the rest of the code base. In some sense, this happens within Subversion already. The *libsvn_ra_local*, *libsvn_ra_n e on*, *libsvn_ra_serf*, and *libsvn_ra_svn* libraries each implement the same interface, all working as plug-ins to *libsvn_ra*. And all four communicate with the Repository layer— *libsvn_ra_local* connects to the repository directly, whereas the other three do so over a network. The *libsvn_fs_base* and *libsvn_fs_fs* libraries are another pair of libraries that implement the same functionality in different ways—both are plug-ins to the common *libsvn_fs* library.

The client itself also highlights the benefits of modularity in the Subversion design. Subversion's *libsvn_client* library is a one-stop shop for most of the functionality necessary for designing a working Subversion client (see "Client Layer" on page 258). So while the Subversion distribution provides only the *svn* command-line client program, several third-party programs provide various forms of graphical client UIs. These GUIs use the same APIs that the stock command-line client does. This type of modularity has played a large role in the proliferation of available Subversion clients and IDE integrations and, by extension, to the tremendous adoption rate of Subversion itself.

Repository Layer

When referring to Subversion's Repository layer, we're generally talking about two basic concepts—the versioned filesystem implementation (accessed via *libsvn_fs*, and supported by its *libsvn_fs_base* and *libsvn_fs_fs* plug-ins), and the repository logic that wraps it (as implemented in *libsvn_repos*). These libraries provide the storage and reporting mechanisms for the various revisions of your version-controlled data. This layer is connected to the Client layer via the Repository Access layer, and is, from the perspective of the Subversion user, the stuff at the "other end of the line."

The Subversion filesystem is not a kernel-level filesystem that one would install in an operating system (such as the Linux ext2 or NTFS), but instead it is a virtual filesystem. Rather than storing "files" and "directories" as real files and directories (the kind you can navigate through using your favorite shell program), it uses one of two available abstract storage backends—either a Berkeley DB database environment or a flat-file representation. (To learn more about the two repository backends, see "Choosing a Data Store" on page 150.) There has even been considerable interest by the development community in giving future releases of Subversion the ability to use other backend database systems, perhaps through a mechanism such as Open Database Connectivity (ODBC). In fact, Google did something similar to this before launching the Google Code Project Hosting service: they announced in mid-2006 that members of its open source team had written a new proprietary Subversion filesystem plug-in that used Google's ultra-scalable Bigtable database for its storage.

The filesystem API exported by *libsvn_fs* contains the kinds of functionality you would expect from any other filesystem API—you can create and remove files and directories, copy and move them around, modify file contents, and so on. It also has features that are not quite as common, such as the ability to add, modify, and remove metadata ("properties") on each file or directory. Furthermore, the Subversion filesystem is a versioning filesystem, which means that as you make changes to your directory tree, Subversion remembers what your tree looked like before those changes. And before the previous changes. And the previous ones. And so on, all the way back through versioning time to (and just beyond) the moment you first started adding things to the filesystem.

All the modifications you make to your tree are done within the context of a Subversion commit transaction. The following is a simplified general routine for modifying your filesystem:

1. Begin a Subversion commit transaction.
2. Make your changes (adds, deletes, property modifications, etc.).
3. Commit your transaction.

Once you have committed your transaction, your filesystem modifications are permanently stored as historical artifacts. Each of these cycles generates a single new revision of your tree, and each revision is forever accessible as an immutable snapshot of "the way things were."

The Transaction Distraction

The notion of a Subversion transaction can become easily confused with the transaction support provided by the underlying database itself, especially given the former's close proximity to the Berkeley DB database code in *libsvn_fs_base*. Both types of transaction exist to provide atomicity and isolation. In other words, transactions give you the ability to perform a set of actions in an all-or-nothing fashion—either all the actions in the set complete with success, or they all get treated as though *none* of them ever happened— and in a way that does not interfere with other processes acting on the data.

Database transactions generally encompass small operations related specifically to the modification of data in the database itself (such as changing the contents of a table row). Subversion transactions are larger in scope, encompassing higher-level operations such as making modifications to a set of files and directories that are intended to be stored as the next revision of the filesystem tree. If that isn't confusing enough, consider the fact that Subversion uses a database transaction during the creation of a Subversion transaction (so that if the creation of a Subversion transaction fails, the database will look as though we had never attempted that creation in the first place)!

Fortunately for users of the filesystem API, the transaction support provided by the database system itself is hidden almost entirely from view (as should be expected from a properly modularized library scheme). It is only when you start digging into the implementation of the filesystem itself that such things become visible (or interesting).

Most of the functionality the filesystem interface provides deals with actions that occur on individual filesystem paths. That is, from outside the filesystem, the primary mechanism for describing and accessing the individual revisions of files and directories comes through the use of path strings such as */foo/bar*, just as though you were addressing files and directories through your favorite shell program. You add new files and directories by passing their paths-to-be to the right API functions. You query for information about them by the same mechanism.

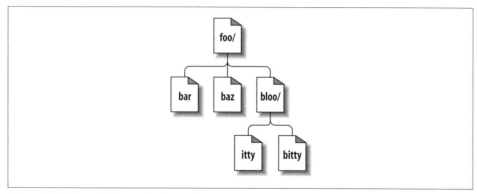

Figure 8-1. Files and directories in two dimensions

Unlike most filesystems, though, a path alone is not enough information to identify a file or directory in Subversion. Think of a directory tree as a two-dimensional system, where a node's siblings represent a sort of left-and-right motion, and navigating into the node's subdirectories represents a downward motion. Figure 8-1 shows a typical representation of a tree as exactly that.

The difference here is that the Subversion filesystem has a nifty third dimension that most filesystems do not have—Time!* In the filesystem interface, nearly every function that has a `path` argument also expects a `root` argument. This `svn_fs_root_t` argument describes either a revision or a Subversion transaction (which is simply a revision in the making) and provides that third dimension of context needed to understand the difference between */foo/bar* in revision 32, and the same path as it exists in revision 98. Figure 8-2 shows revision history as an added dimension to the Subversion filesystem universe.

As we mentioned earlier, the *libsvn_fs* API looks and feels like any other filesystem, except that it has this wonderful versioning capability. It was designed to be usable by any program interested in a versioning filesystem. Not coincidentally, Subversion itself is interested in that functionality. But while the filesystem API should be sufficient for basic file and directory versioning support, Subversion wants more—and that is where *libsvn_repos* comes in.

The Subversion repository library (*libsvn_repos*) sits (logically speaking) atop the *libsvn_fs* API, providing additional functionality beyond that of the underlying versioned filesystem logic. It does not completely wrap each and every filesystem function—only certain major steps in the general cycle of filesystem activity are wrapped by the repository interface. Some of these include the creation and committing of Subversion transactions and the modification of revision properties. These particular

---

* We understand that this may come as a shock to sci-fi fans who have long been under the impression that Time was actually the *fourth* dimension, and we apologize for any emotional trauma induced by our assertion of a different theory.

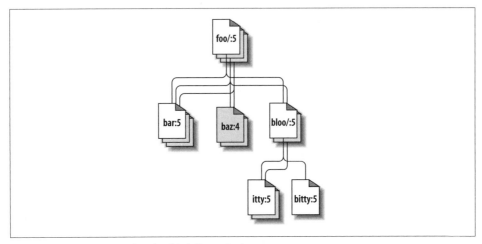

Figure 8-2. Versioning time—the third dimension!

events are wrapped by the repository layer because they have hooks associated with them. A repository hook system is not strictly related to implementing a versioning filesystem, so it lives in the repository wrapper library.

The hooks mechanism is but one of the reasons for the abstraction of a separate repository library from the rest of the filesystem code. The *libsvn_repos* API provides several other important utilities to Subversion. These include the abilities to:

- Create, open, destroy, and perform recovery steps on a Subversion repository and the filesystem included in that repository.
- Describe the differences between two filesystem trees.
- Query for the commit log messages associated with all (or some) of the revisions in which a set of files was modified in the filesystem.
- Generate a human-readable "dump" of the filesystem—a complete representation of the revisions in the filesystem.
- Parse that dump format, loading the dumped revisions into a different Subversion repository.

As Subversion continues to evolve, the repository library will grow with the filesystem library to offer increased functionality and configurable option support.

Repository Access Layer

If the Subversion Repository layer is at "the other end of the line," the Repository Access (RA) layer is the line itself. Charged with marshaling data between the client libraries and the repository, this layer includes the *libsvn_ra* module loader library, the RA modules themselves (which currently includes *libsvn_ra_neon*, *libsvn_ra_local*, *libsvn_ra_serf*, and *libsvn_ra_svn*), and any additional libraries needed by one or more of those RA modules (such as the *mod_dav_svn* Apache module or *libsvn_ra_svn*'s server, *svnserve*).

Since Subversion uses URLs to identify its repository resources, the protocol portion of the URL scheme (usually `file://`, `http://`, `https://`, `svn://`, or `svn+ssh://`) is used to determine which RA module will handle the communications. Each module registers a list of the protocols it knows how to "speak" so that the RA loader can, at runtime, determine which module to use for the task at hand. You can determine which RA modules are available to the Subversion command-line client, and what protocols they claim to support, by running `svn --version`:

```
$ svn --version
svn, version 1.5.0 (r31699)
   compiled Jun 18 2008, 09:57:36

Copyright (C) 2000-2008 CollabNet.
Subversion is open source software, see http://subversion.tigris.org/
This product includes software developed by CollabNet (http://www.Collab.Net/).

The following repository access (RA) modules are available:

* ra_neon : Module for accessing a repository via WebDAV protocol using Neon.
  - handles 'http' scheme
  - handles 'https' scheme
* ra_svn : Module for accessing a repository using the svn network protocol.
  - handles 'svn' scheme
* ra_local : Module for accessing a repository on local disk.
  - handles 'file' scheme
* ra_serf : Module for accessing a repository via WebDAV protocol using serf.
  - handles 'http' scheme
  - handles 'https' scheme

$
```

The public API exported by the RA layer contains functionality necessary for sending and receiving versioned data to and from the repository. And each of the available RA plug-ins is able to perform that task using a specific protocol—*libsvn_ra_dav* speaks HTTP/WebDAV (optionally using SSL encryption) with an Apache HTTP Server that is running the *mod_dav_svn* Subversion server module; *libsvn_ra_svn* speaks a custom network protocol with the *svnserve* program; and so on.

For those who wish to access a Subversion repository using still another protocol, that is precisely why the Repository Access layer is modularized! Developers can simply write a new library that implements the RA interface on one side and communicates with the repository on the other. Your new library can use existing network protocols or you can invent your own. You could use interprocess communication (IPC) calls, or—let's get crazy, shall we?—you could even implement an email-based protocol. Subversion supplies the APIs; you supply the creativity.

Client Layer

On the client side, the Subversion working copy is where all the action takes place. The bulk of functionality implemented by the client-side libraries exists for the sole purpose of managing working copies—directories full of files and other subdirectories that serve as a sort of local, editable "reflection" of one or more repository locations—and propagating changes to and from the Repository Access layer.

Subversion's working copy library, *libsvn_wc*, is directly responsible for managing the data in the working copies. To accomplish this, the library stores administrative information about each working copy directory within a special subdirectory. This subdirectory, named *.svn*, is present in each working copy directory and contains various other files and directories that record state and provide a private workspace for administrative action. For those familiar with CVS, this *.svn* subdirectory is similar in purpose to the *CVS* administrative directories found in CVS working copies. For more information about the *.svn* administrative area, see "Inside the Working Copy Administration Area" on page 259.

Binding Directly—A Word About Correctness

Why should your GUI program bind directly with a *libsvn_client* instead of acting as a wrapper around a command-line program? Besides simply being more efficient, it can be more correct as well. A command-line program (such as the one supplied with Subversion) that binds to the client library needs to effectively translate feedback and requested data bits from C types to some form of human-readable output. This type of translation can be lossy. That is, the program may not display all of the information harvested from the API or it may combine bits of information for compact representation.

If you wrap such a command-line program with yet another program, the second program has access only to already interpreted (and as we mentioned, likely incomplete) information, which it must *again* translate into *its* representation format. With each layer of wrapping, the integrity of the original data is potentially tainted more and more, much like the result of making a copy of a copy (of a copy…) of a favorite audio or video cassette.

But the most compelling argument for binding directly to the APIs instead of wrapping other programs is that the Subversion project makes compatibility promises regarding its APIs. Across minor versions of those APIs (such as between 1.3 and 1.4), no function's prototype will change. In other words, you aren't forced to update your program's source code simply because you've upgraded to a new version of Subversion. Certain functions might be deprecated, but they still work, and this gives you a buffer of time to eventually embrace the newer APIs. These kinds of compatibility promises do not exist for Subversion command-line program output, which is subject to change from release to release.

The Subversion client library, *libsvn_client*, has the broadest responsibility; its job is to mingle the functionality of the working copy library with that of the Repository Access layer, and then to provide the highest-level API to any application that wishes to perform general revision control actions. For example, the function svn_client_checkout() takes a URL as an argument. It passes this URL to the RA layer and opens an authenticated session with a particular repository. It then asks the repository for a certain tree, and sends this tree into the working copy library, which then writes a full working copy to disk (*.svn* directories and all).

The client library is designed to be used by any application. While the Subversion source code includes a standard command-line client, it should be very easy to write any number of GUI clients on top of the client library. New GUIs (or any new client, really) for Subversion need not be clunky wrappers around the included command-line client—they have full access via the *libsvn_client* API to the same functionality, data, and callback mechanisms that the command-line client uses. In fact, the Subversion source code tree contains a small C program (which you can find at *tools/examples/minimal_client.c*) that exemplifies how to wield the Subversion API to create a simple client program.

Inside the Working Copy Administration Area

As we mentioned earlier, each directory of a Subversion working copy contains a special subdirectory called *.svn* that houses administrative data about that working copy directory. Subversion uses the information in *.svn* to keep track of things such as:

- Which repository location(s) are represented by the files and subdirectories in the working copy directory
- Which revision of each of those files and directories is currently present in the working copy
- Any user-defined properties that might be attached to those files and directories
- Pristine (unedited) copies of the working copy files

The Subversion working copy administration area's layout and contents are considered implementation details not really intended for human consumption. Developers are encouraged to use Subversion's public APIs, or the tools that Subversion provides, to access and manipulate the working copy data, instead of directly reading or modifying those files. The file formats employed by the working copy library for its administrative data do change from time to time—a fact that the public APIs do a great job of hiding from the average user. In this section, we expose some of these implementation details sheerly to appease your overwhelming curiosity.

The Entries File

Perhaps the single most important file in the *.svn* directory is the *entries* file. It contains the bulk of the administrative information about the versioned items in a working copy directory. This one file tracks the repository URLs, pristine revision, file checksums, pristine text and property timestamps, scheduling and conflict state information, last-known commit information (author, revision, timestamp), local copy history—practically everything that a Subversion client is interested in knowing about a versioned (or to-be-versioned) resource!

Folks familiar with CVS's administrative directories will have recognized at this point that Subversion's *.svn/entries* file serves the purposes of, among other things, CVS's *CVS/Entries*, *CVS/Root*, and *CVS/Repository* files combined.

The format of the *.svn/entries* file has changed over time. Originally an XML file, it now uses a custom—though still human-readable—file format. While XML was a great choice for early developers of Subversion who were frequently debugging the file's contents (and Subversion's behavior in light of them), the need for easy developer debugging has diminished as Subversion has matured and has been replaced by the user's need for snappier performance. Be aware that Subversion's working copy library automatically upgrades working copies from one format to another—it reads the old formats and writes the new—which saves you the hassle of checking out a new working copy, but it can also complicate situations where different versions of Subversion might be trying to use the same working copy.

Pristine Copies and Property Files

As mentioned before, the *.svn* directory also holds the pristine "text-base" versions of files. You can find those in *.svn/text-base*. The benefits of these pristine copies are multiple—network-free checks for local modifications and difference reporting, network-free reversion of modified or missing files, more efficient transmission of changes to the server—but they come at the cost of having each versioned file stored at least twice on disk. These days, this seems to be a negligible penalty for most files. However, the situation gets uglier as the size of your versioned files grows. Some attention is being given to making the presence of the text-base an option. Ironically, though, it is as your versioned files' sizes get larger that the existence of the "text-base" becomes more crucial—who wants to transmit a huge file across a network just because he wants to commit a tiny change to it?

Similar in purpose to the "text-base" files are the property files and their pristine "prop-base" copies, located in *.svn/props* and *.svn/prop-base*, respectively. Since directories can have properties too, there are also *.svn/dir-props* and *.svn/dir-prop-base* files.

Using the APIs

Developing applications against the Subversion library APIs is fairly straightforward. Subversion is primarily a set of C libraries, with header (*.h*) files that live in the *subversion/include* directory of the source tree. These headers are copied into your system locations (e.g., */usr/local/include*) when you build and install Subversion itself from source. These headers represent the entirety of the functions and types meant to be accessible by users of the Subversion libraries. The Subversion developer community is meticulous about ensuring that the public API is well documented—refer directly to the header files for that documentation.

When examining the public header files, the first thing you might notice is that Subversion's datatypes and functions are namespace-protected. That is, every public Subversion symbol name begins with `svn_`, followed by a short code for the library in which the symbol is defined (such as `wc`, `client`, `fs`, etc.), followed by a single underscore (`_`), and then the rest of the symbol name. Semipublic functions (used among source files of a given library but not by code outside that library, and found inside the library directories themselves) differ from this naming scheme in that instead of a single underscore after the library code, they use a double underscore (`__`). Functions that are private to a given source file have no special prefixing and are declared `static`. Of course, a compiler isn't interested in these naming conventions, but they help clarify the scope of a given function or datatype.

Another good source of information about programming against the Subversion APIs is the project's own hacking guidelines, which you can find online at *http://subversion .tigris.org/hacking.html*. This document contains useful information, which, while aimed at developers and would-be developers of Subversion itself, is equally applicable to folks developing against Subversion as a set of third-party libraries.[†]

The Apache Portable Runtime Library

Along with Subversion's own datatypes, you will see many references to datatypes that begin with `apr_`—symbols from the Apache Portable Runtime (APR) library. APR is Apache's portability library, originally carved out of its server code as an attempt to separate the OS-specific bits from the OS-independent portions of the code. The result was a library that provides a generic API for performing operations that differ mildly—or wildly—from OS to OS. While the Apache HTTP Server was obviously the first user of the APR library, the Subversion developers immediately recognized the value of using APR as well. This means that there is practically no OS-specific code in Subversion itself. Also, it means that the Subversion client compiles and runs anywhere that the Apache HTTP Server does. Currently, this list includes all flavors of Unix, Win32, BeOS, OS/2, and Mac OS X.

[†] After all, Subversion uses Subversion's APIs, too.

In addition to providing consistent implementations of system calls that differ across operating systems,[‡] APR gives Subversion immediate access to many custom datatypes, such as dynamic arrays and hash tables. Subversion uses these types extensively. But perhaps the most pervasive APR datatype, found in nearly every Subversion API prototype, is the `apr_pool_t`—the APR memory pool. Subversion uses pools internally for all its memory allocation needs (unless an external library requires a different memory management mechanism for data passed through its API),[§] and while a person coding against the Subversion APIs is not required to do the same, she *is* required to provide pools to the API functions that need them. This means that users of the Subversion API must also link against APR, must call `apr_initialize()` to initialize the APR subsystem, and then must create and manage pools for use with Subversion API calls, typically by using `svn_pool_create()`, `svn_pool_clear()`, and `svn_pool_destroy()`.

Programming with Memory Pools

Almost every developer who has used the C programming language has at some point sighed at the daunting task of managing memory usage. Allocating enough memory to use, keeping track of those allocations, freeing the memory when you no longer need it—these tasks can be quite complex. And of course, failure to do those things properly can result in a program that crashes itself, or worse, crashes the computer.

Higher-level languages, on the other hand, either take the job of memory management away from you completely or make it something you toy with only when doing extremely tight program optimization. Languages such as Java and Python use *garbage collection*, allocating memory for objects when needed, and automatically freeing that memory when the object is no longer in use.

APR provides a middle-ground approach called *pool-based memory management*. It allows the developer to control memory usage at a lower resolution—per chunk (or "pool") of memory, instead of per allocated object. Rather than using `malloc()` and friends to allocate enough memory for a given object, you ask APR to allocate the memory from a memory pool. When you're finished using the objects you've created in the pool, you destroy the entire pool, effectively deallocating the memory consumed by *all* the objects you allocated from it. Thus, rather than keeping track of individual objects that need to be deallocated, your program simply considers the general lifetimes of those objects and allocates the objects in a pool whose lifetime (the time between the pool's creation and its deletion) matches the object's needs.

URL and Path Requirements

With remote version control operation as the whole point of Subversion's existence, it makes sense that some attention has been paid to internationalization (i18n) support.

[‡] Subversion uses ANSI system calls and datatypes as much as possible.

[§] Neon and Berkeley DB are examples of such libraries.

After all, while "remote" might mean "across the office," it could just as well mean "across the globe." To facilitate this, all of Subversion's public interfaces that accept path arguments expect those paths to be canonicalized—which is most easily accomplished by passing them through the `svn_path_canonicalize()` function—and encoded in UTF-8. This means, for example, that any new client binary that drives the *libsvn_client* interface needs to first convert paths from the locale-specific encoding to UTF-8 before passing those paths to the Subversion libraries, and then to reconvert any resultant output paths from Subversion back into the locale's encoding before using those paths for non-Subversion purposes. Fortunately, Subversion provides a suite of functions (see *subversion/include/svn_utf.h*) that any program can use to do these conversions.

Also, Subversion APIs require all URL parameters to be properly URI-encoded. So, instead of passing *file:///home/username/My File.txt* as the URL of a file named *My File.txt*, you need to pass *file:///home/username/My%20File.txt*. Again, Subversion supplies helper functions that your application can use—`svn_path_uri_encode()` and `svn_path_uri_decode()`, for URI encoding and decoding, respectively.

Using Languages Other Than C and C++

If you are interested in using the Subversion libraries in conjunction with something other than a C program—say, a Python or Perl script—Subversion has some support for this via the Simplified Wrapper and Interface Generator (SWIG). The SWIG bindings for Subversion are located in *subversion/bindings/swig*. They are still maturing, but they are usable. These bindings allow you to call Subversion API functions indirectly, using wrappers that translate the datatypes native to your scripting language into the datatypes needed by Subversion's C libraries.

Significant efforts have been made toward creating functional SWIG-generated bindings for Python, Perl, and Ruby. To some extent, the work done preparing the SWIG interface files for these languages is reusable in efforts to generate bindings for other languages supported by SWIG (which include versions of C#, Guile, Java, MzScheme, OCaml, PHP, and Tcl, among others). However, some extra programming is required to compensate for complex APIs that SWIG needs some help translating between languages. For more information on SWIG itself, see the project's web site at *http://www.swig.org/*.

Subversion also has language bindings for Java. The javahl bindings (located in *subversion/bindings/java* in the Subversion source tree) aren't SWIG-based; they are a mixture of Java and handcoded JNI. Javahl covers most Subversion client-side APIs and is specifically targeted at implementors of Java-based Subversion clients and IDE integrations.

Subversion's language bindings tend to lack the level of developer attention given to the core Subversion modules, but they can generally be trusted as production-ready. A number of scripts and applications, alternative Subversion GUI clients, and other third-party tools are successfully using Subversion's language bindings today to accomplish their Subversion integrations.

It's worth noting here that other options exist for interfacing with Subversion using other languages: alternative bindings for Subversion that aren't provided by the Subversion development community at all. You can find links to these alternative bindings on the Subversion project's links page (at *http://subversion.tigris.org/links.html*), but there are a couple of popular ones we feel are especially noteworthy. First, Barry Scott's PySVN bindings (*http://pysvn.tigris.org/*) are a popular option for binding with Python. PySVN boasts of a more Pythonic interface than the more C-like APIs provided by Subversion's own Python bindings. And if you're looking for a pure Java implementation of Subversion, check out SVNKit (*http://svnkit.com/*), which is Subversion rewritten from the ground up in Java.

SVNKit Versus javahl

In 2005, a small company called TMate announced the 1.0.0 release of JavaSVN—a pure Java implementation of Subversion. Since then, the project has been renamed to SVNKit (available at *http://svnkit.com/*) and has seen great success as a provider of Subversion functionality to various Subversion clients, IDE integrations, and other third-party tools.

The SVNKit library is interesting in that, unlike the javahl library, it is not merely a wrapper around the official Subversion core libraries. In fact, it shares no code with Subversion at all. But while it is easy to confuse SVNKit with javahl, and easier still not to even realize which of these libraries you are using, folks should be aware that SVNKit differs from javahl in some significant ways. First, SVNKit is not developed as open source software and seems to have at any given time only a few developers working on it. Also, SVNKit's license is more restrictive than that of Subversion. Finally, by aiming to be a pure Java Subversion library, SVNKit is limited in which portions of Subversion can be reasonably cloned while still keeping up with Subversion's releases. This has already happened once—SVNKit cannot access BDB-backed Subversion repositories via the `file://` protocol because there's no pure Java implementation of Berkeley DB that is file-format-compatible with the native implementation of that library.

That said, SVNKit has a well-established track record of reliability. And a pure Java solution is much more robust in the face of programming errors—a bug in SVNKit might raise a catchable Java exception, but a bug in the Subversion core libraries as accessed via javahl can bring down your entire Java Runtime Environment. So, weigh the costs when choosing a Java-based Subversion implementation.

Code Samples

Example 8-1 contains a code segment (written in C) that illustrates some of the concepts we've been discussing. It uses both the repository and filesystem interfaces (as can be determined by the prefixes `svn_repos_` and `svn_fs_` of the function names, respectively) to create a new revision in which a directory is added. You can see the use of an APR pool, which is passed around for memory allocation purposes. Also, the code reveals a somewhat obscure fact about Subversion error handling—all Subversion errors must be explicitly handled to avoid memory leakage (and in some cases, application failure).

Example 8-1. Using the Repository Layer

```
/* Convert a Subversion error into a simple boolean error code.
 *
 * NOTE:  Subversion errors must be cleared (using svn_error_clear())
 *        because they are allocated from the global pool, else memory
 *        leaking occurs.
 */
#define INT_ERR(expr)                           \
  do {                                          \
    svn_error_t *__temperr = (expr);            \
    if (__temperr)                              \
      {                                         \
        svn_error_clear(__temperr);             \
        return 1;                               \
      }                                         \
    return 0;                                   \
  } while (0)

/* Create a new directory at the path NEW_DIRECTORY in the Subversion
 * repository located at REPOS_PATH.  Perform all memory allocation in
 * POOL.  This function will create a new revision for the addition of
 * NEW_DIRECTORY.  Return zero if the operation completes
 * successfully, nonzero otherwise.
 */
static int
make_new_directory(const char *repos_path,
                   const char *new_directory,
                   apr_pool_t *pool)
{
  svn_error_t *err;
  svn_repos_t *repos;
  svn_fs_t *fs;
  svn_revnum_t youngest_rev;
  svn_fs_txn_t *txn;
  svn_fs_root_t *txn_root;
  const char *conflict_str;

  /* Open the repository located at REPOS_PATH.
   */
  INT_ERR(svn_repos_open(&repos, repos_path, pool));

  /* Get a pointer to the filesystem object that is stored in REPOS.
   */
  fs = svn_repos_fs(repos);

  /* Ask the filesystem to tell us the youngest revision that
   * currently exists.
   */
  INT_ERR(svn_fs_youngest_rev(&youngest_rev, fs, pool));
```

```c
/* Begin a new transaction that is based on YOUNGEST_REV.  We are
 * less likely to have our later commit rejected as conflicting if we
 * always try to make our changes against a copy of the latest snapshot
 * of the filesystem tree.
 */
INT_ERR(svn_repos_fs_begin_txn_for_commit2(&txn, repos, youngest_rev,
                                           apr_hash_make(pool), pool));

/* Now that we have started a new Subversion transaction, get a root
 * object that represents that transaction.
 */
INT_ERR(svn_fs_txn_root(&txn_root, txn, pool));

/* Create our new directory under the transaction root, at the path
 * NEW_DIRECTORY.
 */
INT_ERR(svn_fs_make_dir(txn_root, new_directory, pool));

/* Commit the transaction, creating a new revision of the filesystem
 * which includes our added directory path.
 */
err = svn_repos_fs_commit_txn(&conflict_str, repos,
                              &youngest_rev, txn, pool);
if (! err)
  {
    /* No error?  Excellent!  Print a brief report of our success.
     */
    printf("Directory '%s' was successfully added as new revision "
           "'%ld'.\n", new_directory, youngest_rev);
  }
else if (err->apr_err == SVN_ERR_FS_CONFLICT)
  {
    /* Uh-oh.  Our commit failed as the result of a conflict
     * (someone else seems to have made changes to the same area
     * of the filesystem that we tried to modify).  Print an error
     * message.
     */
    printf("A conflict occurred at path '%s' while attempting "
           "to add directory '%s' to the repository at '%s'.\n",
           conflict_str, new_directory, repos_path);
  }
else
  {
    /* Some other error has occurred.  Print an error message.
     */
    printf("An error occurred while attempting to add directory '%s' "
           "to the repository at '%s'.\n",
           new_directory, repos_path);
  }

INT_ERR(err);
}
```

Note that in Example 8-1, the code could just as easily have committed the transaction using svn_fs_commit_txn(). But the filesystem API knows nothing about the repository library's hook mechanism. If you want your Subversion repository to automatically perform some set of non-Subversion tasks every time you commit a transaction (e.g., sending an email that describes all the changes made in that transaction to your developer mailing list), you need to use the *libsvn_repos*-wrapped version of that function, which adds the hook triggering functionality—in this case, svn_repos_fs_commit_txn(). (For more information regarding Subversion's repository hooks, see "Implementing Repository Hooks" on page 156.)

Now let's switch languages. Example 8-2 is a sample program that uses Subversion's SWIG Python bindings to recursively crawl the youngest repository revision and to print the various paths reached during the crawl.

Example 8-2. Using the Repository Layer with Python

```python
#!/usr/bin/python

"""Crawl a repository, printing versioned object path names."""

import sys
import os.path
import svn.fs, svn.core, svn.repos

def crawl_filesystem_dir(root, directory):
    """Recursively crawl DIRECTORY under ROOT in the filesystem, and return
    a list of all the paths at or below DIRECTORY."""

    # Print the name of this path.
    print directory + "/"

    # Get the directory entries for DIRECTORY.
    entries = svn.fs.svn_fs_dir_entries(root, directory)

    # Loop over the entries.
    names = entries.keys()
    for name in names:
        # Calculate the entry's full path.
        full_path = directory + '/' + name

        # If the entry is a directory, recurse.  The recursion will return
        # a list with the entry and all its children, which we will add to
        # our running list of paths.
        if svn.fs.svn_fs_is_dir(root, full_path):
            crawl_filesystem_dir(root, full_path)
        else:
            # Else it's a file, so print its path here.
            print full_path

def crawl_youngest(repos_path):
    """Open the repository at REPOS_PATH, and recursively crawl its
    youngest revision."""
```

```
# Open the repository at REPOS_PATH, and get a reference to its
# versioning filesystem.
repos_obj = svn.repos.svn_repos_open(repos_path)
fs_obj = svn.repos.svn_repos_fs(repos_obj)

# Query the current youngest revision.
youngest_rev = svn.fs.svn_fs_youngest_rev(fs_obj)

# Open a root object representing the youngest (HEAD) revision.
root_obj = svn.fs.svn_fs_revision_root(fs_obj, youngest_rev)

# Do the recursive crawl.
crawl_filesystem_dir(root_obj, "")

if __name__ == "__main__":
    # Check for sane usage.
    if len(sys.argv) != 2:
        sys.stderr.write("Usage: %s REPOS_PATH\n"
                         % (os.path.basename(sys.argv[0])))
        sys.exit(1)

    # Canonicalize the repository path.
    repos_path = svn.core.svn_path_canonicalize(sys.argv[1])

    # Do the real work.
    crawl_youngest(repos_path)
```

This same program in C would need to deal with APR's memory pool system. But Python handles memory usage automatically, and Subversion's Python bindings adhere to that convention. In C, you'd be working with custom datatypes (such as those provided by the APR library) for representing the hash of entries and the list of paths, but Python has hashes (called "dictionaries") and lists as built-in datatypes, and it provides a rich collection of functions for operating on those types. So SWIG (with the help of some customizations in Subversion's language bindings layer) takes care of mapping those custom datatypes into the native datatypes of the target language. This provides a more intuitive interface for users of that language.

The Subversion Python bindings can be used for working copy operations, too. In the previous section of this chapter, we mentioned the *libsvn_client* interface and how it exists for the sole purpose of simplifying the process of writing a Subversion client. Example 8-3 is a brief example of how that library can be accessed via the SWIG Python bindings to re-create a scaled-down version of the *svn status* command.

Example 8-3. A Python status crawler

```
#!/usr/bin/env python

"""Crawl a working copy directory, printing status information."""

import sys
import os.path
import getopt
```

```
import svn.core, svn.client, svn.wc

def generate_status_code(status):
    """Translate a status value into a single-character status code,
    using the same logic as the Subversion command-line client."""
    code_map = { svn.wc.svn_wc_status_none        : ' ',
                 svn.wc.svn_wc_status_normal       : ' ',
                 svn.wc.svn_wc_status_added        : 'A',
                 svn.wc.svn_wc_status_missing      : '!',
                 svn.wc.svn_wc_status_incomplete   : '!',
                 svn.wc.svn_wc_status_deleted      : 'D',
                 svn.wc.svn_wc_status_replaced     : 'R',
                 svn.wc.svn_wc_status_modified     : 'M',
                 svn.wc.svn_wc_status_merged       : 'G',
                 svn.wc.svn_wc_status_conflicted   : 'C',
                 svn.wc.svn_wc_status_obstructed   : '~',
                 svn.wc.svn_wc_status_ignored      : 'I',
                 svn.wc.svn_wc_status_external     : 'X',
                 svn.wc.svn_wc_status_unversioned  : '?',
                 }
    return code_map.get(status, '?')

def do_status(wc_path, verbose):
    # Build a client context baton.
    ctx = svn.client.svn_client_ctx_t()

    def _status_callback(path, status):
        """A callback function for svn_client_status."""

        # Print the path, minus the bit that overlaps with the root of
        # the status crawl
        text_status = generate_status_code(status.text_status)
        prop_status = generate_status_code(status.prop_status)
        print '%s%s   %s' % (text_status, prop_status, path)

    # Do the status crawl, using _status_callback() as our callback function.
    revision = svn.core.svn_opt_revision_t()
    revision.type = svn.core.svn_opt_revision_head
    svn.client.svn_client_status2(wc_path, revision, _status_callback,
                                  svn.core.svn_depth_infinity, verbose,
                                  0, 0, 1, ctx)

def usage_and_exit(errorcode):
    """Print usage message, and exit with ERRORCODE."""
    stream = errorcode and sys.stderr or sys.stdout
    stream.write("""Usage: %s OPTIONS WC-PATH
Options:
  --help, -h    : Show this usage message
  --verbose, -v : Show all statuses, even uninteresting ones
""" % (os.path.basename(sys.argv[0])))
    sys.exit(errorcode)

if __name__ == '__main__':
    # Parse command-line options.
    try:
```

```
        opts, args = getopt.getopt(sys.argv[1:], "hv", ["help", "verbose"])
    except getopt.GetoptError:
        usage_and_exit(1)
    verbose = 0
    for opt, arg in opts:
        if opt in ("-h", "--help"):
            usage_and_exit(0)
        if opt in ("-v", "--verbose"):
            verbose = 1
    if len(args) != 1:
        usage_and_exit(2)

    # Canonicalize the repository path.
    wc_path = svn.core.svn_path_canonicalize(args[0])

    # Do the real work.
    try:
        do_status(wc_path, verbose)
    except svn.core.SubversionException, e:
        sys.stderr.write("Error (%d): %s\n" % (e.apr_err, e.message))
        sys.exit(1)
```

As was the case in Example 8-2, this program is pool-free and uses, for the most part, normal Python datatypes. The call to `svn_client_ctx_t()` is deceiving because the public Subversion API has no such function—this just happens to be a case where SWIG's automatic language generation bleeds through a little bit (the function is a sort of factory function for Python's version of the corresponding complex C structure). Also note that the path passed to this program (like the last one) gets run through `svn_path_canonicalize()`, because to *not* do so runs the risk of triggering the underlying Subversion C library's assertions about such things, which translates into rather immediate and unceremonious program abortion.

Summary

One of Subversion's greatest features isn't something you get from running its command-line client or other tools. It's the fact that Subversion was designed modularly and provides a stable, public API so that others—like yourself, perhaps—can write custom software that drives Subversion's core logic.

In this chapter, we took a closer look at Subversion's architecture, examining its logical layers and describing that public API, the very same API that Subversion's own layers use to communicate with each other. Many developers have found interesting uses for the Subversion API, from simple repository hook scripts, to integrations between Subversion and some other application, to completely different version control systems. What unique itch will *you* scratch with it?

CHAPTER 9

Subversion Complete Reference

This chapter is intended to be a complete reference to using Subversion. This includes the command-line client (*svn*) and all its subcommands, as well as the repository administration programs (*svnadmin* and *svnlook*) and their respective subcommands.

The Subversion Command-Line Client: svn

To use the command-line client, type *svn*, the subcommand you wish to use,[*] and any options or targets that you wish to operate on—the subcommand and the options need not appear in a specific order. For example, all of the following are valid ways to use *svn status*:

```
$ svn -v status
$ svn status -v
$ svn status -v myfile
```

You can find many more examples of how to use most client commands in Chapter 2 and commands for managing properties in "Properties" on page 48.

svn Options

While Subversion has different options for its subcommands, all options exist in a single namespace—that is, each option is guaranteed to mean the same thing regardless of the subcommand you use it with. For example, --verbose (-v) always means "verbose output," regardless of the subcommand you use it with.

The *svn* command-line client usually exits quickly with an error if you pass it an option that does not apply to the specified subcommand. But as of Subversion 1.5, several of the options that apply to all—or nearly all—of the subcommands have been deemed acceptable by all subcommands, even if they have no effect on some of them. They appear grouped together in the command-line client's usage messages as global options.

---

[*] Well, you don't need a subcommand to use the --version option, but we'll get to that in just a minute.

This was done to assist folks who write scripts that wrap the command-line client. These global options are as follows:

`--config-dir` *DIR*

> Instructs Subversion to read configuration information from the specified directory instead of the default location (*.subversion* in the user's home directory).

`--no-auth-cache`

> Prevents caching of authentication information (e.g., username and password) in the Subversion runtime configuration directories.

`--non-interactive`

> Disables all interactive prompting. Some examples of interactive prompting include requests for authentication credentials and conflict resolution decisions. This is useful if you're running Subversion inside an automated script and it's more appropriate to have Subversion fail than to prompt for more information.

`--password` *PASSWD*

> Specifies the password to use when authenticating against a Subversion server. If not provided, or if incorrect, Subversion will prompt you for this information as needed.

`--username` *NAME*

> Specifies the username to use when authenticating against a Subversion server. If not provided, or if incorrect, Subversion will prompt you for this information as needed.

The rest of the options apply and are accepted by only a subset of the subcommand. They are as follows:

`--accept` *ACTION*

> Specifies an action for automatic conflict resolution. Possible actions are `postpone`, `base`, `mine-full`, `theirs-full`, `edit`, and `launch`.

`--auto-props`

> Enables auto-props, overriding the `enable-auto-props` directive in the *config* file.

`--change (-c)` *ARG*

> Used as a means to refer to a specific "change" (a.k.a., a revision). This option is syntactic sugar for "-r ARG-1:ARG".

`--changelist` *ARG*

> Instructs Subversion to operate only on members of the changelist named *ARG*. You can use this option multiple times to specify sets of changelists.

`--cl` *ARG*

> An alias for the `--changelist` option.

`--depth` *ARG*

> Instructs Subversion to limit the scope of an operation to a particular tree depth. *ARG* is one of `empty`, `files`, `immediates`, or `infinity`.

`--diff-cmd` *CMD*

> Specifies an external program to use to show differences between files. When *svn diff* is invoked without this option, it uses Subversion's internal diff engine, which provides unified diffs by default. If you want to use an external diff program, use `--diff-cmd`. You can pass options to the diff program with the `--extensions` option (more on that later in this section).

`--diff3-cmd` *CMD*

> Specifies an external program to use to merge files.

`--dry-run`

> Goes through all the motions of running a command, but makes no actual changes—either on disk or in the repository.

`--editor-cmd` *CMD*

> Specifies an external program to use to edit a log message or a property value. See the `editor-cmd` section in "Config" on page 239 for ways to specify a default editor.

`--encoding` *ENC*

> Tells Subversion that your commit message is encoded in the charset provided. The default is your operating system's native locale, and you should specify the encoding if your commit message is in any other encoding.

`--extensions` *(-x) ARGS*

> Specifies an argument or arguments that Subversion should pass to an external diff command. This option is valid only when used with the *svn diff* or *svn merge* commands, with the `--diff-cmd` option. If you wish to pass multiple arguments, you must enclose all of them in quotes (e.g., `svn diff --diff-cmd /usr/bin/diff -x "-b -E"`).

`--file` *(-F) FILENAME*

> Uses the contents of the named file for the specified subcommand, though different subcommands do different things with this content. For example, *svn commit* uses the content as a commit log, whereas *svn propset* uses it as a property value.

`--force`

> Forces a particular command or operation to run. Subversion will prevent you from performing some operations in normal usage, but you can pass the force option to tell Subversion, "I know what I'm doing as well as the possible repercussions of doing it, so let me at 'em." This option is the programmatic equivalent of doing your own electrical work with the power on—if you don't know what you're doing, you're likely to get a nasty shock.

`--force-log`

> Forces a suspicious parameter passed to the `--message` (-m) or `--file` (-F) option to be accepted as valid. By default, Subversion will produce an error if parameters to these options look like they might instead be targets of the subcommand. For example, if you pass a versioned file's path to the `--file` (-F) option, Subversion will assume you've made a mistake, that the path was instead intended as the target

of the operation, and that you simply failed to provide some other—unversioned—file as the source of your log message. To assert your intent and override these types of errors, pass the `--force-log` option to subcommands that accept log messages.

`--help (-h) or (-?)`

If used with one or more subcommands, shows the built-in help text for each. If used alone, it displays the general client help text.

`--ignore-ancestry`

Tells Subversion to ignore ancestry when calculating differences (rely on path contents alone).

`--ignore-externals`

Tells Subversion to ignore externals definitions and the external working copies managed by them.

`--incremental`

Prints output in a format suitable for concatenation.

`--keep-changelists`

Tells Subversion not to delete changelists after committing.

`--keep-local`

Keeps the local copy of a file or directory (used with the *svn delete* command).

`--limit (-l) NUM`

Shows only the first *NUM* log messages.

`--message (-m) MESSAGE`

Indicates that you will specify either a log message or a lock comment on the command line, following this option. For example:

```
$ svn commit -m "They don't make Sunday."
```

`--new ARG`

Uses *ARG* as the newer target (for use with *svn diff*).

`--no-auto-props`

Disables auto-props, overriding the `enable-auto-props` directive in the *config* file.

`--no-diff-deleted`

Prevents Subversion from printing differences for deleted files. The default behavior when you remove a file is for *svn diff* to print the same differences that you would see if you had left the file but removed all the content.

`--no-ignore`

Shows files in the status listing that would normally be omitted since they match a pattern in the `global-ignores` configuration option or the `svn:ignore` property. See "Config" on page 239 and "Ignoring Unversioned Items" on page 60 for more information.

`--no-unlock`

Tells Subversion not to automatically unlock files (the default commit behavior is to unlock all files listed as part of the commit). See "Locking" on page 73 for more information.

`--non-recursive (-N)`

Deprecated. Stops a subcommand from recursing into subdirectories. Most subcommands recurse by default, but some subcommands—usually those that have the potential to remove or undo your local modifications—do not.

`--notice-ancestry`

Pays attention to ancestry when calculating differences.

`--old ARG`

Uses *ARG* as the older target (for use with *svn diff*).

`--parents`

Creates and adds nonexistent or nonversioned parent subdirectories to the working copy or repository as part of an operation. This is useful for automatically creating multiple subdirectories where none currently exist. If performed on a URL, all the directories will be created in a single commit.

`--quiet (-q)`

Requests that the client print only essential information while performing an operation.

`--record-only`

Marks revisions as merged (for use with `--revision`).

`--recursive (-R)`

Makes a subcommand recurse into subdirectories. Most subcommands recurse by default.

`--reintegrate`

Used with the *svn merge* subcommand, merges all of the source URL's changes into the working copy. See "Keeping a Branch in Sync" on page 109 for details.

`--relocate FROM TO [PATH...]`

Used with the *svn switch* subcommand, changes the location of the repository that your working copy references. This is useful if the location of your repository changes and you have an existing working copy that you'd like to continue to use. See *svn switch* for an example.

`--remove ARG`

Disassociates *ARG* from a changelist.

`--revision (-r) REV`

Indicates that you're going to supply a revision (or range of revisions) for a particular operation. You can provide revision numbers, keywords, or dates (in curly braces) as arguments to the revision option. If you wish to offer a range of revisions, you can provide two revisions separated by a colon. For example:

```
$ svn log -r 1729
$ svn log -r 1729:HEAD
$ svn log -r 1729:1744
$ svn log -r {2001-12-04}:{2002-02-17}
$ svn log -r 1729:{2002-02-17}
```

See "Revision Keywords" on page 46 for more information.

`--revprop`

Operates on a revision property instead of a property specific to a file or directory. This option requires that you also pass a revision with the `--revision` (-r) option.

`--set-depth ARG`

Sets the sticky depth on a directory in a working copy to one of `empty`, `files`, `immediates`, or `infinity`.

`--show-revs ARG`

Used to make *svn mergeinfo* display either `merged` or `eligible` revisions.

`--show-updates (-u)`

Causes the client to display information about which files in your working copy are out of date. This doesn't actually update any of your files—it just shows you which files will be updated if you then use *svn update*.

`--stop-on-copy`

Causes a Subversion subcommand that traverses the history of a versioned resource to stop harvesting that historical information when a copy—that is, a location in history where that resource was copied from another location in the repository—is encountered.

`--strict`

Causes Subversion to use strict semantics, a notion that is rather vague unless talking about specific subcommands (namely, *svn propget*).

`--targets FILENAME`

Tells Subversion to get the list of files that you wish to operate on from the filename that you provide instead of listing all the files on the command line.

`--use-merge-history (-g)`

Uses or displays additional information from merge history.

`--verbose (-v)`

Requests that the client print out as much information as it can while running any subcommand. This may result in Subversion printing out additional fields, detailed information about every file, or additional information regarding its actions.

`--version`

Prints the client version info. This information includes not only the version number of the client, but also a listing of all repository access modules that the client can use to access a Subversion repository. With `--quiet` (-q), it prints only the version number in a compact form.

`--with-all-revprops`

Used with the `--xml` option to *svn log*, will retrieve and display all revision properties in the log output.

`--with-revprop ARG`

When used with any command that writes to the repository, sets the revision property, using the `NAME=VALUE` format, `NAME` to `VALUE`. When used with *svn log* in `--xml` mode, this displays the value of `ARG` in the log output.

`--xml`

Prints output in XML format.

svn Subcommands

Here are the various subcommands for the *svn* program. For the sake of brevity, we omit the global options (described in "svn Options" on page 271) from the subcommand descriptions that follow.

---

svn add
Add files, directories, or symbolic links.

Synopsis
```
svn add PATH...
```

Description
Schedule files, directories, or symbolic links in your working copy for addition to the repository. They will be uploaded and added to the repository on your next commit. If you add something and change your mind before committing, you can unschedule the addition using *svn revert*.

Alternate names
None.

Changes
Working copy.

Accesses repository
No.

Options
```
--auto-props
--depth ARG
--force
--no-auto-props
--no-ignore
--parents
--quiet (-q)
--targets FILENAME
```

Examples

To add a file to your working copy:

```
$ svn add foo.c
A         foo.c
```

When adding a directory, the default behavior of *svn add* is to recurse:

```
$ svn add testdir
A         testdir
A         testdir/a
A         testdir/b
A         testdir/c
A         testdir/d
```

You can add a directory without adding its contents:

```
$ svn add --depth=empty otherdir
A         otherdir
```

Normally, the command svn add * will skip over any directories that are already under version control. Sometimes, however, you may want to add every unversioned object in your working copy, including those hiding deeper. Passing the --force option makes *svn add* recurse into versioned directories:

```
$ svn add * --force
A         foo.c
A         somedir/bar.c
A (bin)   otherdir/docs/baz.doc
...
```

svn blame

Show author and revision information inline for the specified files or URLs.

Synopsis

```
svn blame TARGET[@REV]...
```

Description

Show author and revision information inline for the specified files or URLs. Each line of text is annotated at the beginning with the author (username) and the revision number for the last change to that line.

Alternate names

praise, annotate, ann.

Changes

Nothing.

Accesses repository

Yes.

Options

```
--extensions (-x) ARG
--force
--incremental
--revision (-r) ARG
```

```
--use-merge-history (-g)
--verbose (-v)
--xml
```

Examples

If you want to see blame-annotated source for *readme.txt* in your test repository:

```
$ svn blame http://svn.red-bean.com/repos/test/readme.txt
    3        sally This is a README file.
    5        harry You should read this.
```

Even if *svn blame* says that Harry last modified *readme.txt* in revision 5, you'll have to examine exactly what the revision changed to be sure that Harry changed the *context* of the line—he may have adjusted just the whitespace.

If you use the `--xml` option, you can get XML output describing the blame annotations, but not the contents of the lines themselves:

```
$ svn blame --xml http://svn.red-bean.com/repos/test/readme.txt
<?xml version="1.0"?>
<blame>
<target
   path="sandwich.txt">
<entry
   line-number="1">
<commit
   revision="3">
<author>sally</author>
<date>2008-05-25T19:12:31.428953Z</date>
</commit>
</entry>
<entry
   line-number="2">
<commit
   revision="5">
<author>harry</author>
<date>2008-05-29T03:26:12.293121Z</date>
</commit>
</entry>
</target>
</blame>
```

svn cat

Output the contents of the specified files or URLs.

Synopsis

```
svn cat TARGET[@REV]...
```

Description

Output the contents of the specified files or URLs. For listing the contents of directories, see *svn list* later in this chapter.

Alternate names

None.

Changes
Nothing.

Accesses repository
Yes.

Options
```
--revision (-r) REV
```

Examples
If you want to view *readme.txt* in your repository without checking it out:

```
$ svn cat http://svn.red-bean.com/repos/test/readme.txt
This is a README file.
You should read this.
```

 If your working copy is out of date (or you have local modifications) and you want to see the HEAD revision of a file in your working copy, *svn cat -r HEAD FILENAME* will automatically fetch the HEAD revision of the specified path:

```
$ cat foo.c
This file is in my local working copy
and has changes that I've made.

$ svn cat -r HEAD foo.c
Latest revision fresh from the repository!
```

svn changelist
Associate (or deassociate) local paths with a changelist.

Synopsis
```
changelist CLNAME TARGET...

changelist --remove TARGET...
```

Description
Used for dividing files in a working copy into a changelist (logical named grouping) to allow users to easily work on multiple file collections within a single working copy.

Alternate names
cl.

Changes
Working copy.

Accesses repository
No.

Options
```
--changelist ARG
--depth ARG
--quiet (-q)
--recursive (-R)
```

```
--remove
--targets ARG
```

Example
Edit three files, add them to a changelist, then commit only files in that changelist:

```
$ svn cl issue1729 foo.c bar.c baz.c
Path 'foo.c' is now a member of changelist 'issue1729'.
Path 'bar.c' is now a member of changelist 'issue1729'.
Path 'baz.c' is now a member of changelist 'issue1729'.

$ svn status
A       someotherfile.c
A       test/sometest.c

--- Changelist 'issue1729':
A       foo.c
A       bar.c
A       baz.c

$ svn commit --changelist issue1729 -m "Fixing Issue 1729."
Adding          bar.c
Adding          baz.c
Adding          foo.c
Transmitting file data ...
Committed revision 2.

$ svn status
A       someotherfile.c
A       test/sometest.c
```

Note that only the files in changelist *issue1729* were committed.

svn checkout

Check out a working copy from a repository.

Synopsis
```
svn checkout URL[@REV]... [PATH]
```

Description
Check out a working copy from a repository. If *PATH* is omitted, the basename of the URL will be used as the destination. If multiple URLs are given, each will be checked out into a subdirectory of *PATH*, with the name of the subdirectory being the basename of the URL.

Alternate names
co.

Changes
Creates a working copy.

Accesses repository
Yes.

Options

```
--depth ARG
--force
--ignore-externals
--quiet (-q)
--revision (-r) REV
```

Examples

Check out a working copy into a directory called *mine*:

```
$ svn checkout file:///var/svn/repos/test mine
A  mine/a
A  mine/b
A  mine/c
A  mine/d
Checked out revision 20.
$ ls
mine
```

Check out two different directories into two separate working copies:

```
$ svn checkout file:///var/svn/repos/test  file:///var/svn/repos/quiz
A  test/a
A  test/b
A  test/c
A  test/d
Checked out revision 20.
A  quiz/l
A  quiz/m
Checked out revision 13.
$ ls
quiz  test
```

Check out two different directories into two separate working copies, but place both into a directory called *working-copies*:

```
$ svn checkout file:///var/svn/repos/test  file:///var/svn/repos/quiz working-copies
A  working-copies/test/a
A  working-copies/test/b
A  working-copies/test/c
A  working-copies/test/d
Checked out revision 20.
A  working-copies/quiz/l
A  working-copies/quiz/m
Checked out revision 13.
$ ls
working-copies
```

If you interrupt a checkout (or something else interrupts your checkout, such as loss of connectivity, etc.), you can restart it either by issuing the identical checkout command again or by updating the incomplete working copy:

```
$ svn checkout file:///var/svn/repos/test mine
A  mine/a
A  mine/b
^C
svn: The operation was interrupted
```

```
svn: caught SIGINT

$ svn checkout file:///var/svn/repos/test mine
A  mine/c
^C
svn: The operation was interrupted
svn: caught SIGINT

$ svn update mine
A  mine/d
Updated to revision 20.
```

If you wish to check out some revision other than the most recent one, you can do so by providing the --revision (-r) option to the *svn checkout* command:

```
$ svn checkout -r 2 file:///var/svn/repos/test mine
A  mine/a
Checked out revision 2.
```

svn cleanup

Synopsis
```
svn cleanup [PATH...]
```

Description
Recursively clean up the working copy, removing working copy locks and resuming unfinished operations. If you ever get a `working copy locked` error, run this command to remove stale locks and get your working copy into a usable state again.

If, for some reason, an *svn update* fails due to a problem running an external diff program (e.g., user input or network failure), pass the --diff3-cmd to allow cleanup to complete any merging with your external diff program. You can also specify any configuration directory with the --config-dir option, but you should need these options extremely infrequently.

Alternate names
None.

Changes
Working copy.

Accesses repository
No.

Options
```
--diff3-cmd CMD
```

Examples
Well, there's not much to the examples here, as *svn cleanup* generates no output. If you pass no *PATH*, then "." is used:

```
$ svn cleanup

$ svn cleanup /var/svn/working-copy
```

svn commit
Send changes from your working copy to the repository.

Synopsis

```
svn commit [PATH...]
```

Description

Send changes from your working copy to the repository. If you do not supply a log message with your commit by using either the `--file` or `--message` option, *svn* will launch your editor for you to compose a commit message. See the `editor-cmd` list entry in "Config" on page 239.

svn commit will send any lock tokens that it finds and will release locks on all *PATH*s committed (recursively) unless `--no-unlock` is passed.

 If you begin a commit and Subversion launches your editor to compose the commit message, you can still abort without committing your changes. If you want to cancel your commit, just quit your editor without saving your commit message and Subversion will prompt you to either abort the commit, continue with no message, or edit the message again.

Alternate names

ci (short for "check in"; not *co*, which is an alias for the *checkout* subcommand).

Changes

Working copy; repository.

Accesses repository

Yes.

Options

```
--changelist ARG
--depth ARG
--editor-cmd ARG
--encoding ENC
--file (-F) FILE
--force-log
--keep-changelists
--message (-m) TEXT
--no-unlock
--quiet (-q)
--targets FILENAME
--with-revprop ARG
```

Examples

Commit a simple modification to a file with the commit message on the command line and an implicit target of your current directory ("."):

```
$ svn commit -m "added howto section."
Sending        a
Transmitting file data .
Committed revision 3.
```

Commit a modification to the file *foo.c* (explicitly specified on the command line) with the commit message in a file named *msg*:

```
$ svn commit -F msg foo.c
Sending        foo.c
Transmitting file data .
Committed revision 5.
```

If you want to use a file that's under version control for your commit message with `--file`, you need to pass the `--force-log` option:

```
$ svn commit --file file_under_vc.txt foo.c
svn: The log message file is under version control
svn: Log message file is a versioned file; use '--force-log' to override

$ svn commit --force-log --file file_under_vc.txt foo.c
Sending        foo.c
Transmitting file data .
Committed revision 6.
```

To commit a file scheduled for deletion:

```
$ svn commit -m "removed file 'c'."
Deleting       c

Committed revision 7.
```

svn copy

Copy a file or directory in a working copy or in the repository.

Synopsis
```
svn copy SRC[@REV]... DST
```

Description
Copy one or more files in a working copy or in the repository. When copying multiple sources, they will be added as children of *DST*, which must be a directory. *SRC* and *DST* can each be either a working copy (WC) path or URL:

WC → WC
> Copy and schedule an item for addition (with history).

WC → URL
> Immediately commit a copy of WC to URL.

URL → WC
> Check out URL into WC and schedule it for addition.

URL → URL
> Complete server-side copy. This is usually used to branch and tag.

When copying multiple sources, they will be added as children of *DST*, which must be a directory.

If no peg revision (i.e., *@REV*) is supplied, by default the BASE revision will be used for files copied from the working copy, whereas the HEAD revision will be used for files copied from a URL.

 You can only copy files within a single repository. Subversion does not support cross-repository copying.

Alternate names
cp.

Changes
Repository if destination is a URL; working copy if destination is a WC path.

Accesses repository
Yes, if source or destination is in the repository, or if needed to look up the source revision number.

Options
```
--editor-cmd EDITOR
--encoding ENC
--file (-F) FILE
--force-log
--message (-m) TEXT
--parents
--quiet (-q)
--revision (-r) REV
--with-revprop ARG
```

Examples
Copy an item within your working copy (this schedules the copy—nothing goes into the repository until you commit):
```
$ svn copy foo.txt bar.txt
A         bar.txt
$ svn status
A +   bar.txt
```

Copy several files in a working copy into a subdirectory:
```
$ svn cp bat.c baz.c qux.c src
A         src/bat.c
A         src/baz.c
A         src/qux.c
```

Copy revision 8 of *bat.c* into your working copy under a different name:
```
$ svn cp -r 8 bat.c ya-old-bat.c
A         ya-old-bat.c
```

Copy an item in your working copy to a URL in the repository (this is an immediate commit, so you must supply a commit message):

```
$ svn copy near.txt file:///var/svn/repos/test/far-away.txt -m "Remote copy."
```

```
Committed revision 8.
```

Copy an item from the repository to your working copy (this just schedules the copy—nothing goes into the repository until you commit):

```
$ svn copy file:///var/svn/repos/test/far-away -r 6 near-here
A         near-here
```

 This is the recommended way to resurrect a dead file in your repository!

And finally, copy between two URLs:

```
$ svn copy file:///var/svn/repos/test/far-away \
           file:///var/svn/repos/test/over-there -m "remote copy."
```

```
Committed revision 9.
```

```
$ svn copy file:///var/svn/repos/test/trunk \
           file:///var/svn/repos/test/tags/0.6.32-prerelease -m "tag tree"
```

```
Committed revision 12.
```

 This is the easiest way to "tag" a revision in your repository—just *svn copy* that revision (usually HEAD) into your *tags* directory.

And don't worry if you forgot to tag—you can always specify an older revision and tag anytime:

```
$ svn copy -r 11 file:///var/svn/repos/test/trunk \
           file:///var/svn/repos/test/tags/0.6.32-prerelease \
           -m "Forgot to tag at rev 11"
```

```
Committed revision 13.
```

svn delete

Delete an item from a working copy or the repository.

Synopsis
```
svn delete PATH...

svn delete URL...
```

Description
Items specified by *PATH* are scheduled for deletion upon the next commit. Files (and directories that have not been committed) are immediately removed from the working copy unless the

`--keep-local` option is given. The command will not remove any unversioned or modified items; use the `--force` option to override this behavior.

Items specified by URL are deleted from the repository via an immediate commit. Multiple URLs are committed atomically.

Alternate names
del, *remove*, *rm*.

Changes
Working copy if operating on files; repository if operating on URLs.

Accesses repository
Only if operating on URLs.

Options
```
--editor-cmd EDITOR
--encoding ENC
--file (-F) FILE
--force
--force-log
--keep-local
--message (-m) TEXT
--quiet (-q)
--targets FILENAME
--with-revprop ARG
```

Examples
Using *svn* to delete a file from your working copy deletes your local copy of the file, but it merely schedules the file to be deleted from the repository. When you commit, the file is deleted in the repository:

```
$ svn delete myfile
D         myfile

$ svn commit -m "Deleted file 'myfile'."
Deleting      myfile
Transmitting file data .
Committed revision 14.
```

Deleting a URL, however, is immediate, so you have to supply a log message:

```
$ svn delete -m "Deleting file 'yourfile'" \
          file:///var/svn/repos/test/yourfile

Committed revision 15.
```

Here's an example of how to force deletion of a file that has local mods:

```
$ svn delete over-there
svn: Attempting restricted operation for modified resource
svn: Use --force to override this restriction
svn: 'over-there' has local modifications

$ svn delete --force over-there
D         over-there
```

svn diff

Synopsis

```
diff [-c M | -r N[:M]] [TARGET[@REV]...]

diff [-r N[:M]] --old=OLD-TGT[@OLDREV] [--new=NEW-TGT[@NEWREV]] [PATH...]

diff OLD-URL[@OLDREV] NEW-URL[@NEWREV]
```

Description

Display the differences between two paths. You can use *svn diff* in the following ways:

- Use just `svn diff` to display local modifications in a working copy.

- Display the changes made to *TARGET*s as they are seen in *REV* between two revisions. *TARGET*s may be all working copy paths or all *URL*s. If *TARGET*s are working copy paths, N defaults to BASE and M to the working copy; if *TARGET*s are URLs, N must be specified and M defaults to HEAD. The `-c M` option is equivalent to `-r N:M` where N = M-1. Using `-c -M` does the reverse: `-r M:N` where N = M-1.

- Display the differences between *OLD-TGT* as it was seen in *OLDREV* and *NEW-TGT* as it was seen in *NEWREV*. *PATH*s, if given, are relative to *OLD-TGT* and *NEW-TGT* and restrict the output to differences for those paths. *OLD-TGT* and *NEW-TGT* may be working copy paths or *URL[@REV]*. *NEW-TGT* defaults to *OLD-TGT* if not specified. `-r N` makes *OLDREV* default to N; `-r N:M` makes *OLDREV* default to *N* and *NEWREV* default to *M*.

`svn diff OLD-URL[@OLDREV] NEW-URL[@NEWREV]` is shorthand for `svn diff --old=OLD-URL[@OLDREV] --new=NEW-URL[@NEWREV]`.

`svn diff -r N:M URL` is shorthand for `svn diff -r N:M --old=URL --new=URL`.

`svn diff [-r N[:M]] URL1[@N] URL2[@M]` is shorthand for `svn diff [-r N[:M]] --old=URL1 --new=URL2`.

If *TARGET* is a URL, then revs N and M can be given either via the `--revision` option or by using the "@" notation as described earlier.

If *TARGET* is a working copy path, the default behavior (when no `--revision` option is provided) is to display the differences between the base and working copies of *TARGET*. If a `--revision` option is specified in this scenario, though, it means:

`--revision N:M`
> The server compares *TARGET@N* and *TARGET@M*.

`--revision N`
> The client compares *TARGET@N* against the working copy.

If the alternate syntax is used, the server compares *URL1* and *URL2* at revisions N and M, respectively. If either N or M is omitted, a value of HEAD is assumed.

By default, *svn diff* ignores the ancestry of files and merely compares the contents of the two files being compared. If you use `--notice-ancestry`, the ancestry of the paths in question will be taken into consideration when comparing revisions (i.e., if you run *svn diff* on two files with identical contents but different ancestry, you will see the entire contents of the file as having been removed and added again).

Alternate names

di.

Changes

Nothing.

Accesses repository

For obtaining differences against anything but BASE revision in your working copy.

Options

```
--change (-c) ARG
--changelist ARG
--depth ARG
--diff-cmd CMD
--extensions (-x) "ARGS"
--force
--new ARG
--no-diff-deleted
--notice-ancestry
--old ARG
--revision (-r) ARG
--summarize
--xml
```

Examples

Compare BASE and your working copy (one of the most popular uses of *svn diff*):

```
$ svn diff COMMITTERS
Index: COMMITTERS
===================================================================
--- COMMITTERS     (revision 4404)
+++ COMMITTERS     (working copy)
```

See what changed in the file *COMMITTERS* in revision 9115:

```
$ svn diff -c 9115 COMMITTERS
Index: COMMITTERS
===================================================================
--- COMMITTERS     (revision 3900)
+++ COMMITTERS     (working copy)
```

See how your working copy's modifications compare against an older revision:

```
$ svn diff -r 3900 COMMITTERS
Index: COMMITTERS
===================================================================
--- COMMITTERS     (revision 3900)
+++ COMMITTERS     (working copy)
```

Compare revision 3000 to revision 3500 using "@" syntax:

```
$ svn diff http://svn.collab.net/repos/svn/trunk/COMMITTERS@3000 \
           http://svn.collab.net/repos/svn/trunk/COMMITTERS@3500
Index: COMMITTERS
===================================================================
--- COMMITTERS     (revision 3000)
+++ COMMITTERS     (revision 3500)
...
```

Compare revision 3000 to revision 3500 using range notation (pass only the one URL in this case):

```
$ svn diff -r 3000:3500 http://svn.collab.net/repos/svn/trunk/COMMITTERS
Index: COMMITTERS
===================================================================
--- COMMITTERS      (revision 3000)
+++ COMMITTERS      (revision 3500)
```

Compare revision 3000 to revision 3500 of all the files in *trunk* using range notation:

```
$ svn diff -r 3000:3500 http://svn.collab.net/repos/svn/trunk
```

Compare revision 3000 to revision 3500 of only three files in *trunk* using range notation:

```
$ svn diff -r 3000:3500 --old http://svn.collab.net/repos/svn/trunk \
          COMMITTERS README HACKING
```

If you have a working copy, you can obtain the differences without typing in the long URLs:

```
$ svn diff -r 3000:3500 COMMITTERS
Index: COMMITTERS
===================================================================
--- COMMITTERS      (revision 3000)
+++ COMMITTERS      (revision 3500)
```

Use --diff-cmd *CMD* -x to pass arguments directly to the external diff program:

```
$ svn diff --diff-cmd /usr/bin/diff -x "-i -b" COMMITTERS
Index: COMMITTERS
===================================================================
0a1,2
> This is a test
>
```

Lastly, you can use the --xml option along with the --summarize option to view XML describing the changes that occurred between revisions, but not the contents of the diff itself:

```
$ svn diff --summarize --xml http://svn.red-bean.com/repos/test@r2 \
          http://svn.red-bean.com/repos/test
<?xml version="1.0"?>
<diff>
<paths>
<path
   props="none"
   kind="file"
   item="modified"&gt;http://svn.red-bean.com/repos/test/sandwich.txt&lt;/path&gt;
<path
   props="none"
   kind="file"
   item="deleted"&gt;http://svn.red-bean.com/repos/test/burrito.txt&lt;/path&gt;
<path
   props="none"
   kind="dir"
   item="added"&gt;http://svn.red-bean.com/repos/test/snacks&lt;/path&gt;
</paths>
</diff>
```

svn export

Synopsis

```
svn export [-r REV] URL[@PEGREV] [PATH]

svn export [-r REV] PATH1[@PEGREV] [PATH2]
```

Description

The first form exports a clean directory tree from the repository specified by *URL*—at revision *REV* if it is given; otherwise, at HEAD, into *PATH*. If *PATH* is omitted, the last component of the *URL* is used for the local directory name.

The second form exports a clean directory tree from the working copy specified by *PATH1* into *PATH2*. All local changes will be preserved, but files not under version control will not be copied.

Alternate names

None.

Changes

Local disk.

Accesses repository

Only if exporting from a URL.

Options

```
--depth ARG
--force
--ignore-externals
--native-eol EOL
--quiet (-q)
--revision (-r) REV
```

Examples

Export from your working copy (doesn't print every file and directory):

```
$ svn export a-wc my-export
Export complete.
```

Export directly from the repository (prints every file and directory):

```
$ svn export file:///var/svn/repos my-export
A  my-export/test
A  my-export/quiz
...
Exported revision 15.
```

When rolling operating-system-specific release packages, it can be useful to export a tree that uses a specific EOL character for line endings. The **--native-eol** option will do this, but it affects only files that have **svn:eol-style** = **native** properties attached to them. For example, to export a tree with all CRLF line endings (possibly for a Windows *.zip* file distribution):

```
$ svn export file:///var/svn/repos my-export --native-eol CRLF
A  my-export/test
A  my-export/quiz
...
Exported revision 15.
```

You can specify LR, CR, or CRLF as a line-ending type with the `--native-eol` option.

svn help

Synopsis
```
svn help [SUBCOMMAND...]
```

Description
This is your best friend when you're using Subversion and this book isn't within reach!

Alternate names
?, h

The options `-?`, `-h`, and `--help` have the same effect as using the *help* subcommand.

Changes
Nothing.

Accesses repository
No.

Options
None.

svn import

Commit an unversioned file or tree into the repository.

Synopsis
```
svn import [PATH] URL
```

Description
Recursively commit a copy of *PATH* to *URL*. If *PATH* is omitted, "." is assumed. Parent directories are created in the repository as necessary. Unversionable items such as device files and pipes are ignored even if `--force` is specified.

Alternate names
None.

Changes
Repository.

Accesses repository
Yes.

Options
```
--auto-props
--depth ARG
--editor-cmd EDITOR
--encoding ENC
--file (-F) FILE
--force
--force-log
--message (-m) TEXT
```

```
--no-auto-props
--no-ignore
--quiet (-q)
--with-revprop ARG
```

Examples

This imports the local directory *myproj* into *trunk/misc* in your repository. The directory *trunk/misc* need not exist before you import into it—*svn import* will recursively create directories for you:

```
$ svn import -m "New import" myproj \
            http://svn.red-bean.com/repos/trunk/misc
Adding          myproj/sample.txt
...
Transmitting file data ........
Committed revision 16.
```

Be aware that this will *not* create a directory named *myproj* in the repository. If that's what you want, simply add *myproj* to the end of the URL:

```
$ svn import -m "New import" myproj \
            http://svn.red-bean.com/repos/trunk/misc/myproj
Adding          myproj/sample.txt
...
Transmitting file data ........
Committed revision 16.
```

After importing data, note that the original tree is *not* under version control. To start working, you still need to *svn checkout* a fresh working copy of the tree.

svn info

Display information about a local or remote item.

Synopsis

```
svn info [TARGET[@REV]...]
```

Description

Print information about the working copy paths or URLs specified. The information shown for both may include:

- Path
- Name
- URL
- Repository root
- Repository UUID
- Revision
- Node kind
- Last changed author
- Last changed revision
- Last changed date

- Lock token
- Lock owner
- Lock created (date)
- Lock expires (date)

Additional kinds of information available only for working copy paths are:

- Schedule
- Copied from URL
- Copied from rev
- Text last updated
- Properties last updated
- Checksum
- Conflict previous base file
- Conflict previous working file
- Conflict current base file
- Conflict properties file

Alternate names
None.

Changes
Nothing.

Accesses repository
Only if operating on URLs.

Options
```
--changelist ARG
--depth ARG
--incremental
--recursive (-R)
--revision (-r) REV
--targets FILENAME
--xml
```

Examples
svn info will show you all the useful information that it has for items in your working copy. It will show information for files:

```
$ svn info foo.c
Path: foo.c
Name: foo.c
URL: http://svn.red-bean.com/repos/test/foo.c
Repository Root: http://svn.red-bean.com/repos/test
Repository UUID: 5e7d134a-54fb-0310-bd04-b611643e5c25
Revision: 4417
Node Kind: file
Schedule: normal
```

```
Last Changed Author: sally
Last Changed Rev: 20
Last Changed Date: 2003-01-13 16:43:13 -0600 (Mon, 13 Jan 2003)
Text Last Updated: 2003-01-16 21:18:16 -0600 (Thu, 16 Jan 2003)
Properties Last Updated: 2003-01-13 21:50:19 -0600 (Mon, 13 Jan 2003)
Checksum: d6aeb60b0662ccceb6bce4bac344cb66
```

It will also show information for directories:

```
$ svn info vendors
Path: vendors
URL: http://svn.red-bean.com/repos/test/vendors
Repository Root: http://svn.red-bean.com/repos/test
Repository UUID: 5e7d134a-54fb-0310-bd04-b611643e5c25
Revision: 19
Node Kind: directory
Schedule: normal
Last Changed Author: harry
Last Changed Rev: 19
Last Changed Date: 2003-01-16 23:21:19 -0600 (Thu, 16 Jan 2003)
Properties Last Updated: 2003-01-16 23:39:02 -0600 (Thu, 16 Jan 2003)
```

svn info also acts on URLs (note that the file *readme.doc* in this example is locked, so lock information is also provided):

```
$ svn info http://svn.red-bean.com/repos/test/readme.doc
Path: readme.doc
Name: readme.doc
URL: http://svn.red-bean.com/repos/test/readme.doc
Repository Root: http://svn.red-bean.com/repos/test
Repository UUID: 5e7d134a-54fb-0310-bd04-b611643e5c25
Revision: 1
Node Kind: file
Schedule: normal
Last Changed Author: sally
Last Changed Rev: 42
Last Changed Date: 2003-01-14 23:21:19 -0600 (Tue, 14 Jan 2003)
Lock Token: opaquelocktoken:14011d4b-54fb-0310-8541-dbd16bd471b2
Lock Owner: harry
Lock Created: 2003-01-15 17:35:12 -0600 (Wed, 15 Jan 2003)
Lock Comment (1 line):
My test lock comment
```

Lastly, *svn info* output is available in XML format by passing the `--xml` option:

```
$ svn info --xml http://svn.red-bean.com/repos/test
<?xml version="1.0"?>
<info>
<entry
   kind="dir"
   path="."
   revision="1">
<url>http://svn.red-bean.com/repos/test</url>
<repository>
<root>http://svn.red-bean.com/repos/test</root>
<uuid>5e7d134a-54fb-0310-bd04-b611643e5c25</uuid>
</repository>
```

```
<wc-info>
<schedule>normal</schedule>
<depth>infinity</depth>
</wc-info>
<commit
    revision="1">
<author>sally</author>
<date>2003-01-15T23:35:12.847647Z</date>
</commit>
</entry>
</info>
```

svn list

Synopsis
```
svn list [TARGET[@REV]...]
```

Description
List each *TARGET* file and the contents of each *TARGET* directory as they exist in the repository. If *TARGET* is a working copy path, the corresponding repository URL will be used.

The default *TARGET* is ".", meaning the repository URL of the current working copy directory.

With --verbose, *svn list* shows the following fields for each item:

- Revision number of the last commit
- Author of the last commit
- If locked, the letter "O" (see the preceding section on "svn info" for details).
- Size (in bytes)
- Date and time of the last commit

With --xml, output is in XML format (with a header and an enclosing document element unless --incremental is also specified). All of the information is present; the --verbose option is not accepted.

Alternate names
ls.

Changes
Nothing.

Accesses repository
Yes.

Options
```
--depth ARG
--incremental
--recursive (-R)
--revision (-r) REV
--verbose (-v)
--xml
```

Examples

svn list is most useful if you want to see what files a repository has without downloading a

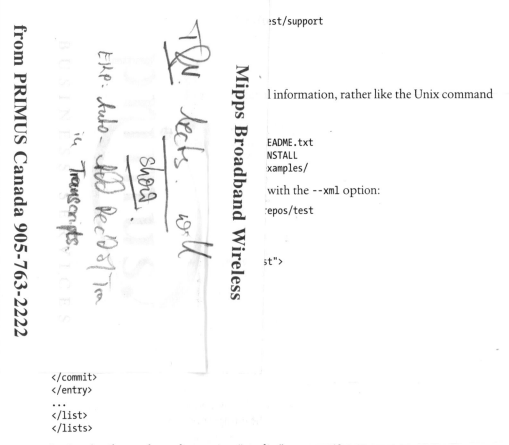

est/support

l information, rather like the Unix command

EADME.txt
NSTALL
xamples/

with the --xml option:

epos/test

st">

```
  </commit>
 </entry>
 ...
 </list>
</lists>
```

For further details, see the earlier section "svn list" on page 42.

---

svn lock

Lock working copy paths or URLs in the repository so that no other user can commit changes to them.

Synopsis

```
svn lock TARGET...
```

Description

Lock each *TARGET*. If any *TARGET* is already locked by another user, print a warning and continue locking the rest of the *TARGET*s. Use --force to steal a lock from another user or working copy.

Alternate names

None.

Changes

Working copy, repository.

Accesses repository

Yes.

Options

```
--encoding ENC
--file (-F) FILE
--force
--force-log
--message (-m) TEXT
--targets FILENAME
```

Examples

Lock two files in your working copy:

```
$ svn lock tree.jpg house.jpg
'tree.jpg' locked by user 'harry'.
'house.jpg' locked by user 'harry'.
```

Lock a file in your working copy that is currently locked by another user:

```
$ svn lock tree.jpg
svn: warning: Path '/tree.jpg is already locked by user 'sally in \
    filesystem '/var/svn/repos/db'

$ svn lock --force tree.jpg
'tree.jpg' locked by user 'harry'.
```

Lock a file without a working copy:

```
$ svn lock http://svn.red-bean.com/repos/test/tree.jpg
'tree.jpg' locked by user 'harry'.
```

For further details, see "Locking" on page 73.

---

svn log

Display commit log messages.

Synopsis

```
svn log [PATH]

svn log URL[@REV] [PATH...]
```

Description

Shows log messages from the repository. If no arguments are supplied, *svn log* shows the log messages for all files and directories inside (and including) the current working directory of your working copy. You can refine the results by specifying a path, one or more revisions, or any combination of the two. The default revision range for a local path is BASE:1.

If you specify a URL alone, it prints log messages for everything the URL contains. If you add paths past the URL, only messages for those paths under that URL will be printed. The default revision range for a URL is HEAD:1.

With --verbose, *svn log* will also print all affected paths with each log message. With --quiet, *svn log* will not print the log message body itself (this is compatible with --verbose).

Each log message is printed just once, even if more than one of the affected paths for that revision were explicitly requested. Logs follow copy history by default. Use `--stop-on-copy` to disable this behavior, which can be useful for determining branch points.

Alternate names
None.

Changes
Nothing.

Accesses repository
Yes.

Options
```
--change (-c) ARG
--incremental
--limit (-l) NUM
--quiet (-q)
--revision (-r) REV
--stop-on-copy
--targets FILENAME
--use-merge-history (-g)
--verbose (-v)
--with-all-revprops
--with-revprop ARG
--xml
```

Examples
You can see the log messages for all the paths that changed in your working copy by running `svn log` from the top:

```
$ svn log
------------------------------------------------------------------------
r20 | harry | 2003-01-17 22:56:19 -0600 (Fri, 17 Jan 2003) | 1 line

Tweak.
------------------------------------------------------------------------
r17 | sally | 2003-01-16 23:21:19 -0600 (Thu, 16 Jan 2003) | 2 lines
...
```

Examine all log messages for a particular file in your working copy:

```
$ svn log foo.c
------------------------------------------------------------------------
r32 | sally | 2003-01-13 00:43:13 -0600 (Mon, 13 Jan 2003) | 1 line

Added defines.
------------------------------------------------------------------------
r28 | sally | 2003-01-07 21:48:33 -0600 (Tue, 07 Jan 2003) | 3 lines
...
```

If you don't have a working copy handy, you can log a URL:

```
$ svn log http://svn.red-bean.com/repos/test/foo.c
------------------------------------------------------------------------
r32 | sally | 2003-01-13 00:43:13 -0600 (Mon, 13 Jan 2003) | 1 line
```

```
Added defines.
------------------------------------------------------------------------
r28 | sally | 2003-01-07 21:48:33 -0600 (Tue, 07 Jan 2003) | 3 lines
...
```

If you want several distinct paths underneath the same URL, you can use the *URL* [*PATH*...] syntax:

```
$ svn log http://svn.red-bean.com/repos/test/ foo.c bar.c
------------------------------------------------------------------------
r32 | sally | 2003-01-13 00:43:13 -0600 (Mon, 13 Jan 2003) | 1 line

Added defines.
------------------------------------------------------------------------
r31 | harry | 2003-01-10 12:25:08 -0600 (Fri, 10 Jan 2003) | 1 line

Added new file bar.c
------------------------------------------------------------------------
r28 | sally | 2003-01-07 21:48:33 -0600 (Tue, 07 Jan 2003) | 3 lines
...
```

The --verbose option causes *svn log* to include information about the paths that were changed in each displayed revision. These paths appear, one path per line of output, with action codes that indicate what type of change was made to the path:

```
$ svn log -v http://svn.red-bean.com/repos/test/ foo.c bar.c
------------------------------------------------------------------------
r32 | sally | 2003-01-13 00:43:13 -0600 (Mon, 13 Jan 2003) | 1 line
Changed paths:
   M /foo.c

Added defines.
------------------------------------------------------------------------
r31 | harry | 2003-01-10 12:25:08 -0600 (Fri, 10 Jan 2003) | 1 line
Changed paths:
   A /bar.c

Added new file bar.c
------------------------------------------------------------------------
r28 | sally | 2003-01-07 21:48:33 -0600 (Tue, 07 Jan 2003) | 3 lines
...
```

svn log uses just a handful of action codes, and they are similar to the ones the *svn update* command uses:

A

The item was added.

D

The item was deleted.

M

Properties or textual contents on the item were changed.

R

The item was replaced by a different one at the same location.

In addition to the action codes that precede the changed paths, *svn log* with the `--verbose` option will note whether a path was added or replaced as the result of a copy operation. It does so by printing (from *COPY-FROM-PATH*:*COPY-FROM-REV*) after such paths.

When you're concatenating the results of multiple calls to the log command, you may want to use the `--incremental` option. *svn log* normally prints out a dashed line at the beginning of a log message, after each subsequent log message, and following the final log message. If you ran *svn log* on a range of two revisions, you would get this:

```
$ svn log -r 14:15
------------------------------------------------------------------------
r14 | ...



------------------------------------------------------------------------
r15 | ...



------------------------------------------------------------------------
```

However, if you wanted to gather two nonsequential log messages into a file, you might do something like this:

```
$ svn log -r 14 > mylog
$ svn log -r 19 >> mylog
$ svn log -r 27 >> mylog
$ cat mylog
------------------------------------------------------------------------
r14 | ...



------------------------------------------------------------------------
------------------------------------------------------------------------
r19 | ...



------------------------------------------------------------------------
------------------------------------------------------------------------
r27 | ...



------------------------------------------------------------------------
```

You can avoid the clutter of the double dashed lines in your output by using the `--incremental` option:

```
$ svn log --incremental -r 14 > mylog
$ svn log --incremental -r 19 >> mylog
$ svn log --incremental -r 27 >> mylog
$ cat mylog
------------------------------------------------------------------------
r14 | ...


------------------------------------------------------------------------
r19 | ...


------------------------------------------------------------------------
r27 | ...
```

The `--incremental` option provides similar output control when using the `--xml` option:

```
$ svn log --xml --incremental -r 1 sandwich.txt
<logentry
    revision="1">
<author>harry</author>
<date>2008-06-03T06:35:53.048870Z</date>
<msg>Initial Import.</msg>
</logentry>
```

 Sometimes when you run *svn log* on a specific path and a specific revision, you see no log information output at all, as in the following:

```
$ svn log -r 20 http://svn.red-bean.com/untouched.txt
------------------------------------------------------------------------
```

That just means the path wasn't modified in that revision. To get log information for that revision, either run the log operation against the repository's root URL, or specify a path that you happen to know was changed in that revision:

```
$ svn log -r 20 touched.txt
------------------------------------------------------------------------
r20 | sally | 2003-01-17 22:56:19 -0600 (Fri, 17 Jan 2003) | 1 line

Made a change.
------------------------------------------------------------------------
```

svn merge

Apply the differences between two sources to a working copy path.

Synopsis

```
svn merge sourceURL1[@N] sourceURL2[@M] [WCPATH]

svn merge sourceWCPATH1@N sourceWCPATH2@M [WCPATH]

svn merge [[-c M]... | [-r N:M]...] [SOURCE[@REV] [WCPATH]]
```

Description

In the first form, the source URLs are specified at revisions *N* and *M*. These are the two sources to be compared. The revisions default to HEAD if omitted.

In the second form, the URLs corresponding to the source working copy paths define the sources to be compared. The revisions must be specified.

In the third form, *SOURCE* can be either a URL or a working copy path (in which case its corresponding URL is used). If not specified, *SOURCE* will be the same as *WCPATH*. *SOURCE* in revision *REV* is compared as it existed between revisions *N* and *M* for each revision range provided. If *REV* is not specified, HEAD is assumed.

`-c M` is equivalent to `-r <M-1>:M`, and `-c -M` does the reverse: `-r M:<M-1>`. If no revision ranges are specified, the default range of `1:HEAD` is used. Multiple `-c` and/or `-r` instances may be specified, and mixing of forward and reverse ranges is allowed—the ranges are internally compacted to their minimum representation before merging begins (which may result in no-op).

WCPATH is the working copy path that will receive the changes. If *WCPATH* is omitted, a default value of "." is assumed, unless the sources have identical basenames that match a file within ".". In this case, the differences will be applied to that file.

Subversion will internally track metadata about the merge operation only if the two sources are ancestrally related—if the first source is an ancestor of the second or vice versa. This is guaranteed to be the case when using the third form. Unlike *svn diff*, the merge command takes the ancestry of a file into consideration when performing a merge operation. This is very important when you're merging changes from one branch into another and you've renamed a file on one branch but not the other.

Alternate names
None.

Changes
Working copy.

Accesses repository
Only if working with URLs.

Options
```
--accept ARG
--change (-c) REV
--depth ARG
--diff3-cmd CMD
--dry-run
--extensions (-x) ARG
--force
--ignore-ancestry
--quiet (-q)
--record-only
--reintegrate
--revision (-r) REV
```

Examples
Merge a branch back into the trunk (assuming that you have an up-to-date working copy of the trunk):

```
$ svn merge --reintegrate \
            http://svn.example.com/repos/calc/branches/my-calc-branch
--- Merging differences between repository URLs into '.':
U    button.c
U    integer.c
U    Makefile
 U   .

$ # build, test, verify, ...

$ svn commit -m "Merge my-calc-branch back into trunk!"
Sending        .
Sending        button.c
Sending        integer.c
Sending        Makefile
Transmitting file data ..
Committed revision 391.
```

To merge changes to a single file:

```
$ cd myproj
$ svn merge -r 30:31 thhgttg.txt
U  thhgttg.txt
```

svn mergeinfo

Query merge-related information. See "Mergeinfo and Previews" on page 113 for details.

Synopsis

```
svn mergeinfo SOURCE_URL[@REV] [TARGET[@REV]...]
```

Description

Query information related to merges (or potential merges) between *SOURCE-URL* and *TARGET*. If the --show-revs option is not provided, display revisions that have been merged from *SOURCE-URL* to *TARGET*. Otherwise, display either merged or eligible revisions as specified by the --show-revs option.

Alternate names

None.

Changes

Nothing.

Accesses repository

Yes.

Options

```
--revision (-r) REV
```

Examples

Find out which changesets your trunk directory has already received, as well as which changesets it's still eligible to receive:

```
$ svn mergeinfo branches/test
Path: branches/test
  Source path: /trunk
    Merged ranges: r2:13
    Eligible ranges: r13:15
```

svn mkdir

Create a new directory under version control.

Synopsis

```
svn mkdir PATH...

svn mkdir URL...
```

Description

Create a directory with a name given by the final component of the *PATH* or *URL*. A directory specified by a working copy *PATH* is scheduled for addition in the working copy, whereas a directory specified by a URL is created in the repository via an immediate commit. Multiple directory URLs are committed atomically. In both cases, all the intermediate directories must already exist unless the --parents option is used.

Alternate names

None.

Changes

Working copy; repository if operating on a URL.

Accesses repository

Only if operating on a URL.

Options

```
--editor-cmd EDITOR
--encoding ENC
--file (-F) FILE
--force-log
--message (-m) TEXT
--parents
--quiet (-q)
--with-revprop ARG
```

Examples

Create a directory in your working copy:

```
$ svn mkdir newdir
A         newdir
```

Create one in the repository (this is an instant commit, so a log message is required):

```
$ svn mkdir -m "Making a new dir." http://svn.red-bean.com/repos/newdir

Committed revision 26.
```

---

svn move   Move a file or directory.

Synopsis

```
svn move SRC... DST
```

Description

This command moves files or directories in your working copy or in the repository.

 This command is equivalent to an *svn copy* followed by *svn delete*.

When moving multiple sources, they will be added as children of *DST*, which must be a directory.

Subversion does not support moving between working copies and URLs. In addition, you can only move files within a single repository—Subversion does not support cross-repository moving. Subversion supports the following types of moves within a single repository:

WC → WC
> Move and schedule a file or directory for addition (with history).

URL → URL
> Complete server-side rename.

Alternate names
mv, rename, ren.

Changes
Working copy; repository if operating on a URL.

Accesses repository
Only if operating on a URL.

Options
```
--editor-cmd EDITOR
--encoding ENC
--file (-F) FILE
--force
--force-log
--message (-m) TEXT
--parents
--quiet (-q)
--revision (-r) REV
--with-revprop ARG
```

Examples
Move a file in your working copy:

```
$ svn move foo.c bar.c
A         bar.c
D         foo.c
```

Move several files in your working copy into a subdirectory:

```
$ svn move baz.c bat.c qux.c src
A         src/baz.c
D         baz.c
A         src/bat.c
D         bat.c
A         src/qux.c
D         qux.c
```

Move a file in the repository (this is an immediate commit, so it requires a commit message):

```
$ svn move -m "Move a file" http://svn.red-bean.com/repos/foo.c \
                            http://svn.red-bean.com/repos/bar.c

Committed revision 27.
```

svn propdel

Synopsis

```
svn propdel PROPNAME [PATH...]

svn propdel PROPNAME --revprop -r REV [TARGET]
```

Description

This removes properties from files, directories, or revisions. The first form removes versioned properties in your working copy, and the second removes unversioned remote properties on a repository revision (*TARGET* determines only which repository to access).

Alternate names

pdel, pd.

Changes

Working copy; repository only if operating on a URL.

Accesses repository

Only if operating on a URL.

Options

```
--changelist ARG
--depth ARG
--quiet (-q)
--recursive (-R)
--revision (-r) REV
--revprop
```

Examples

Delete a property from a file in your working copy:

```
$ svn propdel svn:mime-type some-script
property 'svn:mime-type' deleted from 'some-script'.
```

Delete a revision property:

```
$ svn propdel --revprop -r 26 release-date
property 'release-date' deleted from repository revision '26'
```

svn propedit

Synopsis

```
svn propedit PROPNAME TARGET...

svn propedit PROPNAME --revprop -r REV [TARGET]
```

Description

Edit one or more properties using your favorite editor. The first form edits versioned properties in your working copy, and the second edits unversioned remote properties on a repository revision (*TARGET* determines only which repository to access). See "svn propset" later in this chapter.

Alternate names

pedit, *pe*.

Changes

Working copy; repository only if operating on a URL.

Accesses repository

Only if operating on a URL.

Options

```
--editor-cmd EDITOR
--encoding ENC
--file (-F) ARG
--force
--force-log
--message (-m) ARG
--revision (-r) REV
--revprop
--with-revprop ARG
```

Examples

svn propedit makes it easy to modify properties that have multiple values:

```
$ svn propedit svn:keywords  foo.c
    <svn will launch your favorite editor here, with a buffer open
    containing the current contents of the svn:keywords property. You
    can add multiple values to a property easily here by entering one
    value per line.>
Set new value for property 'svn:keywords' on 'foo.c'
```

svn propget

Print the value of a property.

Synopsis

```
svn propget PROPNAME [TARGET[@REV]...]

svn propget PROPNAME --revprop -r REV [URL]
```

Description

Print the value of a property on files, directories, or revisions. The first form prints the versioned property of an item or items in your working copy, and the second prints unversioned remote properties on a repository revision. See "Properties" on page 48 for more information on properties.

Alternate names

pget, *pg*.

Changes

Working copy; repository only if operating on a URL.

Accesses repository

Only if operating on a URL.

Options

```
--changelist ARG
--depth ARG
--recursive (-R)
--revision (-r) REV
--revprop
--strict
--xml
```

Examples

Examine a property of a file in your working copy:

```
$ svn propget svn:keywords foo.c
Author
Date
Rev
```

The same goes for a revision property:

```
$ svn propget svn:log --revprop -r 20
Began journal.
```

Lastly, you can get *svn propget* output in XML format with the `--xml` option:

```
$ svn propget --xml svn:ignore .
<?xml version="1.0"?>
<properties>
<target
   path="">
<property
   name="svn:ignore">*.o
</property>
</target>
</properties>
```

svn proplist

List all properties.

Synopsis

```
svn proplist [TARGET[@REV]...]

svn proplist --revprop -r REV [TARGET]
```

Description

List all properties on files, directories, or revisions. The first form lists versioned properties in your working copy, and the second lists unversioned remote properties on a repository revision (*TARGET* determines only which repository to access).

Alternate names

plist, *pl.*

Changes

Working copy; repository only if operating on a URL.

Accesses repository

Only if operating on a URL.

Options

```
--changelist ARG
--depth ARG
--quiet (-q)
--recursive (-R)
--revision (-r) REV
--revprop
--verbose (-v)
--xml
```

Examples

You can use *proplist* to see the properties on an item in your working copy:

```
$ svn proplist foo.c
Properties on 'foo.c':
  svn:mime-type
  svn:keywords
  owner
```

With the `--verbose` flag, *svn proplist* is extremely handy, as it also shows you the values for the properties:

```
$ svn proplist --verbose foo.c
Properties on 'foo.c':
  svn:mime-type : text/plain
  svn:keywords : Author Date Rev
  owner : sally
```

Lastly, you can get *svn proplist* output in XML format with the `--xml` option:

```
$ svn proplist --xml
<?xml version="1.0"?>
<properties>
<target
   path=".">
<property
   name="svn:ignore"/>
</target>
</properties>
```

---

svn propset   Set PROPNAME to PROPVAL on files, directories, or revisions.

Synopsis

```
svn propset PROPNAME [PROPVAL | -F VALFILE] PATH...

svn propset PROPNAME --revprop -r REV [PROPVAL | -F VALFILE] [TARGET]
```

Description

Set *PROPNAME* to *PROPVAL* on files, directories, or revisions. The first example creates a versioned, local property change in the working copy, and the second creates an unversioned, remote property change on a repository revision (*TARGET* determines only which repository to access).

Subversion has a number of "special" properties that affect its behavior. See "Subversion Properties" on page 358 for more on these properties.

Alternate names

pset, ps.

Changes

Working copy; repository only if operating on a URL.

Accesses repository

Only if operating on a URL.

Options

```
--changelist ARG
--depth ARG
--encoding ENC
--file (-F) FILE
--force
--quiet (-q)
--recursive (-R)
--revision (-r) REV
--revprop
--targets FILENAME
```

Examples

Set the MIME type for a file:

```
$ svn propset svn:mime-type image/jpeg foo.jpg
property 'svn:mime-type' set on 'foo.jpg'
```

On a Unix system, if you want a file to have the executable permission set:

```
$ svn propset svn:executable ON somescript
property 'svn:executable' set on 'somescript'
```

Perhaps you have an internal policy to set certain properties for the benefit of your coworkers:

```
$ svn propset owner sally foo.c
property 'owner' set on 'foo.c'
```

If you made a mistake in a log message for a particular revision and want to change it, use --revprop and set svn:log to the new log message:

```
$ svn propset --revprop -r 25 svn:log "Journaled about trip to New York."
property 'svn:log' set on repository revision '25'
```

Or, if you don't have a working copy, you can provide a URL:

```
$ svn propset --revprop -r 26 svn:log "Document nap." \
          http://svn.red-bean.com/repos
property 'svn:log' set on repository revision '25'
```

Lastly, you can tell *propset* to take its input from a file. You could even use this to set the contents of a property to something binary:

```
$ svn propset owner-pic -F sally.jpg moo.c
property 'owner-pic' set on 'moo.c'
```

 By default, you cannot modify revision properties in a Subversion repository. Your repository administrator must explicitly enable revision property modifications by creating a hook named `pre-revprop-change`. See "Implementing Repository Hooks" on page 156 for more information on hook scripts.

svn resolve
Resolve conflicts on working copy files or directories.

Synopsis
svn resolve *PATH...*

Description
Resolve "conflicted" state on working copy files or directories. This routine does not semantically resolve conflict markers; however, it replaces *PATH* with the version specified by the `--accept` argument and then removes conflict-related artifact files. This allows *PATH* to be committed again—that is, it tells Subversion that the conflicts have been "resolved." You can pass the following arguments to the `--accept` command, depending on your desired resolution:

base
> Choose the file that was the BASE revision before you updated your working copy—that is, the file that you checked out before you made your latest edits.

working
> Assuming that you've manually handled the conflict resolution, choose the version of the file as it currently stands in your working copy.

mine-full
> Resolve all conflicted files with copies of the files as they stood immediately before you ran *svn update*.

theirs-full
> Resolve all conflicted files with copies of the files that were fetched from the server when you ran *svn update*.

See "Resolve Conflicts (Merging Others' Changes)" on page 30 for an in-depth look at resolving conflicts.

Alternate names
None.

Changes
Working copy.

Accesses repository
No.

Options

```
--accept ARG
--depth ARG
--quiet (-q)
--recursive (-R)
--targets FILENAME
```

Examples

Here's an example where, after a postponed conflict resolution during update, *svn resolve* replaces all the conflicts in file *foo.c* with your edits:

```
$ svn up
Conflict discovered in 'foo.c'.
Select: (p) postpone, (df) diff-full, (e) edit,
        (h) help for more options: p
C    foo.c
Updated to revision 5.

$ svn resolve --accept mine-full foo.c
Resolved conflicted state of 'foo.c'
```

svn resolved

Remove "conflicted" state on working copy files or directories.

Synopsis

```
svn resolved PATH...
```

Description

This command has been deprecated in favor of running `svn resolve --accept working` *PATH*. See "svn resolve" in the preceding section for details.

Remove "conflicted" state on working copy files or directories. This routine does not semantically resolve conflict markers; it merely removes conflict-related artifact files and allows *PATH* to be committed again; that is, it tells Subversion that the conflicts have been "resolved." See "Resolve Conflicts (Merging Others' Changes)" on page 30 for an in-depth look at resolving conflicts.

Alternate names

None.

Changes

Working copy.

Accesses repository

No.

Options

```
--depth ARG
--quiet (-q)
--recursive (-R)
--targets FILENAME
```

Examples

If you get a conflict on an update, your working copy will sprout three new files:

```
$ svn update
C  foo.c
Updated to revision 31.
$ ls
foo.c
foo.c.mine
foo.c.r30
foo.c.r31
```

Once you've resolved the conflict and *foo.c* is ready to be committed, run *svn resolved* to let your working copy know you've taken care of everything.

 You *can* just remove the conflict files and commit, but *svn resolved* fixes up some bookkeeping data in the working copy administrative area in addition to removing the conflict files, so we recommend that you use this command.

svn revert

Undo all local edits.

Synopsis

```
svn revert PATH...
```

Description

Reverts any local changes to a file or directory and resolves any conflicted states. *svn revert* will revert not only the contents of an item in your working copy, but also any property changes. Finally, you can use it to undo any scheduling operations that you may have performed (e.g., files scheduled for addition or deletion can be "unscheduled").

Alternate names

None.

Changes

Working copy.

Accesses repository

No.

Options

```
--changelist ARG
--depth ARG
--quiet (-q)
--recursive (-R)
--targets FILENAME
```

Examples

Discard changes to a file:

```
$ svn revert foo.c
Reverted foo.c
```

If you want to revert a whole directory of files, use the `--depth=infinity` option:

```
$ svn revert --depth=infinity .
Reverted newdir/afile
Reverted foo.c
Reverted bar.txt
```

Lastly, you can undo any scheduling operations:

```
$ svn add mistake.txt whoops
A         mistake.txt
A         whoops
A         whoops/oopsie.c

$ svn revert mistake.txt whoops
Reverted mistake.txt
Reverted whoops

$ svn status
?         mistake.txt
?         whoops
```

 svn revert is inherently dangerous, since its entire purpose is to throw away data—namely, your uncommitted changes. Once you've reverted, Subversion provides *no way* to get back those uncommitted changes.

If you provide no targets to *svn revert*, it will do nothing—to protect you from accidentally losing changes in your working copy, *svn revert* requires you to provide at least one target.

svn status

Print the status of working copy files and directories.

Synopsis

```
svn status [PATH...]
```

Description

Print the status of working copy files and directories. With no arguments, it prints only locally modified items (no repository access). With `--show-updates`, it adds working revision and server out-of-date information. With `--verbose`, it prints full revision information on every item. With `--quiet`, it prints only summary information about locally modified items.

The first six columns in the output are each one character wide, and each column gives you information about different aspects of each working copy item.

The first column indicates that an item was added, deleted, or otherwise changed:

' '

No modifications.

'A'

Item is scheduled for addition.

'D'

Item is scheduled for deletion.

'M'

Item has been modified.

'R'

Item has been replaced in your working copy. This means the file was scheduled for deletion, and then a new file with the same name was scheduled for addition in its place.

'C'

The contents (as opposed to the properties) of the item conflict with updates received from the repository.

'X'

Item is present because of an externals definition.

'I'

Item is being ignored (e.g., with the svn:ignore property).

'?'

Item is not under version control.

'!'

Item is missing (e.g., you moved or deleted it without using *svn*). This also indicates that a directory is incomplete (a checkout or update was interrupted).

'~'

Item is versioned as one kind of object (file, directory, link) but has been replaced by a different kind of object.

The second column tells the status of a file's or directory's properties:

' '

No modifications.

'M'

Properties for this item have been modified.

'C'

Properties for this item are in conflict with property updates received from the repository.

The third column is populated only if the working copy directory is locked (see "Sometimes You Just Need to Clean Up" on page 43):

' '

Item is not locked.

'L'

Item is locked.

The fourth column is populated only if the item is scheduled for addition-with-history:

' '

No history scheduled with commit.

'+'

History scheduled with commit.

The fifth column is populated only if the item is switched relative to its parent (see "Traversing Branches" on page 130):

' '

Item is a child of its parent directory.

'S'

Item is switched.

The sixth column is populated with lock information:

' '

When --show-updates is used, the file is not locked. If --show-updates is *not* used, this merely means that the file is not locked in this working copy.

K

File is locked in this working copy.

O

File is locked either by another user or in another working copy. This appears only when --show-updates is used.

T

File was locked in this working copy, but the lock has been "stolen" and is invalid. The file is currently locked in the repository. This appears only when --show-updates is used.

B

File was locked in this working copy, but the lock has been "broken" and is invalid. The file is no longer locked. This appears only when --show-updates is used.

The out-of-date information appears in the seventh column (only if you pass the --show-updates option):

' '

The item in your working copy is up to date.

'*'

A newer revision of the item exists on the server.

The remaining fields are variable width and delimited by spaces. The working revision is the next field if the --show-updates or --verbose option is passed.

If the --verbose option is passed, the last committed revision and last committed author are displayed next.

The working copy path is always the final field, so it can include spaces.

Alternate names
stat, st.

Changes
Nothing.

Accesses repository
Only if using `--show-updates`.

Options
```
--changelist ARG
--depth ARG
--ignore-externals
--incremental
--no-ignore
--quiet (-q)
--show-updates (-u)
--verbose (-v)
--xml
```

Examples
This is the easiest way to find out what changes you have made to your working copy:

```
$ svn status wc
 M     wc/bar.c
 A  +  wc/qax.c
```

If you want to find out which files in your working copy are out of date, pass the `--show-updates` option (this will *not* make any changes to your working copy). Here you can see that *wc/foo.c* has changed in the repository since we last updated our working copy:

```
$ svn status --show-updates wc
 M           965    wc/bar.c
       *     965    wc/foo.c
 A  +        965    wc/qax.c
Status against revision:    981
```

 `--show-updates` *only* places an asterisk next to items that are out of date (i.e., items that will be updated from the repository if you later use *svn update*). `--show-updates` does *not* cause the status listing to reflect the repository's version of the item (although you can see the revision number in the repository by passing the `--verbose` option).

The most information you can get out of the status subcommand is as follows:

```
$ svn status --show-updates --verbose wc
 M           965      938 sally      wc/bar.c
       *     965      922 harry      wc/foo.c
 A  +        965      687 harry      wc/qax.c
             965      687 harry      wc/zig.c
Head revision:   981
```

Lastly, you can get *svn status* output in XML format with the `--xml` option:

```
$ svn status --xml wc
<?xml version="1.0"?>
<status>
<target
   path="wc">
<entry
```

```
      path="qax.c">
<wc-status
    props="none"
    item="added"
    revision="0">
</wc-status>
</entry>
<entry
    path="bar.c">
<wc-status
    props="normal"
    item="modified"
    revision="965">
<commit
    revision="965">
<author>sally</author>
<date>2008-05-28T06:35:53.048870Z</date>
</commit>
</wc-status>
</entry>
</target>
</status>
```

For many more examples of *svn status*, see "See an overview of your changes" on page 26.

svn switch

Update working copy to a different URL.

Synopsis

```
svn switch URL[@PEGREV] [PATH]

switch --relocate FROM TO [PATH...]
```

Description

The first variant of this subcommand (without the `--relocate` option) updates your working copy to point to a new URL—usually a URL that shares a common ancestor with your working copy, although not necessarily. This is the Subversion way to move a working copy to a new branch. If specified, *PEGREV* determines in which revision the target is first looked up. See "Traversing Branches" on page 130 for an in-depth look at switching.

If `--force` is used, unversioned obstructing paths in the working copy do not automatically cause a failure if the switch attempts to add the same path. If the obstructing path is the same type (file or directory) as the corresponding path in the repository, it becomes versioned but its contents are left untouched in the working copy. This means that an obstructing directory's unversioned children may also obstruct and become versioned. For files, any content differences between the obstruction and the repository are treated like a local modification to the working copy. All properties from the repository are applied to the obstructing path.

As with most subcommands, you can limit the scope of the switch operation to a particular tree depth using the `--depth` option. Alternatively, you can use the `--set-depth` option to set a new "sticky" working copy depth on the switch target. Currently, the depth of a working copy directory can only be increased (telescoped more deeply); you cannot make a directory more shallow.

The --relocate option causes *svn switch* to do something different: it updates your working copy to point to *the same* repository directory, only at a different URL (typically because an administrator has moved the repository to another server, or to another URL on the same server).

Alternate names

sw.

Changes

Working copy.

Accesses repository

Yes.

Options

```
--accept ARG
--depth ARG
--diff3-cmd CMD
--force
--ignore-externals
--quiet (-q)
--relocate
--revision (-r) REV
--set-depth ARG
```

Examples

If you're currently inside the directory *vendors*, which was branched to *vendors-with-fix*, and you'd like to switch your working copy to that branch:

```
$ svn switch http://svn.red-bean.com/repos/branches/vendors-with-fix .
U  myproj/foo.txt
U  myproj/bar.txt
U  myproj/baz.c
U  myproj/qux.c
Updated to revision 31.
```

To switch back, just provide the URL to the location in the repository from which you originally checked out your working copy:

```
$ svn switch http://svn.red-bean.com/repos/trunk/vendors .
U  myproj/foo.txt
U  myproj/bar.txt
U  myproj/baz.c
U  myproj/qux.c
Updated to revision 31.
```

 You can switch just part of your working copy to a branch if you don't want to switch your entire working copy.

Sometimes an administrator might change the location (or apparent location) of your repository—in other words, the content of the repository doesn't change, but the repository's root URL does. For example, the hostname may change, the URL scheme may change, or any part of the URL that leads to the repository itself may change. Rather than check out a new working copy, you can have the *svn switch* command "rewrite" your working copy's administrative metadata to refer to the new repository location. If you use the --relocate option to *svn switch*, Subversion will contact the repository to validate the relocation request (looking for the repository at the new URL, of course), and then do this metadata rewriting. No file contents will be changed as the result of this type of switch operation—this is a metadata-only modification to the working copy:

```
$ svn checkout file:///var/svn/repos test
A  test/a
A  test/b
...

$ mv repos newlocation
$ cd test/

$ svn update
svn: Unable to open an ra_local session to URL
svn: Unable to open repository 'file:///var/svn/repos'

$ svn switch --relocate file:///var/svn/repos file:///tmp/newlocation .
$ svn update
At revision 3.
```

 Be careful when using the --relocate option. If you mistype the argument, you might end up creating nonsensical URLs within your working copy that render the whole workspace unusable and tricky to fix. It's also important to understand exactly when one should or shouldn't use --relocate. Here's the rule of thumb:

- If the working copy needs to reflect a new directory *within* the repository, use just *svn switch*.
- If the working copy still reflects the same repository directory, but the location of the repository itself has changed, use *svn switch* with the --relocate option.

svn unlock

Unlock working copy paths or URLs.

Synopsis

```
svn unlock TARGET...
```

Description

Unlock each *TARGET*. If any *TARGET* is locked by another user or no valid lock token exists in the working copy, print a warning and continue unlocking the rest of the *TARGET*s. Use --force to break a lock belonging to another user or working copy.

Alternate names

None.

Changes
Working copy, repository.

Accesses repository
Yes.

Options
```
--force
--targets FILENAME
```

Examples
Unlock two files in your working copy:

```
$ svn unlock tree.jpg house.jpg
'tree.jpg' unlocked.
'house.jpg' unlocked.
```

Unlock a file in your working copy that is currently locked by another user:

```
$ svn unlock tree.jpg
svn: 'tree.jpg' is not locked in this working copy
$ svn unlock --force tree.jpg
'tree.jpg' unlocked.
```

Unlock a file without a working copy:

```
$ svn unlock http://svn.red-bean.com/repos/test/tree.jpg
'tree.jpg unlocked.
```

For further details, see "Locking" on page 73.

---

svn update
Update your working copy.

Synopsis
```
svn update [PATH...]
```

Description
svn update brings changes from the repository into your working copy. If no revision is given, it brings your working copy up to date with the HEAD revision. Otherwise, it synchronizes the working copy to the revision given by the --revision option. As part of the synchronization, *svn update* also removes any stale locks (see "Sometimes You Just Need to Clean Up" on page 43) found in the working copy.

For each updated item, it prints a line that starts with a character reporting the action taken. These characters have the following meanings:

A

    Added

B

    Broken lock (third column only)

D

    Deleted

U

> Updated

C

> Conflicted

G

> Merged

E

> Existed

A character in the first column signifies an update to the actual file, whereas updates to the file's properties are shown in the second column. Lock information is printed in the third column.

As with most subcommands, you can limit the scope of the update operation to a particular tree depth using the `--depth` option. Alternatively, you can use the `--set-depth` option to set a new "sticky" working copy depth on the update target. Currently, the depth of a working copy directory can only be increased (telescoped more deeply); you cannot make a directory more shallow.

Alternate names
up.

Changes
Working copy.

Accesses repository
Yes.

Options
```
--accept ARG
--changelist
--depth ARG
--diff3-cmd CMD
--editor-cmd ARG
--force
--ignore-externals
--quiet (-q)
--revision (-r) REV
--set-depth ARG
```

Examples
Pick up repository changes that have happened since your last update:

```
$ svn update
A   newdir/toggle.c
A   newdir/disclose.c
A   newdir/launch.c
D   newdir/README
Updated to revision 32.
```

You can also "update" your working copy to an older revision (Subversion doesn't have the concept of "sticky" files like CVS does; see Appendix B):

```
$ svn update -r30
A  newdir/README
D  newdir/toggle.c
D  newdir/disclose.c
D  newdir/launch.c
U  foo.c
Updated to revision 30.
```

 If you want to examine an older revision of a single file, you may want to use *svn cat* instead—it won't change your working copy.

svnadmin

svnadmin is the administrative tool for monitoring and repairing your Subversion repository. For detailed information on repository administration, see the maintenance section for "svnadmin" on page 159.

Since *svnadmin* works via direct repository access (and thus can be used only on the machine that holds the repository), it refers to the repository with a path, not a URL.

svnadmin Options

Options in *svnadmin* are global, just as they are in *svn*:

--bdb-log-keep
> (Berkeley DB-specific.) Disable automatic log removal of database logfiles. Having these logfiles around can be convenient if you need to restore from a catastrophic repository failure.

--bdb-txn-nosync
> (Berkeley DB-specific.) Disables fsync when committing database transactions. Used with the *svnadmin create* command to create a Berkeley DB-backed repository with DB_TXN_NOSYNC enabled (which improves speed but has some risks associated with it).

--bypass-hooks
> Bypass the repository hook system.

--clean-logs
> Remove unused Berkeley DB logs.

--force-uuid
> By default, when loading data into repository that already contains revisions, *svnadmin* will ignore the UUID from the dump stream. This option will cause the repository's UUID to be set to the UUID from the stream.

--ignore-uuid

By default, when loading an empty repository, *svnadmin* will ignore the UUID from the dump stream. This option will force that UUID to be ignored (useful for overriding your configuration file if it has --force-uuid set).

--incremental

Dump a revision only as a diff against the previous revision, instead of the usual fulltext.

--parent-dir *DIR*

When loading a dump file, root paths at *DIR* instead of /.

--pre-1.4-compatible

When creating a new repository, use a format that is compatible with versions of Subversion earlier than Subversion 1.4.

--pre-1.5-compatible

When creating a new repository, use a format that is compatible with versions of Subversion earlier than Subversion 1.5.

--revision (-r) *ARG*

Specify a particular revision to operate on.

--quiet

Do not show normal progress—show only errors.

--use-post-commit-hook

When loading a dump file, runs the repository's post-commit hook after finalizing each newly loaded revision.

--use-post-revprop-change-hook

When changing a revision property, runs the repository's post-revprop-change hook after changing the revision property.

--use-pre-commit-hook

When loading a dump file, runs the repository's pre-commit hook before finalizing each newly loaded revision. If the hook fails, aborts the commit and terminates the load process.

--use-pre-revprop-change-hook

When changing a revision property, runs the repository's pre-revprop-change hook before changing the revision property. If the hook fails, aborts the modification and terminates.

svnadmin Subcommands

Here are the various subcommands for the *svnadmin* program.

svnadmin crashtest

Synopsis

```
svnadmin crashtest REPOS_PATH
```

Description

Open the repository at *REPOS_PATH*, then abort, thus simulating a process that crashes while holding an open repository handle. This is used for testing automatic repository recovery (a new feature in Berkeley DB 4.4). It's unlikely that you'll need to run this command.

Options

None.

Examples

```
$ svnadmin crashtest /var/svn/repos
Aborted
```

Exciting, isn't it?

svnadmin create

Synopsis

```
svnadmin create REPOS_PATH
```

Description

Create a new, empty repository at the path provided. If the provided directory does not exist, it will be created for you.* As of Subversion 1.2, *svnadmin* creates new repositories with the FSFS filesystem backend by default.

While *svnadmin create* will create the base directory for a new repository, it will not create intermediate directories. For example, if you have an empty directory named */var/svn*, creating */var/svn/repos* will work, while attempting to create */var/svn/subdirectory/repos* will fail with an error.

Options

```
--bdb-log-keep
--bdb-txn-nosync
--config-dir DIR
--fs-type TYPE
--pre-1.4-compatible
--pre-1.5-compatible
```

Examples

Creating a new repository is this easy:

```
$ svnadmin create /var/svn/repos
```

In Subversion 1.0, a Berkeley DB repository is always created. In Subversion 1.1, a Berkeley DB repository is the default, but an FSFS repository can be created with the `--fs-type` option:

```
$ svnadmin create /var/svn/repos --fs-type fsfs
```

---

* Remember, *svnadmin* works only with local *paths*, not *URLs*.

svnadmin deltify
Deltify changed paths in a revision range.

Synopsis
```
svnadmin deltify [-r LOWER[:UPPER]] REPOS_PATH
```

Description
svnadmin deltify exists in current versions of Subversion only for historical reasons. This command is deprecated and no longer needed.

It dates from a time when Subversion offered administrators greater control over compression strategies in the repository. This turned out to be a lot of complexity for *very* little gain, and this "feature" was deprecated.

Options
```
--quiet (-q)
--revision (-r) REV
```

svnadmin dump
Dump the contents of the filesystem to *stdout*.

Synopsis
```
svnadmin dump REPOS_PATH [-r LOWER[:UPPER]] [--incremental]
```

Description
Dump the contents of the filesystem to *stdout* in a "dump file" portable format, sending feedback to *stderr*. Dump revisions *LOWER* rev through *UPPER* rev. If no revisions are given, dump all revision trees. If only *LOWER* is given, dump that one revision tree. See "Migrating Repository Data Elsewhere" on page 169 for a practical use.

By default, the Subversion dump stream contains a single revision (the first revision in the requested revision range) in which every file and directory in the repository in that revision is presented as though that whole tree was added at once, followed by other revisions (the remainder of the revisions in the requested range), which contain only the files and directories that were modified in those revisions. For a modified file, the complete full-text representation of its contents, as well as all of its properties, are presented in the dump file; for a directory, all of its properties are presented.

Two useful options modify the dump file generator's behavior. The first is the `--incremental` option, which simply causes that first revision in the dump stream to contain only the files and directories modified in that revision, instead of being presented as the addition of a new tree, and in exactly the same way that every other revision in the dump file is presented. This is useful for generating a relatively small dump file to be loaded into another repository that already has the files and directories that exist in the original repository.

The second useful option is `--deltas`. This option causes *svnadmin dump* to, instead of emitting full-text representations of file contents and property lists, emit only deltas of those items against their previous versions. This reduces (in some cases, drastically) the size of the dump file that *svnadmin dump* creates. There are, however, disadvantages to using this option—deltified dump files are more CPU-intensive to create, cannot be operated on by *svndumpfilter*, and tend not to compress as well as their nondeltified counterparts when using third-party tools such as *gzip* and *bzip2*.

Options

```
--deltas
--incremental
--quiet (-q)
--revision (-r) REV
```

Examples

Dump your whole repository:

```
$ svnadmin dump /var/svn/repos > full.dump
* Dumped revision 0.
* Dumped revision 1.
* Dumped revision 2.
...
```

Incrementally dump a single transaction from your repository:

```
$ svnadmin dump /var/svn/repos -r 21 --incremental > incr.dump
* Dumped revision 21.
```

---

svnadmin help   Help!

Synopsis

```
svnadmin help [SUBCOMMAND...]
```

Description

This subcommand is useful when you're trapped on a desert island with neither a Net connection nor a copy of this book.

Alternate names

?, h.

Options

None.

---

svnadmin hotcopy   Make a hot copy of a repository.

Synopsis

```
svnadmin hotcopy REPOS_PATH NEW_REPOS_PATH
```

Description

This subcommand makes a full "hot" backup of your repository, including all hooks, configuration files, and, of course, database files. If you pass the `--clean-logs` option, *svnadmin* will perform a hot copy of your repository and will then remove unused Berkeley DB logs from the original repository. You can run this command at any time and make a safe copy of the repository, regardless of whether other processes are using the repository.

Options

```
--clean-logs
```

As described in "Berkeley DB" on page 152, hot-copied Berkeley DB repositories are *not* portable across operating systems, nor will they work on machines with a different "endianness" than the machine where they were created.

svnadmin list-dblogs

Ask Berkeley DB which logfiles exist for a given Subversion repository.

Synopsis

```
svnadmin list-dblogs REPOS_PATH
```

Description

Berkeley DB creates logs of all changes to the repository, which allow it to recover in the face of catastrophe. Unless you enable DB_LOG_AUTOREMOVE, the logfiles accumulate, although most are no longer used and can be deleted to reclaim disk space. This command applies only to repositories using the bdb backend. See "Managing Disk Space" on page 164 for more information.

Options

None.

svnadmin list-unused-dblogs

Ask Berkeley DB which logfiles can be safely deleted.

Synopsis

```
svnadmin list-unused-dblogs REPOS_PATH
```

Description

Berkeley DB creates logs of all changes to the repository, which allow it to recover in the face of catastrophe. Unless you enable DB_LOG_AUTOREMOVE, the logfiles accumulate, although most are no longer used and can be deleted to reclaim disk space. This command applies only to repositories using the bdb backend. See "Managing Disk Space" on page 164 for more information.

Options

None.

Examples

Remove all unused logfiles from the repository:

```
$ svnadmin list-unused-dblogs /var/svn/repos
/var/svn/repos/log.0000000031
/var/svn/repos/log.0000000032
/var/svn/repos/log.0000000033

$ svnadmin list-unused-dblogs /var/svn/repos | xargs rm
## disk space reclaimed!
```

svnadmin load

Read a repository dump stream from *stdin*.

Synopsis

```
svnadmin load REPOS_PATH
```

Description

Read a repository dump stream from *stdin*, committing new revisions into the repository's filesystem. Send progress feedback to *stdout*.

Options

```
--force-uuid
--ignore-uuid
--parent-dir
--quiet (-q)
--use-post-commit-hook
--use-pre-commit-hook
```

Examples

This shows the beginning of loading a repository from a backup file (made, of course, with *svnadmin dump*):

```
$ svnadmin load /var/svn/restored < repos-backup
<<< Started new txn, based on original revision 1
     * adding path : test ... done.
     * adding path : test/a ... done.
...
```

Or if you want to load into a subdirectory:

```
$ svnadmin load --parent-dir new/subdir/for/project \
            /var/svn/restored < repos-backup
<<< Started new txn, based on original revision 1
     * adding path : test ... done.
     * adding path : test/a ... done.
...
```

svnadmin lslocks

Print descriptions of all locks.

Synopsis

```
svnadmin lslocks REPOS_PATH [PATH-IN-REPOS]
```

Description

Print descriptions of all locks in repository REPOS_PATH underneath the path PATH-IN-REPOS. If PATH-IN-REPOS is not provided, it defaults to the root directory of the repository.

Options

None.

Examples

This lists the one locked file in the repository at */var/svn/repos*:

```
$ svnadmin lslocks /var/svn/repos
Path: /tree.jpg
UUID Token: opaquelocktoken:ab00ddf0-6afb-0310-9cd0-dda813329753
```

```
Owner: harry
Created: 2005-07-08 17:27:36 -0500 (Fri, 08 Jul 2005)
Expires:
Comment (1 line):
Rework the uppermost branches on the bald cypress in the foreground.
```

svnadmin lstxns

Print the names of all uncommitted transactions.

Synopsis

```
svnadmin lstxns REPOS_PATH
```

Description

Print the names of all uncommitted transactions. See "Removing dead transactions" on page 165 for information on how uncommitted transactions are created and what you should do with them.

Options

None.

Examples

List all outstanding transactions in a repository:

```
$ svnadmin lstxns /var/svn/repos/
1w
1x
```

svnadmin recover

Bring a repository database back into a consistent state.

Synopsis

```
svnadmin recover REPOS_PATH
```

Description

Run this command if you get an error indicating that your repository needs to be recovered. This command applies only to repositories using the **bdb** backend. In addition, if *repos/conf/passwd* does not exist, it will create a default passwordfile.

Options

```
--wait
```

Examples

Recover a hung repository:

```
$ svnadmin recover /var/svn/repos/
Repository lock acquired.
Please wait; recovering the repository may take some time...

Recovery completed.
The latest repos revision is 34.
```

Recovering the database requires an exclusive lock on the repository. (This is a "database lock"; see the sidebar "The Three Meanings of "Lock"" on page 75.) If another process is accessing the repository, then *svnadmin recover* will error:

```
$ svnadmin recover /var/svn/repos
svn: Failed to get exclusive repository access; perhaps another process
such as httpd, svnserve or svn has it open?

$
```

The --wait option, however, will cause *svnadmin recover* to wait indefinitely for other processes to disconnect:

```
$ svnadmin recover /var/svn/repos --wait
Waiting on repository lock; perhaps another process has it open?

### time goes by...

Repository lock acquired.
Please wait; recovering the repository may take some time...

Recovery completed.
The latest repos revision is 34.
```

svnadmin rmlocks

Synopsis
```
svnadmin rmlocks REPOS_PATH LOCKED_PATH...
```

Description
Remove one or more locks from each *LOCKED_PATH*.

Options
None.

Examples
This deletes the locks on *tree.jpg* and *house.jpg* in the repository at */var/svn/repos*:

```
$ svnadmin rmlocks /var/svn/repos tree.jpg house.jpg
Removed lock on '/tree.jpg.
Removed lock on '/house.jpg.
```

svnadmin rmtxns

Synopsis
```
svnadmin rmtxns REPOS_PATH TXN_NAME...
```

Description
Delete outstanding transactions from a repository. This is covered in detail in "Removing dead transactions" on page 165.

Options
```
--quiet (-q)
```

Examples

Remove named transactions:

```
$ svnadmin rmtxns /var/svn/repos/ 1w 1x
```

Fortunately, the output of *lstxns* works great as the input for *rmtxns*:

```
$ svnadmin rmtxns /var/svn/repos/  'svnadmin lstxns /var/svn/repos/'
```

This removes all uncommitted transactions from your repository.

svnadmin setlog   Set the log message on a revision.

Synopsis

```
svnadmin setlog REPOS_PATH -r REVISION FILE
```

Description

Set the log message on revision *REVISION* to the contents of *FILE*.

This is similar to using *svn propset* with the --revprop option to set the svn:log property on a revision, except that you can also use the option --bypass-hooks to avoid running any pre- or post-commit hooks, which is useful if the modification of revision properties has not been enabled in the pre-revprop-change hook.

 Revision properties are not under version control, so this command will permanently overwrite the previous log message.

Options

```
--bypass-hooks
--revision (-r) REV
```

Examples

Set the log message for revision 19 to the contents of the file *msg*:

```
$ svnadmin setlog /var/svn/repos/ -r 19 msg
```

svnadmin setrevprop   Set a property on a revision.

Synopsis

```
svnadmin setrevprop REPOS_PATH -r REVISION NAME FILE
```

Description

Set the property *NAME* on revision *REVISION* to the contents of *FILE*. Use --use-pre-revprop-change-hook or --use-post-revprop-change-hook to trigger the revision property-related hooks (e.g., if you want an email notification sent from your post-revprop-change-hook).

Options

```
--revision (-r) ARG
--use-post-revprop-change-hook
--use-pre-revprop-change-hook
```

Examples

The following sets the revision property `repository-photo` to the contents of the file *sandwich.png*:

```
$svnadmin setrevprop /var/svn/repos -r 0 repository-photo sandwich.png
```

As you can see, *svnadmin setrevprop* has no output upon success.

svnadmin setuuid

Reset the repository UUID.

Synopsis

```
svnadmin setuuid REPOS_PATH [NEW_UUID]
```

Description

Reset the repository UUID for the repository located at *REPOS_PATH*. If *NEW_UUID* is provided, use that as the new repository UUID; otherwise, generate a brand-new UUID for the repository.

Options

None.

Examples

If you've *svnsynced* */var/svn/repos* to */var/svn/repos-new* and intend to use *repos-new* as your canonical repository, you may want to change the UUID for *repos-new* to the UUID of *repos* so that your users don't have to check out a new working copy to accommodate the change:

```
$ svnadmin setuuid /var/svn/repos-new 2109a8dd-854f-0410-ad31-d604008985ab
```

As you can see, *svnadmin setuuid* has no output upon success.

svnadmin upgrade

Upgrade a repository to the latest supported schema version.

Synopsis

```
svnadmin upgrade REPOS_PATH
```

Description

Upgrade the repository located at *REPOS_PATH* to the latest supported schema version.

This functionality is provided as a convenience for repository administrators who wish to make use of new Subversion functionality without having to undertake a potentially costly full repository dump and load operation. As such, the upgrade performs only the minimum amount of work needed to accomplish this while still maintaining the integrity of the repository. While a dump and subsequent load guarantee the most optimized repository state, *svnadmin upgrade* does not.

 You should *always* back up your repository before upgrading.

Options
None.

Examples
Upgrade the repository at path */var/repos/svn*:

```
$ svnadmin upgrade /var/repos/svn
Repository lock acquired.
Please wait; upgrading the repository may take some time...

Upgrade completed.
```

---

svnadmin verify
Verify the data stored in the repository.

Synopsis
```
svnadmin verify REPOS_PATH
```

Description
Run this command if you wish to verify the integrity of your repository. This basically iterates through all revisions in the repository by internally dumping all revisions and discarding the output—it's a good idea to run this on a regular basis to guard against latent hard disk failures and "bitrot." If this command fails—which it will do at the first sign of a problem—that means your repository has at least one corrupted revision, and you should restore the corrupted revision from a backup. (You did make a backup, didn't you?)

Options
```
--quiet (-q)
--revision (-r) ARG
```

Examples
Verify a hung repository:

```
$ svnadmin verify /var/svn/repos/
* Verified revision 1729.
```

svnlook

svnlook is a command-line utility for examining different aspects of a Subversion repository. It does not make any changes to the repository—it's just used for "peeking." *svnlook* is typically used by the repository hooks, but a repository administrator might find it useful for diagnostic purposes.

Since *svnlook* works via direct repository access (and thus can be used only on the machine that holds the repository), it refers to the repository with a path, not a URL.

If no revision or transaction is specified, *svnlook* defaults to the youngest (most recent) revision of the repository.

svnlook Options

Options in *svnlook* are global, just as they are in *svn* and *svnadmin*; however, most options apply to only one subcommand since the functionality of *svnlook* is (intentionally) limited in scope:

`--copy-info`
: Causes *svnlook changed* to show detailed copy source information.

`--no-diff-deleted`
: Prevents *svnlook diff* from printing differences for deleted files. The default behavior when a file is deleted in a transaction/revision is to print the same differences that you would see if you had left the file but removed all the content.

`--no-diff-added`
: Prevents *svnlook diff* from printing differences for added files. The default behavior when you add a file is to print the same differences that you would see if you had added the entire contents of an existing (empty) file.

`--revision (-r)`
: Specifies a particular revision number that you wish to examine.

`--revprop`
: Operates on a revision property instead of a property specific to a file or directory. This option requires that you also pass a revision with the `--revision (-r)` option.

`--transaction (-t)`
: Specifies a particular transaction ID that you wish to examine.

`--show-ids`
: Shows the filesystem node revision IDs for each path in the filesystem tree.

svnlook Subcommands

Here are the various subcommands for the *svnlook* program.

svnlook author

Print the author.

Synopsis
```
svnlook author REPOS_PATH
```

Description
Print the author of a revision or transaction in the repository.

Options
```
--revision (-r) REV
--transaction (-t) TXN
```

Examples

svnlook author is handy, but not very exciting:

```
$ svnlook author -r 40 /var/svn/repos
sally
```

svnlook cat

Print the contents of a file.

Synopsis

```
svnlook cat REPOS_PATH PATH_IN_REPOS
```

Description

Print the contents of a file.

Options

```
--revision (-r) REV
--transaction (-t) TXN
```

Examples

This shows the contents of a file in transaction **ax8**, located at */trunk/README*:

```
$ svnlook cat -t ax8 /var/svn/repos /trunk/README

              Subversion, a version control system.
              =======================================

$LastChangedDate: 2003-07-17 10:45:25 -0500 (Thu, 17 Jul 2003) $

Contents:

     I. A FEW POINTERS
    II. DOCUMENTATION
   III. PARTICIPATING IN THE SUBVERSION COMMUNITY
...
```

svnlook changed

Print the paths that were changed.

Synopsis

```
svnlook changed REPOS_PATH
```

Description

Print the paths that were changed in a particular revision or transaction, as well as *svn update*-style status letters in the first two columns:

'A '

Item added to repository

'D '

Item deleted from repository

'U '

File contents changed

'_U'

Properties of item changed; note the leading underscore

'UU'

File contents and properties changed

Files and directories can be distinguished, as directory paths are displayed with a trailing /
character.

Options

```
--copy-info
--revision (-r) REV
--transaction (-t) TXN
```

Examples

This shows a list of all the changed files and directories in revision 39 of a test repository.
Note that the first changed item is a directory, as evidenced by the trailing /:

```
$ svnlook changed -r 39 /var/svn/repos
A   trunk/vendors/deli/
A   trunk/vendors/deli/chips.txt
A   trunk/vendors/deli/sandwich.txt
A   trunk/vendors/deli/pickle.txt
U   trunk/vendors/baker/bagel.txt
_U  trunk/vendors/baker/croissant.txt
UU  trunk/vendors/baker/pretzel.txt
D   trunk/vendors/baker/baguette.txt
```

Here's an example that shows a revision in which a file was renamed:

```
$ svnlook changed -r 64 /var/svn/repos
A   trunk/vendors/baker/toast.txt
D   trunk/vendors/baker/bread.txt
```

Unfortunately, nothing in the preceding output reveals the connection between the deleted
and added files. Use the --copy-info option to make this relationship more apparent:

```
$ svnlook changed -r 64 --copy-info /var/svn/repos
A + trunk/vendors/baker/toast.txt
    (from trunk/vendors/baker/bread.txt:r63)
D   trunk/vendors/baker/bread.txt
```

svnlook date

Print the datestamp.

Synopsis

```
svnlook date REPOS_PATH
```

Description

Print the datestamp of a revision or transaction in a repository.

Options

```
--revision (-r) REV
--transaction (-t) TXN
```

Examples

This shows the date of revision 40 of a test repository:

```
$ svnlook date -r 40 /var/svn/repos/
2003-02-22 17:44:49 -0600 (Sat, 22 Feb 2003)
```

svnlook diff

Print differences of changed files and properties.

Synopsis

```
svnlook diff REPOS_PATH
```

Description

Print GNU-style differences of changed files and properties in a repository.

Options

```
--diff-copy-from
--no-diff-added
--no-diff-deleted
--revision (-r) REV
--transaction (-t) TXN
```

Examples

This shows a newly added (empty) file, a deleted file, and a copied file:

```
$ svnlook diff -r 40 /var/svn/repos/
Copied: egg.txt (from rev 39, trunk/vendors/deli/pickle.txt)

Added: trunk/vendors/deli/soda.txt
===============================================================================

Modified: trunk/vendors/deli/sandwich.txt
===============================================================================
--- trunk/vendors/deli/sandwich.txt     (original)
+++ trunk/vendors/deli/sandwich.txt     2003-02-22 17:45:04.000000000 -0600
@@ -0,0 +1 @@
+Don't forget the mayo!

Modified: trunk/vendors/deli/logo.jpg
===============================================================================
(Binary files differ)

Deleted: trunk/vendors/deli/chips.txt
===============================================================================

Deleted: trunk/vendors/deli/pickle.txt
===============================================================================
```

If a file has a nontextual `svn:mime-type` property, the differences are not explicitly shown.

svnlook dirs-changed

Print the directories that were themselves changed.

Synopsis

```
svnlook dirs-changed REPOS_PATH
```

Description
Print the directories that were themselves changed (property edits) or whose file children were changed.

Options
```
--revision (-r) REV
--transaction (-t) TXN
```

Examples
This shows the directories that changed in revision 40 in our sample repository:

```
$ svnlook dirs-changed -r 40 /var/svn/repos
trunk/vendors/deli/
```

svnlook help

Synopsis
```
svnlook help

svnlook -h

svnlook -?
```

Description
Displays the help message for *svnlook*. This command, like its brother, *svn help*, is also your friend, even though you never call it anymore and forgot to invite it to your last party.

Alternate names
?, *h*.

Options
None.

svnlook history   Print information about the history of a path in the repository.

Synopsis
```
svnlook history REPOS_PATH [PATH_IN_REPOS]
```

Description
Print information about the history of a path in the repository (or the root directory if no path is supplied).

Options
```
--limit (-l) ARG
--revision (-r) REV
--show-ids
```

Examples
This shows the history output for the path */branches/bookstore* as of revision 13 in our sample repository:

```
$ svnlook history -r 13 /var/svn/repos /branches/bookstore --show-ids
REVISION   PATH <ID>
```

```
 --------   ---------
     13   /branches/bookstore <1.1.r13/390>
     12   /branches/bookstore <1.1.r12/413>
     11   /branches/bookstore <1.1.r11/0>
      9   /trunk <1.0.r9/551>
      8   /trunk <1.0.r8/131357096>
      7   /trunk <1.0.r7/294>
      6   /trunk <1.0.r6/353>
      5   /trunk <1.0.r5/349>
      4   /trunk <1.0.r4/332>
      3   /trunk <1.0.r3/335>
      2   /trunk <1.0.r2/295>
      1   /trunk <1.0.r1/532>
```

svnlook info

Print the author, datestamp, log message size, and log message.

Synopsis

```
svnlook info REPOS_PATH
```

Description

Print the author, datestamp, log message size (in bytes), and log message, followed by a new-line character.

Options

```
--revision (-r) REV
--transaction (-t) TXN
```

Examples

This shows the info output for revision 40 in our sample repository:

```
$ svnlook info -r 40 /var/svn/repos
sally
2003-02-22 17:44:49 -0600 (Sat, 22 Feb 2003)
16
Rearrange lunch.
```

svnlook lock

If a lock exists on a path in the repository, describe it.

Synopsis

```
svnlook lock REPOS_PATH PATH_IN_REPOS
```

Description

Print all information available for the lock at PATH_IN_REPOS. If PATH_IN_REPOS is not locked, print nothing.

Options

None.

Examples

This describes the lock on the file *tree.jpg*:

```
$ svnlook lock /var/svn/repos tree.jpg
UUID Token: opaquelocktoken:ab00ddf0-6afb-0310-9cd0-dda813329753
```

```
Owner: harry
Created: 2005-07-08 17:27:36 -0500 (Fri, 08 Jul 2005)
Expires:
Comment (1 line):
Rework the uppermost branches on the bald cypress in the foreground.
```

svnlook log

Print the log message, followed by a newline character.

Synopsis

```
svnlook log REPOS_PATH
```

Description

Print the log message.

Options

```
--revision (-r) REV
--transaction (-t) TXN
```

Examples

This shows the log output for revision 40 in our sample repository:

```
$ svnlook log /var/svn/repos/
Rearrange lunch.
```

svnlook propget

Print the raw value of a property on a path in the repository.

Synopsis

```
svnlook propget REPOS_PATH PROPNAME [PATH_IN_REPOS]
```

Description

List the value of a property on a path in the repository.

Alternate names

pg, *pget*.

Options

```
--revision (-r) REV
--revprop
--transaction (-t) TXN
```

Examples

This shows the value of the "seasonings" property on the file */trunk/sandwich* in the HEAD revision:

```
$ svnlook pg /var/svn/repos seasonings /trunk/sandwich
mustard
```

svnlook proplist

Print the names and values of versioned file and directory properties.

Synopsis

```
svnlook proplist REPOS_PATH [PATH_IN_REPOS]
```

Description

List the properties of a path in the repository. With --verbose, show the property values, too.

Alternate names

pl, *plist*.

Options

```
--revision (-r) REV
--revprop
--transaction (-t) TXN
--verbose (-v)
```

Examples

This shows the names of properties set on the file */trunk/README* in the HEAD revision:

```
$ svnlook proplist /var/svn/repos /trunk/README
  original-author
  svn:mime-type
```

This is the same command as in the preceding example, but this example shows the property values as well:

```
$ svnlook --verbose proplist /var/svn/repos /trunk/README
  original-author : harry
  svn:mime-type : text/plain
```

svnlook tree   Print the tree.

Synopsis

```
svnlook tree REPOS_PATH [PATH_IN_REPOS]
```

Description

Print the tree, starting at `PATH_IN_REPOS` (if supplied; at the root of the tree otherwise), optionally showing node revision IDs.

Options

```
--full-paths
--non-recursive (-N)
--revision (-r) REV
--show-ids
--transaction (-t) TXN
```

Example

This shows the tree output (with nodeIDs) for revision 13 in our sample repository:

```
$ svnlook tree -r 13 /var/svn/repos --show-ids
/ <0.0.r13/811>
 trunk/ <1.0.r9/551>
  button.c <2.0.r9/238>
  Makefile <3.0.r7/41>
  integer.c <4.0.r6/98>
 branches/ <5.0.r13/593>
  bookstore/ <1.1.r13/390>
   button.c <2.1.r12/85>
```

```
Makefile <3.0.r7/41>
integer.c <4.1.r13/109>
```

svnlook uuid

Synopsis

```
svnlook uuid REPOS_PATH
```

Description

Print the UUID for the repository. The UUID is the repository's *universal unique identifier*. The Subversion client uses this identifier to differentiate between one repository and another.

Options

None.

Example

```
$ svnlook uuid /var/svn/repos
e7fe1b91-8cd5-0310-98dd-2f12e793c5e8
```

svnlook youngest

Synopsis

```
svnlook youngest REPOS_PATH
```

Description

Print the youngest revision number of a repository.

Options

None.

Examples

This shows the youngest revision of our sample repository:

```
$ svnlook youngest /var/svn/repos/
42
```

svnsync

svnsync is the Subversion remote repository mirroring tool. Put simply, it allows you to replay the revisions of one repository into another one.

In any mirroring scenario, there are two repositories: the source repository, and the mirror (or "sink") repository. The source repository is the repository from which *svnsync* pulls revisions. The mirror repository is the destination for the revisions pulled from the source repository. Each of the repositories may be local or remote—they are only ever addressed by their URLs.

The *svnsync* process requires only read access to the source repository; it never attempts to modify it. But obviously, *svnsync* requires both read and write access to the mirror repository.

svnsync is very sensitive to changes made in the mirror repository that weren't made as part of a mirroring operation. To prevent this from happening, it's best if the *svnsync* process is the only process permitted to modify the mirror repository.

svnsync Options

Options in *svnsync* are global, just as they are in *svn* and *svnadmin*:

`--config-dir DIR`
> Instructs Subversion to read configuration information from the specified directory instead of the default location (*.subversion* in the user's home directory).

`--no-auth-cache`
> Prevents caching of authentication information (e.g., username and password) in the Subversion runtime configuration directories.

`--non-interactive`
> In the case of an authentication failure or insufficient credentials, prevents prompting for credentials (e.g., username or password). This is useful if you're running Subversion inside an automated script and it's more appropriate to have Subversion fail than to prompt for more information.

`--quiet (-q)`
> Requests that the client print only essential information while performing an operation.

`--source-password PASSWD`
> Specifies the password for the Subversion server from which you are syncing. If not provided, or if incorrect, Subversion will prompt you for this information as needed.

`--source-username NAME`
> Specifies the username for the Subversion server from which you are syncing. If not provided, or if incorrect, Subversion will prompt you for this information as needed.

`--sync-password PASSWD`
> Specifies the password for the Subversion server to which you are syncing. If not provided, or if incorrect, Subversion will prompt you for this information as needed.

`--sync-username NAME`
> Specifies the username for the Subversion server to which you are syncing. If not provided, or if incorrect, Subversion will prompt you for this information as needed.

svnsync Subcommands

Here are the various subcommands for the *svnsync* program.

svnsync copy-revprops

Copy all revision properties for a revision from the source to the mirror repository.

Synopsis

```
svnsync copy-revprops DEST_URL [REV[:REV2]]
```

Description

Because Subversion revision properties can be changed at any time, it's possible that the properties for some revision might be changed after that revision has already been synchronized to another repository. Because the *svnsync synchronize* command operates only on the range of revisions that have not yet been synchronized, it won't notice a revision property change outside that range. Left as is, this causes a deviation in the values of that revision's properties between the source and mirror repositories. *svnsync copy-revprops* is the answer to this problem. Use it to resynchronize the revision properties for a particular revision or range of revisions.

Options

```
--config-dir DIR
--no-auth-cache
--non-interactive
--quiet (-q)
--source-password ARG
--source-username ARG
--sync-password ARG
--sync-username ARG
```

Examples

Resynchronize revision properties for a single revision:

```
$ svnsync copy-revprops file:///var/svn/repos-mirror 6
Copied properties for revision 6.
$
```

svnsync help

Help!

Synopsis

```
svnsync help
```

Description

This subcommand is useful when you're trapped in a foreign prison with neither a Net connection nor a copy of this book, but you do have a local Wi-Fi network running and you'd like to sync a copy of your repository over to the backup server that Ira The Knife is running over in cell block D.

Options

None.

svnsync initialize

Synopsis

```
svnsync initialize MIRROR_URL SOURCE_URL
```

Description

Verifies that a repository meets the requirements of a new mirror repository—that it has no previous existing version history and that it allows revision property modifications—and records the initial administrative information that associates the mirror repository with the source repository. This is the first *svnsync* operation you run on a would-be mirror repository.

Alternate names

init.

Options

```
--config-dir DIR
--no-auth-cache
--non-interactive
--quiet (-q)
--source-password ARG
--source-username ARG
--sync-password ARG
--sync-username ARG
```

Examples

Fail to initialize a mirror repository due to inability to modify revision properties:

```
$ svnsync initialize file:///var/svn/repos-mirror http://svn.example.com/repos
svnsync: Repository has not been enabled to accept revision propchanges;
ask the administrator to create a pre-revprop-change hook
$
```

Initialize a repository as a mirror, having already created a `pre-revprop-change` hook that permits all revision property changes:

```
$ svnsync initialize file:///var/svn/repos-mirror http://svn.example.com/repos
Copied properties for revision 0.
$
```

svnsync synchronize

Synopsis

```
svnsync synchronize DEST_URL
```

Description

The *svnsync synchronize* command does all the heavy lifting of a repository mirroring operation. After consulting with the mirror repository to see which revisions have already been copied into it, it then begins to copy any not-yet-mirrored revisions from the source repository.

svnsync synchronize can be gracefully canceled and restarted.

As of Subversion 1.5, you can limit *svnsync* to a subdirectory of the source repository by specifying the subdirectory as part of the *SOURCE_URL*.

Alternate names

sync.

Options

```
--config-dir DIR
--no-auth-cache
--non-interactive
--quiet (-q)
--source-password ARG
--source-username ARG
--sync-password ARG
--sync-username ARG
```

Examples

Copy unsynchronized revisions from the source repository to the mirror repository:

```
$ svnsync synchronize file:///var/svn/repos-mirror
Committed revision 1.
Copied properties for revision 1.
Committed revision 2.
Copied properties for revision 2.
Committed revision 3.
Copied properties for revision 3.
...
Committed revision 45.
Copied properties for revision 45.
Committed revision 46.
Copied properties for revision 46.
Committed revision 47.
Copied properties for revision 47.
$
```

svnserve

svnserve allows access to Subversion repositories using Subversion's custom network protocol.

You can run *svnserve* as a standalone server process (for clients that are using the svn:// access method); you can have a daemon such as *inetd* or *xinetd* launch it for you on demand (also for svn://), or you can have *sshd* launch it on demand for the svn+ssh:// access method.

Regardless of the access method, once the client has selected a repository by transmitting its URL, *svnserve* reads a file named *conf/svnserve.conf* in the repository directory to determine repository-specific settings such as what authentication database to use and what authorization policies to apply. See "svnserve, a Custom Server" on page 195 for details of the *svnserve.conf* file.

svnserve Options

Unlike the previous commands we've described, *svnserve* has no subcommands—it is controlled exclusively by options:

`--daemon (-d)`

Causes *svnserve* to run in daemon mode. *svnserve* backgrounds itself and accepts and serves TCP/IP connections on the *svn* port (3690, by default).

`--foreground`

When used together with `-d`, causes *svnserve* to stay in the foreground. This is mainly useful for debugging.

`--inetd (-i)`

Causes *svnserve* to use the *stdin* and *stdout* file descriptors, as is appropriate for a daemon running out of *inetd*.

`--help (-h)`

Displays a usage summary and exits.

`--listen-host=HOST`

Causes *svnserve* to listen on the interface specified by *HOST*, which may be either a hostname or an IP address.

`--listen-once (-X)`

Causes *svnserve* to accept one connection on the `svn` port, serve it, and exit. This option is mainly useful for debugging.

`--listen-port=PORT`

Causes *svnserve* to listen on *PORT* when run in daemon mode. (FreeBSD daemons listen only on tcp6 by default—this option tells them to also listen on tcp4.)

`--pid-file FILENAME`

Causes *svnserve* to write its process ID to *FILENAME*, which must be writable by the user under which *svnserve* is running.

`--root=ROOT (-r=ROOT)`

Sets the virtual root for repositories served by *svnserve*. The pathname in URLs provided by the client will be interpreted relative to this root and will not be allowed to escape this root.

`--threads (-T)`

When running in daemon mode, causes *svnserve* to spawn a thread instead of a process for each connection (e.g., for when running on Windows). The *svnserve* process still backgrounds itself at startup time.

`--tunnel (-t)`

Causes *svnserve* to run in tunnel mode, which is just like the *inetd* mode of operation (both modes serve one connection over *stdin*/*stdout*, and then exit), except that the connection is considered to be preauthenticated with the username of the current UID. This flag is automatically passed for you by the client when running over a tunnel agent such as *ssh*. That means there's rarely any need for *you* to pass this option to *svnserve*. So, if you find yourself typing `svnserve --tunnel` on the command line and wondering what to do next, see "Tunneling over SSH" on page 203.

`--tunnel-user NAME`
> Used in conjunction with the `--tunnel` option, tells *svnserve* to assume that `NAME` is the authenticated user, rather than the UID of the *svnserve* process. This is useful for users who wish to share a single system account over SSH but who want to maintain separate commit identities.

`--version`
> Displays version information and a list of repository backend modules available, and then exits.

svndumpfilter

svndumpfilter is a command-line utility for removing history from a Subversion dump file by either excluding or including paths beginning with one or more named prefixes. For details, see "svndumpfilter" on page 161.

svndumpfilter Options

Options in *svndumpfilter* are global, just as they are in *svn* and *svnadmin*:

`--drop-empty-revs`
> If filtering causes any revision to be empty (i.e., causes no change to the repository), removes these revisions from the final dump file.

`--renumber-revs`
> Renumbers revisions that remain after filtering.

`--skip-missing-merge-sources`
> Skips merge sources that have been removed as part of the filtering. Without this option, *svndumpfilter* will exit with an error if the merge source for a retained path is removed by filtering.

`--preserve-revprops`
> If all nodes in a revision are removed by filtering and `--drop-empty-revs` is not passed, the default behavior of *svndumpfilter* is to remove all revision properties except for the date and the log message (which will merely indicate that the revision is empty). Passing this option will preserve existing revision properties (which may or may not make sense, since the related content is no longer present in the dump file).

`--quiet`
> Does not display filtering statistics.

svndumpfilter Subcommands

Here are the various subcommands for the *svndumpfilter* program.

svndumpfilter exclude

Filter out nodes with given prefixes from the dump stream.

Synopsis

```
svndumpfilter exclude PATH_PREFIX...
```

Description

This can be used to exclude nodes that begin with one or more PATH_PREFIXes from a filtered dump file.

Options

```
--drop-empty-revs
--preserve-revprops
--quiet
--renumber-revs
--skip-missing-merge-sources
```

Examples

If we have a dump file from a repository with a number of different picnic-related directories in it, but we want to keep everything *except* the *sandwiches* part of the repository, we'll exclude only that path:

```
$ svndumpfilter exclude sandwiches < dumpfile > filtered-dumpfile
Excluding prefixes:
    '/sandwiches'

Revision 0 committed as 0.
Revision 1 committed as 1.
Revision 2 committed as 2.
Revision 3 committed as 3.
Revision 4 committed as 4.

Dropped 1 node(s):
    '/sandwiches'
```

svndumpfilter include

Filter out nodes without given prefixes from dump stream.

Synopsis

```
svndumpfilter include PATH_PREFIX...
```

Description

Can be used to include nodes that begin with one or more PATH_PREFIXes in a filtered dump file (thus excluding all other paths).

Options

```
--drop-empty-revs
--preserve-revprops
--quiet
```

```
--renumber-revs
--skip-missing-merge-sources
```

Example
If we have a dump file from a repository with a number of different picnic-related directories in it, but want to keep only the *sandwiches* part of the repository, we'll include only that path:

```
$ svndumpfilter include sandwiches < dumpfile > filtered-dumpfile
Including prefixes:
   '/sandwiches'

Revision 0 committed as 0.
Revision 1 committed as 1.
Revision 2 committed as 2.
Revision 3 committed as 3.
Revision 4 committed as 4.

Dropped 3 node(s):
   '/drinks'
   '/snacks'
   '/supplies'
```

svndumpfilter help
Help!

Synopsis
```
svndumpfilter help [SUBCOMMAND...]
```

Description
Displays the help message for *svndumpfilter*. Unlike other help commands documented in this chapter, there is no witty commentary for this help command. The authors of this book deeply regret the omission.

Options
None.

svnversion

svnversion is a program for summarizing the revision mixture of a working copy. The resultant revision number, or revision range, is written to standard output.

It's common to use this output in your build process when defining the version number of your program:

```
svnversion [OPTIONS] [WC_PATH [TRAIL_URL]]
```

TRAIL_URL, if present, is the trailing portion of the URL used to determine whether *WC_PATH* itself is switched (detection of switches within *WC_PATH* does not rely on *TRAIL_URL*).

When *WC_PATH* is not defined, the current directory will be used as the working copy path. *TRAIL_URL* cannot be defined if *WC_PATH* is not explicitly given.

svnversion Options

Like *svnserve*, *svnversion* has no subcommands—only options:

`--no-newline (-n)`
> Omits the usual trailing newline from the output.

`--committed (-c)`
> Uses the last-changed revisions rather than the current (i.e., highest locally available) revisions.

`--help (-h)`
> Prints a help summary.

`--version`
> Prints the version of *svnversion* and exits with no error.

svnversion Examples

If the working copy is all at the same revision (e.g., immediately after an update), then that revision is printed out:

```
$ svnversion
4168
```

You can add *TRAIL_URL* to make sure the working copy is not switched from what you expect. Note that the *WC_PATH* is required in this command:

```
$ svnversion . /var/svn/trunk
4168
```

For a mixed-revision working copy, the range of revisions present is printed:

```
$ svnversion
4123:4168
```

If the working copy contains modifications, a trailing "M" is added:

```
$ svnversion
4168M
```

If the working copy is switched, a trailing "S" is added:

```
$ svnversion
4168S
```

Thus, here is a mixed-revision, switched working copy containing some local modifications:

```
$ svnversion
4212:4168MS
```

If invoked on a directory that is not a working copy, *svnversion* assumes it is an exported working copy and prints "exported":

```
$ svnversion
exported
```

mod_dav_svn Configuration Directives

This section covers Apache configuration directives for serving Subversion repositories through the Apache HTTP Server. We will briefly describe each Subversion Apache configuration directive here. For an in-depth description of configuring Apache with Subversion, see "httpd, the Apache HTTP Server" on page 207.

Directives

These are the *httpd.conf* directives that apply to *mod_dav_svn*:

DAV svn

> Must be included in any `Directory` or `Location` block for a Subversion repository. It tells *httpd* to use the Subversion backend for mod_dav to handle all requests.

SVNAllowBulkUpdates On|Off

> Toggles support for all-inclusive responses to update-style `REPORT` requests. Subversion clients use `REPORT` requests to get information about directory tree checkouts and updates from *mod_dav_svn*. They can ask the server to send that information in one of two ways: with the entirety of the tree's information in one massive response, or with a *skelta* (a skeletal representation of a tree delta), which contains just enough information for the client to know what *additional* data to request from the server. When this directive is included with a value of `Off`, *mod_dav_svn* will only ever respond to these `REPORT` requests with skelta responses, regardless of the type of responses requested by the client.

> Most folks won't need to use this directive at all. It primarily exists for administrators who wish—for security or auditing reasons—to force Subversion clients to fetch individually all the files and directories needed for updates and checkouts, thus leaving an audit trail of `GET` and `PROPFIND` requests in Apache's logs. The default value of this directive is `On`.

SVNAutoversioning On|Off

> When its value is `On`, allows write requests from WebDAV clients to result in automatic commits. A generic log message is autogenerated and attached to each revision. If you enable autoversioning, you'll likely want to set `ModMimeUsePathInfo` `On` so that mod_mime can set `svn:mime-type` to the correct MIME type automatically (as best as mod_mime is able to, of course). For more information, see Appendix C. The default value of this directive is `Off`.

SVNPath *directory-path*

> Specifies the location in the filesystem for a Subversion repository's files. In a configuration block for a Subversion repository, either this directive or `SVNParent Path` must be present, but not both.

SVNSpecialURI *component*

> Specifies the URI component (namespace) for special Subversion resources. The default is `!svn`, and most administrators will never use this directive. Set this only

if there is a pressing need to have a file named *!svn* in your repository. If you change this on a server already in use, it will break all of the outstanding working copies, and your users will hunt you down with pitchforks and flaming torches.

SVNReposName *name*

Specifies the name of a Subversion repository for use in HTTP GET responses. This value will be prepended to the title of all directory listings (which are served when you navigate to a Subversion repository with a web browser). This directive is optional.

SVNIndexXSLT *directory-path*

Specifies the URI of an XSL transformation for directory indexes. This directive is optional.

SVNParentPath *directory-path*

Specifies the location in the filesystem of a parent directory whose child directories are Subversion repositories. In a configuration block for a Subversion repository, either this directive or SVNPath must be present, but not both.

SVNPathAuthz On|Off|short_circuit

Controls path-based authorization by enabling subrequests (On), disabling subrequests (Off; see "Disabling path-based checks" on page 218), or querying *mod_authz_svn* directly (short_circuit). The default value of this directive is On.

SVNListParentPath On|Off

When set to On, allows a GET of SVNParentPath, which results in a listing of all repositories under that path. The default setting is Off.

SVNMasterURI *url*

Specifies a URI to the master Subversion repository (used for a write-through proxy).

SVNActivitiesDB *directory-path*

Specifies the location in the filesystem where the activities database should be stored. By default, *mod_dav_svn* creates and uses a directory in the repository called *dav/activities.d*. The path specified with this option must be an absolute path.

If specified for an SVNParentPath area, *mod_dav_svn* appends the basename of the repository to the path specified here. For example:

```
<Location /svn>
  DAV svn

  # any "/svn/foo" URL will map to a repository in
  # /net/svn.nfs/repositories/foo
  SVNParentPath          "/net/svn.nfs/repositories"

  # any "/svn/foo" URL will map to an activities db in
  #  /var/db/svn/activities/foo
  SVNActivitiesDB        "/var/db/svn/activities"
</Location>
```

High-Level Logging

This is a list of Subversion action log messages produced by Apache's high-level logging mechanism, each followed by an example of the log message. See "Apache logging" on page 221 for details on logging:

Checkout or export
```
checkout-or-export /path r62 depth=infinity
```

Commit
```
commit harry r100
```

Diffs
```
diff /path r15:20 depth=infinity ignore-ancestry
diff /path1@15 /path2@20 depth=infinity ignore-ancestry
```

Fetch a directory
```
get-dir /trunk r17 text
```

Fetch a file
```
get-file /path r20 props
```

Fetch a file revision
```
get-file-revs /path r12:15 include-merged-revisions
```

Fetch merge information
```
get-mergeinfo (/path1 /path2)
```

Lock
```
lock /path steal
```

Log
```
log (/path1,/path2,/path3) r20:90 discover-changed-paths revprops=()
```

Replay revisions (svnsync)
```
replay /path r19
```

Revision property change
```
change-rev-prop r50 propertyname
```

Revision property list
```
rev-proplist r34
```

Status
```
status /path r62 depth=infinity
```

Switch
```
switch /pathA /pathB@50 depth=infinity
```

Unlock
```
unlock /path break
```

Update
```
update /path r17 send-copyfrom-args
```

mod_authz_svn

This section covers Apache configuration directives for configuring path-based authorization for Subversion repositories served through the Apache HTTP Server. We will briefly describe each Apache configuration directive offered by *mod_authz_svn* for configuring path-based authorization for Subversion repositories served through the Apache HTTP Server. For an in-depth description of using path-based authorization in Subversion, see "Path-Based Authorization" on page 226.

Directives

These are the *httpd.conf* directives that apply to *mod_authz_svn*:

AuthzSVNAccessFile *file-path*
> Consult *file-path* for access rules describing the permissions for paths in the Subversion repository.

AuthzSVNAnonymous On|Off
> Set to Off to disable two special-case behaviors of this module: interaction with the Satisfy Any directive, and enforcement of the authorization policy even when no Require directives are present. The default value of this directive is On.

AuthzSVNAuthoritative On|Off
> Set to Off to allow access control to be passed along to lower modules. The default value of this directive is On.

AuthzSVNNoAuthWhenAnonymousAllowed On|Off
> Set to On to suppress authentication and authorization for requests that anonymous users are allowed to perform. The default value of this directive is On.

Subversion Properties

Subversion allows users to invent arbitrarily named versioned properties on files and directories, as well as unversioned properties on revisions. The only restriction is on properties whose names begin with svn: (those are reserved for Subversion's own use). Although these properties may be set by users to control Subversion's behavior, users may not invent new svn: properties.

Versioned Properties

These are the versioned properties that Subversion reserves for its own use:

svn:executable
> If present on a file, the client will make the file executable in Unix-hosted working copies. See "File Executability" on page 58.

`svn:mime-type`

> If present on a file, the value indicates the file's MIME type. This allows the client to decide whether line-based contextual merging is safe to perform during updates and can also affect how the file behaves when fetched via a web browser. See "File Content Type" on page 57.

`svn:ignore`

> If present on a directory, the value is a list of *unversioned* file patterns to be ignored by *svn status* and other subcommands. See "Ignoring Unversioned Items" on page 60.

`svn:keywords`

> If present on a file, the value tells the client how to expand particular keywords within the file. See "Keyword Substitution" on page 65.

`svn:eol-style`

> If present on a file, the value tells the client how to manipulate the file's line-endings in the working copy and in exported trees. See "End-of-Line Character Sequences" on page 59 and "svn export" earlier in this chapter.

`svn:externals`

> If present on a directory, the value is a multiline list of other paths and URLs the client should check out. See "Externals Definitions" on page 82.

`svn:special`

> If present on a file, indicates that the file is not an ordinary file but a symbolic link or other special object.[*]

`svn:needs-lock`

> If present on a file, tells the client to make the file read-only in the working copy, as a reminder that the file should be locked before editing begins. See "Lock Communication" on page 81.

`svn:mergeinfo`

> Used by Subversion to track merge data. See "Mergeinfo and Previews" on page 113 for details, but you should never edit this property unless you *really* know what you're doing.

Unversioned Properties

These are the unversioned properties that Subversion reserves for its own use:

`svn:author`

> If present, contains the authenticated username of the person who created the revision. (If not present, the revision was committed anonymously.)

---

[*] As of this writing, symbolic links are indeed the only "special" objects. But there might be more in future releases of Subversion.

`svn:date`
> Contains the UTC time the revision was created, in ISO 8601 format. The value comes from the *server* machine's clock, not the client's.

`svn:log`
> Contains the log message describing the revision.

`svn:autoversioned`
> If present, the revision was created via the autoversioning feature. See "Autoversioning" on page 378.

Repository Hooks

The following are the repository hooks that Subversion provides.

---

start-commit
Notification of the beginning of a commit.

Description
The `start-commit` hook is run before the commit transaction is even created. It is typically used to decide whether the user has commit privileges at all.

If the `start-commit` hook program returns a nonzero exit value, the commit is stopped before the commit transaction is even created, and anything printed to *stderr* is marshaled back to the client.

Input Parameter(s)
The command-line arguments passed to the hook program, in order, are:

1. Repository path
2. Authenticated username attempting the commit
3. Colon-separated list of capabilities that a client passes to the server, including `depth`, `mergeinfo`, and `log-revprops` (new in Subversion 1.5).

Common uses
Access control (e.g., temporarily lockout commits for some reason); a means to allow access only from clients that have certain capabilities.

---

pre-commit
Notification just prior to commit completion.

Description
The `pre-commit` hook is run just before a commit transaction is promoted to a new revision. Typically, this hook is used to protect against commits that are disallowed due to content or location (e.g., your site might require that all commits to a certain branch include a ticket number from the bug tracker, or that the incoming log message is nonempty).

If the `pre-commit` hook program returns a nonzero exit value, the commit is aborted, the commit transaction is removed, and anything printed to *stderr* is marshaled back to the client.

Input parameter(s)

The command-line arguments passed to the hook program, in order, are:

1. Repository path
2. Commit transaction name

Common uses

Change validation and control.

post-commit

Notification of a successful commit.

Description

The post-commit hook is run after the transaction is committed and a new revision is created. Most people use this hook to send out descriptive emails about the commit or to notify some other tool (such as an issue tracker) that a commit has happened. Some configurations also use this hook to trigger backup processes.

If the post-commit hook returns a nonzero exit status, the commit *will not* be aborted, since it has already completed. However, anything that the hook printed to *stderr* will be marshaled back to the client, making it easier to diagnose hook failures.

Input parameter(s)

The command-line arguments passed to the hook program, in order, are:

1. Repository path
2. Revision number created by the commit

Common uses

Commit notification; tool integration.

pre-revprop-change

Notification of a revision property change attempt.

Description

The pre-revprop-change hook is run immediately prior to the modification of a revision property when performed outside the scope of a normal commit. Unlike the other hooks, the default state of this one is to deny the proposed action. The hook must actually exist and return a zero exit value before a revision property modification can happen.

If the pre-revprop-change hook doesn't exist, isn't executable, or returns a nonzero exit value, no change to the property will be made, and anything printed to *stderr* is marshaled back to the client.

Input parameter(s)

The command-line arguments passed to the hook program, in order, are:

1. Repository path
2. Revision whose property is about to be modified
3. Authenticated username attempting the property change

4. Name of the property changed

5. Change description: A (added), D (deleted), or M (modified)

Additionally, Subversion passes the intended new value of the property to the hook program via standard input.

Common uses
Access control; change validation and control.

---

post-revprop-change
Notification of a successful revision property change.

Description
The post-revprop-change hook is run immediately after the modification of a revision property when performed outside the scope of a normal commit. As you can derive from the description of its counterpart (the pre-revprop-change hook), this hook will not run at all unless the pre-revprop-change hook is implemented. It is typically used to send email notification of the property change.

If the post-revprop-change hook returns a nonzero exit status, the change *will not* be aborted, since it has already completed. However, anything that the hook printed to *stderr* will be marshaled back to the client, making it easier to diagnose hook failures.

Input parameter(s)
The command-line arguments passed to the hook program, in order, are:

1. Repository path

2. Revision whose property was modified

3. Authenticated username of the person making the change

4. Name of the property changed

5. Change description: A (added), D (deleted), or M (modified)

Additionally, Subversion passes to the hook program, via standard input, the previous value of the property.

Common uses
Property change notification.

---

pre-lock
Notification of a path lock attempt.

Description
The pre-lock hook runs whenever someone attempts to lock a path. It can be used to prevent locks altogether or to create a more complex policy specifying exactly which users are allowed to lock particular paths. If the hook notices a preexisting lock, it can also decide whether a user is allowed to "steal" the existing lock.

If the pre-lock hook program returns a nonzero exit value, the lock action is aborted and anything printed to *stderr* is marshaled back to the client.

---

362 | Chapter 9: Subversion Complete Reference

Input parameter(s)

The command-line arguments passed to the hook program, in order, are:

1. Repository path
2. Versioned path that is to be locked
3. Authenticated username of the person attempting the lock

Common uses

Access control.

---

post-lock

Notification of a successful path lock.

Description

The post-lock hook runs after one or more paths have been locked. It is typically used to send email notification of the lock event.

If the post-lock hook returns a nonzero exit status, the lock *will not* be aborted, since it has already completed. However, anything that the hook printed to *stderr* will be marshaled back to the client, making it easier to diagnose hook failures.

Input parameter(s)

The command-line arguments passed to the hook program, in order, are:

1. Repository path
2. Authenticated username of the person who locked the paths

Additionally, the list of paths locked is passed to the hook program via standard input, one path per line.

Common uses

Lock notification.

---

pre-unlock

Notification of a path unlock attempt.

Description

The pre-unlock hook runs whenever someone attempts to remove a lock on a file. It can be used to create policies that specify which users are allowed to unlock particular paths. It's particularly important for determining policies about lock breakage. If user A locks a file, is user B allowed to break the lock? What if the lock is more than a week old? These sorts of things can be decided and enforced by the hook.

If the pre-unlock hook program returns a nonzero exit value, the unlock action is aborted and anything printed to *stderr* is marshaled back to the client.

Input parameter(s)

The command-line arguments passed to the hook program, in order, are:

1. Repository path

2. Versioned path that is to be locked

3. Authenticated username of the person attempting the lock

Common uses
Access control.

---

post-unlock
Notification of a successful path unlock.

Description
The `post-unlock` hook runs after one or more paths have been unlocked. It is typically used to send email notification of the unlock event.

If the `post-unlock` hook returns a nonzero exit status, the unlock *will not* be aborted, since it has already completed. However, anything that the hook printed to *stderr* will be marshaled back to the client, making it easier to diagnose hook failures.

Input parameter(s)
The command-line arguments passed to the hook program, in order, are:

1. Repository path

2. Authenticated username of the person who unlocked the paths

Additionally, the list of paths unlocked is passed to the hook program via standard input, one path per line.

Common uses
Unlock notification.

364 | Chapter 9: Subversion Complete Reference

Subversion Quick-Start Guide

If you're eager to get Subversion up and running (and you enjoy learning by experimentation), this appendix will show you how to create a repository, import code, and then check it back out again as a working copy. Along the way, we give links to the relevant chapters of this book.

 If you're new to the entire concept of version control or to the "copy-modify-merge" model used by both CVS and Subversion, you should read Chapter 1 before going any further.

Installing Subversion

Subversion is built on a portability layer called APR: the Apache Portable Runtime library. The APR library provides all the interfaces that Subversion needs to function on different operating systems: disk access, network access, memory management, and so on. While Subversion is able to use Apache as one of its network server programs, its dependence on APR *does not* mean that Apache is a required component. APR is a standalone library usable by any application. It does mean, however, that like Apache, Subversion clients and servers run on any operating system that the Apache *httpd* server runs on: Windows, Linux, all flavors of BSD, Mac OS X, NetWare, and others.

The easiest way to get Subversion is to download a binary package built for your operating system. Subversion's web site (*http://subversion.tigris.org*) often has these packages available for download, posted by volunteers. The site usually contains graphical installer packages for users of Microsoft operating systems. If you run a Unix-like operating system, you can use your system's native package distribution system (RPMs, DEBs, the ports tree, etc.) to get Subversion.

Alternatively, you can build Subversion directly from source code, though it's not always an easy task. (If you're not experienced at building open source software packages, you're probably better off downloading a binary distribution instead!) From the Subversion web site, download the latest source code release. After unpacking it, follow the instructions in the *INSTALL* file to build it. Note that a released source package may not contain everything you need to build a command-line client capable of talking to a remote repository. Starting with Subversion 1.4 and later, the libraries Subversion depends on (apr, apr-util, and neon) are distributed in a separate source package suffixed with *-deps*. These libraries are now common enough that they may already be installed on your system. If not, you'll need to unpack the dependency package into the same directory where you unpacked the main Subversion source. Regardless, it's possible that you may want to fetch other optional dependencies, such as Berkeley DB and possibly Apache *httpd*. If you want to do a complete build, make sure you have all of the packages documented in the *INSTALL* file.

If you're one of those folks who likes to use bleeding-edge software, you can also get the Subversion source code from the Subversion repository in which it lives. Obviously, you'll need to already have a Subversion client on hand to do this. But once you do, you can check out a working copy of the Subversion source repository from *http://svn .collab.net/repos/svn/trunk/*:[*]

```
$ svn checkout http://svn.collab.net/repos/svn/trunk subversion
A    subversion/HACKING
A    subversion/INSTALL
A    subversion/README
A    subversion/autogen.sh
A    subversion/build.conf
...
```

The preceding command will create a working copy of the latest (unreleased) Subversion source code into a subdirectory named *subversion* in your current working directory. You can adjust that last argument as you see fit. Regardless of what you call the new working copy directory, though, after this operation completes, you will now have the Subversion source code. Of course, you will still need to fetch a few helper libraries (apr, apr-util, etc.)—see the *INSTALL* file in the top level of the working copy for details.

High-Speed Tutorial

> "Please make sure your seat backs are in their full, upright position and that your tray tables are stored. Flight attendants, prepare for take-off...."

What follows is a quick tutorial that walks you through some basic Subversion configuration and operation. When you finish it, you should have a general understanding of Subversion's typical usage.

---

[*] Note that the URL checked out in the example ends not with svn, but with a subdirectory thereof called trunk. See our discussion of Subversion's branching and tagging model for the reasoning behind this.

The examples used in this appendix assume that you have *svn*, the Subversion command-line client, and *svnadmin*, the administrative tool, ready to go on a Unix-like operating system. (This tutorial also works at the Windows command-line prompt, assuming you make some obvious tweaks.) We also assume you are using Subversion 1.2 or later (run `svn --version` to check).

Subversion stores all versioned data in a central repository. To begin, create a new repository:

```
$ svnadmin create /var/svn/repos
$ ls /var/svn/repos
conf/  dav/  db/  format  hooks/  locks/  README.txt
```

This command creates a new directory, */var/svn/repos*, which contains a Subversion repository. This new directory contains (among other things) a collection of database files. You won't see your versioned files if you peek inside. For more information about repository creation and maintenance, see Chapter 5.

Subversion has no concept of a "project." The repository is just a virtual versioned filesystem, a large tree that can hold anything you wish. Some administrators prefer to store only one project in a repository, and others prefer to store multiple projects in a repository by placing them into separate directories. We discuss the merits of each approach in "Planning Your Repository Organization" on page 147. Either way, the repository manages only files and directories, so it's up to humans to interpret particular directories as "projects." So, while you might see references to projects throughout this book, keep in mind that we're only ever talking about some directory (or collection of directories) in the repository.

In this example, we assume you already have some sort of project (a collection of files and directories) that you wish to import into your newly created Subversion repository. Begin by organizing your data into a single directory called *myproject* (or whatever you wish). For reasons explained in Chapter 4, your project's tree structure should contain three top-level directories named *branches*, *tags*, and *trunk*. The *trunk* directory should contain all of your data, and the *branches* and *tags* directories should be empty:

```
/tmp/myproject/branches/
/tmp/myproject/tags/
/tmp/myproject/trunk/
                foo.c
                bar.c
                Makefile
                ...
```

The *branches*, *tags*, and *trunk* subdirectories aren't actually required by Subversion. They're merely a popular convention that you'll most likely want to use later on.

Once you have your tree of data ready to go, import it into the repository with the *svn import* command (see "Getting Data into Your Repository" on page 18):

```
$ svn import /tmp/myproject file:///var/svn/repos/myproject -m "initial import"
Adding          /tmp/myproject/branches
Adding          /tmp/myproject/tags
Adding          /tmp/myproject/trunk
Adding          /tmp/myproject/trunk/foo.c
Adding          /tmp/myproject/trunk/bar.c
Adding          /tmp/myproject/trunk/Makefile
...
Committed revision 1.
$
```

Now the repository contains this tree of data. As mentioned earlier, you won't see your files by directly peeking into the repository; they're all stored within a database. But the repository's imaginary filesystem now contains a top-level directory named *myproject*, which in turn contains your data.

Note that the original */tmp/myproject* directory is unchanged; Subversion is unaware of it. (In fact, you can even delete that directory if you wish.) To start manipulating repository data, you need to create a new "working copy" of the data, a sort of private workspace. Ask Subversion to "check out" a working copy of the *myproject/trunk* directory in the repository:

```
$ svn checkout file:///var/svn/repos/myproject/trunk myproject
A  myproject/foo.c
A  myproject/bar.c
A  myproject/Makefile
...
Checked out revision 1.
```

Now you have a personal copy of part of the repository in a new directory named *myproject*. You can edit the files in your working copy and then commit those changes back into the repository:

- Enter your working copy and edit a file's contents.
- Run *svn diff* to see unified diff output of your changes.
- Run *svn commit* to commit the new version of your file to the repository.
- Run *svn update* to bring your working copy "up to date" with the repository.

For a full tour of all the things you can do with your working copy, read Chapter 2.

At this point, you have the option of making your repository available to others over a network. See Chapter 6 to learn about the different sorts of server processes available and how to configure them.

Subversion for CVS Users

This appendix is a guide for CVS users new to Subversion. It's essentially a list of differences between the two systems as "viewed from 10,000 feet." For each section, we provide references to relevant chapters when possible.

Although the goal of Subversion is to take over the current and future CVS user base, some new features and design changes were required to fix certain "broken" behaviors that CVS had. This means that, as a CVS user, you may need to break habits—ones that you forgot were odd to begin with.

Revision Numbers Are Different Now

In CVS, revision numbers are per file. This is because CVS stores its data in RCS files; each file has a corresponding RCS file in the repository, and the repository is roughly laid out according to the structure of your project tree.

In Subversion, the repository looks like a single filesystem. Each commit results in an entirely new filesystem tree; in essence, the repository is an array of trees. Each of these trees is labeled with a single revision number. When someone talks about "revision 54," he's talking about a particular tree (and indirectly, the way the filesystem looked after the 54th commit).

Technically, it's not valid to talk about "revision 5 of *foo.c*." Instead, one would say "*foo.c* as it appears in revision 5." Also, be careful when making assumptions about the evolution of a file. In CVS, revisions 5 and 6 of *foo.c* are always different. In Subversion, it's most likely that *foo.c* did *not* change between revisions 5 and 6.

Similarly, in CVS, a tag or branch is an annotation on the file or on the version information for that individual file, whereas in Subversion, a tag or branch is a copy of an entire tree (by convention, into the */branches* or */tags* directories that appear at the top level of the repository, beside */trunk*). In the repository as a whole, many versions of each file may be visible: the latest version on each branch, every tagged version, and of course the latest version on the trunk itself. So, to refine the terms even further, one would often say "*foo.c* as it appears in */branches/REL1* in revision 5."

For more details on this topic, see "Revisions" on page 11.

Directory Versions

Subversion tracks tree structures, not just file contents. It's one of the biggest reasons Subversion was written to replace CVS.

Here's what this means to you, as a former CVS user:

- The *svn add* and *svn delete* commands work on directories now, just as they work on files. So do *svn copy* and *svn move*. However, these commands do *not* cause any kind of immediate change in the repository. Instead, the working items are simply "scheduled" for addition or deletion. No repository changes happen until you run *svn commit*.

- Directories aren't dumb containers anymore; they have revision numbers like files. (Or more properly, it's correct to talk about "directory *foo/* in revision 5.")

Let's talk more about that last point. Directory versioning is a hard problem; because we want to allow mixed-revision working copies, there are some limitations on how far we can abuse this model.

From a theoretical point of view, we define "revision 5 of directory *foo*" to mean a specific collection of directory entries and properties. Now, suppose we start adding and removing files from *foo*, and then commit. It would be a lie to say that we still have revision 5 of *foo*. However, if we bumped *foo*'s revision number after the commit, that would be a lie, too; there may be other changes to *foo* we haven't yet received, because we haven't updated yet.

Subversion deals with this problem by quietly tracking committed adds and deletes in the *.svn* area. When you eventually run *svn update*, all accounts are settled with the repository, and the directory's new revision number is set correctly. *Therefore, only after an update is it truly safe to say that you have a "perfect" revision of a directory.* Most of the time, your working copy will contain "imperfect" directory revisions.

Similarly, a problem arises if you attempt to commit property changes on a directory. Normally, the commit would bump the working directory's local revision number. But again, that would be a lie, as there may be adds or deletes that the directory doesn't yet have, because no update has happened. *Therefore, you are not allowed to commit property changes on a directory unless the directory is up to date.*

For more discussion about the limitations of directory versioning, see "Mixed Revision Working Copies" on page 14.

More Disconnected Operations

In recent years, disk space has become outrageously cheap and abundant, but network bandwidth has not. Therefore, the Subversion working copy has been optimized around the scarcer resource.

The *.svn* administrative directory serves the same purpose as the *CVS* directory, except that it also stores read-only, "pristine" copies of your files. This allows you to do many things offline:

svn status
> Shows you any local changes you've made (see "See an overview of your changes" on page 26)

svn diff
> Shows you the details of your changes (see "Examine the details of your local modifications" on page 28)

svn revert
> Removes your local changes (see "Undoing Working Changes" on page 29)

Also, the cached pristine files allow the Subversion client to send differences when committing, which CVS cannot do.

The last subcommand in the list, *svn revert*, is new. It will not only remove local changes, but also unschedule operations such as adds and deletes. Although deleting the file and then running *svn update* will still work, doing so distorts the true purpose of updating. And, while we're on this subject...

Distinction Between Status and Update

Subversion attempts to erase a lot of the confusion between the *cvs status* and *cvs update* commands.

The *cvs status* command has two purposes: first, to show the user any local modifications in the working copy, and second, to show the user which files are out of date. Unfortunately, because of CVS's hard-to-read status output, many CVS users don't take advantage of this command at all. Instead, they've developed a habit of running *cvs update* or *cvs -n update* to quickly see their changes. If users forget to use the -n option, this has the side effect of merging repository changes they may not be ready to deal with.

Subversion removes this muddle by making the output of *svn status* easy to read for both humans and parsers. Also, *svn update* prints only information about files that are updated, *not* local modifications.

Status

svn status prints all files that have local modifications. By default, the repository is not contacted. While this subcommand accepts a fair number of options, the following are the most commonly used ones:

-u

Contact the repository to determine, and then display, out-of-dateness information.

-v

Show *all* entries under version control.

-N

Run nonrecursively (do not descend into subdirectories).

The *svn status* command has two output formats. In the default "short" format, local modifications look like this:

```
$ svn status
M      foo.c
M      bar/baz.c
```

If you specify the `--show-updates` (-u) option, a longer output format is used:

```
$ svn status -u
M            1047   foo.c
        *    1045   faces.html
        *           bloo.png
M            1050   bar/baz.c
Status against revision:   1066
```

In this case, two new columns appear. The second column contains an asterisk if the file or directory is out of date. The third column shows the working copy's revision number of the item. In the previous example, the asterisk indicates that *faces.html* would be patched if we updated, and that *bloo.png* is a newly added file in the repository. (The absence of any revision number next to *bloo.png* means that it doesn't yet exist in the working copy.)

At this point, you should take a quick look at the list of all possible status codes in "svn status" in Chapter 9. Here are a few of the more common status codes you'll see:

```
A    Resource is scheduled for Addition
D    Resource is scheduled for Deletion
M    Resource has local Modifications
C    Resource has Conflicts (changes have not been completely merged
        between the repository and working copy version)
X    Resource is eXternal to this working copy (may come from another
        repository).  See "Externals Definitions" on page 82
?    Resource is not under version control
!    Resource is missing or incomplete (removed by a tool other than
        Subversion)
```

For more details on *svn status*, see "See an overview of your changes" on page 26.

Update

svn update updates your working copy, and prints only information about files that it updates.

Subversion has combined CVS's P and U codes into just U. When a merge or conflict occurs, Subversion simply prints G or C, rather than a whole sentence about it.

For more details on *svn update*, see "Update Your Working Copy" on page 23.

Branches and Tags

Subversion doesn't distinguish between filesystem space and "branch" space; branches and tags are ordinary directories within the filesystem. This is probably the single biggest mental hurdle that a CVS user will need to cross. Read all about it in Chapter 4.

Since Subversion treats branches and tags as ordinary directories, your project's various lines of development probably live in subdirectories of the main project directory. So remember to check out using the URL of the subdirectory that contains the particular line of development you want, not the project's root URL. If you make the mistake of checking out the root of the project, you may very well wind up with a working copy that contains a complete copy of your project's content for each and every one of its branches and tags.*

Metadata Properties

A new feature of Subversion is that you can attach arbitrary metadata (or "properties") to files and directories. Properties are arbitrary name/value pairs associated with files and directories in your working copy.

To set or get a property name, use the *svn propset* and *svn propget* subcommands. To list all properties on an object, use *svn proplist*.

For more information, see "Properties" on page 48.

Conflict Resolution

CVS marks conflicts with inline "conflict markers," and then prints a C during an update or a merge operation. Historically, this has caused problems because CVS isn't doing enough. Many users forget about (or don't see) the C after it whizzes by on their terminal. They often forget that the conflict markers are even present, and then accidentally commit files containing those conflict markers.

---

* That is, providing you don't run out of disk space before your checkout finishes.

Subversion solves this problem in a pair of ways. First, when a conflict occurs in a file, Subversion records the fact that the file is in a state of conflict and won't allow you to commit changes to that file until you explicitly resolve the conflict. Second, Subversion 1.5 provides interactive conflict resolution, which allows you to resolve conflicts as they happen instead of having to go back and do so after the update or merge operation completes. See "Resolve Conflicts (Merging Others' Changes)" on page 30 for more about conflict resolution in Subversion.

Binary Files and Translation

In the most general sense, Subversion handles binary files more gracefully than CVS does. Because CVS uses RCS, it can only store successive full copies of a changing binary file. Subversion, however, expresses differences between files using a binary differencing algorithm, regardless of whether they contain textual or binary data. That means all files are stored differentially (compressed) in the repository.

CVS users have to mark binary files with -kb flags to prevent data from being garbled (due to keyword expansion and line-ending translations). They sometimes forget to do this.

Subversion takes the more paranoid route. First, it never performs any kind of keyword or line-ending translation unless you explicitly ask it to do so (see "Keyword Substitution" on page 65 and "End-of-Line Character Sequences" on page 59 for more details). By default, Subversion treats all file data as literal byte strings, and files are always stored in the repository in an untranslated state.

Second, Subversion maintains an internal notion of whether a file is "text" or "binary" data, but this notion is *only* extant in the working copy. During an *svn update*, Subversion will perform contextual merges on locally modified text files, but it will not attempt to do so for binary files.

To determine whether a contextual merge is possible, Subversion examines the svn:mime-type property. If the file has no svn:mime-type property, or has a MIME type that is textual (e.g., text/*), Subversion assumes it is text. Otherwise, Subversion assumes the file is binary. Subversion also helps users by running a binary-detection algorithm in the *svn import* and *svn add* commands. These commands will make a good guess and then (possibly) set a binary svn:mime-type property on the file being added. (If Subversion guesses wrong, the user can always remove or hand-edit the property.)

Versioned Modules

Unlike CVS, a Subversion working copy is aware that it has checked out a module. That means if somebody changes the definition of a module (e.g., adds or removes components), a call to *svn update* will update the working copy appropriately, adding and removing components.

Subversion defines modules as a list of directories within a directory property; see "Externals Definitions" on page 82.

Authentication

With CVS's pserver, you are required to log into the server (using the *cvs login* command) before performing any read or write operation—you sometimes even have to log in for anonymous operations. With a Subversion repository using Apache *httpd* or *svnserve* as the server, you don't provide any authentication credentials at the outset—if an operation requires authentication, the server will challenge you for your credentials (whether those are username and password, a client certificate, or even both). So, if your repository is world-readable, you will not be required to authenticate at all for read operations.

As with CVS, Subversion still caches your credentials on disk (in your *~/.subversion/auth/* directory) unless you tell it not to by using the `--no-auth-cache` option.

The exception to this behavior, however, is in the case of accessing an *svnserve* server over an SSH tunnel, using the `svn+ssh://` URL scheme. In that case, the *ssh* program unconditionally demands authentication just to start the tunnel.

Converting a Repository from CVS to Subversion

Perhaps the most important way to familiarize CVS users with Subversion is to let them continue to work on their projects using the new system. And while that can be somewhat accomplished using a flat import into a Subversion repository of an exported CVS repository, the more thorough solution involves transferring not just the latest snapshot of their data, but all the history behind it as well, from one system to another. This is an extremely difficult problem to solve; it involves deducing changesets in the absence of atomicity and translating between the systems' completely orthogonal branching policies, among other complications. Still, a handful of tools claim to at least partially support the ability to convert existing CVS repositories into Subversion ones.

The most popular (and mature) conversion tool is cvs2svn (*http://cvs2svn.tigris.org/*), a Python program originally created by members of Subversion's own development community. This tool is meant to run exactly once: it scans your CVS repository multiple times and attempts to deduce commits, branches, and tags as best it can. When it finishes, the result is either a Subversion repository or a portable Subversion dump file representing your code's history. See the web site for detailed instructions and caveats.

WebDAV and Autoversioning

WebDAV is an extension to HTTP, and it is growing more and more popular as a standard for file sharing. Today's operating systems are becoming extremely web-aware, and many now have built-in support for mounting "shares" exported by WebDAV servers.

If you use Apache as your Subversion network server, to some extent you are also running a WebDAV server. This appendix provides some background on the nature of this protocol, how Subversion uses it, and how well Subversion interoperates with other software that is WebDAV-aware.

What Is WebDAV?

DAV stands for "Distributed Authoring and Versioning." RFC 2518 defines a set of concepts and accompanying extension methods to HTTP 1.1 that make the Web a more universal read/write medium. The basic idea is that a WebDAV-compliant web server can act like a generic file server; clients can "mount" shared folders over HTTP that behave much like other network filesystems (such as NFS or SMB).

The tragedy, though, is that despite the acronym, the RFC specification doesn't actually describe any sort of version control. Basic WebDAV clients and servers assume that only one version of each file or directory exists and that it can be repeatedly overwritten.

Because RFC 2518 left out versioning concepts, another committee was stuck with the responsibility of writing RFC 3253 a few years later. The new RFC adds versioning concepts to WebDAV, placing the "V" back in "DAV"—hence the term "DeltaV." WebDAV/DeltaV clients and servers are often called just "DeltaV" programs, since DeltaV implies the existence of basic WebDAV.

The original WebDAV standard has been widely successful. Every modern computer operating system has a general WebDAV client built in (details to follow), and a number of popular standalone applications are also able to speak WebDAV—Microsoft Office, Dreamweaver, and Photoshop, to name a few. On the server end, Apache HTTP Server has been able to provide WebDAV services since 1998 and is considered the de facto open source standard. Several other commercial WebDAV servers are available, including Microsoft's own IIS.

DeltaV, unfortunately, has not been so successful. It's very difficult to find any DeltaV clients or servers. The few that do exist are relatively unknown commercial products, and thus it's very difficult to test interoperability. It's not entirely clear why DeltaV has remained stagnant. Some opine that the specification is just too complex. Others argue that while WebDAV's features have mass appeal (even the least technical users appreciate network file sharing), its version control features just aren't interesting or necessary for most users. Finally, some believe that DeltaV remains unpopular because there's still no open source server product that implements it well.

When Subversion was still in its design phase, it seemed like a great idea to use Apache as a network server. It already had a module to provide WebDAV services. DeltaV was a relatively new specification. The hope was that the Subversion server module (*mod_dav_svn*) would eventually evolve into an open source DeltaV reference implementation. Unfortunately, DeltaV has a very specific versioning model that doesn't quite line up with Subversion's model. Some concepts were mappable; others were not.

What does this mean, then?

First, the Subversion client is not a fully implemented DeltaV client. It needs certain types of things from the server that DeltaV itself cannot provide, and thus it is largely dependent on a number of Subversion-specific HTTP REPORT requests that only *mod_dav_svn* understands.

Second, *mod_dav_svn* is not a fully realized DeltaV server. Many portions of the DeltaV specification were irrelevant to Subversion and were thus left unimplemented.

There is still some debate in the developer community as to whether it's worthwhile to remedy either of these situations. It's fairly unrealistic to change Subversion's design to match DeltaV, so there's probably no way the client can ever learn to get everything it needs from a general DeltaV server. On the other hand, *mod_dav_svn could* be further developed to implement all of DeltaV, but it's hard to find motivation to do so—there are almost no DeltaV clients to interoperate with.

Autoversioning

Although the Subversion client is not a full DeltaV client, and the Subversion server is not a full DeltaV server, there's still a glimmer of WebDAV interoperability to be happy about: *autoversioning*.

Autoversioning is an optional feature defined in the DeltaV standard. A typical DeltaV server will reject an ignorant WebDAV client attempting to do a PUT to a file that's under version control. To change a version-controlled file, the server expects a series of proper versioning requests: something like MKACTIVITY, CHECKOUT, PUT, CHECKIN. But if the DeltaV server supports autoversioning, write requests from basic WebDAV clients are accepted. The server behaves as though the client *had* issued the proper series of versioning requests, performing a commit under the hood. In other words, it allows a DeltaV server to interoperate with ordinary WebDAV clients that don't understand versioning.

Because so many operating systems have already integrated WebDAV clients, the use case for this feature can be incredibly appealing to administrators working with non-technical users. Imagine an office of ordinary users running Microsoft Windows or Mac OS. Each user "mounts" the Subversion repository, which appears to be an ordinary network folder. They use the shared folder as they always do: open files, edit them, and save them. Meanwhile, the server is automatically versioning everything. Any administrator (or knowledgeable user) can still use a Subversion client to search history and retrieve older versions of data.

This scenario isn't fiction—it's real and it works, as of Subversion 1.2 and later. To activate autoversioning in *mod_dav_svn*, use the SVNAutoversioning directive within the *httpd.conf* Location block, like so:

```
<Location /repos>
  DAV svn
  SVNPath /var/svn/repository
  SVNAutoversioning on
</Location>
```

When Subversion autoversioning is active, write requests from WebDAV clients result in automatic commits. A generic log message is automatically generated and attached to each revision.

Before activating this feature, however, understand what you're getting into. WebDAV clients tend to do *many* write requests, resulting in a huge number of automatically committed revisions. For example, when saving data, many clients will do a PUT of a 0-byte file (as a way of reserving a name), followed by another PUT with the real file data. The single file-write results in two separate commits. Also consider that many applications autosave every few minutes, resulting in even more commits.

If you have a post-commit hook program that sends email, you may want to disable email generation either altogether or on certain sections of the repository; it depends on whether you think the influx of emails will still prove to be valuable notifications. Also, a smart post-commit hook program can distinguish between a transaction created via autoversioning and one created through a normal Subversion commit operation. The trick is to look for a revision property named svn:autoversioned. If present, the commit was made by a generic WebDAV client.

Another feature that may be a useful complement for Subversion's autoversioning comes from Apache's mod_mime module. If a WebDAV client adds a new file to the repository, there's no opportunity for the user to set the svn:mime-type property. This might cause the file to appear as a generic icon when viewed within a WebDAV shared folder, not having an association with any application. One remedy is to have a sysadmin (or other Subversion-knowledgeable person) check out a working copy and manually set the svn:mime-type property on necessary files. But there's potentially no end to such cleanup tasks. Instead, you can use the ModMimeUsePathInfo directive in your Subversion <Location> block:

```
<Location /repos>
  DAV svn
  SVNPath /var/svn/repository
  SVNAutoversioning on

  ModMimeUsePathInfo on

</Location>
```

This directive allows mod_mime to attempt automatic deduction of the MIME type on new files that enter the repository via autoversioning. The module looks at the file's named extension and possibly the contents as well; if the file matches some common patterns, the file's svn:mime-type property will be set automatically.

Client Interoperability

All WebDAV clients fall into one of three categories: standalone applications, file-explorer extensions, or filesystem implementations. These categories broadly define the types of WebDAV functionality available to users. Table C-1 gives our categorization as well as a quick description of some common pieces of WebDAV-enabled software. You can find more details about these software offerings, as well as their general category, in the sections that follow.

Table C-1. Common WebDAV clients

Software	Type	Windows	Mac	Linux	Description
Adobe Photoshop	Standalone WebDAV application	X			Image editing software, allowing direct opening from and writing to WebDAV URLs
cadaver	Standalone WebDAV application		X	X	Command-line WebDAV client supporting file transfer, tree, and locking operations
DAV Explorer	Standalone WebDAV application	X	X	X	Java GUI tool for exploring WebDAV shares
Adobe Dreamweaver	Standalone WebDAV application	X			Web production software able to directly read from and write to WebDAV URLs
Microsoft Office	Standalone WebDAV application	X			Office productivity suite with several components

Software	Type	Windows	Mac	Linux	Description
					able to directly read from and write to WebDAV URLs
Microsoft Web Folders	File-explorer WebDAV extension	X			GUI file-explorer program able to perform tree operations on a WebDAV share
GNOME Nautilus	File-explorer WebDAV extension			X	GUI file explorer able to perform tree operations on a WebDAV share
KDE Konqueror	File-explorer WebDAV extension			X	GUI file explorer able to perform tree operations on a WebDAV share
Mac OS X	WebDAV filesystem implementation		X		Operating system that has built-in support for mounting WebDAV shares
Novell NetDrive	WebDAV filesystem implementation	X			Drive-mapping program for assigning Windows drive letters to a mounted remote WebDAV share
SRT WebDrive	WebDAV filesystem implementation	X			File transfer software, which, among other things, allows the assignment of Windows drive letters to a mounted remote WebDAV share
davfs2	WebDAV filesystem implementation			X	Linux filesystem driver that allows you to mount a WebDAV share

Standalone WebDAV Applications

A WebDAV application is a program that speaks WebDAV protocols with a WebDAV server. We'll cover some of the most popular programs with this kind of WebDAV support.

Microsoft Office, Dreamweaver, Photoshop

On Windows, several well-known applications contain integrated WebDAV client functionality, such as Microsoft's Office,[*] Adobe's Photoshop and Dreamweaver programs. They're able to directly open and save to URLs, and tend to make heavy use of WebDAV locks when editing a file.

---

[*] WebDAV support was removed from Microsoft Access for some reason, but it exists in the rest of the Office suite.

Note that while many of these programs also exist for Mac OS X, they do not appear to support WebDAV directly on that platform. In fact, on Mac OS X, the File→Open dialog box doesn't allow one to type a path or URL at all. It's likely that the WebDAV features were deliberately left out of Macintosh versions of these programs, since OS X already provides such excellent low-level filesystem support for WebDAV.

cadaver, DAV Explorer

cadaver is a bare-bones Unix command-line program for browsing and changing Web-DAV shares. Like the Subversion client, it uses the neon HTTP library—not surprisingly, since both neon and cadaver are written by the same author. cadaver is free software (GPL license) and is available at *http://www.webdav.org/cadaver/*.

Using cadaver is similar to using a command-line FTP program, and thus it's extremely useful for basic WebDAV debugging. It can be used to upload or download files in a pinch, to examine properties, and to copy, move, lock, or unlock files:

```
$ cadaver http://host/repos
dav:/repos/> ls
Listing collection '/repos/': succeeded.
Coll: > foobar                            0  May 10 16:19
       > playwright.el                 2864  May  4 16:18
       > proofbypoem.txt               1461  May  5 15:09
       > westcoast.jpg                66737  May  5 15:09

dav:/repos/> put README
Uploading README to '/repos/README':
Progress: [=============================>] 100.0% of 357 bytes succeeded.

dav:/repos/> get proofbypoem.txt
Downloading '/repos/proofbypoem.txt' to proofbypoem.txt:
Progress: [=============================>] 100.0% of 1461 bytes succeeded.
```

DAV Explorer is another standalone WebDAV client, written in Java. It's under a free Apache-like license and is available at *http://www.ics.uci.edu/~webdav/*. It does everything cadaver does but has the advantages of being portable and being a more user-friendly GUI application. It's also one of the first clients to support the new WebDAV Access Control Protocol (RFC 3744).

Of course, DAV Explorer's ACL support is useless in this case, since *mod_dav_svn* doesn't support it. The fact that both cadaver and DAV Explorer support some limited DeltaV commands isn't particularly useful either, since they don't allow MKACTIVITY requests. But it's not relevant anyway; we're assuming all of these clients are operating against an autoversioning repository.

File-Explorer WebDAV Extensions

Some popular file explorer GUI programs support WebDAV extensions that allow a user to browse a DAV share as though it was just another directory on the local computer and to perform basic tree editing operations on the items in that share. For example, Windows Explorer is able to browse a WebDAV server as a "network place." Users can drag files to and from the desktop, or can rename, copy, or delete files in the usual way. But because it's only a feature of the file explorer, the DAV share isn't visible to ordinary applications. All DAV interaction must happen through the explorer interface.

Microsoft Web Folders

Microsoft was one of the original backers of the WebDAV specification and first started shipping a client in Windows 98, which was known as Web Folders. This client was also shipped in Windows NT 4.0 and Windows 2000.

The original Web Folders client was an extension to Explorer, the main GUI program used to browse filesystems. It works well enough. In Windows 98, the feature might need to be explicitly installed if Web Folders aren't already visible inside My Computer. In Windows 2000, simply add a new "network place," enter the URL, and the WebDAV share will pop up for browsing.

With the release of Windows XP, Microsoft started shipping a new implementation of Web Folders, known as the WebDAV Mini-Redirector. The new implementation is a filesystem-level client, allowing WebDAV shares to be mounted as drive letters. Unfortunately, this implementation is incredibly buggy. The client usually tries to convert HTTP URLs (`http://host/repos`) into Universal Naming Convention (UNC) share notation (`\\host\repos`); it also often tries to use Windows Domain authentication to respond to basic-auth HTTP challenges, sending usernames as `HOST\username`. These interoperability problems are severe and are documented in numerous places around the Web, to the frustration of many users. Even Greg Stein, the original author of Apache's WebDAV module, bluntly states that XP Web Folders simply can't operate against an Apache server.

Windows Vista's initial implementation of Web Folders seems to be almost the same as XP's, so it has the same sort of problems. With luck, Microsoft will remedy these issues in a Vista Service Pack.

However, there seem to be workarounds for both XP and Vista that allow Web Folders to work against Apache. Users have mostly reported success with these techniques, so we'll relay them here.

On Windows XP, you have two options. First, search Microsoft's web site for update KB90730, "Software Update for Web Folders." This may fix all your problems. If it doesn't, it seems that the original pre-XP Web Folders implementation is still buried within the system. You can unearth it by going to Network Places and adding a new network place. When prompted, enter the URL of the repository, but *include a port number* in the URL. For example, you should enter `http://host/repos` as `http://host:80/repos` instead. Respond to any authentication prompts with your Subversion credentials.

On Windows Vista, the same KB90730 update may clear everything up. But there may still be other issues. Some users have reported that Vista considers all `http://` connections insecure, and thus will always fail any authentication challenges from Apache unless the connection happens over `https://`. If you're unable to connect to the Subversion repository via SSL, you can tweak the system registry to turn off this behavior. Just change the value of the `HKEY_LOCAL_MACHINE\SYSTEM\CurrentControlSet\Services \WebClient\Parameters\BasicAuthLevel` key from `1` to `2`. A final warning: be sure to set up the Web Folder to point to the repository's root directory (*/*), rather than some subdirectory such as */trunk*. Vista Web Folders seems to work only against repository roots.

In general, while these workarounds may function for you, you might get a better overall experience using a third-party WebDAV client such as WebDrive or NetDrive.

Nautilus, Konqueror

Nautilus is the official file manager/browser for the GNOME desktop (*http://www .gnome.org*), and Konqueror is the manager/browser for the KDE desktop (*http://www .kde.org*). Both of these applications have an explorer-level WebDAV client built-in, and they operate just fine against an autoversioning repository.

In GNOME's Nautilus, select the File→Open location menu item and enter the URL in the dialog box presented. The repository should then be displayed like any other filesystem.

In KDE's Konqueror, you need to use the `webdav://` scheme when entering the URL in the location bar. If you enter an `http://` URL, Konqueror will behave like an ordinary web browser. You'll likely see the generic HTML directory listing produced by *mod_dav_svn*. When you enter `webdav://host/repos` instead of `http://host/repos`, Konqueror becomes a WebDAV client and displays the repository as a filesystem.

WebDAV Filesystem Implementation

The WebDAV filesystem implementation is arguably the best sort of WebDAV client. It's implemented as a low-level filesystem module, typically within the operating system's kernel. This means that the DAV share is mounted like any other network filesystem, similar to mounting an NFS share on Unix or attaching an SMB share as a drive letter in Windows. As a result, this sort of client provides completely transparent read/ write WebDAV access to all programs. Applications aren't even aware that WebDAV requests are happening.

WebDrive, NetDrive

Both WebDrive and NetDrive are excellent commercial products that allow a WebDAV share to be attached as drive letters in Windows. As a result, you can operate on the contents of these WebDAV-backed pseudodrives as easily as you can against real local hard drives, and in the same ways. You can purchase WebDrive from South River Technologies (*http://www.southrivertech.com*). Novell's NetDrive is freely available online, but it requires users to have a NetWare license.

Mac OS X

Apple's OS X operating system has an integrated filesystem-level WebDAV client. From the Finder, select the Go→Connect to Server menu item. Enter a WebDAV URL, and it appears as a disk on the desktop, just like any other mounted volume. You can also mount a WebDAV share from the Darwin terminal by using the webdav filesystem type with the *mount* command:

```
$ mount -t webdav http://svn.example.com/repos/project /some/mountpoint
$
```

Note that if your *mod_dav_svn* is older than version 1.2, OS X will refuse to mount the share as read/write; it will appear as read-only. This is because OS X insists on locking support for read/write shares, and the ability to lock files first appeared in Subversion 1.2.

Also, OS X's WebDAV client can sometimes be overly sensitive to HTTP redirects. If OS X is unable to mount the repository at all, you may need to enable the BrowserMatch directive in the Apache server's *httpd.conf*:

```
BrowserMatch "^WebDAVFS/1.[012]" redirect-carefully
```

Linux davfs2

Linux davfs2 is a filesystem module for the Linux kernel, whose development is organized at *http://dav.sourceforge.net/*. Once you install davfs2, you can mount a WebDAV network share using the usual Linux mount command:

```
$ mount.davfs http://host/repos /mnt/dav
```

Copyright

Creative Commons Legal Code

Attribution 2.0

License

THE WORK (AS DEFINED BELOW) IS PROVIDED UNDER THE TERMS OF THIS CREATIVE COMMONS PUBLIC LICENSE ("CCPL" OR "LICENSE"). THE WORK IS PROTECTED BY COPYRIGHT AND/OR OTHER APPLICABLE LAW. ANY USE OF THE WORK OTHER THAN AS AUTHORIZED UNDER THIS LICENSE OR COPYRIGHT LAW IS PROHIBITED.

BY EXERCISING ANY RIGHTS TO THE WORK PROVIDED HERE, YOU ACCEPT AND AGREE TO BE BOUND BY THE TERMS OF THIS LICENSE. THE LICENSOR GRANTS YOU THE RIGHTS CONTAINED HERE IN CONSIDERATION OF YOUR ACCEPTANCE OF SUCH TERMS AND CONDITIONS.

1. **Definitions**

    a. "Collective Work" means a work, such as a periodical issue, anthology or encyclopedia, in which the Work in its entirety in unmodified form, along with a number of other contributions, constituting separate and independent works in themselves, are assembled into a collective whole. A work that constitutes a Collective Work will not be considered a Derivative Work (as defined below) for the purposes of this License.

    b. "Derivative Work" means a work based upon the Work or upon the Work and other pre-existing works, such as a translation, musical arrangement, dramatization, fictionalization, motion picture version, sound recording, art reproduction, abridgment, condensation, or any other form in which the Work may be recast, transformed, or adapted, except that a work that constitutes a Collective Work will not be considered a Derivative Work for the purpose of this License. For the avoidance of doubt, where the Work is a musical composition or sound recording, the synchronization of the Work in timed-relation with a moving image ("synching") will be considered a Derivative Work for the purpose of this License.

    c. "Licensor" means the individual or entity that offers the Work under the terms of this License.

    d. "Original Author" means the individual or entity who created the Work.

    e. "Work" means the copyrightable work of authorship offered under the terms of this License.

    f. "You" means an individual or entity exercising rights under this License who has not previously violated the terms of this License with respect to the Work, or who has received express permission from the Licensor to exercise rights under this License despite a previous violation.

2. **Fair Use Rights.** Nothing in this license is intended to reduce, limit, or restrict any rights arising from fair use, first sale or other limitations on the exclusive rights of the copyright owner under copyright law or other applicable laws.

3. **License Grant.** Subject to the terms and conditions of this License, Licensor hereby grants You a worldwide, royalty-free, non-exclusive, perpetual (for the duration of the applicable copyright) license to exercise the rights in the Work as stated below:

   a. to reproduce the Work, to incorporate the Work into one or more Collective Works, and to reproduce the Work as incorporated in the Collective Works;

   b. to create and reproduce Derivative Works;

   c. to distribute copies or phonorecords of, display publicly, perform publicly, and perform publicly by means of a digital audio transmission the Work including as incorporated in Collective Works;

   d. to distribute copies or phonorecords of, display publicly, perform publicly, and perform publicly by means of a digital audio transmission Derivative Works.

   e. For the avoidance of doubt, where the work is a musical composition:

      i. Performance Royalties Under Blanket Licenses. Licensor waives the exclusive right to collect, whether individually or via a performance rights society (e.g. ASCAP, BMI, SESAC), royalties for the public performance or public digital performance (e.g. webcast) of the Work.

      ii. Mechanical Rights and Statutory Royalties. Licensor waives the exclusive right to collect, whether individually or via a music rights agency or designated agent (e.g. Harry Fox Agency), royalties for any phonorecord You create from the Work ("cover version") and distribute, subject to the compulsory license created by 17 USC Section 115 of the US Copyright Act (or the equivalent in other jurisdictions).

   f. Webcasting Rights and Statutory Royalties. For the avoidance of doubt, where the Work is a sound recording, Licensor waives the exclusive right to collect, whether individually or via a performance-rights society (e.g. SoundExchange), royalties for the public digital performance (e.g. webcast) of the Work, subject to the compulsory license created by 17 USC Section 114 of the US Copyright Act (or the equivalent in other jurisdictions).

The above rights may be exercised in all media and formats whether now known or hereafter devised. The above rights include the right to make such modifications as are technically necessary to exercise the rights in other media and formats. All rights not expressly granted by Licensor are hereby reserved.

4. **Restrictions.** The license granted in Section 3 above is expressly made subject to and limited by the following restrictions:

   a. You may distribute, publicly display, publicly perform, or publicly digitally perform the Work only under the terms of this License, and You must include a copy of, or the Uniform Resource Identifier for, this License with every copy or phonorecord of the Work You distribute, publicly display, publicly perform, or publicly digitally perform. You may not offer or impose any terms on the Work that alter or restrict the terms of this License or the recipients' exercise of the rights granted hereunder. You may not sublicense the Work. You must keep intact all notices that refer to this License and to the disclaimer of warranties. You may not distribute, publicly display, publicly perform, or publicly digitally perform the Work with any technological measures that control access or use of the Work in a manner inconsistent with the terms of this License Agreement. The above applies to the Work as incorporated in a Collective Work, but this does not require the Collective Work apart from the Work itself to be made subject to the terms of this License. If You create a Collective Work, upon notice from any Licensor You must, to the extent practicable, remove from the Collective Work any reference to such Licensor or the Original Author, as requested. If You create a Derivative Work, upon notice from any Licensor You must, to the extent practicable, remove from the Derivative Work any reference to such Licensor or the Original Author, as requested.

b. If you distribute, publicly display, publicly perform, or publicly digitally perform the Work or any Derivative Works or Collective Works, You must keep intact all copyright notices for the Work and give the Original Author credit reasonable to the medium or means You are utilizing by conveying the name (or pseudonym if applicable) of the Original Author if supplied; the title of the Work if supplied; to the extent reasonably practicable, the Uniform Resource Identifier, if any, that Licensor specifies to be associated with the Work, unless such URI does not refer to the copyright notice or licensing information for the Work; and in the case of a Derivative Work, a credit identifying the use of the Work in the Derivative Work (e.g., "French translation of the Work by Original Author," or "Screenplay based on original Work by Original Author"). Such credit may be implemented in any reasonable manner; provided, however, that in the case of a Derivative Work or Collective Work, at a minimum such credit will appear where any other comparable authorship credit appears and in a manner at least as prominent as such other comparable authorship credit.

5. **Representations, Warranties and Disclaimer.** UNLESS OTHERWISE MUTUALLY AGREED TO BY THE PARTIES IN WRITING, LICENSOR OFFERS THE WORK AS-IS AND MAKES NO REPRESENTATIONS OR WARRANTIES OF ANY KIND CONCERNING THE WORK, EXPRESS, IMPLIED, STATUTORY OR OTHERWISE, INCLUDING, WITHOUT LIMITATION, WARRANTIES OF TITLE, MERCHANTIBILITY, FITNESS FOR A PARTICULAR PURPOSE, NONINFRINGEMENT, OR THE ABSENCE OF LATENT OR OTHER DEFECTS, ACCURACY, OR THE PRESENCE OF ABSENCE OF ERRORS, WHETHER OR NOT DISCOVERABLE. SOME JURISDICTIONS DO NOT ALLOW THE EXCLUSION OF IMPLIED WARRANTIES, SO SUCH EXCLUSION MAY NOT APPLY TO YOU.

6. **Limitation on Liability.** EXCEPT TO THE EXTENT REQUIRED BY APPLICABLE LAW, IN NO EVENT WILL LICENSOR BE LIABLE TO YOU ON ANY LEGAL THEORY FOR ANY SPECIAL, INCIDENTAL, CONSEQUENTIAL, PUNITIVE OR EXEMPLARY DAMAGES ARISING OUT OF THIS LICENSE OR THE USE OF THE WORK, EVEN IF LICENSOR HAS BEEN ADVISED OF THE POSSIBILITY OF SUCH DAMAGES.

7. **Termination.**

   a. This License and the rights granted hereunder will terminate automatically upon any breach by You of the terms of this License. Individuals or entities who have received Derivative Works or Collective Works from You under this License, however, will not have their licenses terminated provided such individuals or entities remain in full compliance with those licenses. Sections 1, 2, 5, 6, 7, and 8 will survive any termination of this License.

   b. Subject to the above terms and conditions, the license granted here is perpetual (for the duration of the applicable copyright in the Work). Notwithstanding the above, Licensor reserves the right to release the Work under different license terms or to stop distributing the Work at any time; provided, however that any such election will not serve to withdraw this License (or any other license that has been, or is required to be, granted under the terms of this License), and this License will continue in full force and effect unless terminated as stated above.

8. **Miscellaneous.**

   a. Each time You distribute or publicly digitally perform the Work or a Collective Work, the Licensor offers to the recipient a license to the Work on the same terms and conditions as the license granted to You under this License.

   b. Each time You distribute or publicly digitally perform a Derivative Work, Licensor offers to the recipient a license to the original Work on the same terms and conditions as the license granted to You under this License.

   c. If any provision of this License is invalid or unenforceable under applicable law, it shall not affect the validity or enforceability of the remainder of the terms of this License, and without further action by the parties to this agreement, such provision shall be reformed to the minimum extent necessary to make such provision valid and enforceable.

   d. No term or provision of this License shall be deemed waived and no breach consented to unless such waiver or consent shall be in writing and signed by the party to be charged with such waiver or consent.

   e. This License constitutes the entire agreement between the parties with respect to the Work licensed here. There are no understandings, agreements or representations with respect to the Work not specified here. Licensor shall not be bound by any additional provisions that may appear in any communication from You. This License may not be modified without the mutual written agreement of the Licensor and You.

Creative Commons is not a party to this License, and makes no warranty whatsoever in connection with the Work. Creative Commons will not be liable to You or any party on any legal theory for any damages whatsoever, including without limitation any general, special, incidental or consequential damages arising in connection to this license. Notwithstanding the foregoing two (2) sentences, if Creative Commons has expressly identified itself as the Licensor hereunder, it shall have all rights and obligations of Licensor.

Except for the limited purpose of indicating to the public that the Work is licensed under the CCPL, neither party will use the trademark "Creative Commons" or any related trademark or logo of Creative Commons without the prior written consent of Creative Commons. Any permitted use will be in compliance with Creative Commons' then-current trademark usage guidelines, as may be published on its website or otherwise made available upon request from time to time.

Creative Commons may be contacted at *http://creativecommons.org/*.

Index

Symbols

\# (hashes), commenting configuration files
and, 199

* (asterisk)
    variables, as, 228
    wildcards, as, 62

/ (root) directory, 155

:: (double colons), 68

? (question mark)
    --help option, 274
    wildcards and, 62

@ (at sign), granting access control, 229

[ ] (square brackets)
    creating configuration files and, 199
    wildcard characters and, 62

_ (underscores), using public/private symbols,
    261

A

A (add) code, 9, 26

--accept option, 34, 272

--accept theirs-full option, 35

access controls (svnserv.conf), setting, 200

add command, 18, 22, 24, 277
    automatic property setting and, 55
    unversioned items and, 61, 64

administrative directories, 9

ambient depth, 70

anchors (keyword), 65

anon-access variable, 200

Apache Portable Runtime (APR) library, 138,
    261
    installing Subversion and, 365

Apache server, 138, 191, 207–226

configuration, 208–210
portable runtime library, 261

APIs (Application Programming Interface),
    251
    using, 261

Application Programming Interface (API)
    using, 261

APR (Apache Portable Runtime) library, 138,
    261
    installing Subversion and, 365

apr_initialize( ) function, 262

apr_pool_t datatype, 262

asterisk (*)
    variables, as, 228
    wildcards, as, 62

at sign (@), granting access control, 229

atomic transactions, 11

auth section (config file), 239

auth-access variable, 200

authentication
    Apache server options, 210–214
    CVS and, 375
    realms, 199
    requests and responses, 97
    SASL, 201
    svnserve processes and, 198

author command, 337

Author keyword, 66

authorized_keys file, 205

AuthType directive, 211

authz-db variable, 226

AuthzSVNAccessFile directive, 216, 226, 358

AuthzSVNAnonymous directive, 358

AuthzSVNAuthoritative directive, 358

We'd like to hear your suggestions for improving our indexes. Send email to *index@oreilly.com*.

AuthzSVNNoAuthWhenAnonymousAllowed
directive, 358
--auto-props option (svn), 272
auto-props section (config file), 242
automatic property setting, 55
autoversioning, 377–385

B

backdate, 15
backporting bug fixes, 120
backup files, as unversioned items, 60
BASE revision keyword, 31, 46
BDB (see Berkeley DB)
--bdb-log-keep option, 166, 325
--bdb-txn-nosync option, 325
Berkeley DB, 150–153
    configuration, 158
    logfiles, purging, 166
    recovery, 167–169
    repository layer and, 253
    storing data and, 164
    utilities, 163
binary files, 374
blame command, 125, 278
branches, 101–143
    changes, undoing, 115
    creating, 103
    CVS and, 373
    data lifetimes and, 135
    deleted items, resurrecting, 116
    feature, 137
    keeping in sync, 109–113
    maintenance, 134–136
    patterns, 136
    release, 136
    tags, 132
    traversing, 130–132
    vendor, 138–143
BrowserMatch directive (httpd.conf), 385
bug fixes, 120
--bypass-hooks option, 164, 325

C

-c (--change) option, 41, 272
C (conflict) code, 26, 32, 373
C programming language, 251, 263
    API, using, 261
C# programming language, 263

C++ programming language, 263
CA (certificate authority), 213
cadaver, 382
carriage returns (CR), 59
case-sensitivity of keywords, 65
cat command, 38, 279, 338
    repositories, browsing, 41
certificate authority (CA), 213
--change (-c) option, 41, 272
changed command, 338
changelist command, 92, 280
--changelist option, 94, 272
changelists, 91–96
    limitations, 96
    operation filters and, 94–96
changesets, 108, 118
character set conversion errors, 244
cheap copies, copying directories/files, 104
checking in, 10
checking out, 9
checkout command, 19, 281
    externals definitions and, 82
    initial, 19–22
    older repositories, fetching, 42
    sparse directories and, 69
checkpoints, 152
cherrypicking, 118–121
--cl option, 272
--clean-logs option, 185, 325
cleanup command, 44, 283
    locking and, 75
client credentials caching, 97
client interoperability, 380
client layer, 258
clients, 1
command-line client, 233
    external editors and, 244
commands, 17–44
commit command, 10, 22, 36–37, 284
    locking and, 75
    mixed revision working copies and, 14
    revisions and, 11
COMMITTED revision keyword, 46
complex tags, creating, 133
Concurrent Versions System (see CVS)
conf/ directory, 146
conf/svnserve.conf file, 198
--config-dir option (svn), 272, 346
configuration area, 233–242

Dreamweaver, using WebDAV protocol, 381
--drop-empty-revs option, 176, 351
--dry-run option, 114, 273
dump command, 169, 174, 328

E

e (edit) option, 30
EDITOR environment variable, 32, 245
editor-cmd option, 239, 245, 273
--editor-cmd command-line option, 245
editors, using, 244
enable-auto-props option (config file), 240
--encoding option, 273
encryption with SASL, 203
end-of-line (EOL) markers, 59
entries file, 260
environment variables, 157
    localization and, 243
EOL (end-of-line) markers, 59
exclude command, 161, 352
export command, 292
--extensions (-x) options, 29, 273
extensions (file), 58
external diff3, 248
external differencing, 245–249
external editors, using, 244
externals definitions, 82–87

F

-F (--file) option, 244, 273
-F (--file) option, 36
feature branches, 137
--file (-F) option, 36, 244, 273
file changes, 24
file content types, 57
file patterns, 61
file portability, 56–60
    executability, 58
file servers, 2
file sharing, problems with, 2
file-explorer WebDAV extensions, 382–384
file:// access method, 7, 191, 257
filesystem trees, 1
    branching and, 107
    virtual filesystems and, 253
flags (commands), 18
fnmatch system function, 62
--force option, 79, 273

--force-log option, 273
--force-uuid option, 325
--foreground option, 350
format/ directory, 146
--fs-type argument, 155
FSFS, 150, 153
    fsfs-reshard.pl script and, 162
    noncompliant remote filesystems and, 153
fsfs-reshard.py script, 162

G

-g (--use-merge-history) option, 126
G (merGed) code, 30
garbage collecting, 262
GET requests, 219
global section (servers file), 236
global-ignores option, 61, 240
globs, 62, 236
Google Code Project Hosting service, 253
groups section (servers file), 236
GSSAPI (Kerberos), 201
Guile, 263

H

-h (--help) option, 31, 274
.h (header) files, 261
hashes (#), commenting configuration files
        and, 199
HEAD revision keyword, 31, 46
header (.h) files, 261
HeadURL keyword, 66
--help (-h) option, 31, 274
help command, 17, 120, 293, 329, 341, 347,
        353
history, 37–43
history command, 341
hooks, 156
hooks/ directory, 146, 156
hot backups (Berkeley DB), 152
hot-backup.py script, 185
hotcopy command, 185, 329
HTML, 220
htpasswd utility, 211
HTTP protocol, 96, 191
http-auth-types option, 238
http-compression option, 237
http-library option, 238
http-proxy-exceptions option, 237

http-proxy-host option, 237
http-proxy-password option, 237
http-proxy-port option, 237
http-proxy-username option, 237
http-timeout option, 237
http:// protocol, 257
httpd, 153, 207–226
    CVS authentication and, 375
    installing Subversion and, 365
httpd.conf, 208
    authentication, 210
    servers, configuring, 222
https:// protocol, 213, 225, 257

update command, 11, 323
    conflicts and, 123
    locking and, 75
    mixed revision working copies and, 14
    --non-interactive option, 32
    older repositories, fetching, 42
    status command and, 371
    syncing up branches with, 110
    working copies and, 23
    working copies, disposing, 43
upgrade command, 335
URLs
    path requirements and, 262
    repositories and, 7
use-commit-times option (config file), 240
--use-merge-history (-g) option, 126
--use-post-commit-hook option, 326
--use-post-revprop-change-hook option, 326
--use-pre-commit-hook option, 171, 326
--use-pre-revprop-change-hook option, 326
user files, creating, 199
--username option, 22, 99, 272
UUID (Universally Unique Identifier), 184, 187
uuid command, 345

V

-v (--verbose) option, 27, 42, 52, 117
variables (svnserve.conf), 199
vendor branches, 138–143
--verbose (-v) option, 27, 42, 117
    mixed revisions, examining, 14
verify command, 336
version control systems, 2
    branches and, 136
--version option, 96
versioned modules, 374
versioning models, 2–7
virtual filesystems, 253
VISUAL environment variable, 245

W

WebDAV/DeltaV protocol, 191, 207, 225, 377–385
    file-explorer extensions, 382–384
    standalone applications and, 381
WebDrive, 385
wildcard characters, 62

Windows, 97
    Berkeley DB, operating on, 152
    configuring, 234–236
    file:// scheme and, 7
    locale configuration and, 243
    SASL, authenticating with, 202
    svnserve and, 197
    WebDAV protocol and, 383
working copies, 4, 9–11
    changes, making, 23
    mixed revisions and, 14
    updating, 23
    work cycle and, 22
working copy locks, 75
wrapper scripts, 251

X

-x (--extensions) option, 273
-x (--extensions) options, 29
-X (--listen-once) option, 350
XML, 220
XSLT, 220

Y

youngest command, 160, 345

About the Authors

C. Michael Pilato is a core Subversion developer and the primary maintainer of ViewVC. He works remotely from his home state of North Carolina as a senior software engineer on CollabNet's version control team and has been an active open source developer for over seven years. Mike is a proud husband and father who loves traveling and spending quality time with his family. He also enjoys composing and performing music, and harbors not-so-secret fantasies of rock stardom. Until that all works out, though, he is content to spend his modicum of private time doing freelance web design, graphic design, and audio and video production work. Mike has a B.S. in computer science and mathematics from the University of North Carolina at Charlotte.

Ben Collins-Sussman spent five years with CollabNet as one of the original designers and founders of the Subversion project. He is currently a technical lead at Google's Chicago office, where he manages part of the team responsible for Google Code's open source project hosting service. He received his B.S. in mathematics from the University of Chicago. In his spare time away from his wife and kids (of which there is none), he enjoys writing musicals and playing bluegrass banjo.

Brian W. Fitzpatrick leads Google's Chicago engineering efforts. Prior to joining Google, Brian worked on Subversion, cvs2svn, and CVS as a senior software engineer on CollabNet's version control team, and was also a senior engineer at Apple Computer. Brian has been an active open source contributor for over 10 years and is a member of the Apache Software Foundation. Brian has an A.B. in classics from Loyola University Chicago with a major in Latin, a minor in Greek, and a concentration in fine arts and ceramics. Despite growing up in New Orleans and working for Silicon Valley companies for most of his career, he decided years ago that Chicago was his home and stubbornly refuses to move to California.

Colophon

The animals on the cover of *Version Control with Subversion*, Second Edition, are hawksbill sea turtles (*Eretmochelys imbricata*) or Honu'ea, as they are known in Hawaii. The hawksbill is a medium-sized turtle weighing up to 270 pounds, with a shell length of about 3 feet. This sea turtle can be found in tropical reef areas in the Atlantic, Pacific, and Indian oceans. The hawksbill gets its name from its distinctive beak-like mouth, and it is also recognized for its beautiful shell coloring, known as "tortoise shell," which was exploited by the fashion industry for many years. Hawksbill sea turtles are listed as an endangered species in Hawaii and are protected under the state law as well as many other endangered species laws.

Sea turtles are highly migratory and have unique nesting habits. Nesting occurs at night, typically between May and October. First, the females go ashore and look for small, isolated beaches where they can lay their eggs. After they choose a site, usually beyond the tideline, they dig a pit with their flippers and excavate an egg chamber. Sea turtles only nest every two to three years, but they can lay up to six clutches of eggs in one breeding season. A single nesting can contain as many as 230 eggs, with the average being about 130. When the last egg has been laid, the females cover the chamber with sand and return to the sea, leaving the eggs behind.

The eggs incubate in their sand chambers for two to three months, and then hatching takes place over several days. At birth, a hatchling is so small it can fit into the palm of a human hand. The newborn turtles emerge from their chambers in groups at night, when the sand is cool and there is less threat of predators. They immediately head toward the sea, guided by the moonlight and the stars' reflections on the water. But they face severe challenges during this journey, and the mortality rate is high, as many of them fall prey to shorebirds and crabs. The turtles that safely reach the ocean disappear into it and may only venture out again years later.

The cover image is a 19th-century engraving from *Cuvier's Animals*. The cover font is Adobe ITC Garamond. The text font is Linotype Birka; the heading font is Adobe Myriad Condensed; and the code font is LucasFont's TheSansMonoCondensed.

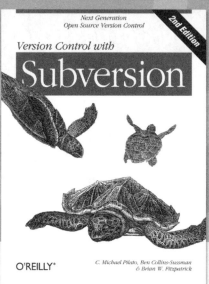